*My congratulations to the organisers on the publication of this volume of Asian Monetary Policy Forum (AMPF) speeches and commissioned papers. This volume brings together the expertise and scholarship of international researchers assembled at AMPF over the years, on issues of direct relevance to policymakers in Asia and beyond. The AMPF has come a long way since its inception. At a time when the global consensus for economic integration is being challenged, the AMPF and Asian Bureau of Finance and Economic Research are well placed to promote informed discussions on related issues through rigorous research. This will allow countries in the region to reap the full benefits of economic integration and achieve growth with financial stability. As the international monetary and financial landscape continues to evolve, I look forward to upcoming Forums to shed light on these policy issues.*

**Deputy Prime Minister Heng Swee Keat**
Coordinating Minister for Economic Policies & Minister for Finance


*Asia's rapid rise and deep integration into the global economic framework has been one of the most significant developments of the last 50 years. Financial markets and services have played pivotal supporting and enabling roles in this dramatic ascent. But this rapid growth, along with wider disruptive forces of change, also brings attendant risks and uncertainties, not least to financial markets. Over the last three decades, the world has witnessed vivid demonstrations of how instabilities in financial markets can become systemic risks, undermining societal security and stability. In this environment of tremendous change, unfolding opportunities and evolving risks, the AMPF and ABFER were instituted to serve as a globally leading platform to explore the most profound and pertinent financial and monetary policy issues facing Asia and the world. This volume will be highly relevant to policymakers, practitioners, and academics, and I congratulate the Forum organizers, the ABFER, Monetary Authority of Singapore, NUS Business School, the University of Chicago Booth, and all Forum participants for their contributions in this illuminating collection of essays.*

**Professor Tan Eng Chye**
President, National University of Singapore

*The last decade has seen an important evolution in the challenges facing central banks, and consequently a — sometimes grudging — expansion in their mandates. Three considerations have been notable: a) the interconnected nature of markets, and the spill-over effects of US monetary policy; b) the increasing complexity of markets, with the growing role of non-bank players post the Global Financial Crisis creating greater opacity; and c) an evolution in the nature of money, with e-wallets and cryptos creating parallel systems that have bearing on money supply and velocity. Central banks have slowly added financial system stability and system efficiency to their price/output mandates. I was privileged to have a ringside seat at many of the meetings of the ABFER and AMPF that served to bring intellectual robustness to the "what and how" debates of appropriate central bank policy response. The current compilation of many of the seminal and thought-provoking ideas is a fascinating look back at some of the key considerations, as well as an excellent guide to the path forward. Its easy reading style makes it as useful to the layman as it is to the practitioner. Highly recommended.*

**Piyush Gupta**
Chief Executive Officer, DBS Bank

*This book collects some of the most important papers and speeches given at the AMPF between 2014 and 2020 by a veritable who's who of thinkers on central banking. It covers issues as diverse as the proper objectives of monetary policy, the choice of exchange rate regime, the pathways to developing bond markets, the role for macro-prudential policies, and the scope for international monetary co-operation, most with a special focus on Asia. As the world emerges from the COVID-19 pandemic, and as it looks for sustainable policies that will promote growth with stability, the articles in this book will be an essential starting point.*

**Raghuram G. Rajan**
Katherine Dusak Miller Distinguished Service Professor of Finance,
University of Chicago Booth School of Business

*The AMPF has become one of the most important meetings for researchers and policymakers in central banking and finance. Like its sister fora — "Jackson Hole" in the US and the "Sintra" in Europe — it attracts outstanding scholars and encourages frank exchanges over current policy issues. The volume edited by Steve Davis, Edward Robinson, and Bernard Yeung brings together the highlights of the first seven years of the Asian Monetary Policy Forum. This is a must-have.*

**Beatrice Weder di Mauro**
President, Centre for Economic Policy Research
Professor of International Economics, Graduate Institute of Geneva;
Distinguished Fellow, INSEAD Emerging Markets Institute, Singapore

*The evolving global economy confronts central banks with an ever-changing array of challenges. This collection, drawn from presentations at the AMPF, brings together the latest insights from academic research and central banking practice. It is an essential reference for anyone who studies or implements monetary policy.*

**James Poterba**
President and CEO, National Bureau of Economic Research,
Mitsui Professor of Economics, MIT

# THE
# ASIAN MONETARY POLICY FORUM

## Insights for
## Central Banking

Editors

### Steven J Davis
University of Chicago
Asian Bureau of Finance and Economic Research

### Edward S Robinson
Monetary Authority of Singapore
Asian Bureau of Finance and Economic Research

### Bernard Yeung
National University of Singapore
Asian Bureau of Finance and Economic Research

**World Scientific**

NEW JERSEY · LONDON · SINGAPORE · BEIJING · SHANGHAI · HONG KONG · TAIPEI · CHENNAI · TOKYO

*Published by*

World Scientific Publishing Co. Pte. Ltd.

5 Toh Tuck Link, Singapore 596224

*USA office:* 27 Warren Street, Suite 401-402, Hackensack, NJ 07601

*UK office:* 57 Shelton Street, Covent Garden, London WC2H 9HE

**National Library Board, Singapore Cataloguing in Publication Data**
Names: Davis, Steven J., editor. | Robinson, Edward S. (Economist), editor. | Yeung, Yin Bernard, 1953–   editor.
Title: The Asian Monetary Policy Forum : insights for central banking / editors, Steven J Davis, Edward S Robinson, Bernard Yeung.
Description: Singapore : World Scientific, [2021] | Includes bibliographic references.
Identifiers: OCN 1245919948 | ISBN 978-981-123-861-1 (hardcover) |
    ISBN 978-981-123-862-8 (ebook for institutions) |
    ISBN 978-981-123-863-5 (ebook for individuals)
Subjects: LCSH: Monetary policy--Asia. | Banks and banking, Central--Asia.
Classification: DDC 332.495--dc23

**British Library Cataloguing-in-Publication Data**
A catalogue record for this book is available from the British Library.

For any available supplementary material, please visit
https://www.worldscientific.com/worldscibooks/10.1142/12323#t=suppl

Desk Editor: Ong Shi Min Nicole

Typeset by Stallion Press
Email: enquiries@stallionpress.com

Printed in Singapore

# About the Editors

**Steven J. Davis** is the William H. Abbott Distinguished Service Professor of International Business and Economics at the University of Chicago Booth School of Business, a senior fellow at the Hoover Institution, senior academic fellow with the Asian Bureau of Finance and Economic Research, and advisor to the US Congressional Budget Office. He is also senior adviser to the Brookings Papers on Economic Activity, past editor of the American Economic Journal: Macroeconomics, and an elected fellow of the Society of Labor Economists.

**Edward Surendran Robinson** is Deputy Managing Director (Economic Policy) and Chief Economist at the Monetary Authority of Singapore. The Economic Policy Group is responsible for the formulation of monetary policy and surveillance of macro-financial developments. He has been with the MAS since 1992, and has an ongoing interest in macro-econometric modelling and studies on structural issues facing the Singapore economy.

**Bernard Yeung** is the Stephen Riady Distinguished Professor in Finance and Strategic Management at the National University of Singapore (NUS) Business School. He is also the President of the Asian Bureau of Finance and Economic Research. He was Dean of NUS Business School from 2008 to 2019. Before joining NUS, he taught at New York University Stern School of Business. He was awarded the Public Administration Silver Medal (2018) in Singapore, Irwin Outstanding Educator Award (2013) from the Academy of Management and is an elected Fellow of the Academy of International Business.

# About the Contributors

## 1. Ravi Menon

Managing Director
Monetary Authority of Singapore

Mr Ravi Menon was appointed Managing Director of the Monetary Authority of Singapore (MAS) in 2011. He was previously Permanent Secretary at the Ministry of Trade & Industry (MTI) and Deputy Secretary at the Ministry of Finance (MOF).

Mr Menon began his career at MAS in 1987. During his 16 years in MAS, he was involved in monetary policy; econometric forecasting; organisational development; banking regulation and liberalisation; and integrated supervision of complex financial institutions. Mr Menon spent a year at the Bank for International Settlements in Basel, as a member of the secretariat to the Financial Stability Forum. A recipient of the Singapore Government's Meritorious Service Medal and Public Administration (Gold) Medal, Mr Menon has served on a variety of boards in the public, private, and people sectors in Singapore. On the international front, Mr Menon is a member of the Financial Stability Board (FSB) Steering Committee. Mr Menon holds a Master's in Public Administration from Harvard University and a Bachelor of Social Science (Honours) in Economics from the National University of Singapore.

## 2. Maurice Obstfeld

Class of 1958 Professor of Economics
University of California, Berkeley
Non-resident Senior Fellow, Peterson Institute for International Economics

Maurice Obstfeld is the Class of 1958 Professor of Economics at UC Berkeley. He joined Berkeley in 1989 as a professor, following appointments at Columbia (1979–1986) and the University of Pennsylvania (1986–1989). He was also a visiting professor at Harvard between 1989 and 1991. He received his Ph.D. from MIT in 1979, following degrees from the University of Pennsylvania and the University of Cambridge. In 2014–2015 he was a Member of President Obama's Council of Economic Advisers, and from 2015–2018 he served as chief economist at the International Monetary Fund. Before that, he served as an honorary adviser to the Bank of Japan's Institute of Monetary and Economic Studies. Among Professor Obstfeld's honors are the Frank Graham Lecture at Princeton, the inaugural Mundell-Fleming Lecture of the International Monetary Fund, the Bernhard Harms Prize and Lecture of the Kiel Institute for World Economy, the L. K. Jha Memorial Lecture at the Reserve Bank of India, and the Richard T. Ely Lecture of the American Economic Association. Professor Obstfeld is a Fellow of the Econometric Society and the American Academy of Arts and Sciences. He is active as a research fellow of the Centre for Economic Policy Research and a research associate of the National Bureau of Economic Research. Most recently, he has joined the Peterson Institute for International Economics in Washington, D.C., as a non-resident senior fellow.

### 3. Barry Eichengreen

George C. Pardee and Helen N. Pardee Professor of Economics and Political Science
University of California, Berkeley

Barry Eichengreen is the George C. Pardee and Helen N. Pardee Professor of Economics and Professor of Political Science at the University of California, Berkeley, where he has taught since 1987. He is a Research Associate of the National Bureau of Economic Research (Cambridge, Massachusetts) and Research Fellow of the Centre for Economic Policy Research (London, England). In 1997–98 he was Senior

Policy Advisor at the International Monetary Fund. He is a fellow of the American Academy of Arts and Sciences (class of 1997).

Professor Eichengreen has held Guggenhim and Fulbright Fellowships and been a fellow of the Center for Advanced Study in the Behavioral Sciences (Palo Alto) and the Institute for Advanced Study (Berlin). From 2004 to 2020 he served as convener of the Bellagio Group of academics and officials. He is a regular monthly columnist for Project Syndicate.

His most recent books are *The Populist Temptation: Economic Grievance and Political Reaction in the Modern Era* (Oxford University Press, 2018), *How Global Currencies Work: Past, Present, and Future* with Livia Chitu and Arnaud Mehl (November 2017), *The Korean Economy: From a Miraculous Past to a Sustainable Future* with Wonhyuk Lim, Yung Chul Park and Dwight H. Perkins (March 2015), *Renminbi Internationalization: Achievements, Prospects, and Challenges*, with Masahiro Kawai (February 2015), *Hall of Mirrors: The Great Depression, The Great Recession, and the Uses — and Misuses — of History* (January 2015), *From Miracle to Maturity: The Growth of the Korean Economy* with Dwight H. Perkins and Kwanho Shin (2012) and *Exorbitant Privilege: The Rise and Fall of the Dollar and the Future of the International Monetary System* (2011) (shortlisted for the Financial Times and Goldman Sachs Business Book of the Year Award in 2011).

Professor Eichengreen was awarded the Economic History Association's Jonathan R.T. Hughes Prize for Excellence in Teaching in 2002 and the University of California at Berkeley Social Science Division's Distinguished Teaching Award in 2004. He is the recipient of a doctor honoris causa from the American University in Paris, and the 2010 recipient of the Schumpeter Prize from the International Schumpeter Society. He was named one of *Foreign Policy Magazine's* 100 Leading Global Thinkers in 2011. He is a past president of the Economic History Association (2010–11 academic year).

## 4. Olivier Blanchard

C. Fred Bergsten Senior Fellow
Peterson Institute for International Economics

Olivier Blanchard joined the Peterson Institute for International Economics as the first C. Fred Bergsten Senior Fellow in October 2015. A citizen of France, Blanchard has spent most of his professional life in Cambridge, MA. After obtaining his PhD in economics from the Massachusetts Institute of Technology (MIT) in 1977, he taught at Harvard University, and returned to MIT in 1982. He was chair of the economics department from 1998 to 2003. In 2008, he took a leave of absence to be the economic counselor and director of the Research Department at the International Monetary Fund. He remains the Robert M. Solow Professor of Economics emeritus at MIT.

He is a macroeconomist, who has worked on a wide range of issues, from the role of monetary and fiscal policy, the nature of speculative bubbles, the nature of the labor market and the determinants of unemployment, transition in former communist countries, and to forces behind the recent global financial crisis. In the process, he has worked with numerous countries and international organizations. He is the author of many books and articles, including two textbooks on macroeconomics, one at the graduate level with Stanley Fischer and the other at the undergraduate level.

He is a past editor of the *Quarterly Journal of Economics* and the *NBER Macroeconomics Annual* and founding editor of *American Economic Journal: Macroeconomics*. He is a fellow and past council member of the Econometric Society, past president of the American Economic Association, and a member of the American Academy of Sciences.

## 5. Jeffrey Frankel

James W. Harpel Professor of Capital Formation and Growth
Harvard University

Jeffrey Frankel is James W. Harpel Professor of Capital Formation and Growth at Harvard University's Kennedy School. He is a Research Associate at the National Bureau of Economic Research. He served at the US President's Council of Economic Advisers in 1983–84 and 1996–99. As CEA Member in the Clinton Administration, Frankel's responsibilities included international economics, macroeconomics, and the environment. Before coming to Harvard in 1999, he was Professor of Economics at the University of California at Berkeley. Born in San Francisco, he graduated from Swarthmore College and received his economics PhD from MIT.

His research interests include commodities, crises, currencies, fiscal policy, international finance, monetary policy, regional blocs, and international environmental issues. RePEc ranks him among the 50 top-cited living economists. He writes a syndicated monthly column and a blog. He also co-directs annually the NBER ISoM and Harvard PEIF conferences.

## 6. Stefan Avdjiev

Adviser for Financial Stability
Bank for International Settlements

Stefan Avdjiev joined the BIS in 2009, immediately after the completion of his PhD in economics. Prior to assuming his current position, he worked as an Economist in the Financial Institutions and the Financial Markets groups of the BIS Monetary and Economic Department (between 2009 and 2014) and as the Deputy Head of International Banking and Financial Statistics (between 2014 and 2020). His recent research has been mainly focused on issues related to financial stability and international finance. He has also conducted and published research in macroeconomics and asset pricing.

## 7. Bat-el Berger

Principal Data Scientist
Bank for International Settlements

Before joining the International Data Hub, Bat-el Berger worked in the International Banking and Financial Statistics unit, supported the Basel Committee on Banking Supervision's quantitative impact studies and worked on research projects in the BIS's Asian Office. She joined the BIS in 2012 after having worked at the International Monetary Fund and the Dutch Ministry of Finance. She holds an MSc in economics from the VU University in Amsterdam and an MSc in behavioural science from the London School of Economics.

## 8. Hyun Song Shin

Economic Adviser and Head of Research
Bank for International Settlements

Hyun Song Shin took up the position of Economic Adviser and Head of Research at the BIS on 1 May 2014. Before joining the BIS, Mr Shin was the Hughes-Rogers Professor of Economics at Princeton University. In 2010, on leave from Princeton, he served as Senior Adviser to the Korean president, taking a leading role in formulating financial stability policy in Korea and developing the agenda for the G20 during Korea's presidency. From 2000 to 2005, he was Professor of Finance at the London School of Economics. He holds a DPhil and MPhil in Economics from Oxford University (Nuffield College) and a BA in Philosophy, Politics and Economics from the same university.

## 9. Pierre-Olivier Gourinchas

S.K. and Angela Chan Professor of Global Management, Haas School of Business
Director, Clausen Centre for International Business and Policy
University of California, Berkeley
Program director, International Macroeconomics & Finance
National Bureau of Economic Research

Pierre-Olivier Gourinchas grew up in Montpellier, France. He attended Ecole Polytechnique and received his PhD in Economics in 1996 from

MIT. He taught at Stanford Graduate School of Business and Princeton University before joining UC Berkeley department of economics.

Professor Gourinchas' main research interests are in international macroeconomics and finance. His recent research focuses on the scarcity of global safe assets, global imbalances and currency wars (with Ricardo Caballero and Emmanuel Farhi); on the International Monetary System and the role of the U.S. dollar (with Hélène Rey); on the Dominant Currency Paradigm (with Gita Gopinath); on the determinants of capital flows to and from developing countries (with Olivier Jeanne); on international portfolios (with Nicolas Coeurdacier); and on the global financial crisis (with Maury Obstfeld).

Professor Gourinchas is the laureate of the 2007 Bernàcer Prize for best European economist working in macroeconomics and finance under the age of 40, and of the 2008 Prix du Meilleur Jeune Economiste for best French economist under the age of 40. In 2012–2013, Professor Gourinchas was a member of the French Council of Economic Advisors to the Prime Minister. From 2009 to 2016 he was the editor-in-chief of the IMF Economic Review and from 2017 to 2019 the managing editor of the Journal of International Economics. He is currently co-editor of the American Economic Review and director of the NBER's International Finance and Macroeconomics Program.

## 10. Markus K. Brunnermeier

Edwards S. Sanford Professor of Economics
Director of the Bendheim Center for Finance
Princeton University

Markus K. Brunnermeier is the Edwards S. Sanford Professor at Princeton University. He is a faculty member of the Department of Economics and director of Princeton's Bendheim Center for Finance. He is also a research associate at NBER, CEPR, and CESifo and a member of the Bellagio Group on the International Economy. He is a Sloan Research

Fellow, Fellow of the Econometric Society, Guggenheim Fellow and the recipient of the Bernácer Prize granted for outstanding contributions in the fields of macroeconomics and finance. He is a member of several advisory groups, including to the U.S. Congressional Budget Office, the German Bundesbank, and previously to the IMF, the Federal Reserve of New York, and the European Systemic Risk Board. Brunnermeier was awarded his Ph.D. by the London School of Economics (LSE).

His research focuses on international financial markets and the macroeconomy with special emphasis on bubbles, liquidity, financial and monetary price stability. He has been awarded several best paper prizes and served on the editorial boards of several leading economics and finance journals. He has tried to establish the concepts: liquidity spirals, CoVaR as systemic risk measure, the Volatility Paradox, Paradox of Prudence, ESBies, financial dominance, the redistributive monetary policy, the Reversal Rate, and Digital Currency Areas. His recent books include *The Euro and the Battle of Ideas* (2016) and *The Resilient Society* (2021).

## 11. Sebastian Merkel

Postdoctoral Research Associate
Princeton University

Sebastian Merkel is a postdoctoral researcher and lecturer at the Department of Economics, Princeton University. He obtained his Ph.D. from University of Mannheim in August 2018. His research interests are in Macroeconomics, Macrofinance, Monetary Economics and Asset Pricing.

## 12. Yuliy Sannikov

The Jack Steele Parker Professor of Economics
Stanford University

Yuliy Sannikov is a theorist who has developed new methods for analyzing continuous time dynamic games using stochastic calculus methods. His work has not only broken new ground in methodology, it has had a substantial influence on applied theory. He has significantly altered the toolbox available for studying dynamic games, and as a result of his contributions, new areas of economic inquiry have become tractable for rigorous theoretical analysis. The areas of application include the design of securities, contract theory, macroeconomics with financial frictions, market microstructure, and collusion.

Sannikov's work is impressive. It is elegant, powerful, and it paves the way for further analysis on lots of problems. The early successes highlighted how even simple and well-studied models could yield new insight. His most recent work has tackled more complex models in finance and macroeconomics. Previous models abstracted from crucial economic forces in the name of tractability, but Sannikov's methods allow models to include the most important forces and thus deliver results that are much more relevant. He is one of the few theorists in many years to have introduced a truly novel tool that changed the way theory is done.

# Foreword

The Asian Monetary Policy Forum (AMPF), into its eighth year, is now among the foremost international fora for serious discussion of the challenges facing monetary policy. It has bridged the gap between academic research and policymaking in the Asian region, and paid special attention to questions facing small open economies. It has however been much more than a regional platform. The papers and discussions at the AMPF have typically drawn on rigorous analysis of the evolving international evidence, and contributed insights that have hopefully been of relevance to scholars and policymakers more broadly.

The AMPF's contribution to policy debate has also come from its robust open-mindedness. It has highlighted questions that remain central as the world seeks to emerge from the COVID-19 pandemic and build back better, and as monetary policy has itself become less effective in many economies with interest rates being close to the zero-lower bound.

The questions are wide open. To cite a few, how should central banks seek to achieve their output and inflation goals, which will in several cases require very accommodative monetary policies for some time to come, without accentuating risks to financial stability? Can macro-prudential polices reliably mitigate these financial risks? How do central banks, especially those already owning a significant proportion of outstanding government debt, avoid expectations that monetary policy actions in future years will be influenced by fiscal needs? More broadly, what discipline of interaction between monetary and fiscal policies, and what width of ambition in the implementation of central bank mandates, will help safeguard central bank independence? What mix of tools should central banks in smaller and developing economies use to gain the benefits of financial globalization while buffering their economies from sudden shifts in global risk attitudes and capital flows? And is there adequate benefit in central banks issuing their own digital currencies, taking into account their risks, or does it suffice to regulate private sector digital tokens and wallets and the payments infrastructure?

I hope the deliberations in this book, as well as the forums to come, will make a meaningful contribution to the evolving thinking on these complex policy issues.

**Tharman Shanmugaratnam**
**Senior Minister, Singapore**
**Chairman, Monetary Authority of Singapore**

# Contents

Introduction

# Asian Monetary Policy Forum: Insights for Central Banking

Steven J. Davis, Edward S. Robinson, and Bernard Yeung[1]

## Introduction

Advances in technology, market liberalization, stronger institutions, and economic growth have propelled a globalization of banking, securities, and currency markets. In turn, financial globalization has facilitated trade, output and cross-border investments in Asia and around the world. Alongside impressive output growth, many Asian countries have grown tremendously with a matching advancement of their businesses in size and sophistication. Their financial systems have expanded and deepened. Their corporates and banks are now engaged in considerable cross-border financial arrangements. The most advanced cities like Tokyo, Singapore, and Hong Kong have become major international financial hubs, providing services that support production, trade and spending, and acting as engines of growth in their own right.

[1] Steven J. Davis is the William H. Abbott Distinguished Service Professor of International Business and Economics, University of Chicago Booth School, Senior fellow at the Hoover Institution, research associate of the National Bureau of Economic Research (NBER) and senior fellow with the Asian Bureau of Finance and Economic Research (ABFER). Email: Steven.Davis@chicagobooth.edu

Edward S. Robinson is Deputy Managing Director (Economic Policy) and Chief Economist, Monetary Authority of Singapore and Advisor, ABFER. Email: Edward_ROBINSON@mas.gov.sg

Bernard Yeung is the Stephen Riady Distinguished Professor of Finance and Strategic Management, National University of Singapore Business School, and President, ABFER. Email: byeung@nus.edu.sg

We are grateful to Liew Yin Sze and Ng Ding Xuan for comments on an earlier draft of this introduction.

As a result, Asian countries have become more exposed to international economic and financial developments, including spillovers that arise from negative shocks and policy shifts in Europe, America, and elsewhere. Prominent examples include the dot.com bust in the early 2000s, the Global Financial Crisis of 2007–2009, a series of sovereign debt and banking crises in Europe since 2010, and the ongoing COVID-19 pandemic. These episodes drove large shifts in trade flows, interest rates, risk premia, capital flows, credit growth, and asset prices in Asian economies. In addition, and for smaller countries in particular, strong capital markets integration places limits on macroeconomic policy options (Rey 2013).

Major shocks have also originated within Asia in recent decades, with the 1997 Asian Financial Crisis as the leading example. Due to inadequate financial supervision frameworks as capital accounts were liberalized, banks and other businesses took on increasing foreign debt on expectations that fixed exchange rate regimes would shield them against adverse currency movements. The subsequent rapid buildup of currency and maturity mismatches set the stage for a devastating financial crisis, triggered by the Thai baht devaluation in July 1997.

Financial globalization brings benefits *and* new sources of economic risk and financial volatility. In response, central bankers have extended their focus beyond price and exchange rate stability to give more attention to the stability and efficiency of the financial system. This expanded domain of concern for central bankers has brought new, often complex, policy challenges. We can learn a great deal from our experiences, sometime harsh, in responding to these challenges and our efforts to address the risks associated with financial globalization. We believe that a deeper understanding can point the way to better policy design and stronger economic performance.

In this spirit, the Monetary Authority of Singapore (MAS), the Asian Bureau of Finance and Economics Research (ABFER), the University of Chicago Booth School of Business, and the National University of Singapore Business School have collaborated since 2014 in organizing the annual Asian Monetary Policy Forum (AMPF). The forum facilitates the exchange of insights among policymakers, practitioners, and senior academicians by delving into pressing monetary policy issues in open-economy settings, with particular attention to Asian countries. The aim is to draw lessons from experience for the benefit of policymakers in Asia and around the world.

The commissioned papers presented at the AMPF offer insights about major developments in the global monetary and financial system, the efficacy of monetary and other policies, and the containment of financial risks. We are grateful to authors, discussants and other participants for their outstanding contributions, and we feel compelled to share the learnings in the broadest possible way. We have compiled the commissioned papers into this book, as a reference to practical and critical thinking about central bank policies in Asia and beyond. We include an edited version of a speech delivered by MAS Managing Director Ravi Menon at the inaugural AMPF.

## Setting the Stage: The Inaugural Asian Monetary Policy Forum

The Global Financial Crisis (GFC) compelled central bankers to reconsider the role of monetary policy in securing financial stability. Ravi Menon addresses this topic in his speech at the first AMPF. In Chapter 1, Menon describes three broad approaches to the issue:

1. Stick to the traditional approach, whereby monetary policy focuses on price stability. Supplement monetary policy with prudential regulations such as capital requirements for financial institutions.
2. Explicitly incorporate financial stability concerns into the conduct of monetary policy — tightening, for example, in response to an unsustainable credit boom.
3. Retain the focus on price stability in the conduct of monetary policy, but deploy a range of macroprudential tools to secure financial stability.

The second approach rests on the insight that monetary policy affects financial stability through the risk-taking channel. "Loose monetary policy can heighten vulnerabilities in the financial system" by lowering risk premiums, thereby promoting risk-taking activities and encouraging banks to expand credit. Conversely, tight monetary policy raises risk premiums, discouraging risk-taking behavior and restraining credit growth. An appealing feature of the second approach, as Menon explains, is that monetary policy can "get in all the cracks" of the financial system. Financial institutions cannot easily evade the effects of tight monetary policy the way they often work around restrictive regulations. Also, the second approach requires only modest departures from well-established and well-understood monetary policy practices. Operationally, the second approach amounts to augmenting the Taylor Rule, so that financial stability concerns influence the central bank's choice of its policy rate.

Menon also explains why relying on monetary policy to secure financial stability may not be enough. First, the policy rate that promotes financial stability may differ from the rate needed for price and output stability. Second, global financial forces may constrain the conduct of monetary policy, an especially important factor for many emerging market economies (EMEs). Third, although monetary policy can get in all the cracks, it may still not be sufficiently potent to fully address serious threats to financial stability. For these reasons, macroprudential policies play an increasingly important role in the central banking toolkit.

Since the outset, many AMPF contributions have addressed concerns related to international capital flows and their implications for monetary policy. The inaugural AMPF commissioned paper by Prof. Maurice Obstfeld, "*Trilemmas and Trade-offs*" (Chapter 2), considers the capacity of emerging market economies (EMEs) to use monetary policy and macroprudential tools to moderate the domestic effects of global financial forces. Obstfeld provides evidence that monetary policy affords EMEs some ability to moderate the effects of external shocks on shorter-term domestic interest rates. Longer-term rates, however, are less responsive to domestic monetary policy and more subject to global financial conditions, even in EMEs that operate with flexible exchange rate systems. Thus, shocks and developments that originate elsewhere can sharply raise the cost of funds in the domestic economy. This work has spurred new research on trilemmas, dilemmas, and even 2.5-lemmas. See Han and Wei (2018), for example.

Issues related to price and financial stability, macroprudential policy, capital flows, exchange rate systems, and related policy tools, arose repeatedly at the Asian Monetary Policy Forums held from 2014 to 2020. Other issues arose as well — including the challenges presented by the dominance of the U.S. dollar in the international monetary and financial system. In the rest of this essay, we summarize some of the key learnings about these matters. We start with a summary of empirical evidence highlighted by the commissioned papers. Next, we turn to policy insights, which we organize according to Prof. Alan Blinder's advice that "good economic policy exploits the market mechanisms where it shines, helps it along where its flaws are easily remedied, and overrules it by government fiat where it fails."[2] Then we discuss foundational work that aims to identify the conditions for a stable financial system, and that highlights complementarities between conventional monetary policy and other central banking tools. We close with remarks about the goals of the AMPF and some outstanding challenges for central bankers.

## Evidence

Several papers in this volume present evidence about the nature of financial globalization and its implications for monetary policy and other aspects of central banking. We sort the empirical evidence into four categories: monetary sovereignty, exchange rate regime choices, the status of international banking and securities markets, and the dominance of the U.S. dollar.

---

[2] See Blinder (2018). Of course, policy, policymakers and the policymaking process have their own limitations and imperfections. Thus, market failure is properly seen as a necessary condition for policy intervention, not a sufficient one.

### Monetary sovereignty

Prof. Obstfeld stresses that a flexible exchange rate regime offers EMEs greater latitude to use monetary policy and macroprudential tools to moderate the domestic economic effects of global financial forces. Examining the experiences of 22 advanced and 33 emerging economies from 1990 to 2013, he shows that monetary authorities retain some degree of interest rate independence at the shorter end of the maturity spectrum when they operate floating exchange rate regimes. However, he also provides evidence that longer-term domestic interest rates are poorly insulated from global influences regardless of the exchange rate regime. Here, "independence" is defined by whether the U.S. interest rate, the rates of multiple base currencies, or the VIX explains movements in home-country interest rates.

These results illustrate that exchange rate regimes matter: monetary sovereignty is preserved to a significant extent outside of fixed exchange rate regimes. Hence, even for small economies buffeted by a global financial cycle, the monetary trilemma is still valid. With open capital markets, monetary authorities have far more room for maneuver than if they peg the exchange rate. However, this latitude is circumscribed by the need for policymaker attention to domestic financial stability.

### Exchange rate regime choices

Prof. Jeffrey Frankel (Chapter 5) stresses that economies have more than two choices when it comes to exchange rate regimes. He tracks the correlation between the change in a currency's foreign exchange value and the change in its foreign exchange reserves (as a fraction of the country's monetary base) over the period 1995 to 2015. The correlations illustrate that, in practice, Asian economies have adopted a variety of foreign exchange regimes, e.g., a fixed-rate regime in Hong Kong, a managed float in Singapore, and an essentially free-floating regime in the Philippines. On the whole, from 1980 to 2010, the proportion of EMEs operating a managed float has increased.

Prof. Frankel also reports regression results that show how an external shock's impact on the real exchange rate varies according to the exchange rate regime. He captures external shocks by using (natural log) measures of the VIX and commodity prices. In Asian regions with an exchange rate peg (e.g., Hong Kong), these shocks do not affect the real exchange rate. In managed float regimes, the impact is greater than zero but less than in jurisdictions with freely floating rates. Thus, the choice of exchange rate regime affects the behavior of real exchange rates and their responsiveness to external shocks, at least in the short term. During the forum, discussants suggested the need to also examine if exchange rate regimes matter for key macroeconomic variables, including price and output volatility.

### Financial globalization

#### Asia's domestic bond markets

In Chapter 3, presented at AMPF 2015, Professor Barry Eichengreen describes the rapid growth of Asian bond markets after the 1997 Asian Financial Crisis (AFC). Asia's domestic bond market capitalization (ex-Japan) rose from 33% of aggregate GDP in 2000 to 57% in 2014. Cross-sectional regressions show that both bond and equity market capitalizations are correlated with per capita GDP. In addition, bond market capitalization is positively associated with the use of common accounting standards and better control of corruption.

Prof. Eichengreen also shows that state-owned banks in China continue to dominate the banking sector and hold most Chinese government bonds. Corporate bonds are mostly issued by state-owned enterprises and have a more diversified investor base. In the equity market, the state used to strictly control new listings.

#### International claims

In Chapter 6, presented at AMPF 2018, Stefan Avdjiev, Bat-el Berger, and Hyun Song Shin review and document several empirical aspects of international lending. While credit cycles may appear similar at the aggregate level, they often differ in their underlying microeconomic features. For example, South Korea experienced a build-up of externally funded bank lending before the AFC and the GFC, as did Spain after the creation of the Euro in 1999. However, South Korea borrowed short term in U.S. dollars, while Spain borrowed long term in Euros. Thus, the Korean cases involved vulnerabilities in the form of currency and maturity mismatches that were not present in the Spanish case.

The authors also show that international bank lending follows identifiable cycles. U.S. banks lent heavily to Latin America in the 80s, Japanese banks lent to Asian countries in the 90s, and European banks lent to emerging economies before the GFC. Using five Asian countries to illustrate, the authors highlight the following pattern: foreign banks lend to domestic banks, which in turn extend short-term dollar-denominated loans to domestic nonfinancial companies. Their evidence underscores how external credit availability and foreign risk-preference cycles affect intermediation in Asian economies and potentially create domestic vulnerabilities associated with term and currency mismatches in assets and liabilities.

As they also stress, the traditional approach to the study of international finance — which presumes a "triple coincidence" in GDP area, currency area, and decision-making unit — can yield misleading impressions when financial flows are important. The currency areas of major funding currencies, especially the U.S. dollar and the Euro, are much broader than their GDP areas. Moreover, the overlap between decision-making units and GDP areas is shrinking, as banks often lend in regions outside their headquarters via securitized market instruments. For instance, European banks held claims on U.S. borrowers of $856 billion in 2002 and more than $2 trillion by 2007. This increase coincided with growth in asset-backed securities from modest levels in the early 2000s to over $2 trillion by 2007. Direct financial intermediation between savers and corporations via capital markets has also grown rapidly.

They also stress that foreign-currency borrowing by EME corporates has aspects of a "carry trade," whereby cheap dollar borrowing, for example, spills over to the domestic economy in the form of easier credit conditions.

When foreign credit conditions tighten or the dollar appreciates, cheap dollar borrowing dries up and domestic credit conditions tighten. Even when the domestic monetary authority holds large dollar reserves, shifts in the cost of dollar borrowing can create sectoral disparities within the domestic economy.

### International monetary system

Policy discussions in central banking circles often turn to spillovers arising from U.S. monetary policy. The pre-eminent role of Fed policy is closely related to the dollar's dominant position in the global monetary and financial system. Prof. Pierre-Olivier Gourinchas considers the dollar's role in Chapter 7, presented at the 2019 AMPF. Among other markers of the dollar's pre-eminence, he notes that global trade invoiced in U.S. dollars is about four times as large as the U.S. share of global trade. On the financial side, 59% of international loans and 63% of international debt securities are denominated in dollars.

As Prof. Gourinchas also shows, the world remains on an informal dollar standard, despite the breakdown of the Bretton Woods system half a century ago. The dollar is the main currency of intervention for most central banks, the main currency in which they accumulate foreign exchange reserves, and the leading anchor currency against which other central banks seek to stabilize their currency values. As he explains, the dollar's dominance in invoicing and payments, in financial claims, and as a currency anchor are mutually reinforcing. If goods are invoiced and transacted in dollars, central banks want stable currency values vis-à-vis the dollar. In addition, private parties often want dollar loans because large portions of their cash flows are in dollars.

## Policy Implications for Central Banks

The AMPF commissioned papers, and the discussions during the forums, yield many useful policy insights. They fit well with Prof. Blinder's advice on how economic policy should interact with the market mechanism. Thus, we organize the insights based on the following functional purposes: (i) addressing structural deficiencies to enable markets to flourish, (ii) correcting distortions, and (iii) intervening to remedy malfunctioning markets.

### Addressing structural deficiencies

Prof. Eichengreen argues in Chapter 3 that governments can help develop domestic capital markets by promulgating sound disclosure and accounting standards. Strong standards attract a broader range of investors in domestic securities, enabling domestic enterprises to more readily raise funds. This is an example of how cross-border financial integration can support the domestic economy. At the same time, Prof. Eichengreen cautions, policymakers must recognize the new financial stability risks that accompany deeper capital markets integration, and they must create policy space for responding to those risks.

This theme arose again at AMPF 2018 in the commissioned paper by Dr. Shin and his co-authors (Chapter 6). The paper reports a rigorous examination of the changing circuitry of cross-border capital flows, which has contributed to rapid growth in the size and complexity of EME financial markets. Accompanying this growth is a build-up of financial risks as seen in the rising pro-cyclicality of bank balance sheets, greater cross-border lending to nonfinancial companies, and greater departures from the "triple coincidence." In a nutshell, greater complexity makes it harder to track currency and term structure mismatches. A quick shift in foreign risk attitudes, currency values, or foreign interest rates can disrupt the domestic economy via domestic banks, nonfinancial corporations, and investment institutions. Governments can help market participants gauge, prepare for, and respond to the potential consequences of such shifts by promoting the timely measurement of risk exposures and their dissemination.

### Correcting distortions

The second Blinder category comprises market-consistent interventions that help correct distortions, such as when pricing behavior diverges from equilibrating levels. The forum's commissioned papers and discussions provide useful insights along this line as well.

Prof. Obstfeld (Chapter 2) shows that a central bank retains the ability to affect short-term interest rates by opting for flexible exchange rates. Prof. Jeffrey Frankel (Chapter 5) further shows that a central bank can intervene to dampen the real exchange rate fluctuations caused by external shocks. Even under a managed float, the monetary authority retains some control over short-term domestic interest rates. In contrast, under a pegged exchange rate, the central bank surrenders interest rate control but shields its real exchange rate from foreign shocks. In other words, the choice is between absorbing external volatility by letting domestic interest rates and the real exchange rate adjust, or by allowing only the interest rate to adjust. The central bank's best policy decision depends on which is preferable: correcting a misaligned real exchange rate, correcting an inappropriate domestic interest rate setting, or some combination of the two.

Dr. Olivier Blanchard (Chapter 4) provides an analytical characterization of how monetary policy shocks transmit internationally, especially when advanced economies face limits on the use of fiscal policy. An easing of U.S. monetary policy raises U.S. aggregate demand and the demand for goods and services produced abroad. Easier U.S. monetary policy also leads to dollar depreciation, dampening U.S. demand for foreign goods and services. These two channels involve countervailing effects on U.S. trading partners. In addition, shifts in the stance of U.S. monetary policy can trigger large portfolio demand shifts, with powerful effects on financial conditions inside emerging market economies. Policymakers need to consider whether these effects involve serious distortions and, if so, how best to respond.

Blanchard sees limited prospects for international monetary policy coordination to address these concerns. Thus, when fiscal policy tools are unavailable or the source of additional problems, Blanchard sees capital controls as natural and useful tools for promoting macroeconomic and financial stability. Other discussions at the 2016 AMPF also make a case for extending the policy toolkit beyond interest rates to include foreign exchange interventions, fiscal measures, and macroprudential policies that correct distortions and forestall risks.

Prof. Gourinchas (Chapter 7) draws attention to policy implications in a dollar-dominated system. As an example, consider the traditional view of how flexible exchange rates facilitate an equilibrating response to a negative shock that lowers domestic demand and the foreign exchange value of the domestic currency. According to the traditional view, prices are slow to adjust and set in units of the producer's own-country currency. It follows that a depreciation of the domestic currency lowers the price of exports and raises the price of imports, at least temporarily. Under this view, a currency depreciation chokes off imports while boosting exports. In contrast, under full dollar invoicing, a depreciation of the domestic currency quickly passes through to increased import prices but leaves export prices unaffected. In this way, dollar invoicing reduces the role of flexible exchange rates in buffering the effects of negative demand shocks.

As a second example, consider the effects of U.S. monetary policy. Under the traditional view, U.S. monetary tightening appreciates the dollar, which is contractionary and can spillover to other countries. Under dollar invoicing, however, dollar appreciation raises foreign import prices. If foreign central banks want to offset this effect on their domestic price levels, they must tighten monetary policy as well. In this way, a contractionary monetary policy move in the United States generates a contractionary monetary policy response abroad under dollar invoicing.

Dollar appreciation also raises the liabilities of countries with net dollar debt and tightens their financial constraints. Therefore, the proper response to U.S. monetary tightening depends on a country's net foreign asset position and the currency denominations of its assets and liabilities. The direction and size of these financial effects differ across countries, as do the trade effects associated with changes in the relative prices of exports and imports. Thus, optimal responses of other central banks to a U.S. monetary tightening are likely to vary across countries.

Overall, the lesson in these discussions is that policymakers must identify the source of distortions and their potential effects. They must then apply suitable remedies, which may vary by country and period. Many conditions can vary, e.g., the speed of adjustment in goods markets, the ability to anticipate and adjust to interest rate and exchange rate changes, the size and currency denominations of assets and liabilities, and the U.S. dollar's position in international trade and the international financial system. All of these factors can affect the appropriate policy responses.

### Direct government interventions

Olivier Blanchard (Chapter 4) makes the case for capital controls in EMEs when advanced economies suffer from a shortage of demand, and they are unable or unwilling to address the demand shortage using fiscal policy tools. Advanced economies then rely too heavily on expansionary monetary policy, causing EME currencies to appreciate and driving gross international capital flows in ways that potentially disrupt EME financial conditions. Monetary policy coordination cannot resolve the problem because of conflicting goals and disagreements about policy effects, which are often highly uncertain. Under these circumstances, judicious capital flow management measures by EMEs might be the right policy choice to mitigate volatility and negative spillovers. This may open up room to use other policies for domestic objectives. Blanchard acknowledges that capital controls come with their own problems and risks. He also remarks that we still have much to learn about how monetary policy in advanced economies affects international capital flows and financial conditions in EMEs. Discussions during the forum emphasized complementarities among policy tools, the need to understand when to use particular tools, and the potential longer-term consequences of each tool.

## An Integrated Policy Framework

As Ravi Menon stresses in Chapter 1, monetary policy objectives have expanded beyond price and exchange rate stability to include financial stability and system efficiency. This expanded domain of concern brings many challenges. In the first place, monetary and financial cycles may not be synchronised. Second, capital market integration weakens policy effectiveness and imposes additional tradeoffs. For example, raising domestic rates to dampen inflation will attract capital inflows and potentially undermine exchange rate and financial stability. It would be desirable to have a framework that holistically brings together objectives, tools and shocks. We also need a framework that yields an internally consistent, integrated analysis of policy tools: interest rates, capital controls, exchange rate interventions, and macroprudential policies.

### Safe assets and policy in a financially globalized world

In Chapter 8, presented at AMPF 2020, Profs. Markus K. Brunnermeier, Sebastian Merkel, and Yuliy Sannikov present a framework built on Brunnermeier and Sannikov (2016; 2019). Their starting point is that financial frictions create demand for safe, liquid assets that maintain value in times of market stress. Safe assets are worth more than the present value of their cash flows because they provide medium-of-exchange, liquidity, collateral, and store-of-value services. For example, the combination of high liquidity and stable value, especially in times of stress, means that safe assets yield insurance services to their holders. These non-cash service flows can give rise to a "bubble" component in the price of certain assets that rests partly on perceptions of their safety, including the expectation that they will continue to provide the safe asset services mentioned above. While this characterization may seem abstract, safe assets are of great practical importance. For example, governments that supply such assets in the form of debt securities can borrow more cheaply and in larger volumes.

In a financially globalized setting, domestically supplied safe assets must compete with international safe assets, which are often denominated in dollars. In equilibrium, the real pecuniary return on the domestic safe asset must exceed that of international assets that offer greater safe-asset services. The pecuniary return on domestic safe assets — which includes a risk premium to account for the possibility that the domestic asset loses its safe status — must also satisfy a domestic sustainability condition. This condition becomes easier to satisfy the smaller the domestic safe-asset risk premium and the faster the domestic economy's growth rate.

In the stylized framework of Prof. Brunnermeier *et al.*, global financial cycles arise from changes in global risk appetites and from shifts in the monetary policy stance of leading safe-asset suppliers, principally the United States. A "risk-on" period often coincides with loose U.S. monetary policy (i.e., low U.S. interest rates), which increases the relative attractiveness of the domestic safe asset, raising its price and lowering its pecuniary yield. Small open economies can then borrow externally at lower costs by using local safe assets as collateral. These conditions facilitate a domestic economic boom and a relaxation of the domestic sustainability condition. However, when U.S. monetary policy tightens, market participants reallocate to U.S. safe assets and a "risk-off" period ensues. The small open economy's safe assets then face greater foreign competition, raising pecuniary yields on the domestic safe asset. The increase in borrowing costs lowers the domestic economy's growth rate, which tightens the domestic sustainability condition. The safe status of domestic safe assets can come under threat, possibly leading to a decline, or even precipitous collapse, in the bubble component of the domestic safe-asset price.

Thus, the ability of small open economies to issue safe assets is affected by foreign monetary policy as well as domestic conditions. The authors use their integrated framework to analyse several possible policies to prevent the bursting of the domestic safe-asset bubble in "risk-off" episodes and to avoid inefficient risk-taking during "risk-on" episodes. These include macro-prudential policies and capital controls to directly restrict portfolio choices, as well as foreign exchange interventions or foreign reserve management to change the mix of assets and liabilities in the domestic economy. They also consider interactions between these policies and conventional monetary policy.

The authors point out that ex-ante macroprudential policies can prevent the bursting of a safe-asset bubble by inhibiting leverage and the asset-price inflation induced by large capital inflows during the boom or risk-on phase. By ensuring that banks retain sufficient capital buffers during the boom phase, the economy has a larger cushion to head off runs in response to falling growth during the risk-off phase. Ex-post macro-prudential policies that force banks to hold more domestic government debt implicitly restrict capital outflows during the bust phase, which can also help the domestic safe asset retain its safe status. In addition, anticipations of ex-post capital controls and exchange rate interventions can help maintain price stability and market liquidity by persuading domestic safe-asset holders that no run will ensue, thereby raising the bubble component of the domestic safe-asset value. Knowing that the bubble will survive even after a rise in the U.S. interest rate, investors become more willing to hold domestic safe assets.

The authors provide a novel perspective on the debate over the validity of the trilemma in international finance. Even if the foreign exchange rate is fully flexible, constraints on the economy's ability to issue domestic safe assets can limit its monetary policy autonomy. For example, expansionary monetary policy in response to a negative domestic shock may undermine the safe status of the domestic safe asset due to competition from international safe assets. Contractionary monetary policy to stabilise inflation may lower the economy's growth rate, tightening the domestic sustainability condition and thereby threatening the status of the domestic safe asset. In this way, monetary policy autonomy can be constrained by foreign competition and domestic growth, even under a flexible exchange rate regime.

By helping to preserve the capacity to issue domestic safe assets, macro-prudential policies, capital controls and exchange rate interventions can create more space for monetary policy. Wise application of these policies can accommodate, or even shape, competition among domestic and international safe assets and also accommodate shifts in global risk appetites in ways that promote financial stability and healthy risk-taking.

Discussants stress that the viability and resilience of domestic safe assets also depends on the quality of domestic governance.[3] In particular, weak public governance that leads to wasteful government over-borrowing without faster growth tightens the domestic sustainability condition. Furthermore, measures aimed at supporting the domestic safe asset, such as capital controls, can distort market competition and development and lead to excessive borrowing in foreign currencies by the private sector. The interactions among the authors and discussants point to the importance of several key factors for a stable system that include good governance, efficient information flows, and prudent public and private sector behavior based on informed and rational expectations.

### *Improving the global financial architecture*

In the framework of Brunnermeier *et al.* (Chapter 8), financial stability rests partly on preserving the bubble component of safe-asset values. To improve financial stability, they stress the need to ensure an adequate and stable supply of safe assets. Under the current global financial architecture, safe assets are asymmetrically supplied: a few countries issue a disproportionate share of global safe assets, as Prof. Gourinchas describes in Chapter 7. The current policy toolkit to deal with shortages of safe assets and instability in their values includes IMF lending facilities, bilateral swap lines between central banks, and the costly accumulation of foreign exchange reserves during normal times.

In view of this asymmetry, and building on Brunnermeier *et al.* (2017) and Prof. Brunnermeier's suggestion in AMPF 2018, the authors propose an international system of Global Safe Bonds (which they call GloSBies). GloSBies are bonds issued from the pooled liabilities of a group of EME countries, which are then tranched into senior and junior grades. The

---

[3] See Prof. Viral Acharya, 2020, http://abfer.org/media/abfer-events-2020/e-ampf/ eAMPF2020_Comments_Viral-Acharya.pdf and Dr. Frank Smet, 2020. http://abfer.org/ media/abfer-events-2020/e-ampf/eAMPF2020_Comments_Frank-Smets.pdf

proposal calls for an international special-purpose vehicle (SPV) that buys a fraction of participating countries' sovereign bonds and requires the participating countries to commit to service the senior tranche first. The aim is for the senior tranche to achieve safe-asset status, lowering funding costs for all participating countries. Under such a system, the authors argue that international investors will tend to allocate larger portfolio shares to junior tranches during risk-on periods and shift to senior tranches during risk-off periods. This should help maintain credit supply to participating countries by generating strong demand for senior bonds in periods of market stress, thereby reducing capital flight from EMEs. This system also benefits from the diversification over the multiple countries that contribute bonds to the pool.

## Concluding Remarks

As we look back to the Asian Monetary Policy Forums from 2014 to 2020, we are greatly pleased to see so many excellent contributions that throw light on the complex policy challenges facing central banks. As we look forward, we see no shortage of open questions for future editions of the AMPF.

One pressing set of issues is how best to deploy monetary and fiscal policies to promote recovery from the devastating economic effects of the COVID-19 pandemic. Another set of issues, intensified by the pandemic, involves the high fiscal deficits and sovereign debt levels in many countries. The risk of major sovereign debt crises looms larger now than before the pandemic, at least in some parts of the world, and there is now less fiscal space to deploy in future crises. The secular fall in nominal and real interest rates, which predates the pandemic, lessens the scope for conventional monetary policy tools and is another major factor behind the expanded use of once-unconventional monetary policy tools. The optimal mix of conventional and unconventional monetary policies, and whether and how to combine them with macroprudential policies, remains an important issue.

The dominant role of the U.S. dollar and U.S. monetary policy is also likely to remain a significant source of tension and policy challenges in the years ahead. One question is whether the United States will remain willing and able to serve as chief supplier of global reserves, borrowing from the rest of the world and running persistent trade deficits. Another question is whether other countries will remain satisfied with that role for the United States. Many, including AMPF participants, have raised concerns about the asymmetric supply of safe assets and the vulnerabilities they create in the current system. Some also propose solutions that call for careful evaluation and analysis.

Advances in distributed-ledger technologies are also shaking up the banking and financial system. Tech companies and central banks are studying, experimenting with, and adopting innovations in payment mechanisms that have great potential to disrupt business models in the banking sector and create new challenges for monetary policy (Duffie 2019). These new technologies offer the promise of large benefits in the form of faster, cheaper payments and better information, but their effects on functional efficiency in the payments system, monetary policy transmission, and financial stability are far from fully understood. These and other issues will find a ready discussion platform at the AMPF, which will continue to bring together central bankers, academics and market participants to analyze the issues and inform debates about policy design.

## References

Acharya, VV (2020). Comments on a safe-asset perspective for an integrated policy framework. Presented at Asian Monetary Policy Forum, Asian Bureau of Finance and Economic Research.

Avdjiev, S, el Berger, B, and Shin, HS (2018). Gauging procyclicality and financial vulnerability in Asia through the BIS banking and financial statistics. Presented at Asian Monetary Policy Forum, Asian Bureau of Finance and Economic Research (Chapter 6, this Volume).

Blanchard, O (2016). Currency wars, coordination, and capital controls. Presented at Asian Monetary Policy Forum, Asian Bureau of Finance and Economic Research (Chapter 4, this Volume).

Blinder, AS (2018). *Advice and dissent: why America suffers when economics and politics collide*. Basic Books.

Brunnermeier, MK, Langfield, S, Pagano, M, Reis, R, Van Nieuwerburgh, S, and Vayanos, D (2017). ESBies: safety in the tranches. *Economic Policy*, 32(90), 175–219.

Brunnermeier, MK, Merkel, S, and Sannikov, Y (2020). A safe-asset perspective for an integrated policy framework. Presented at Asian Monetary Policy Forum, Asian Bureau of Finance and Economic Research (Chapter 8, this Volume).

Brunnermeier, MK and Sannikov, Y (2016). The I theory of money. Working Paper, Princeton University.

Brunnermeier, MK and Sannikov, Y (2019). International monetary theory: a risk perspective. Working Paper, Princeton University.

Duffie, D (2019). Digital currencies and fast payments systems: disruption is coming. Prepared for the Asian Monetary Policy Forum, May.

Eichengreen, BJ (2015). Financial development in Asia: the role of policy and institutions, with special reference to China. Presented at Asian Monetary Policy Forum, Asian Bureau of Finance and Economic Research (Chapter 3, this Volume).

Frankel, J (2019). Systematic managed floating. *Open Economies Review*, 30(2), 255–295. (Presented at Asian Monetary Policy Forum 2017) (Chapter 5, this Volume).

Gourinchas, P-O (2019). The dollar hegemon? evidence and implications for policy makers. Presented at Asian Monetary Policy Forum, Asian Bureau of Finance and Economic Research (Chapter 7, this Volume).

Han, XH and Wei, SJ (2018). International transmissions of monetary shocks: between a trilemma and a dilemma. *Journal of International Economics*, 110, 205–219.

Menon, R (2014). Getting in all the cracks or targeting the cracks? Securing financial stability in the post-crisis era. Opening Remarks at the 2014 Asian Monetary Policy Forum, Singapore (Chapter 1, this Volume).

Obstfeld, M (2015). *Trilemmas and tradeoffs: living with financial globalization*. Central Bank of Chile. (Presented at Asian Monetary Policy Forum 2014) (Chapter 2, this Volume).

Rey, H (2013). Dilemma not trilemma: the global financial cycle and monetary policy independence. In *Global Dimensions of Unconventional Monetary Policy*. Proceedings of the Economic Policy Symposium at Jackson Hole, Federal Reserve Bank of Kansas City.

Smets, FR (2020). Comments on a safe-asset perspective for an integrated policy framework. Presented at Asian Monetary Policy Forum, Asian Bureau of Finance and Economic Research.

# CHAPTER 1

# Chapter 1

# "Getting in All the Cracks or Targeting the Cracks? Securing Financial Stability in the Post-Crisis Era"*

## Ravi Menon[1]

### Monetary Policy at the Crossroads

One of the most pressing questions facing central bankers today concerns the role of monetary policy in helping to secure financial stability. For two decades before the Global Financial Crisis (GFC), central bankers thought they had found the secret sauce of monetary policy. The recipe was simple — an independent central bank, a single target (price stability) and a single instrument (the interest rate). Monetary policy was directed at achieving price and output stability, with the central bank's reaction function well-characterized by the Taylor rule on an ex-post basis.

The recipe worked brilliantly. Sustained price stability and steady economic growth were the order of the day. The result was the Great Moderation. Indeed, monetary policy was getting boring. During this period, monetary policy was unencumbered by financial stability considerations. To be fair, central bankers were not unconcerned about financial stability. But financial stability was seen as the preserve of prudential regulation and supervision. Academic thinking reinforced

---

* This chapter is a slightly edited version of MC Ravi Menon's 2014 AMPF speech.
[1] Opening Remarks by the Managing Director of the Monetary Authority of Singapore at the Asian Monetary Policy Forum (AMPF) on 24 May 2014

policy practice: the macroeconomic models central banks relied on did not map clear linkages between financial and real variables.

Another constraint may have been the perceived difficulty in identifying a financial bubble ex-ante. How does one tell if the value of an asset reflected economic fundamentals or speculative fever? So, when faced with potential financial vulnerabilities, it was deemed better to *clean up* after a bubble had actually burst than to try to *lean against* suspected bubbles.

But beneath the still waters of macroeconomic stability, deadly financial whirlpools were forming. Financial imbalances built up steadily in the advanced economies from the mid-1990s to mid-2000s and culminated in the GFC of 2008/2009. The Crisis sent financial systems into a tailspin and plunged economies into recession. The cost of cleaning up after the bubble had burst proved extremely high. The "*clean versus lean*" debate has been re-ignited, and within the "*lean*" camp there are differences over how to lean. Monetary policy has become interesting again.

## Financial Stability: What We Know and What We Don't

Following the Crisis, there has been growing consensus that it is important for central banks to pay more attention to financial stability. We know now that macroeconomic stability does not guarantee financial stability. Nor does prudential supervision of individual institutions guarantee financial stability at the systemic level.

We also have a much better appreciation of how credit cycles have strong implications for financial stability.

Schularick and Taylor (2009) describe financial crises as "*credit booms gone wrong*",[2] arguing that risks to financial stability stem from both the pace of credit creation as well as the level of credit. Borio and Disyatat

---

[2] Schularick and Taylor (2009)'s phrase is taken from Eichengreen and Mitchener's 2003 BIS working paper on "The Great Depression as a Credit Boom Gone Wrong".

(2011) argue that the amplitude of financial cycles, such as for credit, exceeds that of business cycles due to what they call *"excess elasticity"* of the financial system. Cross-border financial flows amplify domestic credit booms and domestic monetary policy fails to constrain the credit creation process adequately. Mishkin (2008) warns how the bursting of credit-fueled asset price bubbles can lead to episodes of financial instability that are particularly damaging for the economy.

These findings help us better understand the conditions that led to the GFC. And the concerns remain valid in the post-Crisis environment. Central banks have kept policy rates low for long, and purchased assets in large quantities further out along the yield curve. Even though the United States was already "tapering" its asset purchases by end-2013, global financial conditions remain extremely loose. There are signs of growing risk-taking: in the form of leveraged loans, covenant-lite corporate bonds, and narrowing spreads on sub-investment grade paper. The risks to financial stability are nowhere near pre-Crisis levels, but they bear close watching. We must not repeat the mistakes of the past.

But there is as yet no consensus on how to secure financial stability and, in particular, *what* role, if any, should be played by monetary policy.

There are three broad approaches to these questions. The first is to stick to the status quo. Monetary policy remains focused on price stability with macroprudential policies limited to the use of capital buffers to pre-empt insolvencies. In the second approach, monetary policy explicitly takes account of financial stability in addition to price stability. Under the third approach, monetary policy remains focused on price stability, while financial stability is secured with the help of macroprudential policy.

The first approach is well-known and is still the dominant practice in most central banks today, especially in the advanced economies. Under this inflation targeting approach, monetary policy will not try to respond to credit cycle movements or asset bubbles unless they have a demonstrable impact on inflation outcomes. The success of inflation-targeting regimes in central banks around the world have provided ample evidence of the efficacy of this approach. As Lars Svensson (2009) puts it, flexible inflation targeting "remains the best-practice monetary policy before, during, and after the financial crisis."

In the next section, the second and third approaches are considered in more detail.

## Monetary Policy: Getting in All the Cracks

The intellectual underpinning for the second approach is based on the insight that monetary policy has the potential to affect financial stability through several channel; here, I will focus on the importance of the *"risk-taking channel"*.[3] Jeremy Stein (2014) puts it succinctly — *"Monetary policy is fundamentally in the business of altering risk premiums."*

Loose monetary policy can heighten vulnerabilities in the financial system by altering both the perception of risk and the tolerance for risk. In conventional monetary policy, lower policy rates boost incomes and profits, and enhance asset and collateral values. This reduces the incidence of default in banks' asset portfolios, leading to greater leverage and risk-taking.

In unconventional monetary policy, large scale asset purchases by central banks depress returns along the entire yield curve. This provides asset managers the incentive to take on more risk, often in a herd-like fashion.

When interest rates are below the *natural* rate at which desired investment and savings equilibrate, banks will continue to expand credit. When economic agents are determined to take risks, they will find ways to circumvent measures that central banks and regulators have put in place. Non-monetary tools like macroprudential policy will therefore not adequately address the root problem caused by interest rates that are too low.

---

[3] Borio and Zhu (2012) coined the term 'risk-taking' channel of monetary policy to refer to the transmission of monetary policy through its impact on asset and collateral values, which would consequently influence agents' willingness to take on risk.

Under these circumstances, only monetary policy can *"get in all of the cracks"* to plug the vulnerabilities. An increase in short-term interest rates will trigger a more realistic evaluation of asset and collateral values, income flows, and thus risks. This will curtail the extent of leverage created by banks and capital markets and keep asset managers from crowding into risky assets. The effects of monetary policy are all-pervasive, and cannot be easily circumvented.

This approach, if formalized, amounts to augmenting the Taylor rule with an additional term to capture deviations in financial variables from their equilibrium levels.[4] If financial market imbalances are growing, *ceteris paribus*, monetary policy should be tightened, even if it causes further deviations in output from potential in the short term. This approach does not preclude the need for robust financial regulation and supervision. But the key is to *get the price of money right*, to encourage a more realistic perception and tolerance of risks.

While no central bank currently implements monetary policy in this way, the concept behind the approach may not be as abstract as it seems. In practice, central bankers do not ignore financial stability considerations when setting monetary policy.

## Why "Getting in all of the Cracks" May Not Always Work

Relying solely on monetary policy to secure financial stability may not always be sufficient. There are at least three reasons for this. First, monetary policy could be constrained by its traditional mandate: price and output stability. Second, monetary policy could be constrained by global financial factors. Third, monetary policy may get in all the cracks, but it may not be able to fill some of them.

It is useful to illustrate these considerations, by drawing on the Asian experience in recent years. First, it is possible that there is a conflict

---

[4] The augmented Taylor Rule equation is: $i_t = \pi_t + r_t^* + \alpha_\pi(\pi_t - \pi_t^*) + \alpha_y(y_t - y_t^*) + \alpha_f(f_t - f_t^*)$, where f is a variable that measures financial market vulnerability, and $f^*$ is the equilibrium level of that variable.

between the objectives of price stability and financial stability in the short term. Financial and business cycles are not synchronized. The interest rate appropriate for price and output stability may therefore not be consistent with financial stability.

This has been the case in Asia in recent years. When Asian economies recovered fairly quickly from the GFC, their central banks raised interest rates. This was, by a happy coincidence, congruent with the need to stem rapid credit growth that was being fueled by improved economic prospects domestically and easy monetary conditions globally. However, following the Eurozone debt crisis and other domestic shocks, economic activity in Asia slowed, and it became untenable for Asian central banks to raise interest rates further. At the same time, risk-seeking capital flows continued flowing into the region, inducing further increases in credit and asset prices. The business cycle and financial cycle began to diverge.

A second constraint on the effectiveness of monetary policy in dealing with domestic financial stresses is the prominent role played by international liquidity in fueling these stresses. Rey (2013) has observed that global liquidity conditions determined by advanced economies' monetary policies, can, at times, reduce the potency of domestic monetary policy even with exchange rate flexibility.

Obstfeld (2014), taking a more moderate view, argues that monetary independence is still possible, although monetary policy carries a much bigger burden in trying to achieve both financial stability and purely macro objectives, due to the effects of the international financial flows on domestic financial stability.

The recent Asian experience is illustrative. The exuberance in Asian asset markets and consequent build-up of financial risk in recent years has been exacerbated by the global search for yield in a zero interest rate environment. Raising policy rates may not sufficiently alter the extent of risk-taking in these economies. In fact, paradoxically, a central bank that tightens monetary policy to stem domestic borrowing could perversely attract more capital flows into the economy, resulting in stronger credit growth and rising asset prices.

Third, it is not clear that monetary policy can fill all the cracks. Undoubtedly, monetary policy flows into all the cracks by influencing all interest rates in the economy, but some cracks are just too big to fill. Financial vulnerabilities are not evenly spread across the economy and tend to be concentrated in specific sectors and segments. So, even when monetary policy has configured aggregate liquidity and risk-taking settings appropriately, specific pockets of financial market vulnerabilities, e.g., a property bubble, could remain.

Monetary policy is too blunt an instrument for addressing such specific risks to financial stability.

During a property boom, expectations of price appreciation may have a greater influence on current prices. Kuttner and Shim (2013) estimate that a 100 basis point increase in the short-term interest rate would lower real annualized credit growth by less than 1 percentage point in the following quarter and a 100 basis point rate hike reduces real housing price growth by only 1 percentage point. Using monetary policy to defuse a property bubble may therefore require very sharp increases in interest rates to be effective. But this may cause significant collateral damage to other parts of the economy.

**Macroprudential Policy: Targeting the Cracks**

This brings us to the third approach: using macroprudential policy, while monetary policy continues to focus on price and output stability. Macroprudential policies can be more effective for "targeting the cracks" where specific vulnerabilities are concentrated.

But what exactly are macroprudential policies? Some have called macroprudential policy *"old wine in new bottles"*, as many macroprudential tools are the same as the microprudential limits familiar to regulators: loan-to-value ratios, debt-to-income ratios, debt service ratios, and so on.

However, there are some key differences. Unlike microprudential policy which typically involves the adjustment of individual levers, or monetary policy which has a single instrument, macroprudential policy requires a multi-dimensional approach. There is no fixed instrument that has a stable or reliable relationship with financial stability or asset price stability.

Macroprudential policies encompass more than loan-to-value ratios for borrowers and counter-cyclical capital buffers for lenders. Adjusting capital requirements in a counter-cyclical fashion or increasing the risk weights for loans to vulnerable sectors cannot fill the cracks completely. In a boom market characterized by keen competition among banks, higher capital charges do not translate into sufficiently higher lending rates that can restrain demand. A cross-country study by the Basel Committee on Banking Supervision shows that a 1 percentage point increase in capital ratios results in a median rise in lending spreads of only 13 basis points.

Dealing with the magnitude of financial cycles or bubble dynamics that economies typically face from time to time requires some absolute prudential limits. In Singapore, which has been an early experimenter and practitioner in the use of macroprudential policy, we have employed the following limits on property loans as of 2014[5]:

- Loan tenure cap of 35 years.
- Loan-to-value ratios of 80%, 50%, and 40% for the first, second, and third property loans respectively, for tenures less than 30 years; for loan tenures more than 30 years, the loan-to-value ratios are 60%, 30%, and 20%.
- Total debt-service ratio of 60%, taking into account all debt obligations and using a medium-term interest rate of 3.5% for residential properties. (Mortgage rates are generally below 2%.)
- Cap on banks' property-related exposures at 35% of their total exposures.

In fact, macroprudential policies need not even be limited to prudential tools at the disposal of central banks or financial regulators. In the face

---

[5] For the latest settings of Singapore's macroprudential instruments, please refer to this URL on the MAS website: https://www.mas.gov.sg/publications/macroprudential-policies-in-singapore

of abundant global liquidity, credit-based prudential measures may not constrain loan growth or asset price increases sufficiently. Singapore has therefore also adopted fiscal measures such as stamp duties on buyers and sellers of properties as part of the macroprudential toolkit as of 2014:

- The seller's stamp duty ranges from 4% to 16%, while the buyer's stamp duty ranges from 3% to 18%.
- These are essentially transaction taxes that aim to curb the speculative flipping of properties.

Further, it is important to draw a distinction between macroprudential policies and capital flow management measures. Capital flow measures are applied "*at the gate*" seeking to regulate flows into and out of the economy; macroprudential measures are applied "*inside the house*" targeted at sectors where financial vulnerabilities are building up.

Capital flow measures can be highly distortionary and pose long-term costs to the economy. Accordingly, they should not take the place of needed macroeconomic adjustments.

While capital flow measures may be warranted under extreme circumstances to safeguard financial stability. their implementation should be "targeted, transparent, and generally temporary", as the IMF recommends.

Asian economies have deployed macroprudential policies to deal with financial imbalances, to a greater extent than other economies. So far, the results have not been bad. They have largely tempered the credit cycle and the pace of asset price increases, while generally maintaining price and output stability.

## A Synthesis?

The view that central banks ought to pay due consideration to financial stability is gathering momentum. The discussion above has described two alternative approaches to the status quo to achieving this:

The second approach incorporates financial stability considerations in the setting of monetary policy. The third actively uses macroprudential policy to help secure financial stability.

Perhaps the differences between the two approaches are exaggerated. Both approaches require the central bank to integrate monetary policy functions effectively with prudential policies. In the second approach, strong supervisory and regulatory policies have to be in place even as monetary policy adjusts the level of risk-taking in the economy.

In the third approach, monetary policy must be appropriately calibrated to the economy for macroprudential measures to effectively target specific areas of imbalances.

In practice, the difference between the two approaches is likely to be one of degree and emphasis rather than of fundamental principle. Central banks will choose the most appropriate combination of the two approaches, taking into account the structure of their economies and the nature of the threats to financial stability existing at any point in time.

And let us not forget the continued relevance of the traditional approach. Just because central bankers had previously ignored financial stability considerations with costly consequences, we must not overcompensate now by placing such an undue burden on monetary policy to secure financial stability, that it becomes detrimental to price and output stability.

We do not need to reinvent macroeconomics. Nor do we need to discard most of what we know about monetary policy, built from decades of rigorous research and painful experience. Much of that knowledge remains relevant. In thinking about the so-called *new normal*, we should pay equal heed to what is *new* and what remains *normal*. No doubt, we need to update our paradigms to meet new realities. But we do not need to overhaul them.

It is also important to bear in mind that the current situation is highly unusual. We must not fall into the trap of believing that the innovative policy measures being taken now in response to these unusual conditions represent the basis for a new paradigm in the future.

I suspect that when the dust has settled and more normal conditions return, monetary policy regimes will not look drastically different from pre-Crisis days. More central banks will have an eye to financial stability considerations — at least informally — when setting monetary policy. More central banks are also likely to have macroprudential policy toolkits at their disposal, which they will use from time to time but perhaps not on the scale that has been used in Asia in recent years. But in essence, monetary policy will remain largely focused on price and output stability — as it should be.

Perhaps as TS Eliot puts it, the end of all our exploring is to arrive where we started and know the place for the first time.

## References

Bank for International Settlements (2010). An assessment of the long-term economic impact of stronger capital and liquidity requirements. Basel Committee of Banking Supervision.

Borio, C and Disyatat, P (2011). Global imbalances and the financial crisis: Link or no link? BIS Working Papers No. 346.

Borio, C and Zhu, H (2012). Capital regulation, risk-taking and monetary policy: A missing link in the transmission mechanism? *Journal of Financial Stability*, 8(4), 236–251.

Eichengreen, BJ and Mitchener, KJ (2003). The great depression as a credit boom gone wrong. BIS Working Papers No. 137.

IMF (2012). The liberalization and management of capital flows: An institutional view. IMF Staff Paper.

Kuttner, K and Shim, I (2013). Can non-interest rate policies stabilise housing markets? Evidence from a panel of 57 economies. BIS Working Papers No. 433.

Lane, PR (2014). International capital flows and domestic credit conditions. *Macroeconomic Review*, XIII(1), Monetary Authority of Singapore, Economic Policy Group.

Mishkin, FS (2008). How should we respond to asset bubbles? Speech delivered at the Wharton Financial Institutions Center and Oliver Wyman Institute's Annual Financial Risk Roundtable, Philadelphia, Pennsylvania, 15 May.

Obstfeld, M (2014). Trilemmas and tradeoffs: Living with globalization. Paper commissioned for the Asian Monetary Policy Forum (Ch. 2 in *The Asian Monetary Policy Forum: Insights for Central Banking*, Steven J. Davis, Edward S. Robinson, and Bernard Yeung (eds), World Scientific Pte Ltd., 2021).

Rey, H (2013). Dilemma not trilemma: The global financial cycle and monetary policy independence. In *Global Dimensions of Unconventional Monetary Policy*. Proceedings of the Economic Policy Symposium at Jackson Hole, Federal Reserve Bank of Kansas City.

Schularick, M and Taylor, AM (2009). Credit booms gone bust: Monetary policy, leverage cycles and financial crises, 1870–2008. NBER Working Paper No. 15512.

Stein, JC (2014). Comments on 'market tantrums and monetary policy'. Speech delivered at the U.S. Monetary Policy Forum, New York, 28 February.

Svensson, LEO (2009). Flexible inflation targeting — lessons from the financial crisis. Speech delivered at the workshop "Towards a new framework for monetary policy? Lessons from the crisis", organized by the Netherlands Bank, Amsterdam, 21 September.

Taylor, JB (2007). Housing and monetary policy. NBER Working Paper No. 13682.

# CHAPTER 2

# Chapter 2

# Trilemmas and Tradeoffs: Living with Financial Globalization[*]

## Maurice Obstfeld[1]

### Abstract

This paper evaluates the capacity of emerging market economies (EMEs) to moderate the domestic impact of global financial and monetary forces through their own monetary policies. Those EMEs able to exploit a flexible exchange rate are far better positioned than those that devote monetary policy to fixing the rate — a reflection of the classical monetary policy trilemma. However, exchange rate changes alone do not insulate economies from foreign financial and monetary shocks. While potentially a potent source of economic benefits, financial globalization does have a downside for economic management. It worsens the tradeoffs monetary policy faces in navigating among multiple domestic objectives. This drawback of globalization raises the marginal value of additional tools of macroeconomic and financial policy. Unfortunately, the availability of such tools is constrained by a *financial* policy trilemma, distinct from the monetary trilemma. The second trilemma posits the incompatibility of national responsibility for financial policy, international financial integration, and financial stability.

[*] Paper commissioned for the Asian Monetary Policy Forum, Singapore (May 2014). I thank Sandile Hlatshwayo for long-suffering research assistance and comments, and the Risk Research Center at UC Berkeley for financial support. Claudio Borio, Menzie Chinn, Pierre-Olivier Gourinchas, Jonathan Ostry, and Jay Shambaugh also provided helpful comments, as did participants in a seminar at the University of Chicago's Becker-Friedman Institute and the Asian Monetary Policy Forum. I thank my discussants at the 13th BIS Annual Conference (June 2014), Otmar Issing and Takatoshi Ito, as well as participants. Gong Cheng, Menzie Chinn, Michael Klein, Gian Maria Milesi-Ferretti, and Jay Shambaugh graciously provided data. All errors are mine.
[1] Class of 1958 Professor of Economics, University of California, Berkeley. Non-resident Senior Fellow, Peterson Institute for International Economics.

## Introduction

This paper evaluates the capacity of emerging market economies (EMEs) to moderate the domestic impact of global financial and monetary forces through their own monetary policies. I present a case that those EMEs able to exploit a flexible exchange rate are far better positioned than those that devote monetary policy to fixing the rate — a reflection of the classical monetary policy trilemma. Indeed, this ability was critically important in EMEs' widely successful response to the Global Financial Crisis (GFC) of 2007–2009.

However, exchange rate changes alone do not insulate economies from foreign financial and monetary developments. While potentially a potent source of economic benefits, financial globalization does have a downside for economic management. It worsens the tradeoffs monetary policy faces in navigating among multiple domestic objectives. This drawback of globalization raises the marginal value of additional tools of macroeconomic and financial policy.

Unfortunately, the availability of such tools is constrained by a *financial* policy trilemma, distinct from the monetary trilemma. The second trilemma posits the incompatibility of national responsibility for financial policy, international financial integration, and financial stability. It therefore impedes effective national prudential policies when capital markets are open to cross-border transactions.[2]

My argument that independent monetary policy is feasible for financially open EMEs, but limited in what it can achieve, takes a middle ground between more extreme positions in the debate about monetary independence in open economies. On one side, Woodford (2010, p. 14) concludes: "I find it difficult to construct scenarios under which globalization would interfere in any substantial way with the ability of domestic monetary policy to maintain control over the dynamics of inflation." His pre-GFC analysis, however, leaves aside financial-market imperfections and views inflation targeting as the only objective of monetary control. On

---

[2] See Schoenmaker (2013) for a broad survey.

the other side, Rey (2013) argues that the monetary trilemma really is a dilemma, because EMEs can exercise no monetary autonomy from United States policy (or the global financial cycle) unless they impose capital controls.

The outline of this paper is as follows. First, I present an overview of the capital flow problem for EMEs. Then, I review mechanisms through which monetary policies and the financial cycle in advanced economies, especially in the U.S., are transmitted to EMEs. One potent mechanism works through interest rate linkages, but financial conditions can also migrate through other channels. Thus, there is a global financial cycle that does not coincide with global monetary-policy shifts (Borio 2012; Bruno and Shin 2013; Rey 2013), and exchange-rate changes alone do not fully offset its effects. The next section sets out empirical evidence on interest rate independence in EMEs, adding to the existing literature by analyzing long-term interest rates. The results leave no doubt that countries that do not peg their exchange rates exercise considerable monetary autonomy at the short end of the term structure; but long-term interest rates are more highly correlated across countries, with little regard for the exchange-rate regime.

In the penultimate section, I describe the relationship between policy trilemmas and tradeoffs in open economies. I present my argument that the fundamental problem for open EMEs is not ineffective monetary policy *per se*. The problem is a more difficult tradeoff among multiple objectives, the result of a shortage of reliable policy instruments for attaining those objectives simultaneously.[3] A brief final section outlines future research directions and also describes how some limited initiatives in international policy cooperation might soften the harsh tradeoffs that EMEs now face.

## Overview

Since the nineteenth century, emerging and frontier regions have been subject to the ebb and flow of lending from richer countries. Even in

---

[3] In a closely related spirit, Filardo, Genberg, and Hofmann (2014) propose a "three-pillar" policy strategy for emerging economies — one that navigates among price stability, financial stability, and exchange rate goals.

the last century, powerful lending cycles buffeted those regions in the 1920s, in the 1970s through the early 1980s, in the early 1990s, in the middle 2000s, and after 2009.

With the development of emerging financial markets and the general expansion of global finance, however, recent decades have revealed some new patterns. First, many emerging countries that Nurkse (1954) ruled out as portfolio investment destinations based on their colonial history now receive such flows. Perhaps history is not always destiny after all. Second, even emerging economies with persistent current account surpluses — including several Asian economies — may experience *gross* capital inflow surges, the result of rich-country portfolio shifts in favor of emerging assets. Where these portfolio demands are accommodated through the home central bank's intervention, the financial inflows finance foreign reserve increases. Where the central bank instead allows currency appreciation, net private claims by foreigners still rise, albeit gradually over time, as a result of a reduced current account balance.[4] China's case shows how both mechanisms can operate at once. Whether the central bank intervenes or not, domestic financial conditions are affected immediately, though the expansionary effect is probably bigger when intervention occurs and causes an increase in the domestic money supply and domestic bank credit.[5]

---

[4] In a pair of classic contributions, Calvo, Leiderman, and Reinhart (1993; 1996) linked *net* emerging market capital inflow surges to monetary ease in the advanced countries. Their theme remains highly relevant, of course, and is the central focus of this paper. For documentation on *gross* capital flow surges and reversals, see Cowan *et al.* (2008), Forbes and Warnock (2012), and Broner, Didier, Erce, and Schmukler (2013). On long-term cycles in capital flows, see Bacha and Díaz-Alejandro (1982), Eichengreen (1991), and Obstfeld and Taylor (2004). Of course, the pattern of net capital flows remains puzzling, as discussed by Prasad, Rajan, and Subramanian (2007) and Gourinchas and Jeanne (2013). On the importance of financing conditions as reflected in gross capital flows, see Borio and Disyatat (2011).

[5] For some suggestive evidence that this is the case, and that net private capital inflows are likely to create more financial fragility in economies with less flexible exchange-rate regimes, see Magud, Reinhart, and Vesperoni (2014). The theoretical perspective I sketch later in this paper suggests, however, that a more nuanced understanding would come from studying the impacts of *gross* inflows, as analyzed by some of the references listed in the previous footnote.

Capital inflow surges can cause a range of dislocations — not the least of which is to create a range of vulnerabilities to subsequent capital-flow reversals. After the GFC, industrial countries, their recoveries slowed by effects of private and public debt overhang, relied on continuing monetary stimulus in the forms of ultra-low policy interest rates (sometimes coupled with forward guidance) and unconventional quantitative measures. In general, however, the EMEs — at least those that avoided big debt run-ups[6] — had suffered less in the crisis. With economies growing more briskly than those of advanced countries, these EMEs did not require abnormally accommodative monetary policy settings. Currencies, bonds, equities, and real estate appreciated because of the resulting global portfolio shift into EME assets. Appreciation contributed to financial stability (as well as competitiveness) concerns, and countries that resisted exchange-rate change through intervention saw greater pressure on domestic asset prices, on domestic credit growth, and on general product price levels. Those pressures have now left EMEs more vulnerable to a reversal of global financial flows.

Clearly, then, EMEs have an interest in tempering the effects of global portfolio shifts, especially when the sequence is capital feast followed by capital famine. How can EMEs use their macroeconomic tools to do so? Astute observers have long known that *in principle* monetary policy is vital, but cannot furnish the sole response to capital inflow surges. Shortly after the Tequila crisis of two decades ago, for example, Calvo, Leiderman and Reinhart (1996, p. 137) wrote:

> [T]he countries that have been the most successful in managing capital flows ... have implemented a comprehensive policy package and not relied on a single instrument. At the outset of the surge in inflows, these countries reacted by treating inflows as temporary and resisted a nominal exchange rate appreciation; the foreign exchange intervention was mostly sterilized. As the inflows persisted, sterilization efforts were scaled back and the domestic currency was allowed to appreciate. To moderate the extent of the real appreciation

---

[6] See Gourinchas and Obstfeld (2012).

and prevent the economy from overheating, fiscal policy was tightened. To moderate the volume of the inflows and lengthen their maturities, exchange rate flexibility was increased and measures to curb inflows were implemented.

A less productive policy mix has consisted of persistent sterilization (which keeps short-term interest rates comparatively high), heavy intervention in the foreign exchange market (which results in little short-run exchange rate uncertainty) and no controls on short-term capital movements. All of these policies have tended to provide especially strong incentives for short-term capital inflows.

Subsequent research and experience suggested, however, that for some countries, the preceding approach was difficult to implement *in practice* during the 1990s. Perhaps most importantly, currency mismatch and the need for an easily verifiable nominal anchor sometimes imparted a strong policy bias toward exchange-rate stability in EMEs, thereby constraining monetary policy (Hausmann, Panizza, and Stein 2001; Calvo and Reinhart 2002). In the presence of fixed or highly managed exchange rates, a number of policy failures set the stage for the EME crises of the late 1990s.

More recently, the position of EMEs has evolved considerably. As noted above, international financial flows have increased in scale, particularly in gross terms, driven in significant part by international banking flows. At the same time domestic financial systems have expanded and deepened. While for EMEs these changes are not as extreme as for the advanced countries, they are still highly significant and leave EMEs more exposed to shifts in global financial-market sentiment. For example, a big sell-off of domestic assets by foreign investors is likely to induce a significant exchange rate change before enough buyers come forward to restore market equilibrium. EME corporates and banks increasingly issue bonds offshore, and these foreign-currency liabilities — not captured in standard, residence-based net international investment position data — are a potential source of currency mismatch, as well as direct exposure to foreign financing conditions (Turner 2014; Shin 2013).

Cross-border/domestic credit ratio (percent)

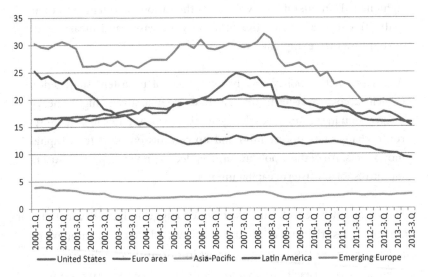

**Figure 1.** Cross-border credit as a fraction of domestic credit, by region
*Source*: BIS, Global Liquidity Indicators

One manifestation of global financial linkages is the importance of cross-border credit, both in local and foreign currency (see Borio, McCauley, and McGuire 2011). Figure 1 shows the ratio of cross-border to domestic bank credit for five regions, as measured in the BIS Global Liquidity Indicators. Three regularities stand out. First, apart from the Asia-Pacific grouping (which mixes advanced and emerging economies), cross-border credit is very significant compared to domestic bank credit — currently in the 10 to 20% range for the other four regions. Second, in all regions, the ratio of cross-border to domestic credit covaries positively with the global credit boom of the mid-2000s and the subsequent collapse — a reflection of the gross financial flows that helped fuel the GFC. Finally, the cross-border bank credit ratio falls secularly in Latin America and emerging Europe, from a very high level at the start of the millennium to a level roughly on the same order as for the U.S. and the euro area. In part, declining reliance on cross-border bank lending reflects domestic financial deepening; in part, it reflects retrenchment in banks' global activities and growth in bond finance after the GFC. While perhaps reduced compared to its level in 2000, considerable exposure

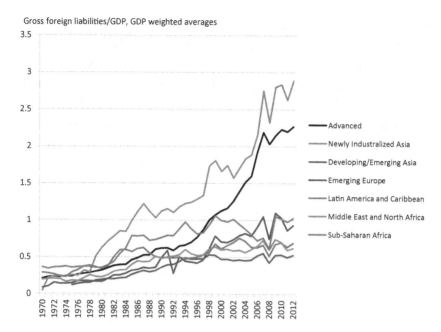

Gross foreign liabilities/GDP, GDP weighted averages

Legend:
- Advanced
- Newly Industralized Asia
- Developing/Emerging Asia
- Emerging Europe
- Latin America and Caribbean
- Middle East and North Africa
- Sub-Saharan Africa

**Figure 2.**  Gross external liabilities relative to GDP, by region
*Source*: Updated data from Lane and Milesi-Ferretti (2007), courtesy Gian Maria Milesi-Ferretti

to global banking fluctuations remains for many EMEs, and evidence indicates that net cross-border debt flows fuel domestic credit growth.[7] Moreover, increasing EME recourse to non-bank funding sources has created new exposures, some not even visible in residence-based data on gross external liabilities, such as the Lane and Milesi-Ferretti (2007) data for selected countries shown in Figure 2.[8]

Counteracting the increased vulnerabilities are some policy and institutional enhancements.[9] Over time, EMEs have shifted their gross liability positions away from debt in the direction of equity instruments

---

[7] Locational banking data such as these (based on the residence principle) may well understate banking exposure, as the head offices of domestic affiliates are likely to divert funding in a crisis. See Cetorelli and Goldberg (2011). Lane and McQuade (2014) document a link between net cross-border debt flows and domestic credit growth.

[8] For this figure I exclude tax havens as well as all countries with GDP below $2 billion in 2012.

[9] See Obstfeld (2014) for a more detailed survey and discussion.

(portfolio equity and FDI). In this respect, international financial integration promotes international risk sharing and therefore can be a stabilizing factor. Figures 3 and 4 illustrate the recent dramatic shift of external liabilities toward equity (see also Lane and Shambaugh 2010 and Prasad 2012).[10] Currency depreciation automatically devalues this portion of external liabilities; but even the remaining external and domestic debt is increasingly denominated in domestic currency (Lane and Shambaugh

Fraction

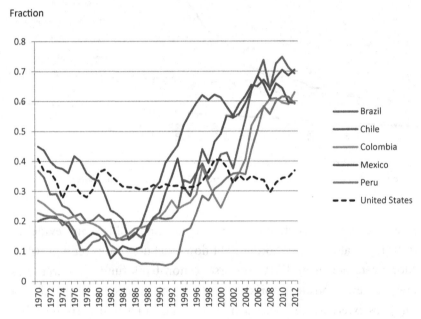

**Figure 3.** External equity liabilities relative to total external liabilities, by country: Western Hemisphere
*Source*: Updated data from Lane and Milesi-Ferretti (2007)

---

[10] In general, the picture in emerging Europe (where some countries are in the euro area) is more mixed and not as favorable to foreign equity finance. The data in the figures of course reflect stock market price fluctuations, but the trends are still clear. Broadly speaking, if one starts in 1970, the data describe a J shape. Prior to gaining access to private lending markets in the 1970s, developing countries relied primarily on FDI for private foreign financing. Access to debt finance allowed a fall in the FDI share. Only much later did portfolio equity inflows become important. The United States is shown in Figure 3 for the purpose of comparison. A caveat to Figures 3 and 4 is that the Lane and Milesi-Ferretti data, which are residence-based, do not capture offshore bond issuance by domestic nationals.

Fraction

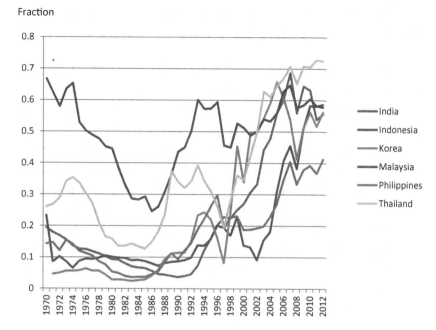

**Figure 4.** External equity liabilities relative to total external liabilities, by country: Asia
*Source*: Updated data from Lane and Milesi-Ferretti (2007)

2010; Miyajima, Mohanty, and Chan 2012; Turner 2012). The growth of domestic bond markets — most advanced among the EMEs in Asia, where corporates are significant players alongside governments — has been an important supporting factor. Moving from a nominal exchange rate anchor to some alternative (often a managed float within the context of an inflation target) has paid dividends for many EMEs, both in providing generally moderate inflation and in relieving the government of the need to defend a definite line in the sand with monetary policy or reserves. The second dividend has generally reduced the incidence of foreign exchange crises, in part by freeing foreign exchange reserves for purposes other than defense of an exchange rate target.[11] Of course, more reliably moderate

---

[11] Ghosh, Ostry, and Qureshi (2014) discuss evidence on the susceptibility of hard and adjustable pegs to crisis. If foreign exchange reserves are not dedicated to defense of the exchange rate, more of them can be used in lender-of-last resort operations in support of domestic entities with short-term foreign-currency liabilities. On the relation between reserve use during the GFC and economic performance, see Dominguez, Hashimoto, and Ito (2012).

inflation itself has helped to promote domestic-currency denomination of domestic and foreign liabilities.

A more effective approach to financial oversight, typically including a macroprudential component, has supplemented these macroeconomic regime changes. Many EMEs, especially in Asia, have accumulated large stocks of foreign exchange reserves that allow the domestic monetary authority to play a lender-of-last-resort role for financial institutions with short-term foreign-current liabilities. Market perceptions that authorities are able and willing to play that role, as many did quite effectively during the GFC, are a stabilizing factor for capital flows. Moreover, large precautionary reserve holdings are complemented by a higher level of capital-account restrictions than in advanced economies; Bussière *et al.* (2014) present evidence on the stabilizing effects of reserve stocks and the use of capital-account measures. Figure 5, which is borrowed from their paper, shows that

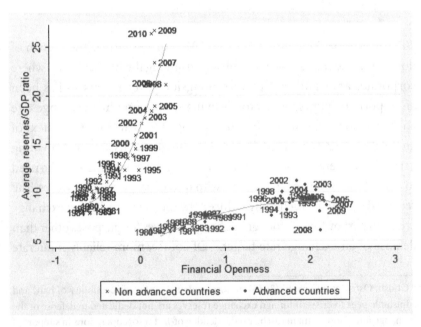

**Figure 5.** Financial openness and international reserves of advanced and developing/emerging countries, by year

*Source*: Bussière et al. (2014), courtesy Menzie Chinn, based on the updated Chinn-Ito (2006) index

while advanced and advancing countries alike have liberalized cross-border financial flows over the past three decades, the developing/emerging group has on average liberalized less and accumulated more international reserves in the process.[12]

To what degree have the preceding structural changes insulated EMEs from monetary shifts and financial cycles in advanced countries? Both during the accommodative phase of advanced-country monetary policies following the GFC, and more lately, as markets have come to anticipate the tapering of accommodation in the United States, EMEs showed their habitual reluctance to let exchange rates bear the full adjustment burden. Indeed, some of the very structural changes cited as enhancements for EME stability could have downsides. Domestic bond markets, if dominated by foreign asset managers and lacking big domestic players such as pension funds and insurance companies, could be quite volatile, with long-term bond returns tightly linked to those in advanced-country markets (Shin 2013).[13] Moreover, if foreign holders of EME-currency bonds hedge the currency risk with counterparts in the issuing country, this potentially creates a currency mismatch: the domestic counterparts have incurred a foreign-currency liability which (leaving aside the associated forward claim to a domestic-currency payment from the bond holders) is equivalent to foreign-currency bond issuance (He and McCauley 2013).

To diagnose and assess the threat from ongoing potential vulnerabilities, it is important to consider carefully the transmission mechanisms between advanced and EME financial markets, and whether there are effective tools that EMEs can use to cope with financial shocks from abroad.

## Transmission Mechanisms

In the early 1970s, inflation surged worldwide. One obvious mechanism driving synchronized global inflation was the system of fixed exchange rates central to the Bretton Woods system, under which all countries

---

[12] Figure 5 uses the Chinn and Ito (2006) measure of capital-account openness.
[13] Highly diversified fund managers might have little incentive to focus on particular countries' economic fundamentals, as argued by Calvo and Mendoza (2000).

pegged to the U.S. dollar (thereby surrendering monetary autonomy) while the U.S. retained monetary discretion (thereby dominating global monetary conditions). The relatively loose monetary policy in the U.S., together with a huge speculative portfolio shift away from the dollar in anticipation of its debasement, led to big increases in foreign exchange reserves and money supplies outside of the United States.

A major motivation for the subsequent move to generally floating exchange rates (at least among industrial economies) was therefore to regain control over domestic inflation. Yet, industrial-country inflation rates did not diverge. They rose in concert in the 1970s, continuing even after the abandonment of fixed exchange rates, and largely fell starting in the following decade. Ciccarelli and Mojon (2010) document a powerful common component in 22 OECD countries' inflation rates over the 1960–2008 period. EME inflation rates remained higher in some countries throughout the 1980s, notably in Latin America, but those rates also converged downward, starting in the 1990s. While trend inflation rates still differ across countries, the cross-country range of variation has become relatively small. The proposition that countries can control their inflation rates over the long term is widely accepted, and observed inflation convergence is regarded as a country- or currency-union-specific phenomenon reflecting synchronized improvements in economic literacy and economic governance.[14]

The degree of national control over short- to medium-term macro developments (including but not restricted to price-level dynamics) is more controversial. When countries' financial markets are linked, even imperfectly, macroeconomic models incorporating realistic good- or asset-market frictions imply that policy and other shocks will be transmitted to trading partners, possibly causing unwanted spillovers even when currency

---

[14] McKinnon (1982) hypothesized that even with floating exchange rates, a high degree of substitutability among the major industrial-country currencies made national inflation dependent on world money-supply growth. If this view were right, even long-term inflation would be out of the hands of any single central bank. There is little theoretical or empirical support for McKinnon's "global monetarist" hypothesis, although some recent authors have used global monetary aggregates as proxy variables for global liquidity conditions. An example of the empirical critiques is Wallace (1984).

exchange rates float freely. Two related questions have been especially prominent in recent debate about the scope for independent and effective monetary policy by EMEs. First, can EMEs offset shifts in advanced-country monetary policies — most importantly U.S. monetary policy — through their own monetary instruments? Second, in the face of a global financial cycle that is in principle distinct from monetary policy cycles — but which also causes portfolio shifts with respect to EME assets — what scope do EMEs have for an effective policy response? Some recent analysis has been pessimistic. Perhaps most provocatively, Rey (2013) argues that EMEs have essentially *no* room for monetary policy that diverges from U.S. conditions: the monetary trilemma is really a dilemma, with independent monetary policy possible if and only if capital markets are segmented from the outside world. On this view, global rather than national liquidity is central.[15]

To assess such arguments, it is useful to review some main mechanisms of transmission of foreign monetary and financial shocks to EME financial markets.[16]

### Direct interest rate linkages

Perhaps most fundamental in a world of integrated financial markets are direct interest rate linkages between countries, which reflect forces of cross-border arbitrage on rates of return. Conventional monetary policy manipulates a short interest rate directly but has effects at all maturities, and these effects induce portfolio shifts into foreign assets. In turn, those portfolio shifts generally affect exchange rates, asset prices, capital accounts, and macroeconomic policies abroad.

If an emerging country fixes its exchange rate against the currency of a central country (for example, the United States), then it has no choice but to match the latter's choice of policy interest rate. Moreover, provided

---

[15] For recent assessments of the concept of global liquidity, see Borio, McCauley, and McGuire (2011), Committee on the Global Financial System (2011), Gourinchas (2012), and Landau (2014).

[16] For complementary discussions see Caruana (2012), He and McCauley (2013), and McCauley, McGuire, and Sushko (2015).

the exchange rate peg is credibly permanent, risk-free nominal interest rates *at all maturities* must match those of the U.S. Thus, U.S. monetary policy is passively imported, in accord with the monetary trilemma.

More generally, exchange-rate flexibility of various types and degrees will alter the international transmission of interest rates. If *e* is the domestic price of the U.S. dollar, *i* the short-term policy rate of interest, and $\rho$ a foreign-currency risk premium, then domestic and U.S. short rates will be linked by an interest-parity relationship of the form:

$$i_t = i_t^{US} + E_t e_{t+1} - e_t + \rho_t.$$

Above, the risk premium $\rho$ might reflect the covariance between the depreciation rate of domestic currency and a stochastic discount factor for domestic currency payments. Now, changes in the U.S. interest rate need not feed one-for-one into $i_t$, depending on the behavior of the exchange rate and the risk premium. For example, if the EME central bank holds its interest rate absolutely constant when the U.S. cuts its interest rate, and the risk premium does not change, then foreign currency will appreciate sharply (a fall in the price of dollars, $e_t$), overshooting its expected future value so as to maintain interest parity. The EME central bank can still set the policy interest rate it prefers, but a sharp exchange rate change may well have effects on its economy that strongly influence the monetary policy response.

A powerful inhibition to allowing full exchange rate adjustment in such circumstances is the negative effect on domestic export competitiveness. The EME central bank may intervene to dampen appreciation, thereby (typically) acquiring international reserves and allowing a jump in the net private capital inflow into its economy. In turn, an increased money supply will likely cause a rise in domestic bank lending. Sterilization of the monetary effects (if somewhat effective) could raise longer term rates at home and (if carried out on a large enough scale) lower them in the U.S., eliciting further pressure through the capital account. The carry-trade dynamics may be reinforced by the perception that the central bank is merely slowing an inevitable appreciation of its currency. The probable effect, in this case, therefore remains transmission of U.S. monetary ease.

Since sterilized foreign exchange intervention is often limited in its effectiveness, stronger efforts to limit currency appreciation are likely to enhance the correlation between the domestic and U.S. policy interest rates. Even when there is no intervention, consequential two-way private gross capital flows could occur, such as increased U.S. bank loans to the EME country, the proceeds of which are deposited in banks abroad. This increase in cross-border credit could well have an impact on domestic financial conditions (as suggested in partial-equilibrium models such as Bruno and Shin 2013); I return to this issue below. Even a fully floating exchange rate cannot provide full insulation from the expansion of gross foreign assets and liabilities.

Further international linkages occur through the longer-term interest rates set in bond markets. These rates affect activity in key economic sectors and drive real wealth through asset-valuation effects. As in the case of short-term interest rates, direct arbitrage between national markets links long-term rates and exchange rates, but long-term rates reflect not only short-term rates, but expected future short rates as well as risk factors. To the extent that monetary policy works through its effect on longer-term interest rates, such as mortgage rates or corporate borrowing rates, stronger international linkages between long-term rates could hamper monetary autonomy, in the sense of requiring sharper changes in short-term rates (and perhaps in forward guidance on those rates) to achieve a given desired result.

To make the discussion more precise, consider the simplest two-period example. Then an approximate term structure model would represent the domestic nominal risk-free yield $i_t^{(2)}$ on a two-period discount bond as depending on an average of current and future expected short rates:

$$i_t^{(2)} = \frac{1}{2}i_t + \frac{1}{2}E_t i_{t+1} + \tau_t.$$

Here, $\tau_t$ is a term premium that might reflect the covariance between future interest rates and a stochastic discount factor for domestic currency payments; and because of the interest parity relationship, $\tau_t$ obviously is closely related to the currency risk premium $\rho_t$ in general equilibrium. Subtracting from this the parallel relationship for the U.S. shows that international long-term rates obey an interest parity relationship of the form:

$$i_t^{(2)} = i_t^{US(2)} + \frac{1}{2}\left(E_t e_{t+1} - e_t\right) + \frac{1}{2}\left(E_t e_{t+2} - E_t e_{t+1}\right) + \frac{1}{2}\rho_t + \frac{1}{2}E_t \rho_{t+1} + \tau_t - \tau_t^{US}.$$

Exchange rate variability matters for long-term risk-free interest rate correlations across countries as well as for short, but to the extent that expected exchange-rate movements tend to slow or be reversed over time, long-rates could be more highly correlated than short rates — perhaps the EME central bank allows short-run movements, but its long-run inflation target is similar to that of the United States and expected real exchange rate changes are small. High international correlation among term premiums could also induce long-rate correlation across countries. For example, He and McCauley (2013) and Turner (2014) argue that U.S. quantitative easing policies that reduce term premiums spill over into a reduction of term premiums abroad.[17] In this way, U.S. unconventional easing may be spread abroad.

Empirically, long-term interest rates tend to be more highly correlated across countries than short-term rates, consistent with results of the next section. Goodhart and Turner (2014) summarize a widely-held view of the evidence:

> Long-term interest rates are more correlated across countries than short-term rates. A central bank operating under a flexible exchange rate regime can set its policy rate independently of the Fed funds rate.
>
> But it has much less power over the long-term rate in its own currency because yields in all bond markets integrated into the financial system tend to rise whenever U.S. yields jump. Bond yields in countries with weaker macroeconomic of financial fundamentals often rise even more.[18]

---

[17] Neely (2013) carries out an econometric study.
[18] See Charles Goodhart and Philip Turner, "Pattern of Policy Tightening is Different

Why is this so? One reason, documented in the next section, is that there is mean reversion in short-term policy rate differentials. In addition, countries' term premiums appear to be increasingly correlated over time and closely linked to U.S. bond premiums; see, for example, Hellerstein (2011) and Dahlquist and Hasseltoft (2012). Our understanding of these premiums in terms of reliable structural models is limited, but they are clearly related to investor risk aversion. In any case, to the extent that long-term rates are strongly subject to global forces, the power of short-term rates to steer the economy could diminish. While recent attention has focused on the effects on EME long-term rates of monetary-policy shifts in the U.S., even U.S. long-term rates appear subject to global influences, as evidenced by several empirical studies. Also related is the anecdotal evidence of the "Greenspan conundrum": the relative constancy of long-term rates in the face of rising policy rates in the mid-2000s.[19]

The apparently high cross-country correlation in term premiums could reflect factors that drive global financial cycles — for example, changes in risk appetite — so I turn the discussion to the impact of international financial developments.[20]

### Transmission of the financial cycle

Like monetary policy, the financial cycle has effects that are transmitted abroad. The level of interest rates certainly can play a catalytic role, among other causes.[21] Changes in credit volumes, including banking flows, can have strong effects across borders. The mid-2000s saw a powerful credit cycle, originating primarily in the U.S. and Europe,

---

This Time," *Financial Times*, April 3, 2014, p. 20. See also Bernanke (2013) and Sheets and Sockin (2013).

[19] Another possibly relevant factor is that uncovered interest parity seems to hold more closely for long-term nominal interest rates than for short-term rates. See Chinn and Quayyum (2012).

[20] Consistent with the financial-cycle view is the evidence of Gonzáles-Rozada and Levy Yeyati (2008) that emerging market bond spreads (on foreign-currency debt) respond strongly to proxies for U.S. risk appetite and liquidity.

[21] For some evidence on the role of interest rates on U.S. bank behavior, see Dell'Ariccia, Laeven, and Suarez (2013).

but also related to the pattern of global current account imbalances. Until the cycle collapsed in September 2008, most EMEs — including those in Asia — navigated it fairly successfully, although some countries experienced problems with capital inflows and appreciation.

A first transmission channel comes from the compression of risk premiums. Consider first the case just under discussion, long-term government bonds. A general decline in risk aversion originating in the U.S. might compress term premiums both at home and abroad. But the latter can be a powerful source of policy spillovers. Looking at the preceding long-term interest parity relation, we can see that, the immediate exchange rate response might have to be quite big if EME long-term rates and the long-term nominal exchange rate do not adjust. For example, a 10 basis point fall in the term premium on a U.S. two-year bond would require a 20 basis point currency appreciation. Just as small movements in exchange rates can be consistent with big discrepancies between short-term interest rates, small discrepancies between long-term rates will require substantial exchange-rate movements unless offset by risk premium changes.

Financial conditions can migrate across borders by relaxing the quantitative borrowing constraints that agents may face. A financial boom in the U.S. will spill over into increased credit supply abroad, appreciating foreign currencies and raising foreign asset values. In turn, those developments will raise collateral values in the recipient countries, with a procyclical effect on their borrowing and asset markets. A number of models suggest different mechanisms through which the process could be, to some degree, self-reinforcing. Examples include Gertler and Karadi (2011), who focus on the franchise value of intermediaries as a limit to lending, and Bruno and Shin (2013), who emphasize the role of currency appreciation in strengthening unhedged borrowers' balance sheets.

If the current account is slow to adjust in the short-run, then a financial inflow will necessarily be matched by an equal outflow. Absent central bank intervention, a higher *private* inflow is matched by a higher *private* outflow. Partial equilibrium models of banking inflows such as Bruno and

Shin (2013) do not capture this consequence.[22] However, the resulting expansion of gross liabilities and assets is quite likely to worsen the balance of financial stability risks, increasing the challenge for macroprudential policy. Challenges for macroeconomic policy could also be accentuated. Goldberg (2013) presents some evidence that a substantial foreign banking presence can reduce monetary independence, as measured by interest-rate independence.

A major spillover channel for easier foreign financial conditions is the compression of corporate spreads, which occurs as domestic financial conditions also ease. Figure 6 shows the behavior of Korean domestic corporate spreads (with the Fed's target policy rate superimposed).[23] Spreads are highly variable, rising with the wave of bankruptcies

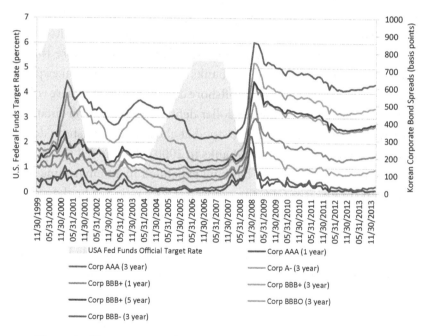

**Figure 6.** Korea, corporate bond spreads versus U.S. Federal funds target
*Source*: Asian Development Bank, Asian Bonds Online

---

[22] The development of general-equilibrium models should therefore be a research priority.
[23] Spreads are for local currency yields computed relative to a Korean government bond of the same tenor.

following the dot-com crash, rising in the Korean credit-card crisis, and falling sharply afterward only to spike upward with the Lehman collapse in September 2008. The relationship to U.S. monetary policy is not mechanical due to the influence of common factors. Starting in mid-2004, for example, the Fed funds rate rose and Korean spreads declined, both in response to the ongoing global boom in credit and liquidity that ended in the GFC.

### Foreign currency credit

While dollar, euro, and yen credit is extended to non-residents, the dollar is dominant, with credit transactions often between two non-U.S. residents (Borio, McCauley, and McGuire 2011). Figure 7 displays some trends. Since 2000, dollar bank credit to non-banks outside of the U.S. has risen from an amount equal to 23% of total U.S. domestic bank credit to about 35% — while U.S. domestic bank credit itself has risen to a level about equal to annual U.S. GDP. Thus, more than a third of global dollar lending by banks to non-banks now takes place outside U.S. borders. Alongside offshore dollar bank credit, there is also significant offshore issuance of dollar debt securities by non-financial borrowers. While such issuance stood at about half of offshore dollar borrowing from banks by non-banks in 2000, the ratio fell sharply up to the GFC as international banking expanded in an environment of low interest rates. The GFC then caused a contraction in bank lending everywhere. More recently, however, offshore dollar bank lending and debt issuance have begun to expand in tandem, with debt issuance rising especially rapidly after the crisis as a result of low long-term dollar interest rates following the Fed's unconventional operations (McCauley, McGuire, and Sushko 2015).

Foreign currency credit presents another transmission channel, most importantly for shocks originating in U.S. financial markets. The effective cost of borrowing in dollars, if those are swapped into domestic currency, is still the domestic interest rate if covered interest parity applies; and a shortage of funding for covered interest arbitrage, as in Ivashina, Scharfstein, and Stein (2012), will only raise the cost of covered dollar

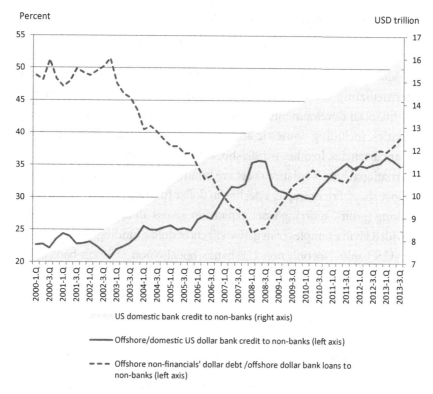

Percent                                                                USD trillion

US domestic bank credit to non-banks (right axis)

——— Offshore/domestic US dollar bank credit to non-banks (left axis)

- - - Offshore non-financials' dollar debt /offshore dollar bank loans to non-banks (left axis)

**Figure 7.** Offshore U.S. dollar bank credit and offshore U.S. dollar debt
*Source*: BIS, Global Liquidity Indicators

borrowing.[24] However, there are channels through which the interest rate on dollar loans and the loans' availability can directly affect credit flows in economies outside the U.S.

Domestic residents who hedge foreign-currency borrowing will still effectively face the domestic interest rate if covered interest parity holds. However, some may engage in carry unhedged trades, either because they are financially unsophisticated or believe (perhaps wrongly) that domestic currency depreciation is very unlikely. Under this scenario, a fall in the cost of unhedged foreign borrowing will be expansionary in

---

[24] Munro and Wooldridge (2012) argue, however, that domestic borrowers may overcome some financial frictions by borrowing in foreign currency and swapping the proceeds into domestic currency.

the short run, though possibly highly contractionary later in the event that significant currency depreciation does occur.

More generally, the heavy participation of global non-U.S. banks in intermediating U.S. dollars creates a potent channel for U.S. monetary and financial developments to influence their balance sheets and lending activities, including domestic and foreign lending denominated in non-dollar currencies. In other words, shocks to the non-dollar component of an international bank's balance sheet are bound to spill over to the rest of the balance sheet. For example, a decline in dollar funding rates is likely to raise banking profits, spurring asset expansion across all currencies. The GFC provided vivid examples of negative effects of dollar funding disruptions on non-U.S. banks. Not only non-U.S. banks, but also non-U.S. non-bank dollar borrowers, whether they borrow from banks or in capital markets, may feel effects of changes in dollar interest rates or dollar funding conditions.

### Implications

A country that pegs its exchange rate to the dollar and has open capital markets will import U.S. monetary policy. While a flexible exchange rate allows the country to control inflation independently, as in Woodford's (2010) exposition, monetary policy has additional objectives and globalization might worsen the tradeoff between these and inflation. Some of these are related to the exchange rate, where big changes could have adverse effects on financial stability or internal resource allocation. Even with exchange-rate flexibility, the influence of monetary policy over long-term interest rates could be reduced compared to a closed economy. Spillovers may be easy to absorb when countries throughout the world face common shocks, but less so when their positions are asymmetric, as was the case in the years immediately following the GFC.

Policy rates of interest are central to financial conditions, and induce portfolio shifts toward EMEs, but other aspects of advanced economy financial conditions can spill across borders to EMEs in the form of incipient or actual net capital flows, and gross flows. These factors potentially have substantial impacts on exchange rates, asset prices, and credit volumes, and thereby on economic activity, inflation, and financial stability. Given the prevalence internationally of dollar credit, movements in U.S. interest rates and financial conditions are likely to be especially important.

## Evidence on Interest Rate Independence

Because some interest rate independence is a necessary condition for an effective monetary policy aimed at domestic goals, a central empirical question is the correlation between domestic and foreign interest rates, and its relation to the exchange rate regime. This section presents some evidence, adding to the findings of previous studies by analyzing long-term nominal rates of interest.[25]

A first test, based on approaches of Shambaugh (2004), Obstfeld, Shambaugh, and Taylor (2005), and Klein and Shambaugh (2013), investigates the average coherence between a short-term nominal interest rate and a base-country rate in panels of countries. More specifically, consider the regression equation linking country $j$'s nominal interest rate to the interest rate of base country $b$:

$$(1) \quad \Delta i_{jt} = \alpha + \beta \Delta i_{bt} + \gamma' X_{jt} + u_{jt}.$$

As shown above, $\beta = 1$ and $\gamma = 0$ under a fully credible currency peg. With some exchange rate flexibility, however, there would generally be less than full pass-through of the base rate to the domestic rate, $\beta < 1$, and the interest rate might also respond to domestic variables included in the vector $X_{jt}$ (for example, through a Taylor rule mechanism). Thus,

---

[25] This section builds on earlier work by Frankel, Schmukler, and Servén (2004), Shambaugh (2004), Obstfeld, Shambaugh, and Taylor (2005), and Klein and Shambaugh (2013). The general conclusion of these studies (which the evidence in this section supports) is that there is some scope for short-run interest rate independence when exchange rates are flexible. Alternative methodologies attempt to identify exogenous monetary shocks but reach broadly similar conclusions to the previous studies; see Miniane and Rogers (2007) and Bluedorn and Bowdler (2010). In a related vein, Sheets and Sockin (2013) argue that U.S. policy rates strongly influence policy rates of the other major industrial countries, but do so primarily by shifting the arguments in those countries' Taylor rules rather than forcing deviations from Taylor rules.

information about the magnitude of $\beta$ and the statistical significance of the coefficient vector $\mathbf{\gamma}$ is informative about the degree of monetary independence. In specification (1), differences of interest rates are preferred to levels so as to avoid spurious regression problems.

In general, there are at least two concerns in interpreting regression (1). First, if a peg is non-credible, it is possible that elements of $X_{jt}$ could affect the domestic interest rate by creating realignment expectations. But in that case, we would also expect to see an amplified response of the home interest rate to changes in the base rate, $\beta > 1$ (and we would not view this as evidence of monetary independence).

A second concern is with unobserved global shocks that are not captured fully by the included vector $X_{jt}$. For example, shifts in global risk tolerance or global liquidity might simultaneously move the base and domestic rates in the same direction. Such an omitted variable would induce a positive correlation between $\Delta i_{bt}$ and $u_{jt}$, raising the OLS estimate of $\beta$ even under substantial monetary independence. (In this case, the upward biased estimate could be indicating positive transmission of the financial cycle, not of monetary policy.) Alternatively, the global shock might be a generalized shift in portfolio preference between base-country bonds and foreign bonds in general (for example, safe-haven inflows to the base country). In this case, $u_{jt}$ would tend to have a negative correlation with $\Delta i_{bt}$, which would induce a downward bias in the OLS estimate of $\beta$. One way to address the issue is to recognize that different countries have different "natural" base rates — the U.S. dollar for Mexico, the euro for Poland, and the South African rand for Botswana, for example. Accounting for this heterogeneity allows one to control for common time effects in the panel version of (1), and thereby attempt to capture unobserved global shocks.

Several researchers have argued that the Chicago Board Options Exchange equity option volatility index (VIX) is a useful summary statistic for the state of the financial cycle, lower values being associated with a greater tolerance for risk-taking (including increases in leverage); see Bruno and Shin (2013) and Rey (2013), among many others. If countries in the sample are matched to their heterogeneous bases, one can enter the percentage change in the VIX as an independent variable in the regressions, rather than time fixed effects. This yields an alternative way to control for shocks to the global cycle that potentially move national and base interest rates simultaneously. If the change in the VIX is a stand-in for global shocks that cause global interest rates to move up or down in concert, then adding the VIX should reduce the estimated coefficient $\hat{\beta}$ in (1). On the other hand, VIX movements could be more highly correlated with portfolio shifts between advanced and emerging markets — the waves of capital flow into or out of the developing world discussed by Calvo, Leiderman, and Reinhart — and in that case, we should expect $\hat{\beta}$ to fall when the VIX change is added as a regressor.

To gauge the additional autonomy loss due to pegging, I will use the interactive specification

$$(2) \quad \beta = \beta_0 + \beta_1 \times PEG,$$

where *PEG* is an indicator variable.

A second type of test, following Frankel, Schmukler, and Servén (2004) and Obstfeld, Shambaugh, and Taylor (2005), considers dynamic adjustment to a long-run levels relationship between home and base-country interest rates. To this end, I will estimate country-$j$ specific equations of the form:

$$(3) \quad \Delta i_{jt} = \sum_{p=1}^{P} \rho_p \Delta i_{jt-p} + \sum_{q=0}^{Q} \beta_q \Delta i_{bt-q} + \sum_{q=0}^{Q} \gamma_q' \Delta X_{jt-q} + \theta \left( i_{jt-1} - \xi\, i_{bt-1} - \omega' X_{jt-1} \right) + u_{jt}.$$

In estimating (3), I do not pool over $j$ because of the likelihood of heterogeneous dynamics across economies. In specification (3), the coefficient $\xi$ is the long-run *levels relationship* between the home and base interest rate, and $-\theta$ is the *adjustment speed* toward that relationship. We would expect $\xi$ to be in the neighborhood of 1, with $-\theta$ an inverse measure of the scope for departure from the long-run relation.

Table 1 reports the result of estimating specification (1) as a pooled or panel regression using my full sample of countries (22 advanced other than

**Table 1:  Pooled and panel regressions of nominal interest rate changes on base-currency changes**

| | (1) US-base SR | (2) Multi-base SR | (3) Multi-base SR with Time Effects | (4) Multi-base SR with VIX Percent Change | (5) US-base LR | (6) Multi-base LR | (7) Multi-base LR with Time Effects | (8) Multi-base LR with VIX Percent Change |
|---|---|---|---|---|---|---|---|---|
| US-base SR change | 0.0605 | | | | | | | |
| | (0.158) | | | | | | | |
| Multi-base SR change | | 0.201 | 0.0121 | 0.241 | | | | |
| | | (0.172) | (0.228) | (0.177) | | | | |
| US-base LR change | | | | | 0.354*** | | | |
| | | | | | (0.0597) | | | |
| Multi-base LR change | | | | | | 0.552*** | 0.433*** | 0.636*** |
| | | | | | | (0.0670) | (0.136) | (0.0616) |
| VIX Percent Change | | | | 0.00252* | | | | 0.00298*** |
| | | | | (0.00131) | | | | (0.000668) |
| Constant | -0.00170** | -0.00154** | 0.000170 | -0.00153** | -0.000798*** | -0.000626*** | -0.00113** | -0.000636*** |
| | (0.000755) | (0.000760) | (0.000724) | (0.000755) | (0.000173) | (0.000166) | (0.000438) | (0.000166) |
| N | 3258 | 3258 | 3258 | 3258 | 3071 | 3071 | 3071 | 3071 |
| adj. R2 | 0.035 | 0.036 | 0.061 | 0.037 | 0.048 | 0.085 | 0.138 | 0.095 |
| Optimal Lags | 5 | 5 | 5 | 5 | 0 | 0 | 0 | 0 |
| p-value for F Test that growth and inflation change variables (and their lags, where applicable) do not enter | 2.13011E-11 | 6.3826E-11 | 1.01883E-06 | 3.12899E-10 | 0.0713856 | 0.183389806 | 0.041894423 | 0.13832495 8 |

Clustered standard errors in parentheses (at country level)

$* p < 0.10$, $** p < 0.05$, $*** p < 0.01$

the U.S. and 34 emerging/developing, dictated by data availability).[26] None of the specifications will include country fixed effects, on the ground that a steady positive or negative country-specific nominal interest rate trend is implausible in my data, but some will include time effects, motivated by the possibility of unobserved global shocks that induce higher interest rates everywhere. The results in Table 1 provide a very crude first pass that accounts for neither exchange-rate regime nor level of development. Nonetheless, the findings display several regularities that prove robust to more nuanced cuts at the data.

Columns (1)–(4) report regressions of short-term nominal interest rate changes (SR) on the short rate change in a base country, whereas columns (5)–(8) do the same for long-term nominal interest rates (LR). Also included (in the $X$ variables that enter equation (1)) are current values and lags of the change in real GDP and the change in CPI inflation, where I use the Bayesian Information Criterion to determine the number of lags to include, up to a maximum of six.[27] Thus, the observations are at quarterly frequency. The short-term interest rate is the quarterly average of end-of-month rates on 90- or 91-day government securities; the long-term rate is the quarterly average of end-of-month rates on 10-year government bonds.

Column (1) assumes that the U.S. dollar is the base currency for all other countries, and the estimated coefficient on its interest rate turns out to be tiny and statistically insignificant. Once countries are matched to more appropriate base currencies, however — the currencies they are most likely to shadow — the estimated coefficient better than triples (to 0.201) but it remains rather small, and insignificant. In column (3), adding time effects to the column (2) specification reduces the coefficient, as one would expect when the time effect captures global shocks that induce positive covariation in policy rates of interest. Adding the change in the VIX in column (4) *raises* $\hat{\beta}$ compared to column (2), but not significantly so.

---

[26] Data coverage is detailed in an appendix. Even where longer data series are available, I generally estimate over the period starting around 1990 so as to capture the regularities that apply during the recent period of high and growing financial globalization. See Klein and Shambaugh (2013) for analysis of longer time series.

[27] To save space, I do not report coefficients on these auxiliary variables.

However, the change in the VIX itself is significant at the 10% level, with a rise in the VIX raising the domestic interest rate. The results are consistent with the view that reductions in global-risk aversion are associated with portfolio shifts toward EMEs.

In all of the column (1)–(4) regressions there is overwhelming evidence for a role of lagged changes in domestic output and inflation — effects that would be absent were domestic interest rates determined entirely by nominal arbitrage without exchange-rate variability. These results, together with the low estimates $\hat{\beta}$, are compatible with substantial interest-rate independence at the short end.

Columns (5)–(8), which analyze long-term rates, present a starkly different picture. In column (5), which takes the U.S. dollar as the universal base, the coefficient on the U.S. bond rate change is significantly different from zero at the 1% level, though significantly below 0.5. Once countries are matched to their most natural base currencies, however, the coefficient rises above 0.5, remaining highly significant. Time effects lower the coefficient (to 0.433), but the change is not significant and the new slope estimate remains significant at the 1% level. Finally, adding the VIX change raises $\hat{\beta}$ substantially, and the VIX variable is itself highly significant, suggesting that the global financial cycle is communicated to long-term interest rates. The effect of a change in the VIX is small but precisely estimated for long-term rates. Interestingly, the auxiliary domestic macro variables usually do not enter this regression with very high significance, and the adjusted $R^2$ in columns (5)–(8) are uniformly higher than those in columns (1)–(4). The LR picture is one of much less interest-rate independence than in the SR case.

Table 2 breaks out the role of exchange rate pegs by adding specification (2) to specification (1), thereby interacting the interest-rate response with the peg indicator.[28] For the SR case in the first four columns,

---

[28] I adapt to quarterly data the de facto currency regime coding method from Klein and Shambaugh (2013), who themselves look at a finer gradation of regimes than just peg or non-peg; see the discussion in the next section. (See also the appendix.) I thank Michael Klein and Jay Shambaugh for providing the files underlying their paper.

Table 2: Exchange-rate pegs versus non-pegs

| | (1) US-base SR | (2) Multi-base SR | (3) Multi-base SR with Time Effects | (4) Multi-base SR with VIX Percent Change | (5) US-base LR | (6) Multi-base LR | (7) Multi-base LR with Time Effects | (8) Multi-base LR with VIX Percent Change |
|---|---|---|---|---|---|---|---|---|
| US-base SR change | 0.0261 (0.178) | | | | | | | |
| Peg * US-base SR change | 0.122 (0.256) | | | | | | | |
| Multi-base SR change | | -0.0256 (0.312) | -0.0948 (0.394) | 0.0290 (0.322) | | | | |
| Peg * Multi-base SR change | | 0.375 (0.310) | 0.278 (0.298) | 0.362 (0.311) | | | | |
| US-base LR change | | | | | 0.348*** (0.0638) | | | |
| Peg * US-base LR change | | | | | 0.0189 (0.158) | | | |
| Multi-base LR change | | | | | | 0.495*** (0.0976) | 0.430*** (0.157) | 0.583*** (0.0870) |
| Peg * Multi-base LR change | | | | | | 0.0964 (0.111) | 0.00816 (0.101) | 0.0890 (0.107) |
| VIX Percent Change | | | | 0.00301* (0.00158) | | | | 0.00297*** (0.000672) |

*(Continued)*

Table 2: (Continued)

| | (1) US-base SR | (2) Multi-base SR | (3) Multi-base SR with Time Effects | (4) Multi-base SR with VIX Percent Change | (5) US-base LR | (6) Multi-base LR | (7) Multi-base LR with Time Effects | (8) Multi-base LR with VIX Percent Change |
|---|---|---|---|---|---|---|---|---|
| Constant | -0.00181** | -0.00116 | 0.00123 | -0.00114 | -0.000836*** | -0.000629*** | -0.00112** | 20.000643*** |
| | (0.000767) | (0.000760) | (0.00138) | (0.000756) | (0.000202) | (0.000162) | (0.000422) | (0.000161) |
| N | 3258 | 3258 | 3258 | 3258 | 3071 | 3071 | 3071 | 3071 |
| adj. R2 | 0.066 | 0.087 | 0.113 | 0.088 | 0.048 | 0.085 | 0.137 | 0.095 |
| Optimal Lags | 5 | 5 | 5 | 5 | 0 | 0 | 0 | 0 |
| p-value for F Test that growth and inflation change variables (and their lags, where applicable) do not enter | 0.000271181 | 5.45319E-05 | 3.56323E-05 | 4.27134E-05 | 0.054861746 | 0.271829271 | 0.138256524 | 0.225336173 |
| p-value for F Test that controls and Peg interaction term coefficients (and lags, where applicable) sum to zero. | 3.95008E-18 | 1.28064E-07 | 1.08185E-08 | 1.24208E-07 | 0.355502 | 0.661292639 | 0.265738535 | 0.569184142 |

Clustered standard errors in parentheses (at country level)

* $p < 0.10$, ** $p < 0.05$, *** $p < 0.01$

positive correlations with the base-currency interest rate change are almost entirely due to being pegged. Adding time effects lowers the estimated SR peg effect somewhat, but leaves it potentially large. Adding the VIX change has little impact compared to column (2). Perhaps surprisingly, the peg interactions are not themselves statistically significant, even at the 10% level. It may be that the limited commitment under a de facto peg allows substantial room for interest-rate deviations from the base, at least for some of currencies.

The LR $\hat{\beta}$s in the last four columns follow the pattern familiar from Table 1. They are reasonably big and very significantly different from zero. While a peg is always estimated to raise the correlation, that result is never statistically significant. It should be noted, however, that because the different base long rates tend to be highly correlated among themselves, adding time effects in this case induces some multicollinearity. As earlier, adding the VIX change raises the estimated coefficient on the base interest rate (both for pegs and non-pegs), and the VIX change itself is highly significant. As in Table 1, the auxiliary output and inflation variables usually are not highly significant in the LR regressions of Table 2, regardless of the exchange rate regime. (These regressions allow the coefficients on the auxiliary variables to differ as between pegs and non-pegs.)

The summary of Table 2 is that there is considerable independence at the short end of the term structure apart from pegged exchange rates, whereas long rates remain significantly correlated with those of base-currency countries even in the absence of a peg (although pegs appear to raise the correlation somewhat compared to non-pegs). As in Table 1, given the base long-term rate, the domestic long-term rate appears less responsive to standard domestic macro variables.

Tables 3 and 4 contrast the results for developing/emerging and advanced economies (with Newly Industrialized Asia placed in the emerging group). Short-term rates for the developing/EME non-pegs appear less tightly linked to base-currency short-rates than for the advanced group of non-pegs; and for the advanced countries, the marginal effect of being pegged is greater for dollar pegs than for pegs in

Table 3: Developing/emerging economy subsample

| | (1) US-base SR | (2) Multi-base SR | (3) Multi-base SR with Time Effects | (4) Multi-base SR with VIX Percent Change | (5) US-base LR | (6) Multi-base LR | (7) Multi-base LR with Time Effects | (8) Multi-base LR with VIX Percent Change |
|---|---|---|---|---|---|---|---|---|
| US-base SR change | -0.313 (0.412) | | | | | | | |
| Peg * US-base SR change | 0.377 (0.430) | | | | | | | |
| Multi-base SR change | | -0.407 (0.515) | -0.260 (0.560) | -0.337 (0.550) | | | | |
| Peg * Multi-base SR change | | 0.480 (0.500) | 0.300 (0.542) | 0.449 (0.513) | | | | |
| US-base LR change | | | | | 0.0590 (0.132) | | | |
| Peg * US-base LR change | | | | | 0.211 (0.188) | | | |
| Multi-base LR change | | | | | | 0.194 (0.125) | 0.622 (0.490) | 0.332*** (0.113) |
| Peg * Multi-base LR change | | | | | | 0.0995 (0.163) | 0.0390 (0.186) | 0.0729 (0.159) |
| VIX Percent Change | | | | 0.00344 (0.00276) | | | | 0.00375** (0.00141) |

| Constant | −0.00230 | −0.00180 | −0.000213 | −0.00178 | −0.00113** | −0.000971*** | −0.00122 | −0.000992*** |
|---|---|---|---|---|---|---|---|---|
| | (0.00153) | (0.00144) | (0.00126) | (0.00144) | (0.000456) | (0.000332) | (0.000832) | (0.000332) |
| N | 1775 | 1775 | 1775 | 1775 | 1286 | 1286 | 1286 | 1286 |
| adj. R2 | 0.073 | 0.099 | 0.153 | 0.099 | 0.005 | 0.014 | 0.088 | 0.022 |
| Optimal Lags | 5 | 5 | 5 | 5 | 0 | 0 | 0 | 0 |
| p-value for F Test that growth and inflation change variables (and their lags, where applicable) do not enter | 0.012799281 | 1.00957E-08 | 6.81558E-10 | 2.26485E-09 | 0.363421235 | 0.073372722 | 0.009637445 | 0.040628087 |
| p-value for F Test that controls and Peg interaction term coefficients (and lags, where applicable) sum to zero. | 1.30925E-12 | 1.64653E-06 | 4.69456E-06 | 1.21227E-06 | 0.319557116 | 0.77502473 | 0.310767234 | 0.744519193 |

Clustered standard errors in parentheses (at country level)

* p < 0.10, ** p < 0.05, *** p < 0.01

general, though there is little difference for developing/EME countries. The time effects regression in column (3) of Table 4 suggests that much of the synchronization of advanced short-term rates with base rates is due to common responses to global shocks. Long-term rate coherence with base rates also seems much greater for advanced economies, with pegs quantitatively important only for advanced countries pegged to the U.S. dollar. By and large the results are not inconsistent with substantial monetary independence in terms of short policy rates, even though the advanced economies move in step to a considerable degree. While the coherence among movements in long-term interest rates is most much more pronounced for advanced countries, advanced-country data series on long rates are much longer, and reflect much thicker markets, so the results in Table 3, columns (5)–(8), should be interpreted cautiously. To the extent that long-term rate co-movement among advanced countries represents forces of arbitrage, it could capture a weakening of the potency of domestic monetary policies and a channel for monetary spillovers from abroad. A final finding in Tables 3 and 4 is the importance of the VIX change for movements in long-term interest rates, given base rate changes — for both country groups, but especially for non-advanced economies.

The apparently higher short-term rate independence for developing/emerging economies, compared to advanced economies, could follow from a greater prevalence of capital controls; recall Figure 5. As Klein and Shambaugh (2013) document, however, only thoroughgoing and long-standing controls seem effective in conferring greater monetary independence, other things equal.

Turn next to estimation of the dynamic relationship (3). The approach of Pesaran, Shin, and Smith (2001) (hereafter PSS) allows for a levels relationship as in (3) between domestic and base rates of interest, even when interest rate levels are stationary. However, different critical regions for test statistics apply depending on whether interest rates are $I(0)$ or $I(1)$. PSS tabulate the appropriate critical values. Because the data are monthly, the vector $X$ in (3) includes only the level of CPI inflation.

Table 4:   Advanced economy subsample

| | (1)<br>US-base SR | (2)<br>Multi-base<br>SR | (3)<br>Multi-base<br>SR with<br>Time Effects | (4)<br>Multi-base<br>SR with VIX<br>Percent Change | (5)<br>US-base LR | (6)<br>Multi-base<br>LR | (7)<br>Multi-base<br>LR with<br>Time Effects | (8)<br>Multi-base<br>LR with<br>VIX Percent<br>Change |
|---|---|---|---|---|---|---|---|---|
| US-base SR change | 0.260*** | | | | | | | |
| | (0.0415) | | | | | | | |
| Peg * US-base SR change | 0.671*** | | | | | | | |
| | (0.0936) | | | | | | | |
| Multi-base SR change | | 0.518*** | 0.306* | 0.546*** | | | | |
| | | (0.133) | (0.152) | (0.129) | | | | |
| Peg * Multi-base SR change | | 0.223 | 0.129 | 0.225 | | | | |
| | | (0.153) | (0.165) | (0.153) | | | | |
| US-base LR change | | | | | 0.484*** | | | |
| | | | | | (0.0502) | | | |
| Peg * US-base LR change | | | | | 0.454*** | | | |
| | | | | | (0.0558) | | | |
| Multi-base LR change | | | | | | 0.753*** | 0.582*** | 0.798*** |
| | | | | | | (0.107) | (0.147) | (0.104) |
| Peg * Multi-base LR change | | | | | | 0.0590 | -0.0317 | 0.0639 |
| | | | | | | (0.124) | (0.0992) | (0.120) |
| VIX Percent Change | | | | 0.00197* | | | | 0.00199*** |
| | | | | (0.00107) | | | | (0.000475) |

*(Continued)*

**Table 4:** *(Continued)*

| | (1)<br>US-base SR | (2)<br>Multi-base SR | (3)<br>Multi-base SR with Time Effects | (4)<br>Multi-base SR with VIX Percent Change | (5)<br>US-base LR | (6)<br>Multi-base LR | (7)<br>Multi-base LR with Time Effects | (8)<br>Multi-base LR with VIX Percent Change |
|---|---|---|---|---|---|---|---|---|
| Constant | −0.00109*** | −0.000694*** | −0.0000462 | −0.000705*** | −0.000675*** | −0.000394*** | −0.00111** | −0.000397*** |
| | (0.000158) | (0.000117) | (0.000145) | (0.000114) | (0.0000939) | (0.0000782) | (0.000481) | (0.0000786) |
| N | 1598 | 1598 | 1598 | 1598 | 1785 | 1785 | 1785 | 1785 |
| adj. R2 | 0.086 | 0.215 | 0.298 | 0.221 | 0.233 | 0.388 | 0.482 | 0.399 |
| Optimal Lags | 0 | 0 | 0 | 0 | 0 | 0 | 0 | 0 |
| p-value for F Test that growth and inflation change variables (and their lags, where applicable) do not enter | 0.00050801 | 0.000189404 | 0.120686741 | 0.000332068 | 0.016935281 | 0.051729132 | 0.048043523 | 0.057385095 |
| p-value for F Test that controls and Peg interaction term coefficients (and lags, where applicable) sum to zero. | 6.16506E-12 | 0.106312651 | 0.880379827 | 0.413387934 | 8.95003E-11 | 0.09259661 | 0.063848163 | 0.204935031 |

Clustered standard errors in parentheses (at country level)

* $p < 0.10$, ** $p < 0.05$, *** $p < 0.01$

Tables 5 and 6 report results for short-term and long-term nominal interest rates, respectively, with all countries measured against the U.S. dollar as base currency. The columns labeled "PSS F stat" indicate whether the hypothesis $\theta = \xi = \omega = 0$ (i.e., no levels relationship) is rejected at the 5% level (indicator = 1) or not (indicator = 0), under the alternative assumptions that the variables in specification (3) are, respectively, I(0) and I(1). Similarly, the columns labeled "PSS T stat" concern the hypothesis $\theta = 0$.

As expected, there is considerable heterogeneity across countries, even within broad country groupings. Looking at country-group averages, however, the values of $\xi$ have a central tendency of being in the neighborhood of 1 for both groups, for both short- and long-term interest rates, though estimates are much more precise for the advanced countries. Thus, the levels relationship (when it exists) is consistent with long-run equality of nominal interest rates at short and long maturities (up to a constant). The average adjustment speed $\theta$ for long rates is nearly the same for both country groups, implying adjustment half-lives of about 14.6–17.5 months. For short-term rates the adjustment speed appears to be quite a bit faster for developing/emerging economies (about a year as opposed to over two years), though once again, the standard error of estimation is comparatively large. The data seem consistent with the existence of a long-term levels relationship in a good number of cases when the data are I(0), but generally less so when the data are I(1). It is particularly hard to detect a levels relationship for developing/emerging short-term rates. It is also very hard to reject the hypothesis $\theta = 0$ for those rates.

These averages, as noted, conceal considerable idiosyncrasies, even within Asia. For example, with respect to short-term interest rates, Hong Kong shows unitary long-run coherence with U.S. rates and an extremely rapid adjustment speed (half-life below 4 months). Singapore's adjustment speed is even more rapid, but its estimated $\xi$ is only 0.39. Malaysia shows both a $\xi$ value of 0.58, and a slow adjustment speed that implies an estimated half-life of about a year and a half. The results for long-term rates are on the whole similar.

| | Coverage | No. of Obs. (based on optimal number of lags) | $\xi$ | $\theta$ | PSS F test stat | PSS F test sig. at 0 | PSS F test sig. at 1 | PSS T test stat | PSS T test sig. at 0 | PSS T test sig. at 1 | Half-life (in months) |
|---|---|---|---|---|---|---|---|---|---|---|---|
| *Advanced* | | | | | | | | | | | |
| 1 Australia | May 1989–Jun 2012 | 271 | 0.43 (0.30) | -0.03 (0.01) | 6.13 | 1 | 1 | -3.69 | 1 | 1 | 26.34 |
| 2 Belgium | May 1989–Jan 2014 | 297 | 1.27 (0.30) | -0.03 (0.01) | 6.36 | 1 | 1 | -3.27 | 1 | 0 | 26.06 |
| 3 Canada | May 1989–Feb 2014 | 297 | 1.07 (0.27) | -0.03 (0.01) | 2.16 | 0 | 0 | -2.53 | 0 | 0 | 21.06 |
| 4 Cyprus | May 1989–Mar 2008 | 227 | 0.58 (0.36) | -0.02 (0.01) | 1.23 | 0 | 0 | -1.67 | 0 | 0 | 34.60 |
| 5 Denmark | May 1989–Jan 2014 | 241 | 1.61 (0.63) | -0.03 (0.01) | 2.12 | 0 | 0 | -2.29 | 0 | 0 | 20.17 |
| 6 France | May 1989–Feb 2014 | 298 | 1.42 (0.36) | -0.03 (0.01) | 3.98 | 1 | 0 | -3.05 | 1 | 0 | 25.78 |
| 7 Germany | May 1989–Feb 2014 | 298 | 1.31 (0.26) | -0.02 (0.01) | 6.86 | 1 | 1 | -3.48 | 1 | 0 | 27.50 |
| 8 Greece | Nov 1992–Feb 2014 | 293 | -2.03 (1.89) | -0.28 (0.05) | 9.50 | 1 | 1 | -5.34 | 1 | 1 | 2.13 |
| 9 Iceland | May 1989–Jan 2013 | 285 | 0.78 (0.23) | -0.10 (0.02) | 11.91 | 1 | 1 | -5.94 | 1 | 1 | 6.27 |

| | | | | | | | | | | | | | |
|---|---|---|---|---|---|---|---|---|---|---|---|---|---|
| 10 | Ireland | Feb 1997–Feb 2014 | 205 | 0.88 (0.15) | -0.06 (0.02) | 5.03 | 1 | 1 | 1 | -3.40 | 1 | 0 | 11.55 |
| 11 | Italy | May 1989–Jan 2014 | 297 | 1.14 (0.40) | -0.03 (0.01) | 4.32 | 1 | 0 | 0 | -3.33 | 1 | 0 | 20.60 |
| 12 | Japan | May 1989–Jan 2014 | 296 | 0.73 (0.44) | -0.01 (0.01) | 1.39 | 0 | 0 | 0 | -1.88 | 0 | 0 | 62.04 |
| 13 | Malta | May 1989–Feb 2014 | 298 | 0.90 (0.20) | -0.03 (0.01) | 6.04 | 1 | 1 | 1 | -3.02 | 1 | 0 | 26.68 |
| 14 | Netherlands | May 1989–Jan 2014 | 297 | 1.48 (0.33) | -0.02 (0.01) | 8.04 | 1 | 1 | 1 | -3.35 | 1 | 0 | 35.77 |
| 15 | Norway | May 1989–Feb 2014 | 296 | 1.18 (0.27) | -0.05 (0.01) | 5.85 | 1 | 1 | 1 | -3.92 | 1 | 1 | 12.46 |
| 16 | Portugal | May 1989–Feb 2014 | 287 | 1.91 (0.74) | -0.01 (0.01) | 2.07 | 0 | 0 | 0 | -2.18 | 0 | 0 | 46.21 |
| 17 | Spain | May 1989–Feb 2014 | 297 | 1.24 (0.39) | -0.02 (0.01) | 5.53 | 1 | 1 | 1 | -3.33 | 1 | 0 | 38.61 |
| 18 | Sweden | May 1989–Jan 2014 | 297 | 1.20 (0.35) | -0.04 (0.01) | 4.72 | 1 | 1 | 0 | -3.61 | 1 | 1 | 17.04 |
| 19 | Switzerland | May 1989–Feb 2014 | 296 | 0.91 (0.28) | -0.03 (0.01) | 4.68 | 1 | 1 | 0 | -3.05 | 1 | 0 | 24.25 |
| 20 | United Kingdom | May 1989–Jan 2014 | 296 | 1.42 (0.22) | -0.03 (0.01) | 3.95 | 1 | 1 | 0 | -3.36 | 1 | 0 | 23.70 |

*(Continued)*

## Table 5: (Continued)

| | Coverage | No. of Obs. (based on optimal number of lags) | ξ | θ | PSS F test stat | PSS F test sig. at 0 | PSS F test sig. at 1 | PSS T test stat | PSS T test sig. at 0 | PSS T test sig. at 1 | Half-life (in months) |
|---|---|---|---|---|---|---|---|---|---|---|---|
| *Devloping/ emerging* | | | | | | | | | | | |
| 1 Albania | Nov 1995– Feb 2014 | 165 | 4.32 (11.52) | -0.03 (0.03) | 0.94 | 0 | 0 | -0.77 | 0 | 0 | 25.48 |
| 2 Argentina | Feb 2008– Feb2014 | 66 | 2.40 (2.83) | -0.10 (0.07) | 1.19 | 0 | 0 | -1.43 | 0 | 0 | 6.35 |
| 3 Armenia | Mar 1995– Nov 2012 | 203 | 1.39 (0.61) | -0.15 (0.03) | 9.56 | 1 | 1 | -4.41 | 1 | 1 | 4.19 |
| 4 Azerbaijan | Mar 1998 –Jan 2008 | 118 | 0.49 (0.21) | -0.10 (0.03) | 5.26 | 1 | 1 | -3.20 | 1 | 0 | 6.74 |
| 5 Brazil | Sep 1997– Sep 2012 | 171 | 0.08 (0.69) | -0.06 (0.02) | 5.12 | 1 | 1 | -3.05 | 1 | 0 | 11.81 |
| 6 Bulgaria | Aug 1997– Dec 2013 | 194 | -0.46 (0.45) | -0.05 (0.02) | 5.75 | 1 | 1 | -2.27 | 0 | 0 | 13.01 |
| 7 Chile | Mar 1998– Feb 2014 | 165 | 0.88 (0.22) | -0.17 (0.03) | 13.96 | 1 | 1 | -6.42 | 1 | 1 | 3.62 |
| 8 China | Feb 2001– Dec 2013 | 155 | 0.14 (0.42) | -0.06 (0.02) | 2.00 | 0 | 0 | -2.44 | 0 | 0 | 11.87 |

| | | | | | | | | | | | | |
|---|---|---|---|---|---|---|---|---|---|---|---|---|
| 9 Colombia | Oct 1993–Jan 2014 | 243 | 1.05 (0.39) | -0.02 (0.01) | 7.05 | 1 | 1 | -3.46 | 1 | 0 | 27.66 |
| 10 Croatia Czech | Feb 2001–Dec 2013 | 155 | 0.14 (0.42) | -0.06 (0.02) | 2.00 | 0 | 0 | -2.44 | 0 | 0 | 11.87 |
| 11 Republic | Oct 1993–Jan 2014 | 243 | 1.05 (0.39) | -0.02 (0.01) | 7.05 | 1 | 1 | -3.46 | 1 | 0 | 27.66 |
| 12 Egypt | Mar 1991–Feb 2014 | 275 | -0.23 (0.46) | -0.05 (0.01) | 6.03 | 1 | 1 | -3.21 | 1 | 0 | 14.51 |
| 13 Fiji | May 1989–Jun 2013 | 290 | 0.46 (0.25) | -0.09 (0.03) | 5.38 | 1 | 1 | -3.56 | 1 | 1 | 7.32 |
| 14 Ghana | Mar 1990–Mar 2013 | 277 | 3.83 (1.85) | -0.02 (0.01) | 2.56 | 0 | 0 | -2.58 | 0 | 0 | 31.97 |
| 15 Guyana | May 1989–Dec 2013 | 274 | 1.05 (1.24) | -0.02 (0.01) | 3.09 | 0 | 0 | -2.53 | 0 | 0 | 39.01 |
| 16 Hong Kong | Aug 1991–Feb 2014 | 271 | 1.09 (0.10) | -0.17 (0.04) | 6.70 | 1 | 1 | -4.41 | 1 | 1 | 3.72 |
| 17 Hungary | Mar 1992–Feb 2014 | 258 | 0.05 (1.01) | -0.03 (0.02) | 1.90 | 0 | 0 | -2.28 | 0 | 0 | 19.89 |
| 18 India | Mar 1993–Jan 2014 | 251 | 0.73 (0.28) | -0.09 (0.03) | 3.29 | 0 | 0 | -3.14 | 1 | 0 | 7.50 |
| 19 Israel | Mar 1992–Jan 2014 | 263 | 1.01 (0.34) | -0.05 (0.01) | 30.97 | 1 | 1 | -4.74 | 1 | 1 | 13.77 |

(Continued)

| | Coverage | No. of Obs. (based on optimal number of lags) | ξ | θ | PSS F test stat | PSS F test sig. at 0 | PSS F test sig. at 1 | PSS T test stat | PSS T test sig. at 0 | PSS T test sig. at 1 | Half-life (in months) |
|---|---|---|---|---|---|---|---|---|---|---|---|
| 20 Kazakhstan | Jun 1994–Feb 2014 | 225 | 1.74 (0.65) | -0.08 (0.02) | 7.84 | 1 | 1 | -4.35 | 1 | 1 | 8.41 |
| 21 Kenya | May 1989–Dec 2013 | 293 | 1.48 (0.96) | -0.06 (0.01) | 6.90 | 1 | 1 | -4.36 | 1 | 1 | 11.73 |
| 22 Kuwait | May 1989–Jan 2005 | 189 | 1.78 (0.79) | -0.02 (0.01) | 2.01 | 0 | 0 | -1.47 | 0 | 0 | 31.50 |
| 23 Kyrgyzstan | Mar 1994–Dec 2013 | 211 | 6.92 (1.71) | -0.15 (0.04) | 4.82 | 1 | 0 | -3.69 | 1 | 1 | 4.30 |
| 24 Latvia | July 1994–Jan 2014 | 234 | 1.19 (1.08) | -0.03 (0.01) | 2.86 | 0 | 0 | -2.74 | 0 | 0 | 22.83 |
| 25 Lebanon | Feb 2003–Feb 2014 | 124 | -0.04 (0.09) | -0.07 (0.02) | 5.82 | 1 | 1 | -3.43 | 1 | 0 | 9.60 |
| 26 Malaysia | Jan 1989–Feb2014 | 298 | 0.58 (0.21) | -0.04 (0.01) | 3.81 | 1 | 0 | -3.22 | 1 | 0 | 17.76 |
| 27 Mexico | May 1989 –Dec 2013 | 293 | 3.14 (1.42) | -0.08 (0.04) | 3.23 | 0 | 0 | -1.82 | 0 | 0 | 8.68 |
| 28 Moldova | May 1995-Feb 2014 | 197 | 2.63 (1.14) | -0.08 (0.03) | 3.57 | 0 | 0 | -3.16 | 1 | 0 | 8.10 |

| | | | | | | | | | | |
|---|---|---|---|---|---|---|---|---|---|---|
| 29 Nepal | May 1989–Dec 2013 | 296 | 0.76 (0.47) | -0.06 (0.02) | 5.14 | 1 | -2.86 | 0 | 0 | 12.23 |
| 30 Nigeria | Mar 1995–Feb 2014 | 228 | 0.53 (0.82) | -0.04 (0.02) | 2.64 | 0 | -2.56 | 0 | 0 | 16.69 |
| 31 Oman | Jun 1996–Feb2014 | 213 | 1.02 (0.09) | -0.11 (0.03) | 5.56 | 1 | -4.00 | 1 | 1 | 6.00 |
| 32 Pakistan | May 1991–Feb 2014 | 274 | 1.27 (0.71) | -0.03 (0.01) | 6.14 | 1 | -2.64 | 0 | 0 | 24.92 |
| 33 Philippines | May 1989–Feb 2014 | 294 | 2.34 (0.52) | -0.06 (0.02) | 5.03 | 1 | -3.67 | 1 | 1 | 11.21 |
| 34 Poland | Jul 1991–Feb 2014 | 260 | 1.12 (0.37) | -0.07 (0.02) | 8.64 | 1 | -3.76 | 1 | 1 | 9.95 |
| 35 Romania | May 1994–Sep 2005 | 130 | 4.47 (2.49) | -0.31 (0.12) | 3.13 | 0 | -2.58 | 0 | 0 | 1.89 |
| 36 Russia | Sep 1994–Feb 2014 | 190 | 1.36 (1.16) | -0.28 (0.06) | 7.98 | 1 | -4.79 | 1 | 1 | 2.08 |
| 37 Rwanda | Mar 1999–Feb 2014 | 179 | -0.08 (0.38) | -0.06 (0.03) | 3.43 | 0 | -2.39 | 0 | 0 | 10.62 |
| 38 Singapore | May 1989–Jan 2014 | 297 | 0.39 (0.05) | -0.23 (0.04) | 13.06 | 1 | -6.21 | 1 | 1 | 2.63 |
| 39 Slovakia | Apr 1993–Dec 2007 | 177 | 1.81 (2.40) | -0.03 (0.02) | 1.82 | 0 | -1.51 | 0 | 0 | 19.87 |

*(Continued)*

Table 5: (Continued)

| | Coverage | No. of Obs. (based on optimal number of lags) | ξ | θ | PSS F test stat | PSS F test sig. at 0 | PSS F test sig. at 1 | PSS T test stat | PSS T test sig. at 0 | PSS T test sig. at 1 | Half-life (in months) |
|---|---|---|---|---|---|---|---|---|---|---|---|
| 40 Slovenia | Mar 2000–Feb 2014 | 159 | 1.73 (0.51) | -0.04 (0.01) | 3.95 | 1 | 0 | -3.10 | 1 | 0 | 17.43 |
| 41 South Africa | May 1989–Jan 2014 | 291 | 1.31 (0.29) | -0.04 (0.01) | 6.10 | 1 | 1 | -4.08 | 1 | 1 | 15.97 |
| 42 South Korea | Nov 2006–Feb 2014 | 88 | 0.53 (0.09) | -0.09 (0.02) | 11.48 | 1 | 1 | -4.99 | 1 | 1 | 7.23 |
| 43 Taiwan | May 1989–Feb 2014 | 298 | 1.02 (0.29) | -0.02 (0.01) | 2.27 | 0 | 0 | -2.38 | 0 | 0 | 35.51 |
| 44 Tanzania | Feb 1994–Jan 2014 | 229 | -0.22 (0.68) | -0.10 (0.03) | 5.64 | 1 | 1 | -3.62 | 1 | 1 | 6.72 |
| 45 Thailand | May 1989–Sep 1989; Mar 1997–Feb 2014 | 178 | 0.25 (0.17) | -0.07 (0.01) | 19.49 | 1 | 1 | -6.89 | 1 | 1 | 9.12 |
| 46 Turkey | May 1989–Feb 2014 | 281 | 1.10 (2.70) | -0.12 (0.04) | 3.62 | 0 | 0 | -3.16 | 1 | 0 | 5.36 |
| 47 Uganda | May 1996–Feb 2014 | 213 | 0.30 (0.54) | -0.09 (0.03) | 5.11 | 1 | 1 | -3.35 | 1 | 0 | 6.97 |

| | | N | ξ | θ | PSS F stat | PSS F stat sig. at 0 | PSS F stat sig. at 1 | PSS T stat | PSS T stat sig. at 0 | PSS T stat sig. at 1 | Half-life (in months) |
|---|---|---|---|---|---|---|---|---|---|---|---|
| 48 Uruguay | Feb 1993–Dec 2013 | 183 | -0.14 (0.30) | -0.27 (0.04) | 12.68 | 1 | 1 | -6.13 | 1 | 1 | 2.23 |
| 49 Venezuela | Feb 1997–Dec 2003 | 83 | -0.33 (2.50) | -0.10 (0.05) | 1.74 | 0 | 0 | 2.18 | 0 | 0 | 6.18 |
| 50 Zambia | May 1998–Feb 2014 | 292 | -1.34 (2.76) | -0.06 (0.02) | 6.95 | 1 | 1 | -3.88 | 1 | 1 | 11.41 |
| *Averages* | | | ξ | θ | | PSS F stat sig. at 0 | PSS F stat sig. at 1 | | PSS T stat sig. at 0 | PSS T stat sig. at 1 | Half-life (in months) |
| Advanced | | | 0.97 (0.42) | -0.05 (0.01) | | 75% | 50% | | 75% | 25% | 25.44 |
| Developing/ Emerging | | | 1.43 (1.39) | -0.09 (0.03) | | 60% | 54% | | 60% | 38% | 13.12 |

Standard errors in parentheses.

ξ: Levels relationship.

θ: Adjustment speed to shocks in the levels relationship.

Sig. at 0: whether we can reject no levels relationship at the 5% level if we assume the data are stationary.

Sig. at 1: whether we can reject no levels relationship at the 5% level if we assume the data are nonstationary. Half-life: The half-life of a shock (in months), based on the adjustment speed.

**Table 6: Long–term interest rate dynamic equations with United States as base currency**

| | Coverage | No. of Obs. (based on optimal number of lags) | ξ | θ | PSS F test stat | PSS F test sig. at 0 | PSS F test sig. at 1 | PSS T test stat | PSS T test sig. at 0 | PSS T test sig. at 1 | Half–life (in months) |
|---|---|---|---|---|---|---|---|---|---|---|---|
| *Advanced* | | | | | | | | | | | |
| 1 Australia | May 1989– Jun 2012 | 271 | 0.74 (0.39) | −0.03 (0.01) | 4.07 | 1 | 0 | −2.28 | 0 | 0 | 24.3 |
| 2 Austria | May 1989– Jan 2014 | 297 | 1.10 (0.11) | −0.06 (0.02) | 6.73 | 1 | 1 | −3.90 | 1 | 1 | 11.4 |
| 3 Belgium | May 1989– Jan 2014 | 297 | 1.20 (0.15) | −0.05 (0.01) | 5.06 | 1 | 1 | −3.35 | 1 | 0 | 14.9 |
| 4 Canada | May 1989– Feb 2014 | 298 | 1.29 (0.11) | −0.05 (0.02) | 3.21 | 0 | 0 | −3.08 | 1 | 0 | 13.2 |
| 5 Cyprus | Jan 1998– Feb 2014 | 194 | 0.01 (0.71) | −0.02 (0.02) | 1.28 | 0 | 0 | −1.48 | 0 | 0 | 30.3 |
| 6 Denmark | May 1989– Jan 2014 | 297 | 1.40 (0.10) | −0.07 (0.02) | 7.50 | 1 | 1 | −4.30 | 1 | 1 | 9.2 |
| 7 Finland | May 1989– Jan 2014 | 297 | 1.71 (0.29) | −0.03 (0.01) | 2.54 | 0 | 0 | −2.70 | 0 | 0 | 22.8 |
| 8 France | May 1989– Feb 2014 | 298 | 1.18 (0.11) | −0.05 (0.01) | 6.29 | 1 | 1 | −3.98 | 1 | 1 | 12.3 |
| 9 Germany | May 1989– Feb 2014 | 298 | 1.15 (0.06) | −0.09 (0.02) | 16.02 | 1 | 1 | −5.84 | 1 | 1 | 7.1 |

| | | | | | | | | | | | | |
|---|---|---|---|---|---|---|---|---|---|---|---|---|
| 10 | Greece | May 1989–Jan 2014 | 255 | -0.90 (2.14) | -0.03 (0.01) | 1.93 | 0 | 0 | -2.33 | 0 | 0 | 21.5 |
| 11 | Iceland | May 2004–Jan 2014 | 117 | 1.09 (0.23) | -0.32 (0.07) | 8.11 | 1 | 1 | -4.73 | 1 | 1 | 1.8 |
| 12 | Ireland | Feb 1997–Jan 2014 | 204 | 0.14 (0.95) | -0.02 (0.02) | 1.48 | 0 | 0 | -1.35 | 0 | 0 | 28.9 |
| 13 | Italy | Mar 1989–Feb 2014 | 297 | 1.58 (0.55) | -0.02 (0.01) | 2.15 | 0 | 0 | -2.48 | 0 | 0 | 30.1 |
| 14 | Japan | May 1989–Jan 2014 | 297 | 0.69 (0.21) | -0.03 (0.01) | 2.70 | 0 | 0 | -2.53 | 0 | 0 | 25.8 |
| 15 | Malta | Feb 2000–Feb 2014 | 169 | 1.18 (0.62) | -0.03 (0.02) | 2.24 | 0 | 0 | -1.43 | 0 | 0 | 24.9 |
| 16 | Netherlands | May 1989–Jan 2014 | 297 | 1.18 (0.08) | -0.07 (0.01) | 9.86 | 1 | 1 | -4.76 | 1 | 1 | 9.8 |
| 17 | Norway | May 1989–Feb 2014 | 298 | 1.26 (0.13) | -0.05 (0.01) | 4.83 | 1 | 0 | -3.75 | 1 | 1 | 12.8 |
| 18 | Portugal | May 1989–Jan 2014 | 264 | 0.99 (0.68) | -0.04 (0.01) | 5.55 | 1 | 1 | -3.97 | 1 | 1 | 17.5 |
| 19 | Spain | May 1989–Feb 2014 | 298 | 1.11 (0.49) | -0.02 (0.01) | 3.21 | 0 | 0 | -2.38 | 0 | 0 | 30.6 |
| 20 | Sweden | May 1989–Jan 2014 | 298 | 1.55 (0.20) | -0.04 (0.01) | 4.53 | 1 | 1 | -3.52 | 1 | 0 | 17.2 |

*(Continued)*

**Table 6:** *(Continued)*

| | Coverage | No. of Obs. (based on optimal number of lags) | ξ | θ | PSS F test stat | PSS F test sig. at 0 | PSS F test sig. at 1 | PSS T test stat | PSS T test sig. at 0 | PSS T test sig. at 1 | Half-life (in months) |
|---|---|---|---|---|---|---|---|---|---|---|---|
| 21 Switzerland | Mar 1989–Feb 2014 | 298 | 0.88 (0.07) | -0.07 (0.02) | 8.69 | 1 | 1 | -4.63 | 1 | 1 | 9.5 |
| 22 United Kingdom | May 1989–Jan 2014 | 297 | 1.37 (0.11) | -0.07 (0.02) | 6.35 | 1 | 1 | -4.02 | 1 | 1 | 9.8 |
| *Developing/ emerging* | | | | | | | | | | | |
| 1 Brazil | Jan 2000–Dec 2006 | 84 | -3.42 (8.78) | | 0.04 | (0.06) | 4.34 | 1 | 0 | 0.75 | 0 |
| 2 Bulgaria | Mar 1998–Nov 2009 | 141 | 0.46 (1.17) | | -0.05 | (0.03) | 1.54 | 0 | 0 | -2.05 | 0 |
| 3 Chile | Sep 2004–Feb 2014 | 94 | 0.39 (0.14) | | -0.21 | (0.05) | 6.31 | 1 | 1 | -3.91 | 1 |
| 4 China | Dec 2006–Feb 2014 | 87 | 0.11 (0.14) | | -0.13 | (0.04) | 4.51 | 1 | 0 | -3.38 | 1 |
| 5 Republic Czech | Jun 2000–Feb 2014 | 165 | 1.16 (0.33) | | -0.06 | (0.02) | 3.43 | 0 | 0 | -2.60 | 0 |
| 6 Fiji | Feb 2001–Jun 2013 | 149 | 0.83 (1.08) | | -0.03 | (0.02) | 1.07 | 0 | 0 | -1.51 | 0 |

| | | | | | | | | | | | |
|---|---|---|---|---|---|---|---|---|---|---|---|
| 7 Hong Kong | Dec 1996–Jan 2014 | 206 | 1.53 | (0.27) | -0.09 | (0.03) | 3.24 | 0 | 0 | -3.08 | 1 |
| 8 Hungary | Mar 1999–Feb 2014 | 180 | 0.11 | (0.29) | -0.12 | (0.04) | 3.70 | 0 | 0 | -3.31 | 1 |
| 9 India | May 1989–Jan 2014 | 297 | 0.98 | (0.44) | -0.03 | (0.01) | 3.15 | 0 | 0 | -2.25 | 0 |
| 10 Israel | Mar 1997–Feb 2014 | 204 | 1.23 | (1.11) | -0.02 | (0.01) | 6.24 | 1 | 1 | -1.46 | 0 |
| 11 Kazakhstan | May 1998–Feb 2014 | 190 | 2.01 | (1.00) | -0.02 | (0.01) | 1.91 | 0 | 0 | -1.81 | 0 |
| 12 Latvia | Feb 1999–Dec 2013 | 177 | -0.05 | (1.12) | -0.03 | (0.01) | 2.42 | 0 | 0 | -2.20 | 0 |
| 13 Malaysia | Mar 1996–Jan 2014 | 215 | 0.64 | (0.23) | -0.04 | (0.02) | 3.78 | 0 | 0 | -2.69 | 0 |
| 14 Mexico | Dec 1999–Feb 2014 | 104 | 0.64 | (0.23) | -0.11 | (0.04) | 3.76 | 0 | 0 | -2.92 | 1 |
| 15 Pakistan | May 1989–Feb 2014 | 290 | -1.12 | (0.69) | -0.02 | (0.01) | 4.43 | 1 | 1 | -1.92 | 0 |
| 16 Philippines | Apr 1999–Jul 2013 | 172 | 2.66 | (0.95) | -0.04 | (0.02) | 1.34 | 0 | 0 | -1.99 | 0 |
| 17 Poland | Jul 1999–Feb 2014 | 176 | 1.44 | (0.40) | -0.06 | (0.02) | 5.25 | 1 | 1 | -3.31 | 1 |

(Continued)

Table 6: (Continued)

| | Coverage | No. of Obs. (based on optimal number of lags) | ξ | θ | PSS F test stat | PSS F test sig. at 0 | PSS F test sig. at 1 | PSS T test stat | PSS T test sig. at 0 | PSS T test sig. at 1 | Half-life (in months) |
|---|---|---|---|---|---|---|---|---|---|---|---|
| 18 | Russia | Feb 1997– Feb 2014 | 205 | 1.82 | (2.20) | -0.07 | (0.04) | 1.94 | 0 | 0 | -1.76 | 0 |
| 19 | Singapore | Aug 1998– Feb 2014 | 185 | 0.64 | (0.06) | -0.19 | (0.04) | 9.83 | 1 | 1 | -5.33 | 1 |
| 20 | Slovakia | Jan 1995– Feb 2014 | 226 | 5.49 | (3.20) | -0.03 | (0.02) | 2.74 | 0 | 0 | -1.62 | 0 |
| 21 | Slovenia | May 2002– Feb 2014 | 142 | -0.56 | (0.39) | -0.09 | (0.03) | 4.82 | 1 | 0 | -3.52 | 1 |
| 22 | South Africa | May 1989– Feb 2014 | 298 | 1.49 | (0.29) | -0.05 | (0.02) | 5.57 | 1 | 1 | -3.62 | 1 |
| 23 | South Korea | Dec 2000– Feb 2014 | 158 | 0.92 | (0.24) | -0.08 | (0.03) | 2.29 | 0 | 0 | -2.59 | 0 |
| 24 | Taiwan | May 1995– Jan 2014 | 227 | 1.16 | (0.25) | -0.03 | (0.01) | 2.45 | 0 | 0 | -2.68 | 0 |
| 25 | Tanzania | Dec 2002– Jan 2014 | 134 | 0.18 | (1.35) | -0.06 | (0.03) | 2.00 | 0 | 0 | -2.42 | 0 |
| 26 | Thailand | May 1989– Feb 2014 | 298 | 1.50 | (0.24) | -0.04 | (0.01) | 9.66 | 1 | 1 | -3.91 | 1 |

| # | Country | Period | n | ξ | (s.e.) | θ | (s.e.) | PSS F stat sig. at 0 | PSS F stat sig. at 1 | PSS T stat sig. at 0 | PSS T stat sig. at 1 | Half-life (in months) |
|---|---------|--------|---|----|--------|----|--------|---------------------|---------------------|---------------------|---------------------|----------------------|
| 27 | Vietnam | Jul 2009–Feb 2014 | 56 | 2.75 | (1.60) | -0.07 | (0.04) | 3.73 | 0 | 0 | -1.90 | 0 |
| 28 | Zambia | Oct 2007–Feb 2014 | 77 | -0.16 | (1.77) | -0.05 | (0.04) | 0.80 | 0 | 0 | -1.14 | 0 |
| *Averages* | Advanced | | | 1.00 | (0.39) | -0.06 | (0.02) | 59% | 45% | 59% | 45% | 17.54 |
| | Devloping/ Emerging | | | 0.89 | (1.07) | -0.06 | (0.03) | 36% | 21% | 36% | 14% | 14.64 |

Standard errors in parentheses.

ξ: Levels relationship.

θ: Adjustment speed to shocks in the levels relationship.

Sig. at 0: whether we can reject no levels relationship at the 5% level if we assume the data are stationary.

Sig. at 1: whether we can reject no levels relationship at the 5% level if we assume the data are nonstationary.

Half-life: The half-life of a shock (in months), based on the adjustment speed.

The overall impression is that nominal interest rates trend strongly with U.S. rates in the long run, in both country groups, but there is usually considerable medium-run scope for interest-rate independence. As before, however, the possibility of unobserved global shocks to interest rates bedevils the interpretation of these results.

## Trilemmas and Tradeoffs

In line with previous research, the results of the preceding section indicate considerable scope for countries that do not peg their exchange rates to vary *short-term* nominal interest rates independently of foreign nominal interest rates. In addition, changes in short-term rates appear to reflect changes in domestic variables such as inflation and output. Independence of *long-term* rates seems lower, regardless of the exchange regime, and the relation of changes in long-term rates to key domestic macro variables is more tenuous.

Rey (2013) summarizes earlier studies and new evidence of her own suggesting that foreign financial shocks beside interest rates spill across national borders, even when exchange rates are flexible. She concludes that:

> [M]onetary conditions are transmitted from the main financial centers to the rest of the world through gross credit flows and leverage, irrespective of the exchange rate regime.... Fluctuating exchange rates cannot insulate economies from the global financial cycle, when capital is mobile. The "trilemma" morphs into a "dilemma" — independent monetary policies are possible if and only if the capital account is managed, directly or indirectly, regardless of the exchange-rate regime.

Because nominal interest-rate independence is demonstrably less where currencies are pegged, one is led to ask: Does this interest-rate independence matter at all? Is there any advantage to having a flexible exchange rate? Rose (2014), for example, shows that it is hard to detect systematic differences between economic outcomes for hard currency pegs and inflation targeting regimes for small economies. As he acknowledges, however, currency regime choice is not exogenous (and, in particular, seems related to the degree of democracy). Di Giovanni and Shambaugh (2008) take a more direct approach to seek benefits from partial independence of interest rates. They demonstrate that comparative interest-rate independence allows countries with flexible exchange rates to shield themselves from the contractionary output effects of higher interest rates abroad. In contrast, countries with pegs suffer more.[29]

Such evidence suggests that, provided an EME's policy interest rate feeds through to other domestic interest rates and demand, its central bank retains a capacity to steer the economy, and the capacity is greater the more the bank is willing to allow exchange rates to fluctuate and depart from the U.S. interest rate. Klein and Shambaugh (2013) present striking confirmation that even countries that dampen exchange rate fluctuations still enjoy some short-term interest-rate independence (though not as much as those that freely float). And of course, countries that manage exchange rates flexibly (or let them float) do not provide a one-way bet for speculators — they seem to be less susceptible to various types of crisis, including growth collapses of the type seen recently in some euro area countries.[30]

Thus, it strikes me as not really fruitful to ask if the exchange-rate regime materially influences the scope for monetary policy independence. Of course it does. It is unquestionably true, as Rey asserts, that "monetary conditions are transmitted from the main financial centers to the rest of the world through gross credit flows and leverage." However, the exchange rate regime is central to the channels of transmission and to the range of policy responses available. The monetary trilemma remains valid.

This is not to say that even monetary independence makes the available menu of options attractive when the capital account is fully open. We learned soon after the fall of the Bretton Woods system in 1973 that floating exchange rates can be helpful in the face of some economic shocks but almost never provide full insulation against disturbances from abroad. Rather, they provide an expanded choice menu for policymakers,

---

[29] Aizenman, Chinn, and Ito (2010) report a similar finding, and also trace over time different country groups' approaches to navigating the monetary trilemma.
[30] See Ghosh, Ostry, and Qureshi (2014). Rose's (2014) discussion points to the recent durability of flexible exchange-rate/inflation targeting regimes.

but with no guarantee that the available choices will be pleasant. This has proven especially true in the face of recent financial cycles in the rich economies. The monetary *trilemma* remains, but the difficulty of the *tradeoffs* that alternative policy choices entail can be worsened by financial globalization.

To understand the tradeoff problem, we need to ask: What exactly does monetary policy autonomy or independence *mean*? I would define it as the ability to pursue a range of domestic goals; and an exchange rate peg clearly precludes this pursuit when capital flows freely across the border. Woodford's (2010) analysis demonstrates that when there is one target only — an inflation rate — then monetary autonomy is possible if the exchange rate floats. Woodford shows within a variety of New Keynesian models that are under a float, the central bank can always shift the dynamic aggregate demand curve to achieve a desired inflation target.

Normally, however, the monetary authority has *multiple* goals, and this is where the tradeoff problem arises.

Even in a hypothetical closed economy, monetary policy faces difficult tradeoffs. The most basic is that between inflation and unemployment. Under certain favorable conditions — essentially, that price pressure (as modeled by a New Keynesian Phillips curve) depends only upon the gap between output and its first-best level — there is no tradeoff, as monetary policy can hit both targets simultaneously. This is Blanchard and Galí's (2007) "divine coincidence." But in general — for example, when there are real wage rigidities — the coincidence fails, and the single instrument of monetary policy has somehow to navigate between the two targets, minimizing a policy loss function subject to a less favorable inflation/ unemployment tradeoff.

Opening up the economy may raise further non-financial problems, because the impact of exchange-rate changes on sectoral resource allocation and income distribution is generally far from neutral. Neither in theory not in practice is there generally a "divine coincidence" for the exchange rate.

Speaking from the central banker's perspective, Fischer (2010) summarizes eloquently:

> Not infrequently we hear central bankers say something like: "We have only one instrument, money growth (or the interest rate), and so we can have only one target, inflation." This view may be based on the targets and instruments approach of Tinbergen, of over fifty years ago, the general result of which was that you need as many instruments as targets. That view is correct if you have to hit the target exactly.
>
> But it is not correct if the problem is set up as is typical in microeconomics, where the goal is to maximize a utility function subject to constraints, in a situation where for whatever reason it is not possible to hit all the targets precisely and all the time. Among the reasons we may not be able to hit our targets precisely and all the time is that there may be more targets than instruments, for instance when the central bank's maximand is a function of output and growth. In that case we have to find marginal conditions for a maximum, and to talk about tradeoffs in explaining the optimum.

Most relevant for the present discussion are the implications for financial stability. The GFC and euro crises underscore that the tradeoff problem arises, even in a closed economy, when monetary policy is additionally burdened with a financial stability remit. In an economy with nominal rigidities, for example, excessive private borrowing may entail negative demand externalities which private agents do not internalize; see, Eggertsson and Krugman (2012) and Farhi and Werning (2013), among others. High debt may then lead to recession and liquidity traps. If authorities do not have available the first-best tools to correct the externalities from debt issuance, then even in an economy characterized by a "divine coincidence" between output and inflation goals, monetary policy might need to deviate from price stability and full employment in order to restrain debt buildups. In the absence of effective macroprudential tools, an optimal monetary policy could be drawn away from exclusive devotion to traditional macroeconomic goals (even if these would be attainable absent financial stability concerns).

In this hypothetical closed-economy setting, monetary policy does not become *ineffective* — "independence" of monetary policy certainly remains — but because authorities now face a *tradeoff* between standard macro-objectives and other targets, they will intentionally set monetary policy so as to miss all targets in a way that balances the marginal costs of the various discrepancies. Monetary policy simply carries a bigger burden than it would without financial-market distortions.

No one would expect this problem to disappear in an open economy, especially when its capital account is full open. And it does not: by themselves, exchange-rate changes would not shut out global financial developments even for policymakers willing to allow exchange rates to float free of intervention. Several theoretical models provide ample confirmation that even in the unrealistically favorable case where national policymakers cooperate, financial frictions that cannot be addressed through other tools will lead to deviations from price stability.[31]

Indeed, the problem confronting monetary policy is likely to be *even worse* in the open economy, because openness to global financial markets will inevitably degrade the effectiveness of the macroprudential tools that are available. The tradeoff between macro stabilization and financial stability becomes even worse, in the sense that the optimal monetary policy will deviate even more from first-best macro stabilization than in the closed economy. If the effects of monetary tools are weakened because of openness, tradeoffs will become harsher still. Even so, independent monetary policy will still be possible; and more so, the less tightly the exchange rate is managed. For example, if a bigger interest rate change is needed to bring about a given demand response in an open economy, this may worsen the macroprudential problem by increasing the fragility of banks and encouraging gross financial inflows.

The proposition that the efficacy of financial stability policies is weakened in the open economy follows from the *financial trilemma*

---

[31] For a recent contribution, see Kolasa and Lombardo (2014).

formulated by Schoenmaker (2013). According to this trilemma, only two of the following three can be enjoyed simultaneously:

1. National control over financial policies.
2. Financial integration with the global market.
3. Financial stability.

For example, it may do little good to place restrictions on lenders within one's jurisdiction if foreign lenders can enter the market and operate without restriction. As another example, direct limitation of residents' domestic foreign-currency borrowing is less effective if the same entities can issue foreign-currency debt in offshore markets.[32]

Moreover, the reliance of financial insurance and resolution policies on the national budget can segment global financial and capital markets along national lines (while also damaging stability), as in the euro area today. In a world of large-scale globalized finance, countries need to preserve precautionary fiscal space against financial crises. Thus, the financial trilemma can imply heavier constraints on fiscal policy as well as on monetary policy in its pursuit of domestic objectives.

Of course, the Basel Committee on Banking Supervision has been grappling with the financial trilemma since 1974, gradually but continually extending the scope and efficacy of international regulatory cooperation. The Basel III blueprint is part of the latest reform wave. Significantly (as observed by Borio, McCauley, and McGuire 2011), Basel III calls for jurisdictional reciprocity in the application of countercyclical capital buffers, so that foreign banks with loans to a country that has invoked the supplementary capital buffer are also subject to the buffer with respect to those loans.[33] By

---

[32] Ostry *et al.* (2012) assess the effects of macroprudential and capital-control policies for a sample of 51 EMEs over 1995–2008. While finding that these policies can favorably influence aggregate indicators of financial fragility, they note the difficulty of using macroprudential policy effectively when activity can migrate to unregulated venues.

[33] See Basel Committee on Banking Supervision (2011, p. 58, n. 49).

raising the effectiveness of domestic authorities' macroprudential tools, this provision reduces the burden on monetary policy.[34]

To summarize: Even for small economies buffeted by a global financial cycle, the monetary trilemma is still valid: with open capital markets, monetary authorities have far more room for maneuver than if they pegged the exchange rate. That does not mean their lives will be easy, however. Because of the financial trilemma, the impact of monetary policy on financial stability will inevitably play a bigger role in their decisions. In the face of a less favorable tradeoff between financial and macro stability, they may well be forced farther from both.

## Conclusion

Smaller economies face downsides in living with globalization. There is an inherent tension between lowering trade barriers — an approach that offers a range of gains from trade — and the implied necessity for exposing oneself to shocks and trends from abroad. These foreign disturbances range from external relative price trends that alter the home income distribution, to financial developments of the type discussed above. Government policies, including monetary and financial policies, have the potential to move the economy to a preferred point on the tradeoff between downsides and benefits.

Inefficacy of one policy instrument, however, raises the burden on the others, leaving the economy worse off in general. I have argued that while globalization places some limits on *monetary* policy, even with flexible exchange rates, the bigger problem is the enhanced difficulty of effective *financial* policy in an open economy: the financial trilemma. As for monetary policy, most emerging economies that have chosen a

---

[34] Some countries are also taking unilateral action. For example, the Federal Reserve in February 2014 required foreign banking organizations with sufficiently large U.S. assets to set up U.S. intermediate holding companies for their American subsidiaries. These holding companies will be subject to U.S. regulation.

resolution of the monetary trilemma based on exchange rate flexibility they have gained.

The paper's analysis raises questions for both future research and policy:

- One of the most potent channels for international monetary and financial transmission clearly runs through long-term interest rates. What factors are most important in determining these correlations — expected short-term rates, term premiums, or currency risk premiums? And what are the implications for domestic monetary control?
- If capital flows create a severe tradeoff problem and macroprudential policies are weakened by imperfect international coordination, then as Rey (2013) points out, the costs and benefits of capital controls come into focus. When are capital controls helpful, what types of controls are even effective, and what globally agreed norms and procedures might allow controls to play a constructive role in the international system? In particular, in what ways does it matter that countries might use capital controls to pursue competitiveness as well as financial stability goals?
- If explicit regular coordination of central bank monetary policies is unrealistic, are there other areas for cooperation that could partially substitute and thereby supplement the Basel process? One potential example is the network of central bank swap lines introduced during the GFC, and established on a permanent basis among six advanced-country central banks in October 2013. This innovation effectively allows the lender-of-last resort function to be practiced in multiple currencies. Could it gradually be extended to a broader set of participant countries?

In discussing measures to mitigate the downsides of financial globalization, it is important to keep the upsides in view. Financial market integration promotes not just gross debt expansion through two-way capital flows, but also international risk sharing. The trend shift from foreign debt to equity finance, illustrated in Figures 3 and 4, is a stabilizing effect of globalization with the potential to make domestic monetary policy more, not less, effective. Thus, policies to discourage debt finance further, including the very high debt levels of globally active banks, have considerable potential to raise national welfare.

## Data Appendix

**Short-term interest rates:** Three-month, local-currency, short-term interest rates come from the Global Financial Data database. Three-month treasury bill rates are used for all countries, other than LIBOR-like three-month money market rates for Azerbaijan, Moldova, Oman, Qatar, and Vietnam. In a few cases (e.g., Kenya), treasury bill rate data are the time series reported by central banks and government statistical agencies. The quarterly data analyzed are averages of end-month rates.

**Long-term interest rates:** Ten-year, local-currency, government bond rates come from Thomson Reuters Datastream and the Global Financial Data database. The quarterly data analyzed are averages of end-month rates.

**Consumer price indices:** Monthly consumer price indices (CPI) are from Thomson Reuters Datastream and Global Financial Data. For Australia, producer price index is used.

**Real GDP:** Quarterly seasonally adjusted GDP data from Thomson Reuters Datastream, OECD, Eurostat, and the Federal Reserve Economic Data (FRED) database of the St. Louis Fed. Where necessary, nominal GDP data were deflated by the GDP deflator and non-seasonally adjusted data were adjusted. Seasonal adjustments were based on the X-12-ARIMA quarterly seasonal adjustment method from the U.S. Census Bureau. The following countries' GDP data were seasonally adjusted by this method: Armenia, Brazil, China, Croatia, Egypt, Hong Kong, Hungary, India, Indonesia, Jordan, Kazakhstan, Latvia, Nigeria, and Poland.

**Pegs/non-pegs:** The paper uses Klein and Shambaugh's (2013) annual de facto coding method to distinguish pegs from non-pegs, but I apply it at quarterly frequency and require that a peg lasts at least eight consecutive quarters. In the present paper, only the most restricted classification of pegs is used (that is, soft pegs, as defined by Klein and Shambaugh, are not considered to be pegs). Pegs are defined as restricted within a +/− 2% band relative to the base country currency. The Klein-Shambaugh soft pegs move within a +/− 5% band.

**Base countries:** From Klein and Shambaugh (2013). The only exceptions are Cyprus and Malta, assigned the base country of Germany rather than France. Taiwan, not included in the Klein-Shambaugh sample, has the U.S. as base country.

**CBOE S&P 500 Volatility Index (VIX):** Quarterly average of end-month data, from Global Financial Data.

Data coverage for the dynamic interest-rate equations is detailed by country in Tables 5 and 6. Coverage for the pooled/panel regressions (Tables 1–4) is as follows:

|    | Advanced | Base currency | LR pooled/panel | SR pooled/panel |
|----|----------|---------------|-----------------|-----------------|
| 1  | Australia | U.S. | Q3 1989–Q4 2013 | Q3 1989–Q4 2013 |
| 2  | Austria | Germany | Q3 1989–Q4 2013 | Q3 1989–Q4 1990 |
| 3  | Belgium | Germany | Q2 1995–Q4 2013 | Q2 1995–Q4 2013 |
| 4  | Canada | U.S. | Q3 1989–Q4 2013 | Q3 1989–Q4 2013 |
| 5  | Cyprus | Germany | Q1 1998–Q4 2013 | Q2 1995–Q1 2008 |
| 6  | Denmark | Germany | Q2 1991–Q4 2013 | Q2 1991–Q4 2013 |
| 7  | Finland | Germany | Q2 1990–Q4 2013 | Q2 2012–Q2 2013 |
| 8  | France | Germany | Q3 1989–Q4 2013 | Q3 1989–Q4 2013 |
| 9  | Germany | U.S. | Q2 1991–Q4 2013 | Q2 1991–Q4 2013 |
| 10 | Greece | Germany | Q2 2000–Q2 2008 | Q2 2000–Q2 2008 |
| 11 | Iceland | U.S./Germany | Q2 2004–Q4 2013 | Q2 1997–Q1 2013 |
| 12 | Ireland | Germany | Q2 1997–Q4 2013 | Q2 1997–Q4 2013 |
| 13 | Italy | Germany | Q2 1991–Q4 2013 | Q2 1991–Q4 2013 |
| 14 | Japan | U.S. | Q3 1989–Q4 2013 | Q3 1989–Q4 2013 |
| 15 | Malta | Germany | Q2 2000–Q4 2007 | Q2 2000–Q4 2007 |
| 16 | Netherlands | Germany | Q3 1989–Q4 2013 | Q3 1989–Q4 2013 |

| 17 | Norway | Germany | Q3 1989–Q4 2013 | Q3 1989–Q4 2013 |
| 18 | Portugal | Germany | Q2 1995–Q4 2013 | Q2 1995–Q4 2013 |
| 19 | Spain | Germany | Q2 1995–Q4 2013 | Q2 1995–Q4 2013 |
| 20 | Sweden | Germany | Q2 1993–Q4 2013 | Q2 1993–Q4 2013 |
| 21 | Switzerland | Germany | Q3 1989–Q4 2013 | Q3 1989–Q4 2013 |
| 22 | United Kingdom | Germany | Q3 1989–Q4 2013 | Q3 1989–Q4 2013 |

| | Non-Advanced | Base currency | LR pooled/panel | SR pooled/panel |
| --- | --- | --- | --- | --- |
| 1 | Albania | Germany | .. | Q2 2005–Q4 2013 |
| 2 | Argentina | U.S. | .. | Q4 2002–Q4 2013 |
| 3 | Armenia | U.S. | .. | Q2 1996–Q4 2013 |
| 4 | Brazil | U.S. | Q1 2000–Q4 2006 | Q2 1995–Q4 2012 |
| 5 | Bulgaria | Germany | Q3 1993–Q3 2009 | Q2 1997–Q1 2008 |
| 6 | Chile | U.S. | Q4 2004–Q4 2013 | Q2 2003–Q3 2012 |
| 7 | China | U.S. | Q1 2007–Q4 2013 | Q3 1997–Q4 2013 |
| 8 | Colombia | U.S. | Q4 2002–Q4 2013 | Q2 2000–Q3 2012 |
| 9 | Croatia | Germany | Q2 2012–Q3 2013 | Q2 2006–Q3 2013 |
| 10 | Czech Republic | Germany | Q3 2000–Q4 2013 | Q1 1996–Q4 2013 |
| 11 | Egypt | U.S. | .. | Q2 2007–Q4 2013 |
| 12 | Ghana | U.S. | .. | Q2 2006–Q2 2013 |
| 13 | Hong Kong | U.S. | Q1 1997–Q4 2013 | Q3 1991–Q4 2013 |
| 14 | Hungary | U.S./Germany | Q2 1999–Q4 2013 | Q2 1995–Q4 2013 |
| 15 | India | U.S. | Q3 2004–Q4 2013 | Q3 2004–Q4 2013 |
| 16 | Indonesia | U.S. | Q3 2009–Q4 2013 | Q2 2000–Q4 2003 |
| 17 | Israel | U.S. | Q2 2006–Q4 2013 | Q2 2006–Q4 2013 |
| 18 | Kazakhstan | U.S. | Q2 1998–Q4 2013 | Q3 1994–Q4 2013 |
| 19 | Kenya | U.S. | Q2 2011–Q3 2013 | Q2 2000–Q3 2013 |
| 20 | Latvia | U.S./Germany | Q1 1999–Q4 2013 | Q2 1995–Q4 2013 |
| 21 | Mexico | U.S. | Q1 2000–Q4 2013 | Q2 1993–Q4 2013 |
| 22 | Nigeria | U.S. | Q2 2009–Q3 2013 | Q3 1995–Q3 2013 |
| 23 | Philippines | U.S. | Q2 1999–Q3 2013 | Q2 1998–Q4 2013 |
| 24 | Poland | Germany | Q3 1999–Q4 2013 | Q2 1996–Q4 2013 |
| 25 | Romania | U.S./Germany | Q2 2012–Q4 2013 | Q2 2000–Q3 2005 |
| 26 | Russia | U.S. | Q2 2003–Q3 2013 | Q2 2003–Q3 2013 |
| 27 | Singapore | Malaysia | Q3 1998–Q4 2013 | Q3 1989–Q4 2013 |
| 28 | Slovakia | Germany | Q2 1997–Q4 2013 | Q2 1997–Q4 2007 |

| 29 | Slovenia | Germany | Q2 2002–Q4 2013 | Q3 2000–Q4 2013 |
|----|----------|---------|-----------------|-----------------|
| 30 | South Africa | U.S. | Q3 1989–Q4 2013 | Q3 1989–Q4 2013 |
| 31 | South Korea | U.S. | Q1 2001–Q4 2013 | Q4 2006–Q4 2013 |
| 32 | Taiwan | U.S. | Q2 1995–Q4 2013 | Q3 1989–Q4 2013 |
| 33 | Thailand | U.S. | Q2 1993–Q4 2013 | Q2 1997–Q4 2013 |
| 34 | Turkey | U.S. | Q2 2012–Q4 2013 | Q2 1998–Q4 2013 |

## References

Aizenman, J, Chinn, MD, and Ito, H (2010). The emerging global financial architecture: tracing and evaluating new patterns of the trilemma configuration. *Journal of International Money and Finance*, 29(June), 615–641.

Bacha, EL and Díaz Alejandro, CF (1982). *International Financial Intermediation: A Long and Tropical View*, Essays in International Finance 147. Princeton, NJ: International Finance Section, Department of Economics, Princeton University.

Basel Committee on Banking Supervision (2011). Basel III: A global framework for more resilient banks and banking systems. Bank for International Settlements, last revised June 2011.

Bernanke, BS (2013). Long-term interest rates. Speech delivered at the Federal Reserve Bank of San Francisco, 1 March. Available at: http://www.federalreserve.gov/newsevents/speech/bernanke20130301a.pdf

Blanchard, OJ and Galí, J (2007). Real wage rigidities and the new Keynesian model. *Journal of Money, Credit, and Banking*, 39(1), Supplement, 35–65.

Bluedorn, JC and Bowdler, C (2010). The empirics of international monetary transmission: identification and the impossible trinity. *Journal of Money, Credit, and Banking*, 42(June), 679–713.

Borio, C (2012). The financial cycle and macroeconomics: what have we learnt? BIS Working Papers No. 395, December.

Borio, C and Disyatat, P (2011). Global imbalances and the financial crisis: link or no link? BIS Working Papers No. 346, May.

Borio, C, McCauley, R, and McGuire, P (2011). Global credit and domestic credit booms. *BIS Quarterly Review*, (September), 43–57.

Broner, F, Didier, T, Erce, A, and Schmukler, SL (2013). Gross capital flows: dynamics and crises. *Journal of Monetary Economics*, 60, 113–133.

Bruno, V and Shin, HS (2013). Capital flows and the risk-taking channel of monetary policy. NBER Working Paper No. 18942, April.

Bussière, M, Cheng, G, Chinn, M, and Lisack, N (2014). For a few dollars more: reserves and growth in times of crises. NBER Working Paper No. 19791, January.

Calvo, GA, Leiderman, L, and Reinhart, CM (1993). Capital inflows and real exchange rate appreciation in Latin America: the role of external factors. *IMF Staff Papers*, 40(March), 108–151.

Calvo, GA, Leiderman, L, and Reinhart, CM (1996). Inflows of capital to developing countries in the 1990s. *Journal of Economic Perspectives*, 10(Spring), 123–139.

Calvo, GA and Mendoza, EG (2000). Rational contagion and the globalization of securities markets. *Journal of International Economics*, 51(1), 79–113.

Calvo, GA and Reinhart, CA (2002). Fear of floating. *Quarterly Journal of Economics*, 117(May), 379–408.

Caruana, J (2012). International monetary policy interactions: challenges and prospects. Speech delivered at the CEMLA-SEACEN Conference, Punta del Este, Uruguay, 16 November. Available at: http://www.bis.org/speeches/sp121116.pdf

Cetorelli, N and Goldberg, LS (2011). Global banks and international shock transmission: evidence from the crisis. *IMF Economic Review*, 59(1), 41–76.

Chinn, MD and Ito, H (2006). What matters for financial development? Capital controls, institutions, and interactions. *Journal of Development Economics*, 81(October), 163–192.

Chinn, MD and Quayyum, S (2012). Long horizon uncovered interest parity re-assessed. University of Wisconsin, October (mimeo).

Ciccarelli, M and Mojon, B (2010). Global inflation. *Review of Economics and Statistics*, 92(August), 524–535.

Committee on the Global Financial System (2011). Global liquidity — concept, measurement and policy implications. CGFS Papers No. 45, Bank for International Settlements, November.

Cowan, K, De Gregorio, J, Micco, A, and Neilson, C (2008). Financial diversification, sudden stops, and sudden starts. In K Cowan, S Edwards, and RO. Valdés (Eds.), *Current Account and External Financing*. Santiago, Chile: Central Bank of Chile.

Dahlquist, M and Hasseltoft, H (2012). International bond risk premia. Stockholm School of Economics and University of Zurich, August (mimeo).

Dell'Ariccia, G, Laeven, L, and Suarez, G (2013). Bank leverage and monetary policy's risk-taking channel: evidence from the United States. IMF Working Paper WP/13/143, June.

di Giovanni, J and Shambaugh, JC (2008). The impact of foreign interest rates on the economy: the role of the exchange rate regime. *Journal of International Economics*, 74, 341–361.

Dominguez, KME, Hashimoto, Y, and Ito, T (2012). International reserves and the global financial crisis. *Journal of International Economics*, 88(November), 388–406.

Eggertsson, GB and Krugman, P (2012). Debt, deleveraging, and the liquidity trap: a Fisher-Minsky-Koo approach. *Quarterly Journal of Economics*, 127(August), 1469–1513.

Eichengreen, B (1991). Trends and cycles in foreign lending. In H Siebert (Ed.), *Capital Flows in the World Economy: Symposium 1990*. Tübingen, Germany: J.C.B. Mohr.

Farhi, E and Werning, I (2013). A theory of macroprudential policies in the presence of nominal rigidities. NBER Working Paper No. 19313, August.

Filardo, A, Genberg, H, and Hofmann, B (2014). Monetary analysis and the global financial cycle: an Asian central bank perspective. BIS Working Papers No. 463.

Fischer, S (2010). Myths of monetary policy. *Israel Economic Review*, 8(2), 1–5.

Forbes, KJ and Warnock, FE (2012). Capital flow waves: surges, stops, flight, and retrenchment. *Journal of International Economics*, 88, 235–251.

Frankel, J, Schmukler, SL, and Servén, L (2004). Global transmission of interest rates: monetary independence and currency regime. *Journal of International Money and Finance*, 23, 701–733.

Gertler, M and Karadi, P (2011). A model of unconventional monetary policy. *Journal of Monetary Economics*, 58(January), 17–34.

Ghosh, AR, Ostry, JD, and Qureshi, MS (2014). Exchange rate management and crisis susceptibility: a reassessment. *IMF Economic Review*, 63(1), 238–276.

Goldberg, LS (2013). Banking globalization, transmission, and monetary policy autonomy. *Penning-och Valutapolitik*, (3), 161–193.

Gonzáles-Rozada, M and Levy Yeyati, E (2008). Global factors and emerging market spreads. *Economic Journal*, 118(November), 1917–1936.

Goodhart, C and Turner, P (2014). Pattern of policy tightening is different this time. *Financial Times*, 3 April 3, p. 20.

Gourinchas, P-O (2012). Global imbalances and global liquidity. In R Glick and MM Spiegel (Eds.), *Asia's Role in the Post-Crisis Global Economy*, 2011 Asia Economic Policy Conference. San Francisco: Federal Reserve Bank of San Francisco.

Gourinchas, P-O and Jeanne, O (2013). Capital flows to developing countries: the allocation puzzle. *Review of Economic Studies*, 80(October), 1484–1515.

Gourinchas, P-O and Obstfeld, M (2012). Stories of the twentieth century for the twenty-first. *American Economic Journal: Macroeconomics*, 4(January), 226–265.

Hausmann, R, Panizza, U, and Stein, E (2001). Why do countries float the way they float? *Journal of Development Economics*, 66, 387–414.

He, D and McCauley, RN (2013). Transmitting global liquidity to East Asia: policy rates, bond yields, currencies and dollar credit. BIS Working Papers No. 431, October.

Hellerstein, R (2011). Global bond risk premiums. Staff Report No. 499, Federal Reserve Bank of New York, June.

Ivashina, V, Scharfstein, DS, and Stein, JC (2012). Dollar funding and the lending behavior of global banks. Harvard University, October (mimeo).

Klein, MW and Shambaugh, JC (2013). Rounding the corners of the policy trilemma: sources of monetary policy autonomy. NBER Working Paper No. 19461, September.

Kolasa, M and Lombardo, G (2014). Financial frictions and optimal monetary policy in an open economy. *International Journal of Central Banking*, 10(March), 43–94.

Landau, J-P (2014). Global liquidity: public and private. In *Global Dimensions of Unconventional Monetary Policy*. Proceedings of 2013 Economic Policy Symposium at Jackson Hole, Federal Reserve Bank of Kansas City.

Lane, PR and McQuade, P (2014). Domestic credit growth and international capital flows. *Scandinavian Journal of Economics*, 116(January), 218–252.

Lane, PR and Milesi-Ferretti, GM (2007). The external wealth of nations, mark ii: revised and extended estimates of foreign assets and liabilities, 1970–2004. *Journal of International Economics*, 73(November), 223–250.

Lane, PR and Shambaugh, JC (2010). Financial exchange rates and international currency exposures. *American Economic Review*, 100(March), 518–540.

Magud, NE, Reinhart, CM, and Vesperoni, ER (2014). Capital inflows, exchange rate flexibility, and credit booms. *Review of Development Economics*, 18(3), 415–430.

McCauley, RN, McGuire, P, and Sushko, V (2015). Global dollar credit: links to U.S. monetary policy and leverage. *Economic Policy*, 30(82), 187–229.

McKinnon, RI (1982). Currency substitution and instability in the world dollar standard. *American Economic Review*, 72(June), 320–333.

Miniane, J and Rogers, JH (2007). Capital controls and the international transmission of U.S. monetary shocks. *Journal of Money, Credit, and Banking* 39(August), 1003–1035.

Miyajima, K, Mohanty, MS, and Chan, T (2012). Emerging market local currency bonds: diversification and stability. BIS Working Papers No. 391, November.

Munro, A and Wooldridge, P (2012). Motivations for swap-covered foreign currency borrowing. In *Currency Internationalisation: Lessons from the Global Financial Crisis and Prospects for the Future in Asia and the Pacific*. BIS Papers No. 61, January. Available at: http://www.bis.org/publ/bppdf/bispap61.htm

Neely, CJ (2013). Unconventional monetary policy had large international effects. Working Paper 2010-018E, Federal Reserve Bank of St. Louis, August.

Nurkse, R (1954). International investment to-day in the light of nineteenth-century experience. *Economic Journal*, 64(December), 744–758.

Obstfeld, M (2014). Never say never: commentary on a policymaker's reflections. *IMF Economic Review*, 62, 656–693.

Obstfeld, M, Shambaugh, JC, and Taylor, AM (2005). The trilemma in history: tradeoffs among exchange rates, monetary policies, and capital mobility. *Review of Economics and Statistics*, 87(August), 423–438.

Obstfeld, M and Taylor, AM (2004). *Global Capital Markets: Integration, Crisis, and Growth*. Cambridge, UK: Cambridge University Press.

Ostry, JD, Ghosh, AR, Chamon, M, and Qureshi, MS (2012). Tools for managing financial-stability risks from capital flows. *Journal of International Economics*, 88, 407–421.

Pesaran, MH, Shin, YC, and Smith, RJ (2001). Bounds testing approaches to the analysis of levels relationships. *Journal of Applied Econometrics*, 16(May/June), 289–326.

Prasad, ES (2012). Role reversal in global finance. In *Achieving Maximum Long-Run Growth*. Proceedings of 2011 Economic Policy Symposium at Jackson Hole, Federal Reserve Bank of Kansas City.

Prasad, E, Rajan, R, and Subramanian, A (2007). The paradox of capital. *Finance & Development*, 44(1).

Rey, H (2014). Dilemma not trilemma: the global financial cycle and monetary policy independence. In *Global Dimensions of Unconventional Monetary Policy*. Proceedings of the 2013 Economic Policy Symposium at Jackson Hole, Federal Reserve Bank of Kansas City.

Rose, AK (2014). Surprising similarities: recent monetary regimes of small economies. University of California, Berkeley, February (mimeo).

Schoenmaker, D (2013). *Governance of International Banking: The Financial Trilemma.* Oxford, UK: Oxford University Press.

Shambaugh, JC (2004). The effect of fixed exchange rates on monetary policy. *Quarterly Journal of Economics*, 119(February), 300–351.

Sheets, N and Sockin, RA (2013). Why are long-term rates so correlated across countries? The role of U.S. monetary policy. *Perspectives*, Citi Research, 5 September.

Shin, HS (2013). The second phase of global liquidity and its impact on emerging economies. Speech delivered at the 2013 Asia Economic Policy Conference, Federal Reserve Bank of San Francisco, 7 November. Available at: http://www.princeton.edu/~hsshin/www/FRBSF_2013.pdf

Turner, P (2012). Weathering financial crisis: domestic bond markets in EMEs. In *Weathering Financial Crises: Bond Markets in Asia and the Pacific.* BIS Papers No. 63, January. Available at: http://www.bis.org/publ/bppdf/bispap63.htm

Turner, P (2014). The global long term interest rate, financial risks and policy choices in EMEs. BIS Working Papers No. 441, February.

Wallace, MS (1984). World money or domestic money: which predicts U.S. inflation best? *Journal of International Money and Finance*, 3(August), 241–244.

Woodford, M (2010). Globalization and monetary control. In J Galí and M Gertler (Eds.), *International Dimensions of Monetary Policy.* Chicago: University of Chicago Press.

# CHAPTER 3

# Chapter 3

# Financial Development in Asia: The Role of Policy and Institutions, with Special Reference to China*

Barry Eichengreen[1]

## Introduction

Approximately a decade and a half ago I wrote a series of papers on financial development and integration in Asia focusing on the role of openness in fostering financial deepening and economic growth.[2] In subsequent years there has been much water under the bridge, not just additional years of financial experience but also a global financial crisis. This commission from the Asian Monetary Policy Forum thus offers a welcome opportunity to revisit these issues.

The questions then were framed by the Asian financial crisis. The problem as seen through that lens was that Asia had relatively underdeveloped securities markets, rendering it dependent on bank finance and offshore funding. Banks, the Asian crisis had shown, can become a problem when they grow so large that they are too big to save and too big to fail. They can be a hotbed of insider dealing or, in popular parlance of that time, "crony capitalism." They can be unstable when they rely excessively on the interbank market for short-term, offshore, foreign-currency-denominated borrowing. Asian countries would be

---

* Prepared for the second annual Asian Monetary Policy Forum. Some of the analysis below draws on ongoing work with Pipat Luengnaruemitchai, whose collaboration is acknowledged with thanks. I am also grateful for help from Coby Hu and Joseph Root.
[1] Barry Eichengreen is the George C. Pardee and Helen N. Pardee Professor of Economics and Political Science, University of California, Berkeley.
[2] See Eichengreen (2006) and Eichengreen and Luengnaruemitchai (2006; 2008).

better off, according to the then conventional wisdom, if they developed better-diversified financial systems, reducing their dependence on bank intermediation and offshore funding. Deep and liquid securities markets that supplemented these traditional sources of finance could serve as a valuable "spare tire," in the much-cited words of Alan Greenspan.[3]

Time has been kinder to some elements of this conventional wisdom than others. Certainly, subsequent experience has underscored the problems of moral hazard and opportunism that arise in connection with the operation of large, complex financial institutions. It has provided more evidence of the prevalence of "crony capitalism" while highlighting that such problems are by no means peculiar to emerging markets or Asia. It has pointed up the dangers of being too big to fail. We have Iceland and others as reminders of the risks of allowing banks to utilize excessively short-term, offshore, foreign-currency funding. And we have the 2008–2009 crisis and subsequent contrasts in the development of the U.S. and European economies as object lessons in the advantages of well-diversified financial systems.[4]

The global credit crisis is also a reminder that agency problems exist not just in banks but also in securities markets. Adverse selection and moral hazard was rife in derivatives markets prior to 2009.[5] When problems then arose, they threatened to take down banks with positions in dubious securities. And when the banks developed problems, they further diminished the attractions of debt securities issued by both the banks themselves and their guarantors.[6] These dynamics are a reminder that securities markets are no panacea. They may not even be a functional spare tire.

Moreover, the crisis challenged the presumption that deeper, more sophisticated financial markets are better. It caused observers to ask

---

[3] The reference is to Greenspan (1999).

[4] This is not to argue that the more heavily bank-based nature of Europe's financial system is the entire explanation for its more intractable crisis and recession, but it is certainly part of the story (see Eichengreen 2015).

[5] For examples of the now large literature developing this point see Gorton (2009), Brunnermeier (2009), Beltran and Thomas (2010) and Kau, Keenan, Lyubomov, and Slawson (2012).

[6] These relationships even acquired their own name: the diabolic loop (Lane 2012).

whether there was such a thing as excessive financialization — whether too much finance might be bad for growth.[7] It pointed up the question of what kind of financial system is best for advancing not just growth but also other social goals.

Another thing that visibly changed in the intervening ten years is the greater prominence of China in any discussion of Asian and global financial markets. China figures prominently by virtue of its size and the fact that its economy grew at high single-digit rates for the better part of the last decade. Developments and policy challenges in China necessarily command more attention, since what happens in China doesn't stay in China, financially or otherwise.

These are the issues addressed in this chapter. I start in Section 2 ("Definitions and Data") by describing the data used to measure the depth of domestic financial markets. In Section 3 ("Where Asia Stands") I revisit the analysis in Eichengreen and Luengnaruemitchai (2006), again asking how Asia compares with other regions and how much progress was been made in the course of the subsequent decade. Section 4 ("Opening and Institutions as a Critical Nexus") then focuses on the critical nexus, namely that between financial opening, economic and social institutions, and financial development.

Dealing with that nexus is a particular challenge for China, the country that holds the key to Asia's financial future. China's prospects are therefore the focus of Section 5 ("China's Challenge"). Section 6 ("Exzcessive Financialization?") asks whether there is such a thing as excessive financialization and whether Asian countries are at risk of succumbing to it. Section 7 ("Conclusion"), in concluding, draws these diverse strands together.

## Definitions and Data

Eichengreen and Luengnaruemitchai (2006) used Bank for International Settlements (BIS) data on debt securities outstanding to compare the

---

[7] See Cecchetti and Kharroubi (2012), Arcand, Berkes, and Panizza (2012) and Sahay *et al.* (2015); I return to these studies below.

depth and development of bond markets in Asia with other regions. We found that Asian countries had smaller bond markets than countries with a comparable per capita GDP in other parts of the world. That difference was attributable in part to the existence in these countries of large, relatively concentrated banking systems, which worked to slow the development of alternative sources of debt finance; to failure to adhere to internationally recognized accounting standards; to levels of transparency and bureaucratic quality that compared unfavorably with those in advanced countries; and to restrictions on capital-account transactions.

In the subsequent decade, the Asian Bond Market Initiative (ABMI) has encouraged information sharing and applied peer pressure to adopt international accounting standards, strengthen contract enforcement, and upgrade supervision and regulation. The Asian Bond Market Forum (ABMF) was created to foster harmonization and standardization of market practices and regulations. Together with relaxation of restrictions on capital account transactions, this has encouraged financial integration and increased the diversity of the investor base.[8] The question is how much difference these policy efforts have made.

A complication in comparing our earlier results with those for the more recent period is that the BIS changed its definitions and procedures for calculating private and international debt securities outstanding by country. As described by Gruic and Wooldridge (2012), prior to mid-2012 the BIS built up estimates of total and international debt securities outstanding — and by implication the difference, namely domestic debt securities outstanding — using issue-level data. It defined an international (for our purpose, foreign) issue as a security placed with international (for our purposes, foreign) investors. The currency of denomination of the issue, the governing law to which it was subject, and the location of primary and secondary markets (active trading) in the securities in question were used to determine the investors, domestic or international, at which an issue was targeted. By and large, the three criteria were

---

[8] On the ABMI and ABMF see Kawashima (2013).

consistent with one another: domestic debt securities were denominated in the local currency, subject to local governing law, and registered and traded at home. In practice they were held primarily by domestic residents.

Subsequently the three criteria began to diverge.[9] In late 2012 the BIS therefore changed its procedures to reflect this fact and the availability of data gathered by national agencies on non-resident holdings of debt securities issued by residents, whether registered domestically or abroad. Now the BIS distinguishes domestic from international debt securities simply according to where they are issued (according to the location of the primary market).[10] The new procedure was used to construct revised series, where possible, back to the early 1990s, and the BIS stopped publishing and supporting the old series.

The change in procedures makes little difference for estimates of market size prior to the turn of the century.[11] More recently, however, the new and old series diverge. Specifically, the new series shows signs of exceeding the old series by growing absolute and relative amounts.[12]

Thus, comparing our earlier statistical results through 2002, based on the old BIS series, to a new set of results through 2013, based on the new BIS series (only the new BIS series being available for 2013), would be comparing apples with oranges. We therefore compare our earlier results through 2002 with an updated set of results through mid-2012 using the old BIS series, which is no longer supported or published by the institution

---

[9] While bonds issued abroad were generally subject to foreign governing law (Greek government bonds issued in London were subject to English law), there were exceptions. Similarly, in a minority of cases, bonds registered and issued on foreign markets could be denominated in the local currency.

[10] The vast majority of these securities issued in the local market are denominated in the local currency, although as Gruic and Wooldridge (2012) note there are also instances where issues placed on the domestic market were denominated in foreign currency (they point to the example of euro-denominated bonds issued in Croatia by that country's government).

[11] See Graph 3 in Gruic and Woodridge (2012).

[12] Much of the difference reflects debt securities issued on the local market but subject to foreign governing law.

but can still be recovered from its website. This is appropriate when we seek to ask whether our earlier findings on the determinants of domestic market development have changed.

In addition, we can compare new results through 2002 (or for that matter, any earlier year) with results for the recent period, extending through 2013, using the new BIS series. With this second approach we are unable to replicate our earlier results, since methods and procedures used to construct the dependent variable, retrospectively as well as currently, are different. But using the new series enables us to extend the analysis through 2013. And the new series is arguably more appropriate for analyzing the determinants of local market development in recent years insofar as it paints a more accurate picture of the recent period.

It is important to be clear on what questions these data on domestic debt securities, new and old, can and cannot address. They can help us understand how Asia compares with other regions in terms of the depth of local markets. Other sources can then be used to shed light on additional aspects of local market development such as big-ask spreads and turnover. BIS statistics on domestic debt securities, and specifically the new series, do not tell us who is holding those securities. They do not speak to the question of whether emerging markets, and Asian countries specifically, are at risk as a result of having sold a significant fraction of domestic debt to footloose foreign investors. Other sources of evidence on this question are mixed, though the idea that foreign investors are especially prone to flee when there is an increase in volatility affecting emerging markets has gained currency, as it were, as a result of the decline in inflows into dedicated emerging market mutual funds at the time of the "taper tantrum" in 2013 and again when expectations developed that the U.S. Federal Reserve was poised to raise interest rates.[13] The point here is that the data analyzed in this paper are not suitable for addressing this question.

---

[13] An early influential paper by Frankel and Schmukler (1997), using data for Mexico, tends to discount the hypothesis. An analysis more supportive of the idea that nonresident investors are "prone to run" is Kim and Wei (1999).

Similarly, our analysis of the development of domestic debt markets in Asia (and generally) does not speak to the currency-mismatch problem. An earlier literature addresses this.[14] A number of commentators have recently pointed to the dollar-denominated debts of corporations, including the foreign subsidiaries of Asian corporations, as posing special risks to stability in an environment where the dollar exchange rate strengthens and U.S. policy rates are poised to rise.[15] But the point is that, in a world where Asian corporates issue foreign-currency-denominated securities abroad (and borrow from international banks) and where foreigners hold claims in the local markets of emerging economies (denominated in those local currencies), BIS data on domestic debt securities will not shed light on the extent of (gross) currency exposures and (net) currency mismatches. The risks associated with such exposures are an important issue that warrants attention from both regulators and market participants, but — to repeat — they are not the topic of this paper.

## Where Asia Stands

The stock of outstanding domestic debt securities issued in East Asian countries excluding Japan has expanded enormously since the turn of the century. Where the value outstanding was just US$1.2 trillion in 2002, it rose to more than $3.6 trillion in 2008, $5.2 trillion in 2010, $6.8 trillion in 2012 and 8.2 trillion in 2014 (Figure 1).

A trio of observations suggest themselves before declaring this growth to be a success. First, this expansion is less impressive when measured against the GDP of the countries in question.[16] Second, this period (and its

---

[14] The reference is to Eichengreen and Hausmann (1999) and Eichegreen, Hausmann, and Panizza (2008).

[15] See for example Nordvig (2014). There is also the issue that the conventional statistics may capture these obligations inadequately, as Nordvig emphasizes; see also Avdjiev, Chui and Shin (2014). In addition, there are the foreign-currency-denominated obligations incurred by agents other than the corporate sector, Eastern European households' borrowing in U.S. dollars and Swiss francs, for example. These obligations to banks will in any case not be captured by data on debt securities. Again, they are not the topic of this paper.

[16] Between 2000 and 2014, the aggregate bond market increased by 9.8 times while the aggregate GDP increased by 5.7 times.

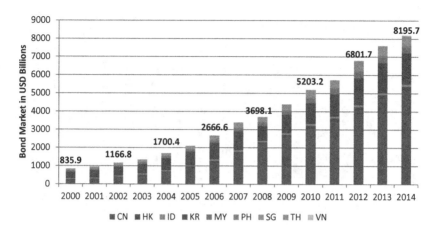

**Figure 1.** Local bond market in Asia (ex. Japan)

*Note:* Calculated using data for December of each year.

*Source:* Asian Development Bank.

first part in particular) was one of enormous increase in reliance on debt securities not just in Asia but in countries around the world. Real interest rates that were low by historical standards encouraged issuance, while the growth of a class of dedicated institutional investors, both domestic and international, fostered take-up.[17] Third, the majority of the increase in the issuance of debt securities in East Asia ex Japan, and by implication the majority of the outstanding stock at the end of the period, was accounted for by additional issuance by just one country, China.

The resulting impact is uneven for Asia as a whole. Figure 2 shows domestic securities outstanding as a percent of the aggregate GDP for the principle East Asian countries without Japan. Figure 3 shows domestic debt securities outstanding as a share of own country GDP for the principal East Asian countries. Bonds issued by financial institutions, as well as by nonfinancial corporations and governments, are included. Leaving aside Japan, whose economic and financial history is different and whose public-debt situation is unique, it shows that Korea and Malaysia have the deepest bond markets, so measured, with ratios of debt securities to GDP on the order of 100%. China's ratio, at roughly half this amount,

---

[17] In addition, the inability or unwillingness of international banks to lend to Asian corporates during the global crisis may have boosted corporate issuance in the region unsustainably.

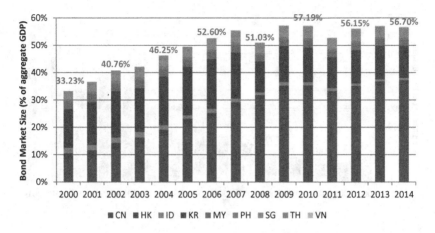

**Figure 2.** Local bond markets in Asia (%GDP, aggregate)

*Note:* GDP as estimated by the IMF. Figures exclude Japan.

*Source:* Asian Development Bank and IMF.

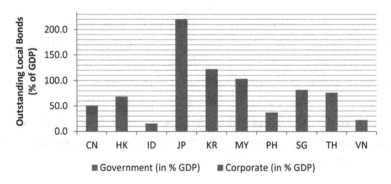

**Figure 3.** Size of local bond market as % of GDP, end 2014

*Source:* Asian Development Bank and IMF.

is notably lower. To put these figures in perspective, note that the ratio for East Asia ex Japan is slightly below that for Latin America but slightly above that for the countries of Central and Eastern Europe — see Table 1.

To be sure, not everything else is equal across these countries. Notably, levels of economic development, as captured by the level of GDP per capita, vary widely with obvious implications for bond market development. In terms of the average relationship between per capita GDP and bond market capitalization, shown in Figure 4, Indonesia and Vietnam underperform, while Malaysia and Korea overperform.

**Table 1.** Total outstanding external finance (in percentages of GDP)

| | Domestic credit to private sector by banks | Market capitalization | Outstanding Domestic Debt Securities | | |
| | | | Issued by corporate issuers | Issued by public sector | Issued by financial institutions |
| --- | --- | --- | --- | --- | --- |
| **East Asia ex Japan** | | | | | |
| China | 133.66 | 44.93 | 8.09 | 18.05 | 15.26 |
| Hong Kong | 198.53 | 421.93 | 5.04 | 34.15 | 10.91 |
| Malaysia | 117.60 | 156.04 | 36.93 | 53.92 | 24.99 |
| Singapore | 116.20 | 144.34 | 0.57 | 39.87 | 7.00 |
| South Korea | 136.69 | 96.54 | 33.91 | 41.44 | 20.18 |
| Thailand | 115.56 | 104.65 | 12.02 | 50.28 | 0.88 |
| Average of above | **134.05** | **68.02** | **11.73** | **23.84** | **15.28** |
| **Latin America** | | | | | |
| Argentina | 14.12 | 5.68 | 0.99 | 7.91 | 0.42 |
| Brazil | 68.54 | 54.69 | 0.46 | 69.74 | 23.31 |
| Chile | 73.19 | 117.68 | 10.67 | 33.89 | 2.80 |
| Mexico | 20.22 | 44.25 | 3.37 | 26.24 | 13.07 |
| Average of above | **47.88** | **48.84** | **1.97** | **46.87** | **16.01** |
| **Central Europe** | | | | | |
| Czech Republic | 53.77 | 17.97 | 5.72 | 27.69 | 8.55 |
| Hungary | 55.72 | 16.62 | 0.40 | 49.84 | 5.72 |
| Poland | 53.09 | 35.82 | 0 | 40.95 | 2.89 |

*(Continued)*

**Table 1.** (*Continued*)

|  | Domestic credit to private sector by banks | Market capitalization | Issued by corporate issuers | Issued by public sector | Issued by financial institutions |
|---|---|---|---|---|---|
| **Average of above** | **53.66** | **28.44** | **1.49** | **39.00** | **4.73** |
| Developed Countries |  |  |  |  |  |
| Australia | 122.24 | 83.84 | 3.10 | 29.99 | 40.88 |
| Canada | 170.01 | 110.69 | 9.94 | 62.23 | 16.86 |
| Japan | 106.92 | 61.82 | 14.45 | 203.93 | 17.58 |
| New Zealand | 158.65 | 46.54 | 0 | 31.07 | 0 |
| United States | 49.49 | 115.50 | 21.22 | 82.02 | 60.04 |
| Euro Area* | 124.21 | 50.18 | 7.73 | 60.89 | 38.45 |
| **Average of above** | **91.94**[18] | **83.84** | **14.37** | **90.81** | **43.23** |
| Other |  |  |  |  |  |
| Anglo-Saxon Nations[19] | 78.85 | 112.42 | 16.50 | 73.66 | 48.95 |
| Asia, including Japan | 124.34 | 65.80 | 12.71 | 88.33 | 16.10 |

*Note:* Data from 2012 and 2013. Author's calculations. Data from Bank for International Settlements, World Bank and Reuters Datastream.

*Euro Area includes Austria, Belgium, Cyprus, Finland, France, Germany, Greece, Ireland, Italy, Luxembourg, Malta, Netherlands, Portugal, Slovakia, Slovenia, Spain. Outstanding domestic debt is calculated as an aggregate, dividing the debt securities in the entire Euro area by the aggregate GDP of the Euro area.

[18] Average excluding Slovakia due to missing data. In addition, calculated using total private credit for Canada and New Zealand.

[19] Anglo-Saxon Nations include Australia, Canada, New Zealand, the United Kingdom, and the United States.

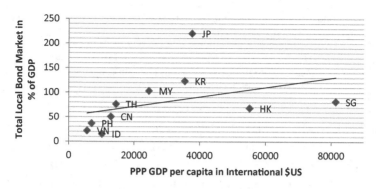

**Figure 4.** Bond markets and PPP GDP per capita, end 2014
*Source:* Asian Development Bank and IMF.

These small-sample comparisons are sensitive to outliers.[20] One way of dealing with this is by expanding the sample so as to reduce the weight on extreme observations. This is done in Table 2, which uses the new BIS series and the largest sample of countries for which the institution provides estimates of total debt market capitalization, international debt securities outstanding, and by implication, domestic bond market capitalization. The latter, scaled by GDP, is regressed on per capita GDP and a dummy variable for Asian countries. From the point of view of this broad international comparison, Asian countries had smaller bond markets than predicted in 1996 but larger bond markets than predicted in 2012, providing some support for the fruitfulness of efforts to development of domestic markets in debt securities in the interim.

Given the caveats the BIS provides on the comparability of its data on total debt issuance and on international debt securities, which are built up from different sources, it may be safer to limit the analysis to countries for which the institution directly estimates domestic debt market capitalization. When this is done in Table 3, the previous picture is preserved. Once upon a time (circa 1996), debt securities outstanding as a share of GDP were significantly lower than in other regions even

---

[20] However, which countries to classify as outliers is less clear. Leaving out Japan would flatten the regression line, while leaving out Hong Kong and Singapore would steepen it. Leaving out all three would limit deviations of the position of the remaining countries, including those cited at the end of the last paragraph, from the resulting regression line.

**Table 2.** Bond market capitalization as a share of GDP by per capita income and region, 1996–2011, new BIS series, full sample

| Sample | (1) 1996 | (2) 2012 | (3) 1996 | (4) 2012 | (5) Full sample | (6) <2002 | (7) >=2002 |
|---|---|---|---|---|---|---|---|
| Ln GDP per capita | | | 0.119 | 0.315 | 0.056 | 0.077 | 0.065 |
| | | | (3.04)** | (3.69)** | (5.78)** | (9.68)** | (6.43)** |
| Asian country | −0.356 | 0.145 | −0.291 | 0.306 | −0.090 | −0.143 | 0.348 |
| | (2.51)* | (0.56) | (2.18)* | (1.29) | (2.86)** | (2.57)* | (8.22)** |
| Constant | 0.362 | 0.748 | −0.739 | −2.410 | −0.166 | −0.387 | −0.165 |
| | (6.58)** | (7.36)** | (2.02)* | (2.80)** | (1.73) | (5.39)** | (1.79) |
| Observations | 53 | 53 | 53 | 53 | 1302 | 772 | 530 |
| R-squared | 0.11 | 0.01 | 0.25 | 0.22 | | | |
| Number of groups | | | | | 53 | 53 | 53 |

*Notes*: Absolute value of t statistics in parentheses; *significant at 5%; **significant at 1%. All regressions are estimated using panel Generalized Least Squares, allowing for autocorrelation within the panel and cross-sectional correlation.
*Source*: See text.

**Table 3.** Bond market capitalization as a share of GDP by per capita income and region, 1996–2011, new BIS series, limited sample

| Sample | (1) 1996 | (2) 2012 | (3) 1996 | (4) 2012 | (5) Full sample | (6) <2002 | (7) >=2002 |
|---|---|---|---|---|---|---|---|
| Ln GDP per capita | | | 0.051 | 0.212 | 0.053 | 0.049 | 0.155 |
| | | | (1.51) | (2.77)** | (4.44)** | (7.44)** | (11.58)** |
| Asian country | −0.243 | 0.335 | −0.225 | 0.429 | 0.050 | −0.126 | 0.270 |
| | (2.20)* | (1.54) | (2.07)* | (2.04)* | (0.91) | (3.20)** | (6.44)** |
| Constant | 0.267 | 0.589 | −0.186 | −1.473 | −0.161 | −0.164 | −0.908 |
| | (5.09)** | (5.36)** | (0.61) | (1.96) | (1.47) | (2.70)** | (7.07)** |
| Observations | 31 | 31 | 31 | 31 | 767 | 467 | 310 |
| R-squared | 0.14 | 0.08 | 0.21 | 0.27 | | | |
| Number of groups | | | | | 31 | 31 | 31 |

*Notes*: Absolute value of t statistics in parentheses; *significant at 5%; **significant at 1%. All regressions are estimated using panel Generalized Least Squares, allowing for autocorrelation within the panel and cross-sectional correlation.
*Source*: See text.

after controlling for per capital GDP. Now, however, they are significantly higher. Significance levels are more erratic when we use the old BIS series (Table 4), but the overall picture is preserved. As Levinger and Li (2014, p. 3) put it, Asia's bond markets have moved from being the region's financial weak link to becoming "a role model for other emerging market countries trying to build resilience...."

Tables 5 and 6 follow Eichengreen and Leungnarimitchai in controlling for additional determinants of bond market capitalization and distinguishing public- and private-sector bonds. Table 6 in addition distinguishes the period through 2002, as analyzed in that earlier paper, from subsequent years. In Table 5 many of the earlier patterns continue to carry over, such as the association of certain institutional variables (stronger accounting standards, better control of corruption as indicated by higher values of the measure used in the table) with bond market capitalization, and the positive association with capital account openness. Table 6 shows that the spotty significance of this last variable reflects the combination of a significant effect prior to 2002 with an insignificant

**Table 4.** Bond market capitalization as a share of GDP by per capita income and region, 1996–2011, old BIS series

| Sample | (1) 1996 | (2) 2011 | (3) 1996 | (4) 2011 | (5) Full sample | (6) <2002 | (7) >=2002 |
|---|---|---|---|---|---|---|---|
| Ln GDP per capita | | | 0.169 | 0.213 | 0.044 | 0.052 | 0.138 |
| | | | (4.56)** | (3.42)** | (4.17)** | (3.88)** | (16.92)** |
| Asian country | −0.157 | 0.234 | −0.063 | 0.315 | 0.096 | −0.047 | 0.219 |
| | (1.05) | (1.21) | (0.50) | (1.99) | (1.69) | (0.96) | (8.18)** |
| Constant | 0.527 | 0.630 | −1.035 | −1.512 | 0.189 | 0.001 | −0.693 |
| | (8.57)** | (8.14)** | (2.99)** | (2.40)* | (1.81) | (0.01) | (8.34)** |
| Observations | 47 | 50 | 47 | 50 | 1082 | 587 | 495 |
| R-squared | 0.02 | 0.03 | 0.34 | 0.22 | | | |
| Number of groups | | | | | 50 | 48 | 50 |

*Notes*: Absolute value of t statistics in parentheses; *significant at 5%; **significant at 1%. All regressions are estimated using panel Generalized Least Squares, allowing for autocorrelation within the panel and cross-sectional correlation.

*Source*: See text.

Table 5. Determinants of issuance of domestic debt securities, by sector of issuer, % of GDP 1996–2013 extended sample, new BIS data

| | (1) Total Debt | (2) Total Debt | (3) Total Debt | (4) Private Debt | (5) Private Debt | (6) Private Debt | (7) Public Debt | (8) Public Debt |
|---|---|---|---|---|---|---|---|---|
| GDP, PPP (constant 2011 international billion $) | 0.001 (9.94)*** | 0.001 (8.40)*** | -0.001 (2.05)** | 0.001 (6.65)*** | 0.001 (7.59)*** | -0.001 (2.05)** | 0.001 (3.95)*** | 0.001 (3.72)*** |
| Exports of goods and services (% of GDP) | -0.002 (2.67)*** | -0.002 (3.17)*** | -0.001 (0.14) | -0.001 (2.75)*** | -0.001 (1.27) | -0.001 (0.14) | -0.001 (1.47) | -0.001 (2.81)*** |
| Asian Country | -0.253 (2.02)** | -0.217 (1.75)* | 0.015 (0.31) | 0.102 (3.02)*** | 0.117 (3.63)*** | 0.015 (0.31) | 0.015 (0.30) | -0.007 (0.15) |
| Dummy for English Legal Origin | -0.210 (2.37)** | -0.228 (2.45)** | -0.046 (0.95) | -0.038 (1.40) | -0.015 (0.56) | -0.046 (0.95) | -0.062 (2.56)** | -0.039 (1.54) |
| Distance from Equator | -0.760 (2.17)** | -0.771 (2.11)** | 0.145 (0.96) | 0.270 (2.93)*** | 0.217 (2.36)** | 0.145 (0.96) | -0.182 (1.65)* | -0.223 (2.16)** |
| Investment Profile | -0.008 (1.87)* | -0.007 (1.84)* | 0.004 (2.23)** | 0.000 (0.19) | 0.000 (0.15) | 0.004 (2.23)** | -0.008 (2.89)*** | -0.009 (3.45)*** |
| Law and Order | 0.008 (0.64) | 0.004 (0.31) | -0.003 (0.52) | 0.001 (0.33) | 0.003 (0.84) | -0.003 (0.52) | -0.002 (0.20) | -0.004 (0.62) |
| GDP per capita, PPP (constant international thousand $) | 0.000 (2.57)** | 0.000 (4.68)*** | 0.000 (2.37)** | 0.000 (5.10)*** | 0.000 (6.66)*** | 0.000 (2.37)** | 0.000 (4.14)*** | 0.000 (6.56)*** |
| Control of Corruption | -0.014 (1.48) | -0.020 (2.08)** | -0.007 (1.30) | 0.002 (0.44) | 0.002 (0.56) | -0.007 (1.30) | -0.012 (1.97)** | -0.013 (2.29)** |
| Accounting Standards | 0.006 (1.71)* | 0.005 (1.38) | -0.007 (2.87)*** | -0.004 (3.12)*** | -0.003 (2.77)*** | -0.007 (2.87)*** | 0.004 (2.52)** | 0.003 (2.05)** |

| | (1) | (2) | (3) | (4) | (5) | (6) | (7) | (8) |
|---|---|---|---|---|---|---|---|---|
| Domestic Credit to Private Sector by Banks (% of GDP) | 0.001 (2.94)*** | 0.001 (1.31) | 0.001 (3.72)*** | 0.001 (4.29)*** | 0.001 (4.58)*** | 0.001 (3.72)*** | 0.001 (3.14)*** | 0.001 (1.19) |
| Bureaucratic Quality | -0.006 (0.40) | -0.012 (0.71) | -0.004 (0.37) | -0.001 (0.19) | -0.008 (1.23) | -0.004 (0.37) | -0.002 (0.19) | 0.001 (0.05) |
| SD log Interest Rate | -0.022 (0.82) | -0.015 (0.55) | -0.046 (3.19)*** | 0.005 (0.49) | -0.000 (0.04) | -0.046 (3.19)*** | 0.054 (5.22)*** | 0.047 (4.47)*** |
| SD_change log Xrate | -0.376 (2.87)*** | -0.363 (2.84)*** | 0.057 (0.88) | 0.022 (0.37) | 0.050 (0.80) | 0.057 (0.88) | 0.057 (1.89)* | -0.232 (3.26)*** |
| Budget Balance (% of GDP) | -0.011 (4.51)*** | | | -0.000 (0.52) | | | -0.012 (8.00)*** | |
| Chinn Ito Capital Controls Measure | 0.015 (1.41) | 0.015 (1.42) | -0.001 (0.17) | 0.004 (0.71) | 0.002 (0.45) | -0.001 (0.17) | 0.015 (2.43)** | 0.006 (1.12) |
| Cash surplus/deficit (% of GDP) | | -0.013 (7.97)*** | | | -0.003 (4.55)*** | | | -0.010 (9.77)*** |
| Outstanding Domestic Debt Securities Issued by Private Sector (% of GDP) | | | 1.448 (45.45)*** | | | 0.448 (14.06)*** | | |
| Constant | 0.491 (1.90)* | 0.477 (1.83)* | 0.461 (3.58)*** | 0.030 (0.40) | -0.026 (0.36) | 0.461 (3.58)*** | -0.152 (1.25) | -0.019 (0.16) |
| Observations | 458 | 493 | 441 | 458 | 493 | 441 | 458 | 493 |
| Number of groups (countries) | 32 | 32 | 20 | 32 | 32 | 20 | 32 | 32 |

Absolute value of z statistics in parentheses

*Significant at 10%; **Significant at 5%; ***Significant at 1%.

**Table 6.** Determinants of issuance of domestic debt securities, total debt, % of GDP, 1996–2013 and subperiods, extended sample, new BIS data

| | (1)<br>Total Debt (Pre 2002) | (2)<br>Total Debt (Post 2002) |
|---|---|---|
| GDP, PPP (constant 2011 international billion $) | 0.001<br>(8.78)*** | 0.001<br>(6.08)*** |
| Exports of goods and services (% of GDP) | 0.000<br>(0.37) | −0.004<br>(5.48)*** |
| Asian Country | −0.388<br>(8.81)*** | 0.239<br>(2.12)** |
| Dummy for English Legal Origin | 0.118<br>(2.09)** | 0.033<br>(0.37) |
| Distance from Equator | 0.065<br>(0.39) | 0.246<br>(0.77) |
| Domestic Credit to Private Sector by Banks (% of GDP) | 0.001<br>(2.34)** | 0.002<br>(3.85)*** |
| Bureaucratic Quality | 0.011<br>(1.01) | −0.029<br>(0.64) |
| Control of Corruption | −0.011<br>(1.59) | 0.011<br>(0.62) |
| Accounting Standards | −0.008<br>(4.81)*** | −0.004<br>(1.35) |
| Investment Profile | −0.001<br>(0.02) | −0.041<br>(4.50)*** |
| Law and Order | 0.002<br>(0.40) | −0.040<br>(2.03)** |
| GDP per capita, PPP (constant international thousand $) | 0.001<br>(4.04)*** | 0.001<br>(4.38)*** |
| GDP, PPP (constant 2011 international $) | 0.001<br>(3.54)*** | 0.001<br>(2.74)*** |
| SD_change in log Xrate | −0.400<br>(6.39)*** | 0.113<br>(1.24) |
| Chinn Ito Capital Controls Measure | 0.031<br>(5.97)*** | −0.006<br>(0.29) |
| Constant | 0.744<br>(5.96)*** | 0.768<br>(3.92)*** |
| Observations | 373 | 340 |
| Number of groups (countries) | 32 | 32 |

Absolute value of z statistics in parentheses
*Significant at 10%; **Significant at 5%; ***Significant at 1%.

effect thereafter, perhaps because capital accounts were more widely open, leaving less variation in the variable, in the second subperiod. The key point, though, is that what was a negative coefficient on the dummy variable for Asian countries turns positive in the second subperiod, as if a set of regional economies with relatively underdeveloped bond markets, so measured, have more than corrected the problem.

An obvious concern is that these results are being driven by Japan, which is a more advanced economy, financially and otherwise, than most of the countries in the sample (and specifically than the emerging markets that are the subject of this paper), and which has an exceptionally large public debt. Tables 7 and 8 replicate Tables 5 and 6 but drop Japan from the countries captured by the Asia dummy. Again, it appears that Asia-ex-Japan countries have smaller bond markets than countries in other regions with comparable characteristics over the sample period as a whole (though significance levels vary). For the earlier (pre-2003) period, the Asia-ex-Japan effect is negative and consistently significant, confirming the earlier result. That effect then goes to zero in the second subperiod, confirming that the observations for Japan were in large part responsible for the significantly positive effect in Table 6 for the recent decade.[21]

Table 7 shows why. For total debt, the Asia-ex-Japan variable is negative for the period as a whole. But when private and public debt are distinguished, we now see that the private debt variable enters positively (Asia-ex-Japan corporates and banks now issue even more debt domestically than their observable characteristics would lead one to expect), while the public debt variable enters positively (unlike Japan, Asian governments issue less debt than those characteristics would lead one to expect).

There is again wide variation across Asian countries in other measures of bond market development. Figure 5 shows the bond market turnover ratio (average daily trading as a share of amounts outstanding) for both the corporate and government segments, where available. The liquidity of the government segment, so measured, exceeds that of the corporate

---

[21] The signs and significance levels of most of the other variables discussed above are largely unchanged.

Table 7. Determinants of issuance of domestic debt securities, by sector of issuer, % of GDP 1996–2013 extended sample, excluding Japan, new BIS data

| | (1) Total Debt | (2) Total Debt | (3) Total Debt | (4) Private Debt | (5) Private Debt | (6) Private Debt | (7) Public Debt | (8) Public Debt |
|---|---|---|---|---|---|---|---|---|
| GDP, PPP (constant 2011 international billion $) | 0.001 (10.70)*** | 0.001 (9.26)*** | -0.001 (2.39)** | 0.001 (6.49)*** | 0.001 (7.48)*** | -0.001 (2.39)** | 0.001 (3.80)*** | 0.001 (3.06)*** |
| Exports of goods and services (% of GDP) | -0.002 (2.97)*** | -0.002 (3.94)*** | -0.001 (0.27) | -0.001 (2.12)*** | -0.001 (1.55) | -0.001 (0.27) | -0.001 (1.01) | -0.001 (2.78)*** |
| Asian Country | -0.242 (2.10)** | -0.180 (1.61) | 0.037 (0.58) | 0.026 (0.71) | 0.068 (1.80)* | 0.037 (0.58) | -0.072 (1.48) | -0.110 (2.57)** |
| Dummy for English Legal Origin | -0.112 (1.22) | -0.095 (1.07) | -0.033 (0.61) | -0.034 (1.19) | -0.026 (0.90) | -0.033 (0.61) | -0.088 (2.44)** | -0.066 (1.82)* |
| Distance from Equator | -0.495 (1.48) | -0.375 (1.25) | 0.136 (0.71) | 0.194 (1.81)* | 0.126 (1.22) | 0.136 (0.71) | -0.326 (2.68)*** | -0.360 (3.39)** |
| Investment Profile | -0.009 (1.99)** | -0.008 (2.08)** | 0.004 (2.15)** | 0.001 (0.38) | 0.000 (0.18) | 0.004 (2.15)** | -0.008 (2.75)*** | -0.007 (2.94)*** |
| Law and Order | 0.008 (0.64) | 0.004 (0.31) | -0.003 (0.52) | 0.001 (0.33) | 0.003 (0.84) | -0.003 (0.52) | -0.002 (0.20) | -0.004 (0.62) |
| GDP per capita, PPP (constant international thousand $) | 0.000 (2.60)*** | 0.000 (4.87)*** | 0.000 (2.69)*** | 0.000 (4.22)*** | 0.000 (6.43)*** | 0.000 (2.69)*** | 0.000 (3.22)*** | 0.000 (6.79)*** |
| Control of Corruption | -0.020 (2.03)** | -0.023 (2.33)** | -0.006 (1.19) | 0.002 (0.42) | 0.002 (0.51) | -0.006 (1.19) | -0.013 (2.13)** | -0.011 (1.88)* |

| | | | | | | | | |
|---|---|---|---|---|---|---|---|---|
| Accounting Standards | 0.003 | 0.002 | -0.007 | -0.003 | -0.002 | -0.007 | 0.005 | 0.003 |
| | (0.83) | (0.56) | (2.93)*** | (2.35)** | (1.83)* | (2.93)*** | (2.63)*** | (1.85)* |
| Domestic Credit to Private Sector by Banks (% of GDP) | 0.002 | 0.001 | 0.001 | 0.001 | 0.001 | 0.001 | 0.001 | 0.000 |
| | (3.34)*** | (1.77)* | (3.63)*** | (4.58)*** | (4.61)*** | (3.63)*** | (3.82)*** | (1.20) |
| Bureaucratic Quality | -0.004 | -0.027 | -0.004 | -0.002 | -0.006 | -0.004 | -0.001 | 0.008 |
| | (0.26) | (1.43) | (0.40) | (0.35) | (1.09) | (0.40) | (0.12) | (0.68) |
| SD log Interest Rate | -0.003 | -0.003 | -0.050 | 0.001 | -0.006 | -0.050 | 0.039 | 0.029 |
| | (0.13) | (0.16) | (2.74)*** | (0.08) | (0.53) | (2.74)*** | (3.40)*** | (2.66)*** |
| SD_change log Xrate | -0.389 | -0.357 | 0.077 | 0.025 | 0.024 | 0.077 | -0.217 | -0.313 |
| | (3.06)*** | (2.83)*** | (1.19) | (0.39) | (0.36) | (1.19) | (2.84)*** | (4.70)*** |
| Budget Balance (% of GDP) | -0.010 | | | -0.001 | | | -0.012 | |
| | (4.40)*** | | | (0.45) | | | (7.70)*** | |
| Chinn Ito Capital Controls Measure | 0.015 | 0.023 | -0.001 | 0.001 | 0.002 | -0.001 | 0.010 | 0.006 |
| | (1.59) | (2.16)** | (0.13) | (0.26) | (0.35) | (0.13) | (1.57) | (1.23) |
| Cash surplus/deficit (% of GDP) | | -0.013 | | | -0.003 | | | -0.010 |
| | | (7.78)*** | | | (4.43)*** | | | (10.22)*** |
| Outstanding Domestic Debt Securities Issued by Private Sector (% of GDP) | | | 1.449 | | | 0.449 | | |
| | | | (46.32)*** | | | (14.35)*** | | |
| Constant | 0.500 | 0.524 | 0.462 | 0.094 | 0.008 | 0.462 | -0.059 | 0.182 |
| | (1.86)* | (1.93)* | (3.32)*** | (1.14) | (0.10) | (3.32)*** | (0.48) | (1.52) |
| Observations | 458 | 493 | 441 | 458 | 493 | 441 | 458 | 493 |
| Number of groups (countries) | 32 | 32 | 20 | 32 | 32 | 20 | 32 | 32 |

Absolute value of z statistics in parentheses

*significant at 10%; **significant at 5%; ***significant at 1%.

**Table 8.** Determinants of issuance of domestic debt securities, total debt, % of GDP, 1996–2013 and subperiods, extended sample, excluding Japan, new BIS data

| | (1) Total Debt (Pre 2002) | (2) Total Debt (Post 2002) |
|---|---|---|
| GDP, PPP (constant 2011 international billion $) | 0.001 (10.01)*** | 0.001 (8.74)*** |
| Exports of goods and services (% of GDP) | 0.000 (0.90) | −0.004 (5.70)*** |
| Asian Country | −0.372 (9.48)*** | 0.047 (0.69) |
| Dummy for English Legal Origin | 0.151 (2.89)*** | 0.184 (2.15)** |
| Distance from Equator | 0.153 (1.00) | −0.509 (1.69)* |
| Domestic Credit to Private Sector by Banks (% of GDP) | 0.001 (0.94) | 0.003 (6.05)*** |
| Bureaucratic Quality | 0.009 (0.88) | 0.003 (0.09) |
| Control of Corruption | −0.011 (1.79)* | 0.008 (0.47) |
| Accounting Standards | −0.008 (5.01)*** | 0.001 (0.56) |
| Investment Profile | −0.001 (0.33) | −0.037 (4.13)*** |
| Law and Order | 0.005 (0.99) | −0.038 (2.02)** |
| GDP per capita, PPP (constant international thousand $) | 0.001 (3.45)*** | 0.001 (4.67)*** |
| GDP, PPP (constant 2011 international $) | 0.001 (0.87) | 0.001 (1.32) |
| SD_change in log Xrate | −0.368 (5.78)*** | −0.012 (0.14) |
| Chinn Ito Capital Controls Measure | 0.028 (5.53)*** | −0.025 (1.52) |
| Constant | 0.692 (5.59)*** | 0.683 (3.76)*** |
| Observations | 373 | 340 |
| Number of groups (countries) | 32 | 32 |

Absolute value of z statistics in parentheses *significant at 10%; **significant at 5%; ***significant at 1%.

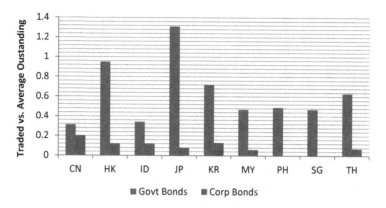

**Figure 5.** Bond market turnover ratio, end 2014

*Note:* End 2013 data for Philippines are latest available.

*Source:* Asian Development Bank.

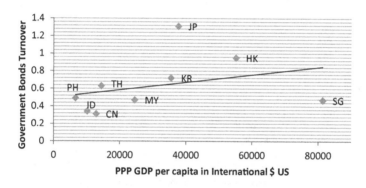

**Figure 6.** Bond market turnover and PPP GDP per capita, end 2014

*Note:* End 2013 data on turnover for Philippines are latest available.

*Source:* See text.

segment across the region, although the difference, interestingly, is least pronounced in China.

Figure 6 then arrays total turnover against per capita GDP. It suggests that China is a slight outlier in the negative direction.[22] For comparison, recall that corporate bond market turnover in the United States is much

---

[22] Again, Japan, Singapore and Hong Kong are the outliers, although not all in the same directions as in Figure 4; again, omitting the three of them reduces the extent to which the position of other countries deviates from the average relationship in the region.

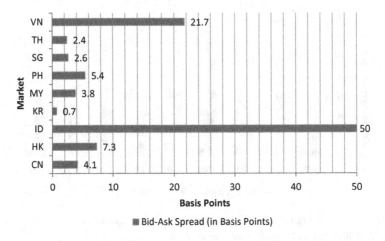

**Figure 7.** Local currency government bond bid-ask spreads, 2013
*Source:* Asian Development Bank.

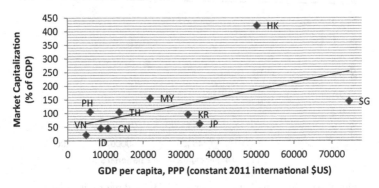

**Figure 8.** Equity market capitalization and GDP per capita
*Note:* 2012 data unless otherwise stated.
*Source:* World Bank.

higher, on the order of 80%.[23] Another measure of market liquidity is the bid-ask spread available for the government segment; on this metric (Figure 7), China is less of an outlier.

Equity markets are historically later to develop, although this may be changing, with changes in the information environment.[24] Figures 8 and 9

---

[23] It was even higher, on the order of 120 per cent, prior to the credit crisis.

[24] "Pecking-order" theories of financial development described below are based on the view that debt markets have developed, historically, before deep and liquid equity markets, owing to high costs of monitoring giving rise to agency problems for outside investors.

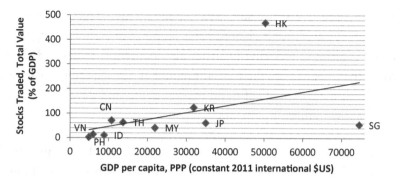

**Figure 9.** Equity market turnover and GDP per capita

*Note:* 2012 data unless otherwise stated.

*Source:* See text.

show equity market capitalization and turnover, along with per capita GDP. China is slightly below the level of market capitalization predicted by the average relationship in the region, but displays a slightly higher than predicted rate of turnover.

## Opening and Institutions as a Critical Nexus

Among the most controversial potential determinants of financial development is financial opening. And nowhere are financial opening and its effects more controversial than in Asia.

On the one hand, opening the capital account is a way of introducing the chill winds of competition into the financial sector.[25] Domestic intermediaries are exposed to foreign financial technology and managerial expertise. Access to offshore markets offers additional funding opportunities. It limits the ability of policymakers to maintain ceilings on deposit rates (as in China — see Section 5 below), relaxing a further constraint on bank funding.[26] It permits intermediaries to diversify their portfolios internationally and offer a better mix of risk and return. It

---

[25] An early important contribution to this view was Claessens, Demirguc-Kunt, and Huizinga (2001). The more cautious view from the vantage point of 2014 is Claessens and Van Horen (2014).

[26] This, recall, was the emphasis of McKinnon (1973) and Shaw (1973).

creates a more diverse investor base, making for higher levels of turnover and market liquidity. These arguments all point to early opening of the capital account as fostering financial development.[27] Tables 5–8 above, where the openness of the capital account is among the positive and significant determinants of bond market depth and development, are consistent with these arguments.

At the same time, capital account opening heightens exposure to financial disturbances originating abroad, which can result in additional volatility, especially in smaller, more specialized, less developed economies. Access to foreign funding can amplify the adverse effects of existing financial distortions, rendering the removal of restrictions on the capital account welfare reducing.[28] Banks, as well as nonbank financial intermediaries and even nonfinancial corporations, enjoying implicit guarantees will see access to offshore funding as an opportunity to lever up their bets.[29] If that offshore funding is denominated in foreign currency or the country lacks an autonomous monetary policy owing to the nature of its exchange rate regime, then the resulting currency mismatch can prove destabilizing. When bad news arrives, capital inflows can give way to sudden stops and capital outflows, with devastating consequences for financial stability. And nothing is more damaging to financial deepening and development than financial instability.[30]

There is some support for both views, which may be just another way of saying that there is overwhelming evidence for neither. Klein and Olivei (2007) analyze a cross-section of countries and find that countries with open capital accounts display significantly higher levels of financial depth and economic growth, holding other factors constant. Utilizing historical

---

[27] 19th century experience points in the same direction.

[28] This is of course a classic illustration of the theory of the second best.

[29] As in the case of banks in Thailand and Korea prior to 1998 and nonfinancial corporations in a variety of Asian countries in recent years (including the debt issued offshore by subsidiaries and therefore missed by the conventional residency-based statistics — see Nordvig 2014 and Avdjiev, Chui, and Shin 2014).

[30] This last point is emphasized even more in the literature on Latin America, given the historical prevalence of financial instability there (see inter alia Didier and Schmukler 2013).

evidence, Rajan and Zingales (2003) argue that financial openness, has a positive impact on financial development and efficiency.[31] Baltagi, Demetriades, and Law (2009) use panel data and an instrumental variables strategy to test this hypothesis, with largely supportive results. My own earlier work (Eichengreen and Luengnaruemitchai 2006) focusing on bond market capitalization, using the IMF's measure of de jure capital account regimes and analyzing data for 41 countries from 1990 through 2001, supports the view that countries with open capital accounts have deeper bond markets. Ishola (n.d.), in contrast, finds no impact of financial opening on financial development in a sample of African countries. Chinn (2000) similarly detects no relationship between financial openness and bank credit to the private sector, albeit some impact on equity market development.

There is also some support for the so-called "threshold view" that the positive effects dominate only when a country achieves a critical level of institutional strength and regulatory quality. Thus, Chinn and Ito (2006) find that a higher level of financial openness contributes to the development of equity markets only when a threshold level of institutional quality is reached. Specifically, that threshold depends more on the general quality of bureaucracy, the strength of the legal system, and control of corruption than it does on finance-focused measures like the quality of supervision and regulation. This suggests that the preconditions for financial opening to have favorable effects involve more than just strengthening the financial system narrowly defined.

A related literature suggests that financial development does more to stimulate economic growth in countries with strong institutions. Chen and Quang (2012) find that only countries with relatively high-quality institutions derive growth benefits from financial opening. Klein (2003) finds an inverted U-shaped relationship between the responsiveness of growth to capital account openness and government quality, where neither countries with very low quality governmental institutions nor countries

---

[31] This is especially the case, they argue, when that financial openness is combined with trade openness.

with the highest quality benefit significantly.[32] The Klein and Olivei study cited above finds that the positive relationship between capital account openness and growth is due mostly to variation within the subsample of high-income countries, which is similarly suggestive of an institutional threshold below which no effects, large or small, are evident.

Also relevant is the question of how opening the capital account affects the quality of institutions and regulation. If the answer is "positively and quickly," then reservations about the impact of opening on financial development where institutional quality is poor need not detain us, since institutions will adapt to accommodate the policy. Rajan and Zingales (2003) argue along these lines, suggesting that opening undermines the market power of incumbents and limits the risk of regulatory capture. Others argue that just as a faster car needs more responsive steering in order to not run off the road, a more open economy needs more responsive regulation in order to avoid financial crashes, and those responsible for it, seeing no alternative, will be compelled to supply it.

From a practical standpoint, the question is how quickly the response occurs, and what the costs are in the event of delay. Here the literature is not helpful. There is a dearth of work on the impact of financial opening on institutional development, in contrast to the literature considering the impact of trade on institutions, which is considerable (see e.g., Acemoglu and Robinson, 2005; Levchenko 2010).

## China's Challenge

At the time of writing, China's financial system is fourth largest in the world, behind only those of the United States, the Euro Area and Japan.[33] Thus, what happens in China financially will have important

---

[32] Where most of the curvature in the U reflects the limited benefits to countries at the low end.

[33] Here financial size is measured as bank lending and the market value of outstanding bonds and equity combined, as in Cruz, Gao, and Song (2014).

consequences for the development of financial markets and economies in Asia and worldwide.

China's financial depth compares less favorably when scaled by GDP. By this metric, the country lags behind not just the advanced economies but also Thailand, Korea and Taiwan, among others. Thailand, Korea and Taiwan have higher per capita incomes, of course. In fact, China's financial depth scaled by GDP is commensurate to that of other countries with comparable per capita incomes, either now or (in the case of the now-advanced countries) historically.

If there is a problem then, it is with not the size but the structure of China's financial markets. As in other countries at China's stage of economic development, the country's financial system remains heavily bank based. Because the information and contracting requirements of arms-length transactions on securities markets are demanding, such markets are late to develop. Until they do, financial services are provided by banks, which cultivate relationships and invest in monitoring technologies so as to be able to assemble information on behalf of investors and to discipline borrowers.[34] Over time, bond, equity and derivatives markets then acquire depth and gain liquidity (according to the pecking-order theory, bond markets first, equity markets later).[35] The growth of these markets presupposes the existence of a relatively elaborate apparatus of underwriters, rating agencies, custodians, clearing and settlement platforms, and systems for policing the markets, both self-policing by organized exchanges, and regulatory oversight by autonomous securities commissions.

Until all this happens, banks remain the dominant source of external finance. So it is in China, where banks account for 60% of the sum of bank

---

[34] This point was influentially made by Gerschenkron (1964). Banks, it can be argued, are also preferred by government officials (and other powerful incumbents) because they provide convenient mechanisms for channeling funds in preferred directions (a capacity that is lost or at least diluted with the development of anonymous, atomistic securities markets).

[35] It should be acknowledged that there is some disagreement in the historical literature about the general validity of this pecking-order view.

lending and stock and bond market capitalization, substantially higher than in other large financial markets (those of the U.S., the Euro Area, Japan, the U.K. and Australia being the leaders).[36] The relative weight of banks in finance is roughly comparable to that in Germany in the 1980s or South Korea in the1990s (in both of which securities markets gained additional capital market share subsequently).The weight of banks is, if anything, higher in China than in other emerging markets at a comparable stage of economic development, reflecting the close control the authorities have exercised over the operation of the Chinese economy and the utility of banks as a policy lever.

Necessarily then, developing the Chinese financial system starts with reforming and strengthening the banks.[37] The big Chinese banks, which account for the bulk of bank intermediation, are still majority state owned. Although they are officially commercialized — supposed to operate at arm's length from the government — whether they in fact take decisions on the basis of commercial or political motives can be questioned. Reflecting this, the World Bank, in a study undertaken jointly with the Development Research Center, a Chinese government think tank, has recommended fully privatizing the banks, which would eliminate much of the remaining ambiguity about their motives.[38]

But commercialization will produce positive results only if the authorities at the same time remove the presumption that the banks enjoy an implicit guarantee. The decision to move ahead with implementation of deposit insurance starting in May 2015, which guarantees deposits rather than the banks themselves, is a necessary step in this direction.

Strengthening the banking system also requires regulatory rationalization. Traditionally the People's Bank of China (PBOC) has set a ceiling for deposit rates and a floor for lending rates, ensuring a spread that

---

[36] Only the Euro Area comes close. Whether these statistics fully capture the role of non-bank financial intermediaries and their liabilities can be questioned, of course — see the discussion below of the shadow banking system.

[37] Some of the following discussion, especially portions connected to renminbi internationalization, are taken from Eichengreen (2014).

[38] See Davis (2013).

makes for healthy profits for state owned banks. In July 2013 regulators lifted some controls over bank lending rates with the goal of permitting the banks to compete more intensively in extending corporate loans. But the authorities were slower to relax other controls, notably those on deposits, reflecting worries that banks would otherwise engage in "unhealthy" competition for deposits and make excessively risky investments in the effort to meet their deposit-rate commitments. Even once most of these controls were officially lifted, deposit rates were still subject to the PBOC's window and pricing guidance. Such guidance encourages the growth of the shadow banking system as a way of circumventing them (Sun 2018). Effective privatization and commercialization will require fully freeing deposit and lending rates so that banks with profitable investment opportunities can compete for both borrowers and funding without having to create unregulated off-balance-sheet financial products. That in turn will require strengthening regulatory oversight of the banks' lending and investment practices to ensure that deposit-rate competition doesn't give rise to excessive risk on the asset side of the banks' balance sheets.

Finally, strengthening the banking system requires widening the regulatory perimeter. It requires strengthening supervision and regulation of not just the banks but also their off-balance sheet subsidiaries, including investment companies, wealth management products and on-line accounts that constitute the shadow banking system. Estimates of the size of the shadow banking system vary, given vagaries of data and definition: they generally range from 50 to 80% of GDP.[39] But even 50% is substantial, given that bank lending is officially on the order of 110% of GDP. Many of China's trust funds and other nonbank investment vehicles are in fact operated by banks that use them to attract funding by offering higher interest rates than permitted on conventional bank deposits, as well as to extend loans that would require them to hold costly capital and provisions were they to be held on the banks' balance sheets. In turn, the managers of these vehicles have an incentive to seek out risky loan opportunities in the hope of earning income sufficient to meet their interest-rate commitments.

---

[39] A variety of these estimates are reported in Wang (2014).

In July 2013 the China Bank Regulatory Commission took a first step in addressing these concerns by requiring commercial banks to register wealth management products prior to selling them to the public. Deposit rate deregulation, by reducing the incentive to create such products as a way of attracting household savings, would be a further step in this direction.

To be effective, supervision will have to extend to other nonbank entities that compete increasingly with the banks. Nonbank firms, both state-owned enterprises (SOEs) and others, use their excess funds to extend credit through trust loans and entrusted loans to other firms, taking land and other property as collateral.[40] Here too banks are involved as intermediaries between the ultimate borrower and lender, allowing restrictions on entrusted loans to be evaded. How banks and others active in this market would hold up in the face of a sharp property market decline or a manufacturing slowdown is an open question. But none of this changes the point that fostering effective and sustainable financial development requires bringing shadow banking into the light.

Bond markets, while starting out behind, are growing relative to the banks. Again, China's size implies that its bond market accounts for a very large fraction of East-Asia-ex-Japan bond market capitalization, on the order of two thirds, while China's bond market is now the third largest in the world, behind only those of the United States and Japan (as noted above). Issuance is growing rapidly — in absolute terms, compared to its rate of increase in other Asian countries, and relative to the growth of the Chinese economy itself — by approximately 20% per annum.

Reassuringly, corporate issuance is expanding most rapidly. While corporate issues account for only about a third of the stock of bonds

---

[40] Trust loans are made by trust companies, which gather funds from individuals and financial institutions, while entrusted loans use corporate earnings and reserves; these are extended within corporate groups, but a significant portion is between unrelated third parties; see Borst and Lardy (2015).

outstanding, they account for half of all new issues.[41] This is a sign that the bond market is increasingly serving the financial needs of the economy.

At the same time, the bond market displays weaknesses. The market is smaller relative to GDP than in other emerging markets such as Brazil, Malaysia, Thailand and South Africa. It is dominated by short-term issuance: nearly 40% of new issuance is of bonds with a maturity under one year, as if investors are reluctant to commit to long-term finance.[42] China is an exception to the general pattern across Asia of lengthening corporate bond maturities, giving rise to worries about rollover risk. Banks still buy many of the longer-term issues, as if much bond issuance is effectively bank lending in disguise.

Corporate issuance, for its part, is dominated by majority-state-owned enterprises, suggesting that the private sector is even more underserved than suggested by the government-bond-corporate-bond breakdown.[43] Borst and Lardy (2015) find that SOEs account directly or indirectly for 90% of corporate bond issuance. As of 2013, only 7 of the top 30 corporate issuers were not majority government owned, and all seven in question were banks. Moreover, a substantial fraction of government bond issuance takes the form of bonds issued by three state-owned policy banks (the China Development Bank, the Export-Import Bank of China, and the Agricultural Development Bank of China) and guaranteed by the central government. The three state banks are presumably stepping in by issuing and then lending for projects for which the private sector finds it difficult to access bond finance. This is all the more striking given the reluctance of the authorities to allow debt issuers to default (given the presence of an implicit guarantee).

---

[41] Again in 2014H1. Over the four years ending in 2014H1, the corporate bond market doubled in size relative to Chinese GDP.

[42] In March 2015 the Finance Ministry announced a plan for provincial governments to refinance RMB 1 tr. in debt (most bank loans and trust loans) as bonds so as to lower rollover risk and reduce funding costs. When the first tranche of this debt was marketed in April, demand from the banks and investors generally was underwhelming.

[43] Similarly, a substantial fraction of the bonds issued by financial institutions are issued by majority-state-owned banks.

In addition, upwards of two thirds of government bonds are held by banks, Chinese banks in particular, as previously noted. This is in contrast to the situation in other Asian countries with relatively well-developed bond markets, where they are held by private investors, pension funds and other provident funds.[44] Given that much corporate bond issuance is by state-owned companies, whose bonds are then purchased by state-owned banks, one wonders how many of these transactions are policy directed as opposed to arm's length. This raises the possibility of a diabolic loop if, say, local governments get into trouble, infecting bank balance sheets, or banks get into trouble and engage in fire-sales of assets that demoralize the bond market.

Nor is this the diverse investor base to which the architects of deep and liquid bond markets aspire. Banks are not active traders. The dominance of banks on the buy side may thus account for the relatively limited liquidity of the secondary market (as measured by turnover, or amount traded as a share of the value of bonds outstanding), in government bonds in particular. Bid-ask spreads in the local currency government bond market compare unfavorably with those in Korea, Singapore and Thailand (Figure 7). Interestingly, China compares more favorably in terms of turnover in the corporate segment of the bond market, where the investor base is more diverse and commercial banks hold less than 40% of total issuance. This contrasts with the experience of other countries where government bonds typically trade more than corporate bonds, reflecting the latter's lack of uniformity, again pointing to China's lack of investor diversity.

The authorities and market participants can do a number of things about these problems. To increase the diversity of the investor base, China opened the interbank bondmarket, where most bonds are traded, to qualified foreign institutional investors (licensed commercial and central banks) in 2012, subject to a quota limit. The National Association of Financial Market Institutional Investors (NAFMII), the self-organizing

---

[44] Japan is an exception to this generalization in that a substantial fraction of government bonds outstanding are held by the central bank.

association of bond dealers and investors overseen by the central bank, has taken steps to enhance the transparency of the interbank market and ameliorate contracting problems (issuing "Guidelines for Book Building and Issuance," a "Code of Conduct for Issuers," "Rules on Bondholders Meetings," etc.). The State Council has authorized trading of government debt futures to enable investors to hedge risks, with the goal of encouraging participation and enhancing market liquidity.

In addition, the authorities have mandated that all transactions on the interbank market be conducted through the National Interbank Funding Center and required legal documentation of transfers of ownership. In part this is a crackdown on so-called "proxy holding trades," where a financial institution transfers a bond from one account to another, both belonging to the same individual or financial institution, as a way for the institution in question to boost its standing in industry league tables for trading volumes. On other occasions, it is alleged, the sale is completed at an inflated price in order to create bookkeeping profits. The result was a drop in daily trading volumes, suggesting that historical turnover figures are inflated and market liquidity, so measured, is even less than previously thought.

The decision in 2014 to allow Chaori, the solar-cell company, to default was a step toward addressing moral hazard in the bond markets by weakening the implicit guarantee. A second step was then taken in April of 2015 when the government of the city of Ordos refused to guarantee the bonds of the troubled Sundry Group of construction companies. Also, in April, property developer Kaisa Group missed an interest payment on its dollar-denominated debt, and state-owned power equipment manufacturer Baoding Tianwei Group failed to make a payment on its domestic debt. However, whether removing the implicit guarantee will encourage greater efficiency or create an additional risk, only time will tell.

The Chinese corporate sector has the highest debt-to-equity ratio in the region, reflecting the explosive growth of the corporate bond market and historical underdevelopment of equity markets. Stock market capitalization, at about 40% of GDP, compares unfavorably to that in other emerging markets like Brazil, India, and Korea. Moreover, a non-negligible (if declining) share of that capitalization is made up of non-negotiable state-owned shares, causing the official Chinese figures to paint a somewhat exaggerated picture. Controlling for free float (eliminating negotiable shares held by important private stakeholders) is likely to redraw the picture further in the same direction. The rate of growth of capitalization is similarly disappointing by international standards, reflecting high volatility on the Shanghai and Shenzhen markets.

Historically, turnover has been relatively high, despite the lack of access of foreign investors to substantial segments of the market. In contrast to the situation in the bond market, retail investors have been willing to participate actively, as a result of which market liquidity compares favorably with the situation in other countries at comparable levels of per capita GDP. But turnover has fallen in some years, reflecting disenchantment among retail investors and complaints about market transparency and integrity (insider trading and corporate governance scandals).

A further constraint on market development is close control by the government of new listings. Applications for public listings must be approved by the China Securities Regulatory Commission. The commission appears to time listings so as to manipulate share prices. When prices fall, applications for new listings are delayed or disapproved, which has been the situation in recent years. Similarly, the government has pressured SOEs and banks to purchase shares when prices are depressed, limiting price discovery and raising additional questions about market integrity.

In May 2014 the State Council circulated a new policy document on capital market development reaffirming its commitment to develop equity markets and to increase the share of direct financing in total external finance, although it did not specify the steps it was prepared to take. Some of these are obvious, including speeding approval of public listings while strengthening disclosure and corporate governance requirements for corporations with public listings.[45] They include refraining from arm-twisting banks and SOEs to buy shares when prices are weak.

A key question is whether China should move faster to liberalize the capital account as a way of fostering financial development and liquidity. This issue arises most immediately in connection with efforts to internationalize the renminbi, it being unlikely that the currency will acquire meaningful unit of account, means of payment and store of value functions internationally so long as access and use across borders are restricted. But the question can also be asked by those concerned about financial development more broadly. Lack of a diverse investor base is a problem for the bond market, and it can become a problem for the equity market if domestic retail investors retreat. More rapidly liberalizing the access of foreign investors would be a way of addressing this problem, and Chinese policymakers have already begun going down this road (as noted above).

Some observers warn that this strategy for attempting to compress the process of building more liquid financial markets has risks (see Yu 2013). Corporates, both nonfinancial and financial, may respond to the appetite of issue-hungry foreigners by issuing reckless amounts of debt. Banks with easier access to foreign funding may lever up their balance sheets. Corporates with governance and transparency problems may bring initial public offerings to market prematurely. Increased exposure to international capital flows may heighten macroeconomic volatility if it precedes the transition to a more flexible exchange rate.

All these are good arguments for why the Chinese authorities should resist the temptation to rely on capital account liberalization as a driver of domestic financial development and instead attend to basics, where the basics include strengthening not just supervision and regulation but also rule of law and bureaucratic quality more generally.

---

[45] Some streamlining already occurred at the end of 2013 with the issuance of new guidelines for initial public offerings by the China Securities Regulatory Commission.

## Excessive Financialization?

The idea that too much financial depth and development ("excessive financialization") might be deleterious to economic stability and growth is not new; for earlier examples see Tobin (1984) and Epstein (1996). But this concern went mainstream with the growth of financial sectors in the decade leading up to the global credit crisis and the crisis itself. In the advanced countries this acceleration in the growth of the financial sector coincided with evidence of a slowdown in output and productivity growth economy-wide that became apparent even before the crisis (a review of the evidence is Gordon 2012). Many of the countries that then suffered the most serious growth setbacks during and after the crisis (Iceland, Ireland, the United Kingdom and the United States) were those with the largest financial sectors.

At least two studies attempt to identify the point where the contribution of financial depth diminishes and turns negative.[46] Arcand, Berkes, and Panizza (2012) run workhorse regressions from the cross-country empirical literature on financial development and growth, including not just credit to the private sector over GDP but also its square. While the ratio enters positively, as in earlier studies, the squared term registers with a negative, statistically significant coefficient. Using a variety of specifications and estimators, Arcand *et al.* consistently find that the effect turns negative when the ratio reaches 100%. Cecchetti and Kharroubi (2012) use panel regression and a different sample of countries, also finding a peak in the inverted U-shaped relationship between the private credit ratio and growth at 100%. In addition, they find an inverted U-shaped relationship between financial-sector employment growth and

---

[46] A third study, by Sahay *et al.* (2015), constructs an eclectic index of financial development that includes not just bank credit to the private sector but also a measure of market-based intermediation, and considers not just financial depth but also measures of access to and efficiency of financial institutions and markets. Like the studies cited in the text, they too find that the contribution of financial development to growth is bell shaped and eventually turns negative. The authors do not provide individual country values of their index, so it is hard to say where Asian countries lie along the bell.

economy-wide productivity growth with a peak at slightly below 4% of total employment.

On this metric (private credit as share of GDP), Singapore, Malaysia, China, South Korea, Thailand and Hong Kong are all above the level where the contribution of credit to economic growth turns negative. If the results of these studies are taken literally, they suggest that in all these countries financial deepening has gone far enough.

The controversy surrounding other magic numbers should leave us skeptical about the precision of such numerical thresholds. In the present instance there are special cases; much of the credit recorded as going to the private sector in Hong Kong, for example, may in fact be going to Chinese borrowers (and being funded by Chinese lenders). High income countries typically possess the largest and best-developed financial sectors; their growth may slow not because of any pernicious effects of excessive financialization but because they are mature economies that have approached the technological frontier.[47] Existing studies fail to identify the *channels* through which additional financial depth depresses growth, which is what they must do in order to convince. In any case, the structure and performance of the financial sector, and not simply its size, are likely matter for output and productivity growth.[48]

Implicit in this last observation is an important implication for Asian policymakers: financial development means enhancing the performance and efficiency of the financial sector, not simply raising the private credit/GDP ratio. The message is the same as for capital formation: at some point simply pushing up the capital/labor ratio encounters diminishing returns, and countries need to focus on the quality (that is to say, the efficiency)

---

[47] The studies cited in the preceding paragraph include per capita GDP and various other country characteristics in an effort to control for this possibility, but the danger of omitted variables remains.

[48] Cecchetti and Kharroubi (2012) experiment with various measures of the structure of the financial sector (bank credit as opposed to total credit) without materially affecting the results. Still, whether they adequately control for the performance of the financial sector can still be questioned.

and not just the quantity of investment. This of course is the essence of the rebalancing debate in China, and it applies to financial development as well as physical capital formation. Pushing up the private credit ratio is the easier task. The Chinese authorities instruct the banks to lend more, and the banks respond. But at some point, simply expanding the supply of credit will reach the point of diminishing returns. Improving the efficiency of a given level of intermediation then becomes even more important.

Policymakers should also scrutinize the distortions to which critics of excessive financialization point in order to avoid creating or compounding them. A large and complex financial system may heighten crisis risk and hamstring efforts to contain the adverse macroeconomic effects (Easterly, Islam, and Stiglitz 2000; Rajan 2006). This should direct the attention of officials to policies that address threats to stability and create policy space for responding, and to the growing importance of such measures as the financial sector grows. Asian countries on the front lines of the 1997–1998 crisis recognized this fact, building larger foreign reserves and negotiating regional networks of swap lines and credits as crisis-containment devices.

Similarly, the distortion may be that the social returns to employment in the financial sector are lower than the private returns, as suggested by Tobin (1984). This may be the case if compensation practices are flawed (bonuses that flow from excessive risk taking cannot be clawed back), because implicit guarantees subsidize financial sector employment, or because financiers redistribute wealth rather than creating it. If so, less employment in the nonfinancial sector may mean less innovation and growth. Korean officials, to take an example, might usefully ask whether their aspirations of making Seoul a financial hub for East Asia are compatible with their desire to maintain the country's competitive position in high-tech products now that the share of employment in the financial sector is approaching Cecchetti and Kharroubi's cutoff of 4%.[49]

---

[49] The earlier caution in the text that magic numbers should not be taken too literally suggests that exactly *how* the Korean authorities go about promoting Seoul as a financial center will make all the difference.

## Conclusion

The Asian crisis of 1997–1998 was attributed, in part, to the failure of economies to build deeper, more liquid and better diversified financial systems.[50] Asian countries, the argument went, relied too heavily on banks for financial services. Those banks in turn relied excessively on short-term, offshore, foreign-currency-denominated funding, exposing host economies to sudden stops and destabilizing exchange rates. This situation reflected the reliance on bank finance that is characteristic of the early stages of economic and financial development and the telescoped nature of the development process in Asia. It reflected weaknesses in the contracting and regulatory environment that gave banks, which rely on long-term relationships and dedicated monitoring technologies, a leg up in the competition for financial business. It reflected the convenience to policymakers of a financial system dominated by banks, which could be relied on to channel credit in particular directions. And it reflected the uneven nature of capital account liberalization, which gave politically favored banks preferential access to offshore funding.

The implication was that Asian countries should develop better diversified financial systems in which security markets, and bond markets in particular, play a larger role.[51] Studies showed that local bond markets were smaller than in other regions and smaller than the economic and financial characteristics of Asian economies would have led one to predict. Following the crisis, this perceived problem was addressed by initiatives at the national and regional levels, including the ABMI, an effort to pool information and expertise on the development of local bond markets, and the ABMF, a mechanism for fostering financial standardization and increased demand in the region for local-currency bonds.

---

[50] The "in part" is important, since a full accounting of the Asian crisis would necessarily acknowledge important roles for other factors both internal and external to the region.
[51] This emphasis on bond markets in turn reflected the presumption, noted above, that equity markets have even more formidable prerequisites and are later to develop, although, as also noted above, this presumption can be questioned.

Economies in the region have made progress in the desired direction. Asian countries no longer stand out as having stunted bond markets. The conclusion holds most strongly for corporate bond markets, which matter most. Evidently, Asian policymakers have succeeded in advancing their objective of building better diversified financial systems.

At the same time, problems remain. Currency mismatches on bank balance sheets may be more closely scrutinized by supervisors and regulators, but nonfinancial corporations continue to borrow offshore, incurring unhedged foreign-currency obligations.[52] This behavior reflects the low cost of funding in offshore bond markets, owing to the low-interest-rate policies of the Federal Reserve and other advanced-country central banks, but also the failure of local bond markets to provide the same services. Domestic bond markets still lack liquidity by the standards of the leading international financial centers. Lack of liquidity, as manifested in turnover rates and bid-ask spreads, reflects the uneven development of the relevant trading platforms and technologies and the absence of a more diverse investor base.

These observations in turn create a temptation to rely on capital account liberalization — to throw open domestic markets to foreign investors — as a way of jump-starting the financial-development process. Doing so promises to increase the diversity of the investor base, boost trading and turnover, and enhance market liquidity at a stroke. But this strategy comes with risks, as Asian countries have learned the hard way. Foreign funds, when they pour in, can push local markets up to uncomfortable heights, from which a fall can be injurious. Such were the worries of policymakers in emerging markets complaining prior to 2013 about the foreign capital flooding into their markets from advanced countries with near-zero interest rates. When flows turn around, markets quickly become illiquid. The so-called "taper tantrum" of mid-2013, when Federal Reserve officials unexpectedly suggested that the security purchase

---

[52] The most prominent study highlighting this problem is Avdjiev, Chui, and Shin (2014), as noted above.

program and low interest rates of the U.S. central bank might soon come to an end, highlighted the dangers.[53]

The implication is that capital account liberalization designed to "jump-start" the process of building larger and more liquid financial markets is an approach with considerable risks. The benefits of capital account liberalization exceed the costs only when prerequisites are met. This conclusion, supported by international evidence and recent Asian history, is an important one for Chinese policymakers to take to heart, given their self-avowed strategy of seeking to develop a better diversified financial system in part by encouraging foreign investor participation in local security markets and internationalizing the renminbi.

The bottom line, which comes through clearly in the literature on "excessive financialization," is that policymakers should focus less on headline measures of financial depth and liquidity like market capitalization and turnover, and more on the efficiency of the financial system in meeting the needs of households and firms. Asian policymakers drew an analogous conclusion about fixed investment from the 1997–1998 financial crisis: that they needed to focus less on the volume of investment and more on its efficiency. They now need to apply the same lesson to the development of the financial system.

## References

Acemoglu, D and Robinson, J (2005). The rise of Europe: Atlantic trade, institutional change, and economic growth. *American Economic Review*, 95, 546–579.

Arcand, J-L, Berkes, E, and Panizza, U (2012). Too much finance? IMF Working Paper No.12/161, June.

Avdjiev, S, Chui, M, and Shin, HS (2014). Non-financial corporations from emerging markets and global capital flows. *BIS Quarterly Review*, (December), 67–77.

---

[53] As described in Eichengreen and Gupta (2015). The capital account regulations of these and other emerging markets are described by Baumann and Gallagher (2013).

Baltagi, B, Demetriades, P, and Law, SH (2009). Financial development and openness: Evidence from panel data. *Journal of Development Economics*, 89, 285–296.

Baumann, B and Gallagher, K (2013). Post-crisis capital account regulation in South Korea and South Africa. Working Paper No. 320, Amherst: Political Economy Research Institute, University of Massachusetts, April.

Beltran, D and Thomas, C (2010). Could asymmetric information alone have caused the collapse of private-label securitization? International Finance Discussion Paper No. 1010, Washington D.C.: International Finance Division, Board of Governors of the Federal Reserve System, October.

Borst, N and Lardy, N (2015). Maintaining financial stability in the People's Republic of China during financial liberalization. Working Paper 15–4, Washington, D.C.: Peterson Institute for International Economics, March.

Brunnermeier, M (2009). Deciphering the liquidity and credit crunch 2007–2008. *Journal of Economic Perspectives*, 23, 77–100.

Cecchetti, S and Kharroubi, E (2012). Reassessing the impact of finance on growth. BIS Working Paper No. 381, July.

Chen, JZ and Quang, T (2012). International financial integration and economic growth: New evidence on threshold effects. CNRS Working Paper No. 2012–06, University of Paris Ouest Nanterre La Defense.

Chinn, M (2000). The compatibility of capital controls and financial development: A selective survey and empirical evidence. *Pacific Economic Papers*, 27, 1–26.

Chinn, M and Ito, H (2006). What matters for financial development? Capital controls, institutions and interactions. *Journal of Development Economics*, 81, 163–192.

Claessens, S, Demirguc-Kunt, A, and Huizinga, H (2001). How does foreign entry affect domestic banking markets? *Journal of Banking and Finance*, 25, 891–911.

Claessens, S and Van Horen, N (2014). Foreign banks: Trends, impact and financial stability. *Journal of Money, Credit and Banking*, 46, 891–911.

Cruz, PC, Gao, YN, and Song, L (2014). The People's Republic of China's financial markets: Are they deep and liquid enough for renminbi internationalization? ADBI Working Paper No. 477, April.

Davis, B (2013). World bank mulling sweeping proposals for China reform. *Wall Street Journal*, 1 August. Available at: http://online.wsj.com/article/SB10 0014241278873241362045786416225999923676.html.

Didier, T and Schmukler, S (2013). *Emerging Issues in Financial Development: Lessons from Latin America*. Washington, D.C.: The World Bank.

Easterly, W, Islam, R, and Stiglitz, J (2000). Shaken and stirred: Explaining growth volatility. Presentation at *Annual Bank Conference on Development Economics*. Washington, D.C.: World Bank, 91–211.

Eichengreen, B (2006). The development of Asian bond markets. In *Asian Bond Markets: Issues and Prospects*, BIS Occasional Paper No. 30, Bank for International Settlements.

Eichengreen, B (2014). Pathways to renminbi internationalization. In *Internationalization of the Renminbi: Pathways, Implications and Opportunities* (pp. 5–51). Sydney: Centre for International Finance and Regulation.

Eichengreen, B (2015). *Hall of Mirrors: The Great Depression, the Great Recession, and the Uses — and Misuses — of History*. New York: Oxford University Press.

Eichengreen, B and Gupta, P (2015). Tapering talk: The impact of expectations of reduced federal reserve security purchases on emerging markets. *Emerging Markets Review*, 25, 1–15.

Eichengreen, B and Hausmann, R (1999). Exchange rates and financial fragility. In *New Challenges for Monetary Policy*. Kansas City: Federal Reserve Bank of Kansas City, 329–368.

Eichengreen, B, Hausmann, R, and Panizza, U (2008). Currency mismatches, debt intolerance and original sin: Why they are not the same and why it matters. In P Collier and JW Gunning (Eds.), *Globalization and Poverty*. Cheltenham: Edward Elgar.

Eichengreen, B and Luengnaruemitchai, P (2006). Why doesn't Asia have bigger bond markets? In *Asian Bond Markets, Issues and Prospects*, BIS Occasional Paper No. 30, Bank for International Settlements, 40–77.

Eichengreen, B and Luengnaruemitchai, P (2008). Bond markets as conduits for capital flows: How does Asia compare? In T Ito and A Rose (Eds.), *International Financial Issues in the Pacific Rim*. Chicago: University of Chicago Press.

Epstein, G (Ed.) (1996). *Financialization and the World Economy*. Cheltenham: Edward Elgar.

Frankel, J and Schmukler, S (1997). Country fund discounts, asymmetric information and the Mexican crisis of 1994: Did local residents turn pessimistic before international investors? In G Tavlas (Ed.), *Currency Crashes: Causes, Consequences and Policy Responses* (pp. 81–104). Boston: Kluwer.

Gerschenkron, A (1964). *Economic Backwardness in Historical Perspective*. Cambridge, MA: Harvard University Press.

Gordon, R (2012). Is US economic growth over? Faltering innovation confronts the six headwinds. CEPR Policy Insight No. 63, London: Centre for Economic Policy Research, September.

Gorton, G (2008). The panic of 2007. *Proceedings of Payments System Research Conference*. Kansas City, MO: Federal Reserve Bank of Kansas City, 131–262.

Greenspan, A (1999). Lessons from the global crises. Remarks by Chairman Alan Greenspan before the World Bank Group and International Monetary Fund, Washington, D.C., 27 September. Available at: http://www.federalreserve.gov/Boarddocs/speeches/1999/199909272.htm.

Gruic, B and Wooldridge, P (2012). Enhancements to the BIS debt securities statistics. *BIS Quarterly Review*, (December), 63–76.

Ishola, M (n.d.). Globalization and financial development in sub-saharan Africa. University of Leicester (unpublished manuscript).

Kau, J, Keenan, D, Lyubimov, C, and Slawson, C (2012). Asymmetric information in the subprime mortgage market. *Journal of Real Estate Finance and Economics*, 44, 67–89.

Kawashima, K (2013). Asian bond market initiative (ABMI). Ministry of Finance, Japan, 5 April (unpublished manuscript).

Kim, WC and Wei, S-J (1999). Foreign portfolio investors before and during a crisis. OECD Working Paper No. 210, February.

Klein, M (2003). Capital account openness and the varieties of growth experience. NBER Working Paper No. 9500, February.

Klein, M and Olivei, G (2007). Capital account liberalization, financial depth and economic growth. *Journal of International Money and Finance*, 27, 861–875.

Lane, P (2012). The European sovereign debt crisis. *Journal of Economic Perspectives*, 26, 49–68.

Levinger, H and Li, C (2014). What's behind recent trends in Asian corporate bond markets? *Deutsche Bank Current Issues: Emerging Markets*, 31 January.

McKinnon, R (1973). *Money and Capital in Economic Development*. Washington, D.C.: Brookings Institution.

Nordvig, J (2014). Hidden debt in emerging markets. *Nomura FX Insights*, 23 March.

Rajan, R (2006). Has financial development made The world riskier? Proceedings of the 2005 Economic Policy Symposium at Jackson Hole, Federal Reserve Bank of Kansas City, 311–369.

Rajan, R and Zingales, L (2003). The great reversals: The politics of financial development in the twentieth century. *Journal of Financial Economics*, 69, 5–50.

Sahay, R, Čihák, M, N'Diaye, P, Barajas, A, Bi, R, Ayala, D, Gao, Y, Kyobe, A, Nguyen, L, Saborowski, C, Svirydzenka, K, and Yousefi, SR (2015). Rethinking financial deepening: Stability and growth in emerging markets. Staff Discussion Note 15/08, Washington, D.C.: IMF, May.

Shaw, E (1973). *Financial Deepening in Economic Development*. New York: Oxford University Press.

Sun, RR (2018). Requiem for the interest-rate controls in China. CFDS Discussion Paper No. 2018/4, Henan, China: Center for Financial Development and Stability, Henan University.

Tobin, J (1984). On the efficiency of the financial system. *Lloyds Bank Review*, 153, 1–15.

Wang, Y (2014). China's shadow banking sector valued at 80% of GDP. *Forbes*, 2 May. Available at: http://www.forbes.com/sites/ywang/2014/05/21/chinas-shadow-banking-valued-at-80-of-gdp/

Yu, YD (2013). China's capital account liberalization. Institute of World Economics and Politics, Chinese Academy of Social Sciences, October (unpublished manuscript).

# CHAPTER 4

# Chapter 4

# Currency Wars, Coordination, and Capital Controls*

Olivier Blanchard[1]

## Abstract

The strong monetary policy actions undertaken by advanced economies' central banks have led to complaints of "currency wars" by some emerging market economies, and to widespread demands for more macroeconomic policy coordination. This chapter revisits these issues. It concludes that, while advanced economies' monetary policies indeed have had substantial spillover effects on emerging market economies, there was and still is little room for coordination. It then argues that, from the viewpoints of both macro and financial stability, restrictions on capital flows were and are the more natural instrument to achieve a better outcome.

## Introduction

In September 2010, Guido Mantega, then minister of finance of Brazil, declared, "We are in the midst of an international currency war, a general weakening of currency. This threatens us because it takes away our competitiveness." His complaint was relayed and amplified by others, notably by Raghu Rajan, then governor of the Central Bank of India. In April 2014 for example, Rajan said, "The disregard for spillovers could put the global economy on a dangerous path of unconventional

* Prepared for the Asian Monetary Policy Forum, Singapore, May 2016. Thanks to Vivek Arora, Tam Bayoumi, Ricardo Caballero, Steve Cecchetti, Bill Cline, Xavier Gabaix, Taka Ito, Olivier Jeanne, Sebnem Kalemli-Ozcan for discussions and comments, and to Julien Acalin for outstanding research assistance

[1] C. Fred Bergsten Senior Fellow, Peterson Institute for International Economics.

monetary policy tit for tat. To ensure stable and sustainable economic growth, world leaders must re-examine the international rules of the monetary game, with advanced and emerging economies alike adopting more mutually beneficial monetary policies."

Complaints by emerging market economies about advanced economies' monetary policies, together with calls for coordination, have been a staple of the last seven years. The purpose of this paper is to examine the validity of these complaints and the scope for coordination. It reaches two conclusions. The scope for coordination was and is limited. Restrictions on capital flows were and are the more natural instrument to achieve a better outcome.

The chapter is organized as follows. Section 1 ("Cross-border Effects") briefly reviews the cross-border effects of advanced economies' monetary policies on emerging economies, through goods markets, foreign exchange markets, and financial markets. Section 2 ("The Scope for Coordination") examines the scope for coordination, and concludes that it was and still is rather limited. It argues that, given the limits on fiscal policy, restrictions on capital flows were and still are the appropriate macroeconomic instrument to achieve better outcomes, both in advanced economies and in emerging economies. Section 3 ("Monetary Policy, Capital Controls and FX Intervention") returns to the effects of capital flows on the financial systems in emerging economies, and argues for a second role for restrictions on capital flows, not only as a macroeconomic tool but also as a financial stability tool.

## Cross-border Effects

Expansionary monetary policy in advanced economies (AEs in what follows), conventional or unconventional, has affected emerging market economies (EMs in what follows) through three channels: increased exports, exchange rate appreciation, and the effects of capital flows on the financial system. The first two are fairly well understood; the crisis has led economists to looking at the third one more closely.[2]

---

[2] For a set of studies of the various cross-border effects, see the "Selected Issues" part of the 2011 IMF United States Spillover Report.

### *Expansionary AE monetary policy leads to a higher demand for EM exports*

This channel is straightforward: Lower interest rates lead to higher AE output, thus to higher AE imports, including higher imports from EMs. It is useful for later to get a sense of potential magnitudes: For most EMs, exports to AEs represent between 5% and 10% of their GDP.[3] For example, Chinese exports to the AEs are equal to 10% of Chinese GDP, Brazilian and Indian exports are equal to 5% of their respective GDPs.[4] Using these numbers suggests small effects of higher output in AEs: A 1% increase in AE output leads to an increase of 0.10% in Chinese output, and less than half that in the other two countries.

The relevant numbers are however higher. First, for any EM, higher AE output leads not only to a direct increase in exports to AEs, but to an indirect effect through higher induced output in other EM countries. Second, the elasticity of AE imports to GDP is higher than unity, reflecting the share of investment in imports, and the higher cyclicality of investment. Recent estimates suggest an elasticity between 1.5 and 2.0.[5]

Overall, this suggests that an increase in U.S. output of 1% may lead, through higher imports (at a given exchange rate), to an increase in output in China around 0.2%, and to a smaller number for most other emerging markets. Putting things together, and with all the proper caveats, if we assume that a 1% sustained decrease in the AE real policy rate — or the equivalent of a 1% decrease in the policy rate in the case QE is used to decrease long rates instead — leads to a 1% increase in AE output, this suggests effects ranging from 0.1% to 0.2% of GDP in EMs, with the size of the effect depending on the ratio of exports to AEs to GDP.

This heterogeneity in the size of the effects of AE growth on EMs is amplified through another related channel, namely the effect of AE

---

[3] Data from http://wits.worldbank.org/
[4] Given the relevance of supply chains, and the fact that higher exports mechanically imply higher imports, the numbers somewhat overstate the relevant numbers.
[5] For example, Bussière *et al.* 2020.

output on commodity prices. An increase in AE output increases the demand for commodities and therefore increases their price. This implies further heterogeneity of the effects on AE output on EMs. Net commodity exporters benefit more from an increase in U.S. output, commodity importers benefit less and possibly not at all.

### Expansionary AE monetary policy leads to EM exchange rate appreciation

This effect has been in evidence since the beginning of the crisis, although monetary policy has been only one of the factors moving exchange rates. The acute phase of the crisis was dominated by an increase in market risk aversion and by repatriations of funds by AE banks, leading to large capital outflows and depreciations of EM currencies despite a sharp decrease in AE policy rates. Thereafter, low interest rates in advanced economies led to a return of capital flows to EMs. Adjustments in policies, current or anticipated, have led to large exchange rate movements, among them the "taper tantrum" of 2013 when the Fed indicated that it would slow down its purchases of bonds, leading to large depreciations in a number of EMs.

EM policy makers have complained about the "unconventional" character of monetary policy in this context, but there is no reason to think that, with respect to exchange rate movements, unconventional monetary expansion works very differently from conventional monetary policy: To the extent that unconventional policy decreases spreads on domestic bonds, whatever their type or maturity, it makes them less attractive, and leads to depreciation.

Depreciation in turn leads to an increase in net exports. The argument has been made that exchange rate changes no longer improve the trade balance. The evidence suggests however that they still do. A recent International Monetary Fund (IMF) study concludes that the (appropriately modified to account for incomplete passthrough) Marshall-Lerner condition still holds: A real depreciation of 10% leads, on average, to an increase in real net exports over time of 1.5% of GDP, with a fairly wide range from 0.5% to 3.0% of GDP, reflecting in part the variation in export shares across AEs and EMs.[6]

Again, it is useful for later to do a back-of-the-envelope computation. Assuming that uncovered interest parity holds at least as an approximation, assuming that AE real interest rates are expected to be lower than EM interest rates by 1% for, say, 3 years, this implies an initial EM real appreciation of 3%. Putting this together with the previous numbers, and with all the proper caveats, the exchange rate channel suggests an average decrease in EM real net exports of 0.45% of GDP, with a range going from 0.15% to 0.9% of GDP, taking place over a number of years. For later reference, note that there is clearly more uncertainty about the strength of this second channel than about the first.

### Expansionary AE monetary policy affects EMs' financial systems

Perhaps the loudest complaints aimed at AE monetary policies have been those aimed at gross inflows, at the so-called "tsunamis of liquidity"[7] triggered by AE monetary policies, and their perceived adverse effects on EMs' financial stability.

The image of tsunamis of liquidity rushing into EM financial systems, is a very powerful one. It is however also a very misleading one. A decrease in the AE policy rate indeed leads AE investors to increase their demand for EM assets. Thus, at a given exchange rate, it indeed leads to an increase in gross inflows to EMs. In the absence of FX intervention, and on the assumption that net exports only adjust over time, these gross inflows must however be matched by equal gross outflows in order for the foreign exchange market to clear. Put another way, whatever "tsunami" of inflows is triggered by monetary policy must be matched by an equal tsunami of outflows: "Net tsunamis" must be equal to zero. This is achieved through

---

[6] IMF World Economic Outlook (2015, Chapter 3).
[7] I believe the expression was first used by Dilma Rousseff in 2012.

the decrease in the AE exchange rate — equivalently the appreciation of the EM currency.

This does not mean however that EM policy makers are wrong when they think that AE monetary policy affects their financial system. Empirical work, in particular by Helène Rey, suggests that U.S. monetary policy indeed has important and complex effects on other countries' financial systems.[8] Why might this be? It is fair to say that, despite a great deal of recent and on-going research, we do not yet have a good sense of the specific channels and of their relative importance. For this reason, I shall leave the effect of AE monetary policy on financial stability out of the model in the next section. I shall however return to the issue in Section 3, review what we know and do not know, and discuss potential implications.

## The Scope for Coordination

Do these cross-border effects, these spillovers, imply a scope for coordination, as the Rajan quote in the introduction suggests? The first step in exploring the answer is to define coordination more precisely, and here I want to take exception with some of the existing rhetoric:

Coordination is not about more communication. Surely, in the current environment, a better understanding of each other's macroeconomic policies can only help. Thus, G7 or G20 meetings and discussions are clearly desirable. This is however too unambitious a definition of coordination.

Coordination is not about asking some countries to modify their policies to help others, even if it is at their own expense. This is too ambitious a definition of coordination, and unlikely to ever happen. The argument that countries play repeated games, and thus may be willing to sacrifice in the short run in order to have others do the same in the future if and when needed, is unlikely to convince policy makers.

---

[8] For example, see Miranda-Agrippino and Rey (2015).

Coordination is not about asking policy makers to take into account "spillbacks", i.e. the effects of their policies on their country through their effects on other countries.[9] This may be the case if, for example, AE policies lead to major difficulties in EMs, which lead in turn to doubts about financial claims on EMs, which, finally, lead to financial problems for AE banks. Typically, these spillbacks are small, and, in any case, policy makers should take them into account. This does not qualify as coordination.

Coordination is not about asking policy makers to follow policies which they feel they cannot or simply do not want to adopt. I feel that this is part of what the "G20 map" process, which is the G20 version of coordination, does.[10] It suggests to countries that they should do more structural reforms, and appropriately modify monetary and fiscal policies. This may be the right advice, but if it is correct, countries should do much of it on their own, whether or not other countries do what is asked of them.

I shall instead take coordination to mean a set of changes in policies which makes all countries better off. More formally, I shall ask whether the decentralized equilibrium, which I shall take to be the Nash equilibrium, is efficient, or whether it can be improved upon.[11,12]

With this definition, the general answer is simple and well known: If countries have as many non-distorting instruments as they have targets, then the Nash equilibrium is efficient. Coordination cannot deliver a better outcome for all countries. A general discussion of whether countries have as many instruments as targets can get very abstract and sterile. One can think of targets as being the output gap,

---

[9] See for example Caruana (2016).

[10] See https://www.imf.org/external/np/exr/facts/g20map.htm for a description of the process, and the 2012 Umbrella Report for G-20 Mutual Assessment Process (http://www.imf.org/external/np/g20/pdf/062012.pdf) for more details.

[11] This is the standard academic definition and the one used for example by Jeff Frankel (2015) in the paper he presented last year at this Forum, called "International coordination". His paper touches on many of the same points I do.

[12] I leave aside the international provision of public goods, such as the provision of liquidity by the IMF or by central banks, the harmonisation of financial regulations, etc. These are obviously important, but are a very different form of coordination.

inflation, the exchange rate, financial stability, and instruments as being monetary policy, fiscal policy, macroprudential policy, FX intervention, capital controls. Simple counting of instruments and targets is unlikely to resolve the issue: Some of the policy instruments are likely to create distortions, so that they enter both as targets (minimizing the distortion) and as instruments. If all instruments are distortionary for example, then it follows that there will always be more targets than instruments and there will always be room for coordination to improve the outcome. But if the distortions are small, the gains from coordination may be limited. It is more useful to work through a simple formal model and show what this implies.

### A two-country Mundell Fleming model

For my purposes, let me start with a simple and old fashioned two-country Mundell-Fleming model. The model is old fashioned in two ways: First, it is static and not derived from micro foundations.[13] Given the logic behind the conclusions, I am confident that they would hold in a more micro-founded and more general model. Second, it leaves out the third channel discussed earlier, the effects of AE monetary policy on EM financial stability. The reason is that I feel we/I do not know how to best extend the model to capture these effects. Thus, I leave this extension to an informal discussion in the next section.

The model has two (blocks of) countries, a domestic economy (as a stand in for advanced economies) and a foreign economy (as a stand in for emerging market economies). Foreign variables are denoted by a star. Domestic output is given by:

$$Y = A + NX$$

$$A = G - cR + X$$

$$NX = a(Y^* - Y) - bE$$

---

[13] For a treatment of the scope for coordination in a micro founded model, see Obstfeld and Rogoff (2002).

Domestic output, $Y$ is equal to the sum of absorption, $A$, and net exports, $NX$. Absorption depends on fiscal policy, summarized by $G$, on the monetary policy rate, $R$, and on a shock to domestic demand, $X$. Net exports depend positively on foreign output, $Y^*$, negatively on domestic output, $Y$, and negatively on the real exchange rate, $E$.

Symmetrically, foreign output is given by:

$$Y^* = A^* - NX$$

$$A^* = G^* - cR^* + X^*$$

$$NX = a(Y^* - Y) - bE$$

Finally, following UIP, the exchange rate depends on the difference between the domestic and the foreign policy rates. Under the UIP interpretation, the coefficient $d$ measures the expected persistence of the interest differential:

$$E = d(R - R^*)$$

A decrease in the domestic policy rate over the foreign policy rate leads to a depreciation of the domestic currency — equivalently to an appreciation of the foreign currency. Absent shocks, $G$, $G^*$, $X$, $X^*$ are normalized to zero. Equilibrium output in the absence of shocks, which I take to be potential output, is equal to zero. So are net exports, interest rates and the exchange rate.

Each country cares about the deviation of output from potential and about the deviation of net exports from zero.

$$\Omega = \min Y^2 + \alpha\, NX^2$$

$$\Omega^* = \min Y^{*2} + \beta\, NX^2$$

Note, in relation to the previous discussion, that neither monetary nor fiscal policies are assumed to affect output in the way characterized above, and not to create additional distortions.

To start with, assume that each country can use both fiscal and monetary policy. As they are two targets and two non-distorting instruments in each country, the theorem applies: The Nash equilibrium is efficient, and there is no room for coordination. Suppose we capture what has happened during the crisis by assuming that, starting from steady state in both countries — so all variables are equal to zero — the domestic economy is hit by an adverse demand shock, so $X < 0$. Then, the Nash equilibrium is trivially characterized: The domestic economy uses fiscal policy, $G = -X$ to offset the shock, and the foreign economy does not need to change either $G^*$ or $R^*$.[14]

One may worry about the fact that, in the model and clearly counterfactually, the two countries have the tools to completely offset the shock, and can return to the pre-shock equilibrium. This is not essential. The shock may be (and indeed was) a more complex one, affecting for example the supply side, so that the countries want to return to a different equilibrium after the shock. And the model is easily extended to limit the ability of policy to offset the shocks. If for example, decisions about fiscal and monetary policy are taken before $X$ is fully revealed, the economies will be affected by the shock, but the efficiency of the Nash equilibrium will remain. Coordination cannot improve the outcome.

### Coordination when fiscal policy cannot be used

Why does the above result feel too strong? Probably because the potential role attributed to fiscal policy is too optimistic. Policy makers may/do care about the fiscal balance, in which case, formally, there are now three targets and only two instruments. Related, and more relevant at this point, given the large increase in debt associated with the crisis, are the perceived limits on the current use of fiscal policy. Indeed, a recurring

---

[14] Actually, the equilibrium set of policies is not unique. One can verify that any equilibrium where $R$ and $R^*$ move together, implying no change in the exchange rate, and $G$ and $G^*$ adjust so as to maintain demand constant in each country is efficient. But this is a curiosity.

theme of policy discussions has been the extreme reliance on monetary policy due to the sharp limits on the use of fiscal policy.

What happens if we assume that fiscal policy cannot be used, so that $G = G^* = 0$?[15] In this case, each country has two targets and only one instrument. The Nash equilibrium is inefficient, and there is a set of policies which improve welfare in both countries.

The set of utilities which can be achieved through coordination is obtained by maximizing a weighted average of the two countries' welfare functions, $\Omega + \lambda \Omega^*$ for different values of $\lambda$. Figure 1 plots the Nash equilibrium, $A$, and the utility frontier for a given set of parameters (the qualitative feature of the figure does not depend on the specific set of parameters.) All the points to the southwest of $A$ yield higher welfare for both countries.[16]

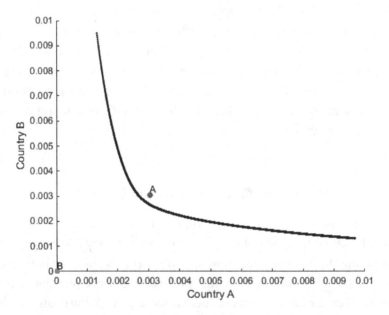

**Figure 1.** AE and EM welfare under Nash and Doordination

---

[15] Equivalently, we could assume that fiscal policy can be used, but that it creates distortions, with these distortions entering the objective function. This would lead to a more limited role for fiscal policy, and the essence of the results below would go through.
[16] Given that we are minimizing a loss function, the closer to the origin, the better.

The improvement in welfare is small, and this conclusion is consistent with the literature, starting with Oudiz *et al.* (1984). Given however the simplicity of the model and the lack of a serious calibration, this conclusion should not be given too much weight. More important is the question of what form coordination should take. Should coordination lead AEs to adopt a more or a less aggressive monetary policy?

The answer turns out to depend on the sign of $(ac - bd)$. This expression has a simple interpretation. The first term, $ac$, reflects the strength of the first channel (higher AE output, leading to a stronger demand for EM exports) above, with $c$ measuring the effect of the policy rate on domestic demand, and $a$ measuring the share of imports. The second term, $bd$ reflects the strength of the second channel (EM appreciation, leading to a decrease demand for EM exports), with $d$ measuring the effect of the policy rate on the exchange rate, and $b$ measuring the effect of the exchange rate on net exports.

When the first channel dominates the second, the net effect of a decrease in the domestic policy rate is to increase foreign net exports and foreign output. The coordination equilibria (I use "equilibria" as there is a (small) range of equilibria which dominate the Nash equilibrium, namely all the points to the southwest of A) are associated with a stronger response of the domestic policy rate, a weaker response of the foreign policy rate than under Nash. When the second channel dominates the first however, the coordination equilibria are associated with a weaker response of the domestic policy rate, a stronger response of the foreign rate.

Table 1 shows the outcomes for two sets of parameters. The shock is taken to be a decrease in domestic demand, $X$ by 1, while $X^*$ is unchanged. The parameters $a$, $b$, $c$ and $d$ are the same in both cases, and equal

**Table 1.** Policy rates under Nash and Coordination

| $a$ | $b$ | $R$ (Nash) | $R^*$ (Nash) | $\lambda$ | $R$ (Coord) | $R^*$ (coord) |
|-----|-----|-----------|-------------|-----------|------------|--------------|
| .4 | 0.2 | −.868 | −.131 | 1 | −.882 | −.117 |
| .2 | 0.4 | −.767 | −.230 | 1 | −.759 | −.241 |

respectively to 0.5, 0.5, 1.0 and 1.0. The two lines differ in the values of $a$ and $b$ (and thus the implied value of $ac - bd$, which is positive in the first case, negative in the second).

The coordinated equilibria which dominate the Nash equilibrium all have very similar interest rates, so we can just look at one of them. The table reports the Nash equilibrium domestic and foreign interest rates, and those associated with one of the dominating coordinated equilibria, the equilibrium associated with $\lambda = 1$. In the first case, the first channel dominates, and coordination yields a stronger response of the domestic rate, −88.2 bps compared to −86.8 bps. In the second case, the second channel dominates, and coordination yields a weaker response, −75.9 bps compared to −76.7 bps.[17]

These results point to the practical problem in achieving coordination in this context, namely whether we know which way the inequality goes. The history of the last seven years is one of major disagreements about the strength of the two effects, and by implication, disagreements about what coordination should achieve.

To go back to the quotes at the beginning, both Guido Mantega and Raghu Rajan emphasized the second channel, the effect on AE monetary policy on the exchange rate. To again quote Rajan: "Rather the mandates of systemically influential central banks should be expanded to account for spillovers, forcing policy makers to avoid unconventional measures with substantial adverse effects on other economies, particularly if the domestic benefits are questionable". In terms of our model, Rajan had in mind a small effect of the policy rate on domestic demand, a small value for $c$. In the limit where $c$ tends to zero, this is indeed a zero sum game between the two countries, and coordination should lead to smaller policy rate cuts. Thus, the use of the term "currency wars".

Advanced economy policy makers, on the other hand, have emphasized the first channel. Strong AE growth, they have argued, is

---

[17] The differences between the rates under Nash and coordination are small, but again, the calibration is too crude for this aspect to be given too much weight.

essential for the world in general, and for EMs in particular. In terms of the model, they have emphasized the importance of $a$, the effect of AE output on AE imports. In his 2015 Mundell Fleming lecture, which deals very much with the same topics as this paper, Ben Bernanke (2017) argued, "U.S. growth during the recent recovery has certainly not been driven by exports, and, as I will explain, the "expenditure-augmenting" effects of U.S. monetary policies (adding to global aggregate demand) tend to offset the "expenditure-switching" effects (adding to demand in one country at the expense of others).

Who is right? The back of the envelope computations given in Section 1 suggest that it is hard to assess which way the inequality works. Simulations using IMF models and reported in IMF spillover reports suggest that monetary expansion in AEs was on net good for emerging economies. Such a simulation is reported in Table 2. It shows the dynamic effects of an AE monetary expansion in response to a decrease in domestic demand in AEs, on both AE and EM output, from year 1 to 6.[18] In that simulation, the net effects on EMs are small, but positive.

While such a simulation is much more sophisticated than the simple computations in Section 1, it still comes with many caveats. In particular, it comes with large differences across EMs. EM countries with strong trade links to AEs, such as China, may indeed be better off, and be in favor of more AE expansion. EM countries with weaker links to AEs, such as Brazil or India, may be worse off, and want less AE expansion; this may explain why Brazil and India may have been among the most vocal critics of AE policy. In short, given the diverging views, coordination means something different for AE and EM policy makers, so it is unlikely to happen.

**Table 2.**  Effects of an AE monetary expansion on AEs and EMs

| Year | 1 | 2 | 3 | 4 | 5 | 6 |
|------|------|------|------|------|------|------|
| Advanced Economies | 1.00 | 1.60 | 1.38 | 0.94 | 0.61 | 0.39 |
| Emerging Economies | 0.17 | 0.39 | 0.39 | 0.33 | 0.28 | 0.22 |

---

[18] The table shows the difference between output with monetary expansion and output without monetary expansion. Courtesy of the IMF modelling team.

### A deus ex machina? Capital controls

If, because of limits on fiscal policy, the Nash equilibrium is inefficient and the room for coordination is limited, can policy makers improve on the Nash outcome? The short answer is yes, if they are willing to use an additional instrument, restrictions on capital flows, capital controls.[19]

The logic for why capital controls are useful in this context is straightforward. Advanced economies suffer from a lack of domestic demand. As we saw earlier, if they could freely use fiscal policy, they could just offset the decrease in domestic demand through a fiscal expansion. This would return both countries to the pre-shock equilibrium levels of output and exchange rate. If fiscal policy is not available, they must use monetary policy. Monetary policy however not only increases domestic demand but also affects the exchange rate through interest differentials. Capital controls can, at least within the logic of the model, eliminate the effect of the interest differential on the exchange rate.

This argument can be formalized as follows. Extend the equation for the exchange rate to:

$$E = d(R - (R^* - x))$$

where $x$ may be interpreted as a tax per unit on foreign inflows (such as has been used in Chile, or more recently in Brazil). Assume, as above, that fiscal policy cannot be used, that AEs can use monetary policy, and EMs can use monetary policy $R$ and the tax $x$. Assume again that the shock is a decrease in $X$ by 1.

Then the Nash equilibrium takes a simple form. AEs decrease the policy rate $R$ by $1/c$. EMs increase $x$ by $1/c$, leaving the exchange rate unchanged. AE output and net exports return to their pre-shock level

---

[19] Many economists have questioned whether fiscal policy is really not available. They have argued that, even at the currently high debt levels, there may be room for fiscal expansion. I leave this debate aside. All I need for the argument made here is that there are some limits on the use of fiscal expansion.

(zero, by normalization). In terms of Figure 1, the two countries achieve the point at the origin, a large improvement relative to the Nash or the coordinated equilibrium absent controls. Not only do EMs protect themselves, but AEs also benefit from being able to use monetary policy without having to worry about the exchange rate.

In short, (varying) capital controls are the logical macroeconomic instrument to use when fiscal policy is not available. It reduces the problems associated with an increased reliance on monetary accommodation. Such an endorsement of capital controls comes with many caveats. Before listing them, I turn to the case for capital controls as a financial instrument.

## Monetary Policy, Capital Controls and FX Intervention

In the previous section, I left aside the third channel, i.e. the potential effects of AE monetary policy on gross inflows into EMs and on the EM financial system. But, as I discussed earlier, many of the EM complaints have been aimed precisely at those gross inflows and their perceived adverse effects on financial stability.

How does AE monetary policy affect gross flows to EMs and the EM financial system? Despite a lot of recent work, the answers are less clear than one would like, on both theoretical and empirical grounds.

### Gross flows and AE monetary policy. Theoretical considerations

Return to the "tsunami" argument briefly discussed in Section 1. Does expansionary AE monetary policy trigger larger gross flows to EMs? Simple arithmetic will again help here. Assume that gross inflows into EMs and gross outflows from EMs are given by:

$$FI = \alpha + \beta(d(R^* - R - z) + E)$$

$$FO = \alpha^* - \beta^*(d(R^* - R - \gamma z + E)$$

Equilibrium in the foreign exchange market is given by:

$$FI = FO + FX$$

where $FX$ is foreign exchange intervention, and the current account is assumed not to change in the short run so I ignore it here.[20]

Both inflows and outflows are now assumed to be less than fully elastic with respect to expected returns. Both $\alpha$ and $\alpha^*$, and $\beta$ and $\beta^*$ are allowed to differ, reflecting potentially different preferences and types of AE and EM investors.

The variable $z$ shifts inflows and outflows; it can be thought of as reflecting a risk premium, reflecting the convolution of perceptions of risk and risk aversion; its effect may be different for AE and EM investors, and this is captured by the presence of coefficient $\gamma$. For example, "risk off" may lead AE investors to become more risk averse, while having less of an effect on EM investors, in which case $\gamma < 1$.

Note that as $\beta$ and $\beta^*$ go to infinity, and $z$ is equal to zero, the equilibrium tends to the uncovered interest parity condition $E = d(R - R^*)$.

Suppose now that the AE central bank decreases its policy rate $R$ by $\Delta R < 0$, that the EM central bank does not adjust its policy rate, so $\Delta R^* = 0$, and does not intervene, so $FX = 0$. Solving for the equilibrium gives:

$$\Delta E = d\Delta R \ \ and \ \ \Delta FI = \Delta FO = 0$$

In words, the exchange rate adjusts so as to keep expected relative returns the same, just as under the UIP condition, and the decrease in the exchange rate leads to unchanged gross inflows (and outflows). This

---

[20] This assumption is surely correct over short periods of time, such as the minute or the day. Over time, net exports will adjust in response to the movement in the exchange rate, and the equation should be modified to include $NX$. The conclusions below — namely that, in the short run, changes in gross inflows have to be matched by changes in gross outflows — would still apply.

is true despite less than fully elastic flows, different preferences of AE and EM investors, and possibly different risk premia.[21]

How can the result of unchanged gross flows be overturned? In one of two ways: Demands for domestic and foreign investors differ in more fundamental ways than introduced here. I do not however have a sense of what plausible deviations to introduce.

Or monetary policy works partly through its effects on the risk premium. Suppose for example that lower AE rates decrease the risk premium $z$ by $\Delta z$. Then:

$$\Delta E = d \; \frac{\beta + \beta^* \gamma}{\beta + \beta^*} \; \Delta z$$

$$\Delta FI = \Delta FO = d \; \frac{\beta^* (\gamma - 1)}{\beta + \beta^*} \; \Delta z$$

If $\gamma$ is less than one, that is if EM investors are less sensitive to $z$ than AE investors, then the exchange rate appreciation is more limited, and gross inflows and outflows increase. Thus, if a decrease in the policy rate is associated with a decrease in the risk premium, and if $\gamma < 1$, then a monetary expansion is associated with higher gross flows.

This line of explanation suggests a complex relation between monetary policy — conventional or unconventional — and gross flows. For example, QE1 may have reassured AE investors that U.S. markets would be less dysfunctional, leading to a return of AE investors to the U.S., and a decrease in gross flows to EMs. In contrast, QE2 may have had little effect on perceived risk, and led AE investors to increase gross flows to EMs. The taper tantrum may have led to a decrease in gross flows to EMs not so much by tightening future U.S. monetary conditions but rather by increasing uncertainty about the course of future U.S. monetary policy.

---

[21] This remains true even if $R^*$ adjusts. The adjustment has an effect on the exchange rate, not on the gross flows.

### Gross flows and AE monetary policy. Empirical evidence

Despite a large number of empirical studies, the evidence on the effects of AE monetary policy on gross flows is also unclear. The empirical difficulties are many, from the usual difficulty of identifying monetary policy shocks, compounded since the crisis by the zero bound and the lack of movement in the policy rate, to the use of unconventional instruments, to the issue of separating out expected and unexpected monetary policy actions, to quality or coverage issues with the flow data.

A number of studies have found an effect of monetary policy on specific gross flows.[22] Bruno and Shin (2015) for example, using a VAR methodology over the pre-crisis period (1995:4 to 2007:4), find an effect of the federal funds rate on cross-border bank to bank flows; the effect is however barely significant. Fratzscher *et al.* (2018), using daily data on portfolio equity and bond flows, find significant effects of different monetary policy announcements and actions since the beginning of the crisis.[23] Their results however point to the complexity of the effects of apparently largely similar monetary measures. For example, they find QE1 announcements decreased bond flows to EMs, while QE2 announcements increased them. In terms of the equations above, this indeed suggests that, in each case, monetary policy worked partly through its effects on the risk premium.

These studies cannot settle however the issue of whether total gross inflows increase with AE monetary expansions: The increase in the inflows the researchers have identified may be offset by a decrease in other inflows. Studies of total inflows, or of the set of inflows adding up to total inflows, yield mixed conclusions. A representative and careful paper, by Cerutti *et al.* (2019), using quarterly flows over 2001:2 to 2013:2, suggests two main conclusions. The most significant observable variable in explaining flows into EMs is the VIX index: An increase in the VIX leads to a decrease in inflows to EMs. The coefficients on the monetary

---

[22] For obvious reasons, I ignore the studies which look at the effects of policy on net flows.

[23] See also Koepke (2018).

policy variables, namely the expected change in the policy rate and the slope of the yield curve, typically have the expected sign, but are rarely significant. Together, these two variables explain only a small part of overall variations in capital flows.

Thus, on both theoretical and empirical grounds, the relation of monetary policy to gross inflows into EMs is less clear than is often believed by policy makers and even by researchers.[24]

### Gross inflows and EM financial systems. Other channels?

Leaving aside the effects if any on the volume of gross flows, how may AE monetary policy affect the EM financial systems? One can think of two channels:

The first channel, which the Asian crisis put in evidence, is through the effect of the exchange rate itself on the financial system. To the extent that financial institutions, the government, firms, or households, have FX-denominated claims and liabilities, the appreciation triggered by AE monetary policy will affect their balance sheets. Even if financial institutions are largely hedged, unhedged positions by the others will affect the value of their claims, and affect financial stability. The effects on financial stability are likely to vary in magnitude, and even in sign, across countries, depending on the structure of FX claims. In general, given that most EM countries still borrow largely in foreign currency, the effect of an appreciation triggered by AE monetary policy, should be favorable. The exact structure of claims and liabilities will however matter.

The second channel is through changes in the composition of gross inflows and outflows triggered by AE monetary policy. If for example foreign investors increase their holdings of sovereign bonds and domestic

---

[24] This suggests that statements like "The empirical literature has long established that U.S. interest rates are an important driver of international portfolio flows, with lower rates "pushing" capital to emerging markets" (Koepke 2018) are too strong. To be clear, the issue is not whether they affect exchange rates — they do — but whether they lead to large increases in gross flows — which is less settled.

investors decrease theirs, then the effects on the financial system are likely to be limited. If instead, inflows take the form of additional funds to domestic banks, and outflows come from a decrease in holdings of sovereign bonds, then this is likely to lead to an increase in domestic credit supply. Depending on its nature and intensity, this increase may be desirable, or instead lead to an unhealthy credit boom.

It is clear for example that, at the beginning of the crisis, the repatriation of funds by AE banks had such a composition effect. The decrease in funding in EM banks by AE banks was not compensated by an increase in funding of EM banks by EM investors, leading to a tightening of credit. The issue at hand is however about the effects of monetary policy per se. Just as for the effect of AE monetary policy on overall gross flows, the evidence on the composition of the flows triggered by AE monetary policy is not clear. In Cerutti *et al.* (2019), for example, there is no clear difference between the estimated effects of monetary policy variables on bank, portfolio debt and portfolio equity flows.

Thus, overall, it is difficult to conclude that AE monetary policy has had major, predictable, effects on EM financial systems. Nevertheless, it is a clearly a potentially important dimension that EM policy makers must monitor. This takes us back to the issue of capital controls, now in the context of financial stability.

### Capital controls versus FX intervention

While the use of capital controls has been limited, many countries have relied on FX intervention to limit the movements in exchange rate caused by AE monetary policy. From the point of view of the previous section, i.e. leaving implications for gross inflows aside, controls and FX intervention are largely substitutes. Under the assumption that the elasticity of flows to return differentials is finite — a necessary condition for FX intervention to have an effect — both can limit the effects of lower AE interest rates on the exchange rate, and achieve the same macroeconomic outcome. If however, we take into account the third channel discussed in this section, the two have very different implications. Capital controls, by assumption, can limit gross inflows. FX intervention, by limiting the exchange rate adjustment, increases gross inflows. This can be seen straightforwardly from above. If, in response to a decrease in the AE policy rate, FX intervention keeps the exchange rate unchanged, gross flows increase by

$$\Delta FI = -bd\Delta R > 0$$

Thus, if the purpose is to limit the effects of AE monetary policy on the EM financial system, capital controls dominate FX intervention.

## Conclusions

I have looked at the interactions between AE and EM macro policies since the beginning of the crisis, interactions characterized by complaints of "currency wars" and demands for more coordination. I have offered three main sets of conclusions.

In AEs, limits on fiscal policy have led since the beginning of the crisis to an over reliance on monetary policy. This potentially opens the scope for coordination. Whether coordination would entail an increase or a decrease in interest rates in AEs is however difficult to assess, with AEs and EMs disagreeing about the sign. This has made and still makes coordination de facto impossible to achieve.

If there are limits on the use of fiscal policy, leading to the overreliance on monetary policy and undesirable effects on the exchange rate, the natural instrument in this context is the use of capital controls by EMs. It allows AEs to use monetary policy to increase domestic demand, while shielding EMs from the undesirable exchange rate effects. In the context of limits on fiscal policy, controls are a natural macroeconomic instrument. Given the high levels of debt in many countries, this is likely to remain the case for some time to come.

Despite some progress, how AE monetary policy affects EM financial systems remains largely to be understood, both theoretically and empirically. To the extent that AE monetary policy leads to gross inflows into EMs, to the extent that these gross flows affect the EM financial systems, and to the extent that EMs want to avoid these effects, capital controls rather than FX intervention are the right instrument.

These conclusions come with the usual and strong caveats. Technical and political issues associated with the use of capital controls as contingent instruments are still relevant. This is not an unconditional endorsement of controls, but an exploration and a starting point to a discussion.

## References

Bernanke, B (2017). Federal reserve policy in an international context. *IMF Economic Review*, 65(1), 1–32.

Bruno, V and Shin, HS (2015). Capital flows and the risk-taking channel of monetary policy. *Journal of Monetary Economics*, 71, 119–132.

Bussière, M, Gaulier, G, and Steingress, W (2020). Global trade flows: Revisiting the exchange rate elasticities. *Open Economies Review*, 31(1), 1–54.

Caruana, J (2016). The international monetary and financial system: Eliminating the blind spot. In O Blanchard, R Rajan, K Rogoff and LH Summers (Eds.), *Progress and Confusion: The State of Macroeconomic Policy* (pp. 245–254), Cambridge, MA: IMF and MIT Press.

Cerutti, E, Claessens, S, and Puy, D (2019). Push factors and capital flows to emerging markets: Why knowing your lender matters more than fundamentals. *Journal of International Economics*, 119, 133–149.

Frankel, J (2015). International coordination. NBER Working Paper No. 21878.

Fratzscher, M, Lo Duca, M, and Straub, R (2018). On the international spillovers of U.S. quantitative easing. *The Economic Journal*, 128(608), 330–377.

IMF (2011). United States spillover report, July.

IMF (2015). World economic outlook, exchange rates and trade flows: Disconnected? October, Chapter 3.

Koepke, R (2018). Fed policy expectations and portfolio flows to emerging markets. *Journal of International Financial Markets, Institutions and Money*, 55, 170–194.

Mantega, G (2010). Brazil in 'currency war" alert. *Financial Times*, 27 September.

Miranda-Agrippino, S and Rey, H (2015). World asset markets and the global financial cycle. CEPR Discussion Paper No. DP10936.

Obstfeld, M and Rogoff, K (2002). Global implications of self-oriented national monetary rules. *The Quarterly Journal of Economics*, 117(2), 503–535.

Oudiz, G, Sachs, J, Blanchard, OJ, Marris, SN, and Woo, WT (1984). Macroeconomic policy coordination among the industrial economies. *Brookings Papers on Economic Activity*, 1984(1), 1–75.

Rajan, R (2014). Containing competitive monetary easing. *Project Syndicate*, 28 April.

# CHAPTER 5

# Chapter 5

# Systematic Managed Floating[*]

Jeffrey Frankel[1]

## Abstract

A majority of countries neither freely float their currencies nor firmly peg. But most of the remainder in practice also don't obey such
well-defined intermediate exchange rate regimes as target zones. This
paper proposes to define an intermediate regime, to be called "systematic managed floating," as an arrangement where the central bank
regularly responds to changes in total exchange market pressure by
allowing some fraction to be reflected as a change in the exchange
rate and the remaining fraction to be absorbed as a change in foreign exchange reserves. An operational criterion for judging systematic managed floaters is a high correlation between exchange rate
changes and reserve changes. The paper rejects the view that exchange
rate regimes make no difference. In regressions to test effects on real
exchange rates, we find that positive external shocks tend to cause real
appreciation for most systematic managed-floaters; more strongly so
for pure floaters; and not at all for most firm peggers. Two measures
of exogenous external shocks are used: (i) for commodity-exporters,
a country-specific index of global prices of the export commodities
and (ii) for other Asian emerging market economies, the VIX.

---

[*] The paper was originally presented at the 4th Asian Monetary Policy Forum, Singapore,
26 May, 2017, organized under the auspices of the Asian Bureau of Finance and Eco-
nomic Research (ABFER), with support from the University of Chicago Booth School
of Business, the National University of Singapore Business School and the Monetary
Authority of Singapore (MAS). The author would like to thank Shruti Lakhtakia and
Tilahun Emiru for assiduous research assistance, Andrew Rose and Sebnem Kalemli-
Ozcan for useful discussion, and Rose and Assaf Razin for discussant comments at the
AMPF conference. Tables 2.1-2.4 draw on new joint research with Danxia Xie. Revised
January 20, 2019.
[1] James W. Harpel Professor of Capital Formation and Growth, Harvard University

## Introduction

According to textbook theory, when countries choose their exchange rate regime they are choosing the extent to which they will be able to run an independent monetary policy despite external shocks. On the one hand, a firmly fixed exchange rate gives up the ability to set an independent monetary policy, unless capital controls or other impediments are used to break the link between domestic and foreign interest rates. On the other hand, a free-floating exchange rate maximizes insulation of the domestic real economy: an adverse foreign shock causes a nominal and real depreciation of the domestic currency, which works to moderate what would otherwise be negative real effects on the domestic trade balance, output and employment. In response to a positive foreign shock, currency appreciation dampens its real effects as well.

There are also intermediate regimes that lie at various points along the spectrum between fixed and floating exchange rates. These intermediate regimes include managed floats, bands, basket pegs, crawls, and other arrangements.[2] The argument for the intermediate regimes is that they allow an intermediate degree of monetary independence in return for an intermediate degree of exchange rate flexibility.

The contribution of this paper is to suggest that there exists another intermediate exchange rate regime: the systematically managed float. To operationalize the classification of currency arrangement as a systematically managed float, Part 2(b) ("Identifying countries that are systematic managed floaters") of the paper identifies it simply by the statistical condition that there is a high positive correlation between the change in foreign exchange reserves and the change in the foreign exchange value of the currency. Part (3) ("Effects of external shocks") examines whether choosing a systematically managed float makes a difference.

To illustrate, consider the history of Emerging Market economies (EMs) since the turn of the century. As an aggregate class they have,

---

[2] E.g., for Asia: Williamson (2001), Ito (2001), and Frankel (2003).

broadly speaking, experienced four periods of big alternating shifts in the external environment for their balance of payments. In the first period from 2003 to mid-2008, the external environment was positive, as U.S. monetary policy was easy, commodity prices were rising, and international investors were not especially concerned about risk as they reached for any EM returns that were even a little higher than those on offer in the advanced countries. The second period was the Global Financial Crisis (GFC) that began in mid-2008 and eased a year later. This was a negative shock for EM economies: risk perceptions leapt and commodity prices plummeted. The third period, in 2010–2011, was essentially a repeat of the first, with a favorable financial environment and a recovery in commodity prices leading to substantial EM inflows. Fourth was the period that began with the Taper Tantrum of May 2013 and continued at least through 2018: an end to the period of U.S. monetary ease and a new fall in commodity prices led to EM outflows.

Central banks in different EM countries responded differently to these external shocks. Figure 1 (adapted from Goldman Sachs) shows responses of Asian central banks to the positive shock of 2010. Reserve accumulation is on the vertical axis and currency appreciation on the horizontal axis. On the one hand, Korea and Singapore appear as relatively more-managed floaters, intervening in the foreign exchange market somewhat more and appreciating less. On the other hand, India, Malaysia, Thailand and the Philippines, took the positive shock mostly in the form of increases in the value of their currencies and not primarily as increased reserves.

Figure 2 shows responses to the "taper tantrum" of May–August 2013, when Federal Reserve Chairman Ben Bernanke announced the intention to begin phasing down U.S. quantitative easing by the end of the year, which produced an immediate rise in U.S. interest rates and a reversal of EM capital flows. Again, Singapore mostly intervened while India and the Philippines mostly took the adverse shock as a change in the exchange rate, that is, a depreciation.

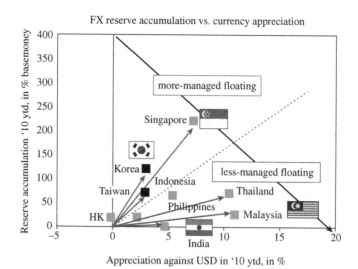

**Figure 1.**  Reactions of Asian central banks to 2010 inflows

*Data*: Haver Analytics and Bloomberg.

*Source*: GS Global ECS Research 10/13/2010.

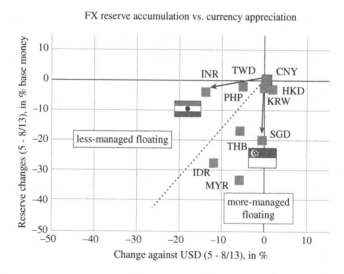

**Figure 2.**  Reactions of central banks to outflows of May–August, 2013, taper tantrum

*Source*: Goldman Sachs Global Investment Research.

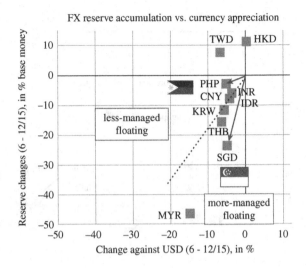

**Figure 3.** Reactions of central banks to outflows of June–December, 2015, China tantrum

*Source*: Goldman Sachs Global Investment Research.

Finally, Figure 3 shows responses to the "China tantrum" of the second half of 2015. Once again, Singapore intervened in the foreign exchange market, while the Philippines took the negative shock more in the form of a depreciation of its currency.

These are just three episodes. But they illustrate how some countries choose to manage their floats more heavily and others less.

One supposes that the countries that allowed greater movements in their nominal exchange rates in response to these positive and negative external shocks also achieved greater movements in their real exchange rates and may have done so with the intention of mitigating the effects of the shocks on their balance of payments and real economies. Hong Kong in this sample is the one economy that is committed to intervening heavily enough to keep its exchange rate fixed against the dollar, and is willing to give up its monetary independence for the other advantages that this stability brings (reducing costs to international trade and investment and providing a credible anchor for monetary policy). So far, so consistent with the conventional textbook framework.

But the textbook framework has been challenged. The paper reviews the challenges in Part 1 ("Four challenges to the conventional wisdom"). Part 2 ("What countries actually do") reviews some of the problems with identifying what exchange rate regime a country follows in practice and offers some evidence on a set of Asian and other currencies. Part 3 ("Effects of external shocks") seeks to determine whether the regime makes a difference for the real exchange rate. The focus is on three regimes: firm fixing, free floating and, especially, systematically managed floating.

### Four challenges to the conventional wisdom

The conventional wisdom about the role of regime choices has been assaulted from several directions. Many of the assaults fall under four rubrics: (a) "the corners hypothesis," (b) "dilemma vs. trilemma," (c) "intervention ineffectiveness" and (d) "exchange rate disconnect." We review these four challenges, as a prelude for defending the conventional view.

a.   The corners hypothesis
Sometimes known as the vanishing intermediate regime, the corners hypothesis is the claim that in a modern world of high capital mobility, the intermediate regimes are no longer viable. Countries are forced to choose between free floating, on the one hand, and hard pegs on the other hand. Hard pegs are exchange rates that are firmly fixed through such institutions as currency boards, official dollarization or monetary union.

What are the origins of the corners hypothesis? A precursor is Friedman (1953, p.164): "In short, the system of occasional changes in temporarily rigid exchange rates seems to me the worst of two worlds: it provides neither the stability of expectations that a genuinely rigid and stable exchange rate could provide in a world of unrestricted trade…nor the continuous sensitivity of a flexible exchange rate."

Such intermediate regimes as target zones or bands became popular in the 1980s. The earliest known reference rejecting them in favor of the firm-fixing and free-floating corners is by Eichengreen (1994). The context was not emerging markets, but rather the European exchange rate mechanism (ERM). In the ERM crisis of 1992–1993, Italy, the United Kingdom, and others were forced to devalue or drop out altogether, and the bands were subsequently widened substantially so that France could stay in. This crisis suggested to some that the strategy that had been planned previously — a gradual transition to the euro, where the width of the target zone was narrowed in a few steps — might not be the best way to proceed after all. Crockett (1994) made the same point. Obstfeld and Rogoff (1995) concluded, "A careful examination of the genesis of speculative attacks suggests that even broad-band systems in the current EMS style pose difficulties, and that there is little, if any, comfortable middle ground between floating rates and the adoption by countries of a common currency." The lesson that "the best way to cross a chasm is in a single jump" was seemingly borne out subsequently, when the leap from wide bands to the new single currency proved successful in 1998–1999.

In the aftermath of the East Asia crises of 1997–1998, the hypothesis was applied to emerging markets and was rapidly adopted by the financial establishment as the new conventional wisdom. Four prominent examples were Council on Foreign Relations (1999), Fischer (2001), Summers (1999), and Meltzer (2000).[3]

But there never was a good theoretical rationale for the corners hypothesis and recent empirical results have re-asserted the viability of intermediate regimes.

On the theoretical side, nothing has changed the traditional logic that intermediate exchange rate regimes deliver an intermediate degree of insulation from foreign shocks in return for an intermediate degree of nominal exchange rate stability. One example of such an intermediate regime is the band, which was well-modeled in the target zone literature

---

[3] Ghosh, Ostry, and Qureshi (2015) offer a more recent empirical evaluation.

initiated by Krugman (1991). Another example is the adjustable peg, which can be modeled as an escape clause invoked in the event of a sufficiently big shock, as modeled by Obstfeld (1997).

Or consider a systematically managed float: If the central bank responds to potentially large inflows by intervening in the foreign exchange market to buy up half of the increased supply of foreign exchange, allowing the other half of the shock to show up as an increase in the value of its currency, then it gets half of the exchange rate stability and half of the impact of the shocks. (It is perhaps surprising that the systematic management has seldom been formalized before now.) These are all counter-examples to the corners hypothesis.

Beyond the normative question as to whether intermediate regimes are advisable is the evidence from classification schemes on what countries are actually doing. A large and growing percentage of International Monetary Fund (IMF) members continue to choose managed floats and other intermediate regimes.[4] To me, it seems that the corners hypothesis is dead.[5]

b. The challenge to the trilemma

Traditional textbook theory says that floating exchange rates help insulate small countries against global financial factors such as foreign monetary conditions, each country choosing the monetary policy that suits its own economic conditions. "Dilemma, not trilemma" represents the claim that floating exchange rates do not in fact insulate countries from foreign shocks and that only capital controls can do that.

The textbook theory is part of the long-standing principle in international macroeconomics (often associated with Robert Mundell) that

---

[4] E.g., Ghosh, Ostry, and Qureshi (2015). Their "managed float" category has grown to be the largest category of exchange rate regime, with the proviso: "'Managed floating', however, is a nebulous concept." (The proviso suggests the utility of defining a regime that we can call systematically managed floating.)
[5] The most recent classification scheme, by Ilzetzki, Reinhart, and Rogoff (2017) again does not support a trend to the corners. The classification studies are discussed in Part 2 of the paper.

goes by the name of "the Impossible Trinity." Also called the "trilemma," the proposition states that even though a country might wish to have a fixed exchange rate, highly integrated financial markets, and the ability to set its own monetary policy, it cannot have all three of these things. The logic is simple. If there are no differences between the domestic currency and foreign currencies and no barriers to the cross-border movement of capital, then the domestic interest rate is tied to the world interest rate. The domestic country loses the ability to set its own interest rate.

One familiar graphical interpretation of the Impossible Trinity or Trilemma shows the three desirable characteristics as three sides of a triangle: exchange rate stability, financial market integration, and monetary independence. Now consider challenges (a) and (b). The corners hypothesis is the claim that financial integration forces a country to choose between the firmly-fixed vertex and the free-floating vertex, while the contrary position is that nothing stops a country from choosing an intermediate point anywhere along the side of the triangle. The "dilemma" view is very different: the triangle collapses into a single line segment, running from "monetary independence via capital controls" to "open capital markets," with the choice of exchange rate regime not relevant for monetary independence.[6]

This area of research is of particular interest during a time when the Fed is pursuing a series of increases in U.S. interest rates, which might lead international investors to pull funds out of emerging countries and trigger new crises as sometimes in the past.

Do floating rates in fact insulate countries from foreign interest rates as the traditional textbook view advertises? Rey (2014) has led a new wave of skepticism on this score.[7] She finds that one global factor explains an

---

[6] Complicating matters, some graphical interpretations depict capital controls, firm fixes, and floating as the three sides of the triangle instead of the three corners. In this case an intermediate regime, such as half-floating and half-independence, cannot be represented by identifying a point along the side of the triangle, but is instead described as "rounding the corners" (Klein and Shambaugh 2015).

[7] Also Miranda-Agrippino and Rey (2015), Devereux and Yetman (2014), and Edwards (2015).

important part of the variance of a large cross section of returns of risky assets around the world. This time-varying global factor can be interpreted as the perceived importance of risk, as reflected in a measure such as the VIX. U.S. monetary policy is, in turn, a driver of this global factor and of international credit flows and leverage.

It is possible that transmission of liquidity and risk effects may invalidate the insulation proposition. Some say that the power to set independent monetary policy was compromised when interest rates hit the zero lower bound after 2008. After all, many countries with floating exchange rates suffered effects of the U.S.-originated GFC. Farhi and Werning (2014) find theoretically that capital market imperfections may prevent floating rates from performing the shock absorption role claimed in traditional macroeconomic analysis and that in such circumstances taxation of capital flows can be welfare-improving.

To argue that floating rates do not automatically insulate against foreign disturbances is to take on a straw man, however. Given the importance of international capital flows and other transmission mechanisms, the claim in favor of floating is not that it automatically gives complete insulation even when domestic monetary policy remains passive. The claim is, rather, that it allows the freedom to respond to shocks so as to achieve the desired level of domestic demand. Indeed there is no shortage of empirical studies finding that floating does help countries retain an important degree of monetary autonomy.[8]

c.   The challenge to intervention effectiveness

Another challenge is the claim that foreign exchange intervention is powerless to affect nominal exchange rates (unless it is non-sterilized, in which case it is just another kind of monetary policy), let alone real exchange rates. This view was originally rooted in models in which the exchange rate was determined by the supply and demand for money; if

---

[8] The studies include Aizenman, Chinn, and Ito (2010; 2011), Di Giovanni and Shambaugh (2008), Han and Wei (2018), Klein and Shambaugh (2012; 2015), Obstfeld (2015), Obstfeld, Shambaugh and Taylor (2005), Shambaugh (2004), and Frankel, Schmukler and Servén (2004). Nelson (2018) critiques Rey.

intervention was sterilized so as to leave the money supply unchanged, then it had no effect. It was thought that non-monetary claims against the government did not have an effect on market interest rates and exchange rates. This was because among advanced countries (the only ones that floated at the time), financial markets were highly liquid, international capital flows unencumbered, default risk a non-issue, and government debt perhaps considered rendered irrelevant by Ricardian equivalence. Uncovered interest parity held because investors were able to arbitrage away international differences in expected returns. If a European or Japanese central bank bought dollar bonds, but then sold an equal number of domestic bonds so as to leave the monetary base unchanged, it was thought to have no effect. The ineffectiveness of sterilized intervention was accepted not just among most academics but also among many central bankers.[9]

There have long been good arguments on the other side of the debate, including theories that go back to portfolio balance models, as well as empirical results.[10] Foreign exchange intervention could be effective regardless whether it changed the monetary base.[11]

Given the experience since the 2008 GFC, it is perhaps puzzling that sterilized intervention is still often presumed ineffective. Among advanced countries that experience includes: quantitative easing, where the composition of assets underlying a given monetary base is thought to make a difference; a surprising relapse to imperfect international integration of financial markets illustrated by a new failure of covered interest parity,[12]

---

[9] E.g., Truman (2003).

[10] Some studies of the effectiveness of intervention by advanced-country central banks include Beine, Bénassy-Quéré, and Lecourt (2002), Dominguez (2006), Dominguez, Fatum, and Vacek (2013), Dominguez and Frankel (1993a;b), Fatum and Hutchison (2003; 2010), Humpage (1999) Ito (2003), Kearns and Rigobon (2005), and Obstfeld (1990). Surveys include Edison (1993), Menkhoff (2010), and Sarno and Taylor (2001).

[11] The venerable "signaling hypothesis" (Mussa 1981) may be a red herring. First, why would a central bank choose such an opaque way of signaling its intentions? Second, what practical difference does it make whether or not sterilized intervention implies that money supplies will change some day, if that day may lie in the distant future?

[12] Avdjiev, Du, Koch, and Shin (2019).

let alone uncovered interest parity; a reversal in the previous trend of diminishing home bias; and the unexpected loss of full creditworthiness represented by triple-A ratings by the U.S. and some other major high-income (but high-debt) countries. More than just money matters.

In any case, if one considers the effectiveness of intervention and managed floating these days, one is usually looking at Emerging Markets, since far more of them are managed floaters than was the case before the turn of the century, when they targeted exchange rates, while the largest industrialized countries have ceased foreign exchange intervention altogether.[13] Among EM countries the failure of interest parity and the impact of outstanding stocks of government debt are nothing new. Hence the notion that sterilized intervention can have effects comes more naturally in the case of EM economies.

Of the recent studies of foreign exchange intervention in EM currencies, most focus on just one or two countries.[14] Fratzscher *et al.* (2019) manages to marshal data from an impressive sample of 33 countries. Its conclusions are broadly similar to those regarding intervention by major central banks in an earlier era. First, intervention can be effective. Second, it tends to be more effective when seeking to move the exchange rate in the direction of longer-term equilibrium. Third, operations are more likely to be effective when orally communicated.

d.   Exchange rate disconnect

The fourth challenge to the conventional view is the "exchange rate disconnect," which says that the nominal exchange rate has no implications for real economic factors such as the real exchange rate, trade, or output. This covers a broad range of papers, from empirical studies to theoretical models. The empirical studies fail to find correlations between nominal

---

[13] At least for the time being. Frankel (2016) reports the G7's post-millennium renunciation of foreign exchange intervention.

[14] Besides Fratzscher *et al.* (2019), other recent studies of EM intervention include Adler, Lisack and Mano (2015), Adler and Tovar (2011), Blanchard, Adler, and de Carvalho Filho (2015), Daude, Levy-Yeyati and Nagengast (2016), Disyatat and Galati (2007) and the collection introduced by Mohanty (2013). Menkhoff (2013) surveys the earlier ones.

exchange rates and real variables.[15] The theoretical models (including Real Business Cycle models) have the property that shocks have the same effect on the real exchange rate regardless whether the currency floats, in which case the shock appears in the nominal exchange rate, or is fixed, in which case the same shock shows up in price levels instead. The strong claim in this case is that it doesn't matter whether foreign exchange intervention is sterilized or not, nor whether it affects the nominal exchange rate or not: the same real exchange rate emerges regardless.

### What countries actually do

This section of the paper considers the exchange rate regimes that countries follow. Our empirical focus will ultimately fall on three: firm fixing, free floating, and systematically-managed floating.

a.   Classification systems
     i.  De facto vs. de jure

It is well-established that de facto regimes need not correspond to de jure, that what a country does in practice often differs from what it says it does officially. To take three cases: countries that say they fix their exchange rate often in practice adjust it at the first serious sign of trouble[16]; countries that say they float often can't refrain from intervening in the market[17]; and countries that say they follow a basket peg often keep the weights secret so that they can depart from the basket without immediate detection.[18] The rampant discrepancies have led to a collection of studies that attempt to estimate and report the true de facto regimes.[19]

---

[15] Including Devereux and Engel (2002), Flood and Rose (1999), and Rose (2011).
[16] Obstfeld and Rogoff (1995) and Klein and Marion (1997).
[17] The famous "fear of floating": Calvo and Reinhart (2002) and Reinhart (2000).
[18] E.g., Frankel, Fajnzylber, Schmukler, and Servén (2001).
[19] Some of the prominent de facto classification schemes are Ghosh, Gulde, and Wolf (2000), Ilzetzki, Reinhart and Rogoff (2017), Reinhart and Rogoff (2004), Bénassy-Quéré, Coeuré, and Mignon (2004), and Levy-Yeyati and Sturzenegger (2001; 2003; 2005). Surveys of the literature on classification of exchange rate regimes include Klein and Shambaugh (2012), Rose (2011), and Tavlas, Dellas and Stockman (2008).

The IMF discontinued reporting the regime claims of its members at face value and began to offer its own de facto schemes.[20] It seems likely, however, that they are still heavily influenced by the claims of member governments, whereas academic researchers are more likely to go wherever the data lead them (which is not always the right way, it must be admitted).

ii. Disagreement among de facto classification schemes

It has become evident that the various de facto classification schemes, though designed to get at the "true answer," disagree widely among themselves.[21] A table in Frankel *et al.* (2004) showed that the classifications of three prominent schemes coincided with the IMF de jure classification only 50.4% of the time, averaging across the three. But they coincided with each other even less, only 38.6% of the time![22] Similarly, a table in Bénassy-Quéré *et al.* (2004) showed three de facto schemes on average correlated .69 with the IMF de jure scheme, but only .63 with each other. A table in Shambaugh (2004) reported for three de facto schemes an average of 80% agreement with the de jure listings, but only 78% among themselves. Finally, a table in Klein and Shambaugh (2012) showed that three de facto schemes coincided with the IMF classification 62% of the time, and coincided with each other also 62% of the time. All-in-all, the evidence is clear that the evidence of the classification schemes is not clear.[23]

iii. Reasons for disagreement

There are three reasons why the classification schemes give such different answers: differences in estimation techniques or other methodology; murkiness of true regimes; and frequent changes.

---

[20] Bubula and Ötker-Robe (2002).

[21] E.g., Eichengreen and Razo-Garcia (2013).

[22] Correlation of the flexibility rankings of the regimes shows an average of .40 between the three de facto schemes and the IMF de jure scheme, but a correlation of only .88 among the three themselves.

[23] In all four studies, one of the de facto classification schemes considered is Levy-Yeyati and Sturzenegger (2001). In Frankel (2004) the other two are Reinhart and Rogoff (2004) and Ghosh, Gulde, and Wolf (2000). In Bénassy-Quéré *et al.* (2004) the other two are their own and Bubula and Ötker-Robe (2002). In Shambaugh (2004) and Klein and Shambaugh (2012) they are his own and Reinhart and Rogoff (2004).

1.  Differences in methodology. Some schemes work off of the official classifications, re-classifying countries when necessary.[24] Other approaches estimate de facto regimes from observed data alone. Among the latter, some look simply at the volatility of the exchange rate, without comparing it to the variability of reserves.[25] Admittedly, if the variance of the currency vis-à-vis the dollar or other major currency is essentially zero, that is evidence of a fixed exchange rate. But it does not follow that the flexibility of exchange rate regimes can be ranked according to the variability of the exchange rate. One should compare the variance of the exchange rate changes to the variance of reserve changes. Only if the latter is large relative to the former can the regime be pronounced highly flexible. Otherwise, a large exchange rate variance might in truth be due to large external shocks. Conversely an exchange rate may show relatively low variability, but this might be due to small shocks rather than a heavily managed exchange rate. That is the proper inference if foreign exchange reserves are even more stable or if there is direct evidence of little or no foreign exchange intervention. To take the example of Figure 1, the Singapore dollar appreciated more in 2010 than the Indian rupee, but this was apparently because it experienced a bigger shock (measured by total exchange market pressure), perhaps because it is a smaller more open economy, and not because its regime has higher flexibility. Reinhart (2000) and Calvo and Reinhart (2002) compared exchange rate variability with reserve variability to show how de facto exchange rate regimes differed from de jure characterizations. The classification scheme of Levy-Yeyati and Sturzenegger (2001; 2003) is entirely based on a comparison of the variance of exchange rate changes versus the variance of reserve changes.

2.  Murky regimes. Relatively few countries follow a single clean regime. Reinhart and Rogoff (2004), for example, argue that there should be a category of free-falling currencies and point out that it is misleading to characterize them as floating merely because the

---

[24] Tavlas, Dellas, and Stockman (2008).
[25] Shambaugh (2004) and Ilzetzki, Reinhart and Rogoff (2017).

changes are so large. Rose (2011) more generally calls many countries' regimes neither fixed nor floating, but "flaky."

3. Changeability. For many countries, if they do follow a peg or other clear regime, it is often not for very long. They tend every few years to change parameters (devaluing, widening a band, changing weights in a basket, etc.) or to switch regimes altogether. One can cope with frequent changes by estimating equations for short sub-periods or using the Bai-Perron econometric technique which allows for endogenous estimation of structural breaks. A country that follows no systematic regime for longer than a year or two at a time should perhaps be treated as having no systematic regime at all, joining those in the murky category.

b. Identifying countries that are systematic managed floaters

Within the large set of countries that are neither firm fixers nor free floaters, we would like to try to identify the subset that systematically manage their floats. We are not interested in the murky regimes. We have no particular hypothesis in their case. By contrast, in the last part of the paper, we have a hypothesis that we want to test for the managed floaters: that they experience external shocks as accommodating movements in their real exchange rate, to a greater extent than the firm fixers do, but to a lesser extent than the free floaters.

How do we identify the systematic managed floaters? We take as a starting point those that are identified as managed floaters by the IMF or by one of the other classification schemes such as Ilzetzki, Reinhart, and Rogoff (2017). But we have something more specific in mind, represented by the word "systematic." We mean that when faced with Exchange Market Pressure, they tend generally to take a particular portion of it in the form of currency appreciation and the remainder in the form of higher foreign exchange reserves, where the portion lies somewhere between all (which would be free floating) and nothing (which would be firm fixing).

One way to approach the problem is to run a regression of changes in the exchange rate against Exchange Market Pressure. A coefficient that is significantly greater than zero and significantly less than one indicates a systematic managed float. We elaborate below, with updated estimates of the regimes followed by a number of Asian countries.

A second way to approach the problem is to treat reserve changes rather than exchange rate changes as the dependent variable. One estimates a central bank reaction function by running a regression of foreign exchange intervention against the exchange rate. A significant coefficient implies that the country is a systematic managed floater. We do that for the case of Turkey (with a focus on two alternative measures of intervention) in the section that follows the next.

But there is a problem. Why should intervention be considered the dependent variable and the exchange rate the independent variable? Or why, on the other hand, should the exchange rate be considered the independent variable? In truth, aren't they both endogenous in the case of a managed float? Accordingly, we also offer a new, third, approach, which makes no presumption as to causality.

i.   A simple-minded criterion for systematic managed floaters
We here propose an amazingly simple-minded test to identify systematic managed floaters. Whether its crudeness is considered a vice or its elegance is considered a virtue, it at least has the desirable property of making no presumption about direction of causality.

The test is to compute for each country the correlation of the change in the foreign exchange value of the currency (in percent) with the change in reserves (as a percentage of the monetary base). If the correlation is positive and high enough to clear some threshold, it is judged a systematic managed floater. At one extreme, a truly fixed exchange rate will show a correlation of zero, because the exchange rate by definition never changes. At the other extreme, a purely floating exchange rate will again show a coefficient of zero, because reserves by definition never change. But it is not just the residents of fixed and floating corners that will fail to meet this criterion. Most countries that are normally classified as intermediate regimes will fail the criterion as well, their intervention being much more episodic than that. Only those that respond to exchange market pressure systematically will show a high positive correlation.[26]

A correlation coefficient of 1, hypothetically, would mean that the management of the float is perfectly systematic. A separate question is how aggressive the management is. Assume a constant of proportionality $\phi$ between percentage exchange rate changes and percentage reserve changes:

$$\Delta s = \phi \, (\Delta Res)/MB, \tag{1}$$

where $\Delta s \equiv$ the change in the log of the foreign exchange value of the domestic currency; $\Delta Res \equiv$ the change in the central bank's holdings of foreign exchange reserves; $MB \equiv$ monetary base; and $\phi \equiv$ the parameter that captures how flexible is the exchange rate regime.

At one extreme, if the constant $\phi$ is zero then the regime in the limit is so heavily managed that it once again collapses into a peg. At the far extreme, as the constant goes to infinity, the currency is so lightly managed that in the limit it becomes a float. In between, a finite $\phi$ implies an intermediate degree of management, which is what we have in mind. But, again, the question whether the intervention is systematic (high correlation coefficient) is independent of the question whether the intervention is aggressive (low $\phi$).

There is one dimension on which the correlation test may lose its claim to elegance. That is the question of what the numeraire currency in which the exchange rate and value of foreign exchange reserves is measured is. We start by using the dollar, which will give the right answer for many countries. But some countries gauge the value of their currency in terms of other major countries or a weighted average of trading partners. This

---

[26] We compute the correlation on changes rather than levels, in part to avoid non-stationarity. One property of working with first differences is that the criterion will not be impaired by a long-term trend in reserves, if the central bank seeks to build them up, nor by a long-term trend in the exchange rate. (Such a trend is to be expected under a crawling peg — the "C" in BBC or Band-Basket-Crawl).

obviously needs to be considered for those that formally declare a role for a basket in their regime, but it is likely true at an implicit level of others too.

We can address this problem with alternative approaches such as using the SDR as the numeraire or experimenting on a case-by-case basis. A well-specified way to estimate the implicit weights in a currency basket is described in the following section. For the moment we will be content with the dollar numeraire.

Table 1 reports the coefficient of correlation between the percentage change in the foreign exchange value of the domestic currency and the change in foreign exchange reserves, scaled by the monetary base. The countries with the highest correlation, strongly suggesting systematic

**Table 1.** Correlation between $\Delta$ s and ($\Delta$ Res)/ MB (January 1997–December 2015)

| Asian Economies (Non-Commodity-Exporters) | |
|---|---|
| Hong Kong | 0.0446 |
| India | 0.4453 |
| Korea, Rep. | 0.5530 |
| Malaysia | 0.2685 |
| Philippines | 0.3023 |
| Singapore | 0.6074 |
| Thailand | 0.2643 |
| Turkey | 0.2950 |
| Vietnam | 0.1142 |
| **Commodity Exporters** | |
| Australia | 0.1755 |
| New Zealand | 0.2199 |
| South Africa | 0.2736 |
| Brazil | 0.2884 |
| Chile | 0.1007 |
| Colombia | 0.2100 |
| Indonesia | −0.0061 |
| Peru | 0.2758 |
| Papua New Guinea | 0.2396 |
| Mongolia | 0.1889 |

**Table 1.**  (*Continued*)

| | |
|---|---|
| Canada | 0.1021 |
| Kazakhstan | 0.1506 |
| Kuwait | −0.1025 |
| Russia | 0.2637 |
| Saudi Arabia | −0.0319 |
| Bahrain | 0 |
| Qatar | 0 |
| United Arab Emirates | 0.0437 |
| Brunei | 0.0465 |

*Note*: s is the log of the exchange rate defined as the dollar price of the domestic currency.

management of their floating currencies, are Singapore, Korea and India. Others that are also above a threshold of 0.25, and which are thereby also judged to have systematically managed floats, are Malaysia, Philippines, Thailand, Turkey, South Africa, Peru and Russia. As expected, countries known to have firm pegs have coefficients well below the threshold, close to or equal to zero: Hong Kong, Kuwait, Saudi Arabia, Bahrain, Qatar, the United Arab Emirates (UAE), and Brunei. Also below the threshold are countries that are thought to float freely: Australia, Canada, Chile, and New Zealand. In Part 3 of the paper we see whether these categories make a difference for insulation from external shocks.

ii.   Estimates of de facto exchange rate regimes for some Asian countries

Frankel and Wei (1994) ran regressions to estimate weights on the dollar, yen and other major currencies in the implicit baskets guiding the exchange rates of smaller Asian countries. At a time when many saw the yen as becoming increasingly important in East Asia, the finding was that the dollar was still by far the dominant currency in most cases.[27] The exercise is a rare case in which, under the null hypothesis

---

[27] Among other similar papers estimating weights were Bénassy-Quéré (1999) and Bénassy-Quéré, Coeuré, and Mignon (2004). Ogawa (2006) and Frankel and Wei (2008) are among those who applied the technique to discern China's exchange rate policy when it moved away from a dollar peg after 2005. More recently, China's yuan has itself joined

of a true basket peg, the estimation should produce, not just statistically significant coefficients, but an $R^2$ close to 1.0. But few countries in Asia or elsewhere claim to peg to a basket and fewer still actually follow through de facto. At most, a regression of the local currency value against other major currencies tells us the weights in a loose anchor around which the exchange rate is allowed to vary.

Frankel and Wei (2008) synthesized (i) the weight-estimation methodology with (ii) a technique to estimate the degree of systematic intervention to dampen fluctuations relative to the basket. This was achieved by adding Exchange Market Pressure (EMP) as another right-hand side variable along with the values of the major foreign currency. The change in Exchange Market Pressure is defined as the percentage increase in the foreign exchange value of the currency plus the increase in foreign exchange reserves (over some denominator such as the monetary base).[28] If $\beta$, the coefficient on $EMP$, is estimated to be close to zero, the regime is a peg (to the basket, whatever its component or components may be). If $\beta$ is estimated to be close to 1, it is a pure float. For most countries, it is in between, suggesting an intermediate exchange rate regime.

$$\Delta \log H_t = c + \sum\nolimits_{j=1}^{k} (w_j \Delta \log X_{j,t}) + \beta \Delta EMP_t + u_t \qquad (2)$$

where $H$ is the value of the home currency $i$ (measured in terms of a numeraire unit, in this case the SDR); $X_j$ is the value of the dollar, euro, yen, or other foreign currencies $j$ that are candidates for components of the basket, measured in terms of the same numeraire; and $\Delta EMP_t$ is Exchange Market Pressure $\equiv \Delta \log H_t + (\Delta Res)/MB_t$. The flexibility parameter in equation (2) is directly related to the flexibility parameter in equation (1):

---

the list of candidate units in the regression to determine the regimes followed by other Asian countries. E.g., Subramanian (2011a; 2011b) claims a rising share for the yuan.

[28] Exchange Market Pressure was originally introduced by Girton and Roper (1977). Here we impose a priori constraint that a one percentage increase in the foreign exchange value of the currency and a one percentage increase in the supply of the currency (the change in reserves as a share of the monetary base) have equal weights, whereas Girton and Roper and others have normalized by standard deviations.

$$\beta = \phi / (1 + \phi).$$

Frankel and Xie (2010) further refined the Frankel-Wei methodology by adapting the econometric technique of Bai and Perron (2003) to allow endogenous estimation of structural break points, so that parameters could change. Appendix Tables 2 and 3 apply the technique to weekly data from the period 1999–2009 for India and Thailand, which have been candidates for a basket-basket-crawl (BBC) at some parts of their recent history. The equations are estimated in rate of change form, to eliminate non-stationarity. Both for Thailand and for India the estimate for $\beta$, the coefficient on EMP, was significantly greater than zero but significantly less than 1, suggesting systematic managed floating. For Thailand, the weight on the dollar moved in the range .6 to .8, with the remaining weight falling on the euro and yen. For India, the weight on the dollar went as high as .9 in the early 2000s.

Even though we label them "systematic," it is noteworthy that there are several structural breaks in the parameters. For Thailand, the flexibility parameter $\beta$ is significantly greater than zero and less than 1 for all four-time sub-periods within 1999–2009, suggesting relatively consistent behavior. For India, the same is true of the parameter in four out of six sub-periods, but it is insignificantly different from zero in two out of six.

Similar estimates from the period 1999–2009 for seven other Asian currencies are reported in an online Appendix,[29] with structural breaks again identified by the week. Singapore, the Philippines, and South Korea show managed floats throughout the period. The technique shows China starting to qualify as a managed float in 2006. For Malaysia we cannot reject free floating in 1999 or fixing in 2000–2005 and 2008–2009, but the ringgit shows a managed float in between. For Indonesia we cannot reject free floating in 2001–2002, but the rupiah shows managed floating thereafter. Turkey shows variable behavior during 1999–2000 but managed floating starts in 2001.

---

[29] "Frankel-Xie" appendix at https://scholar.harvard.edu/frankel/exchange-rates-terms/fixed-vs-floating-exchange-rate-regimes.

Next we update the estimates to 2017, for four of the Asian currencies that are of the most interest. Again, the technique allows estimation of the weights in the implicit basket that the authorities treat as the anchor or reference rate (as in Frankel and Wei 1994), while also estimating the parameter that calibrates the degree of exchange rate flexibility relative to that basket (as in Frankel and Wei 2008) and estimating endogenously possible structural breaks in any of these parameters (as in Frankel and Xie 2010). The data set runs from 1999 to 2017. The exchange rate observations are daily, which requires interpolation of the components of monthly reserve data to compute the EMP variable.

The updated results are shown in Tables 2.1–2.4. All four currencies qualify for systematic managed floats, if one overlooks the many small structural breaks in the parameters. (We use a .01 significance level for defining a structural break.) For Singapore the flexibility parameter appears higher during March 2013–February 2017 than it did before, above .7. For Korea, the estimated flexibility parameter has risen over time, from .7 to .9. For India, the flexibility parameter appears higher during November 2008–February 2017 than earlier, well above .9.

For China, the managed float starts in July 2005 (Frankel 2009). In recent years, the estimated weight on the dollar has declined from .9 to .5. The flexibility parameter appears quite high during the period August 2010–April 2017: above .9. One might suspect that this is a sign of asymmetric response by the Chinese authorities to recent outflows and depreciation, as compared to the earlier period of inflows and appreciation. But in fact the parameter changes on the post-2014 downside do not particularly run in that direction. The value of the RMB in terms of dollars peaked in January 2014. Since that date, net capital outflows have mostly been pushing in the opposite direction from the preceding 10 years. Holdings of foreign exchange reserves by the People's Bank of China peaked in June 2014, at $4.0 trillion, and went down by almost a trillion dollars subsequently.

Singapore's basket has allocated a significant weight to China's RMB during the period since January 2008, at the expense of the U.S. dollar.

**Table 2.** Estimation of implicit weights and flexibility parameter, for four Asian currencies, updated to 2017[1]

2.1 China: RMB's exchange rate regime before the exchange rate reform of july 21, 2005, daily M1:1999–M6:2005, identifying break points in renminbi regime, daily M7:2005–M4:2017

| Variables | (1) 1/1/1999–7/20/2005 | (2) 7/22/2005–6/5/2007 | (3) 6/6/2007–8/8/2008 | (4) 8/11/2008–8/24/2010 | (5) 8/25/2010–11/4/2011 | (6) 11/7/2011–1/9/2013 | (7) 1/10/2013–2/3/2015 | (8) 2/4/2015–4/28/2017 |
|---|---|---|---|---|---|---|---|---|
| U.S. $ | 0.999*** | 0.896*** | 0.692*** | 0.864*** | 0.449*** | 0.461*** | 0.490*** | 0.500*** |
|  | (0.000) | (0.013) | (0.025) | (0.025) | (0.014) | (0.011) | (0.009) | (0.005) |
| Euro € | −0.000 | 0.057*** | 0.192*** | 0.091*** | 0.343*** | 0.331*** | 0.327*** | 0.319*** |
|  | (0.000) | (0.013) | (0.025) | (0.014) | (0.009) | (0.007) | (0.007) | (0.005) |
| JP Y | 0.000 | 0.028*** | 0.057*** | 0.024*** | 0.120*** | 0.098*** | 0.073*** | 0.075*** |
|  | (0.000) | (0.007) | (0.008) | (0.005) | (0.006) | (0.004) | (0.003) | (0.003) |
| ΔEMP | 0.001 | 0.161*** | 0.454*** | 0.216*** | 0.915*** | 0.935*** | 0.904*** | 0.931*** |
|  | (0.001) | (0.022) | (0.039) | (0.043) | (0.021) | (0.016) | (0.014) | (0.010) |
| Constant | −0.000 | −0.000*** | −0.000*** | −0.000*** | −0.001*** | −0.000*** | −0.000*** | 0.000*** |
|  | (0.000) | (0.000) | (0.000) | (0.000) | (0.000) | (0.000) | (0.000) | (0.000) |
| Observations | 1,634 | 467 | 296 | 512 | 301 | 294 | 517 | 559 |
| R² | 1.000 | 0.986 | 0.968 | 0.996 | 0.994 | 0.996 | 0.994 | 0.997 |
| GB£ | 0.001 | 0.019 | 0.059 | 0.021 | 0.088 | 0.110 | 0.109 | 0.106 |

***p<0.01, **p<0.05, *p<0.1. (Robust standard errors in parentheses.)

Δ EMP ≡ Δlog $H_t$ + (ΔRes)/$MB_t$ (daily interpolation).

[1]Thanks to Danxia Xie. The methodology is from Frankel and Wei (2008), but allowing for endogenously estimated structural breaks as in Frankel and Xie (2010).

**Table 2.2** India: Identifying break points in India's exchange rate regime, daily M8:2005-M2:2017

| Variables | (1) 8/2/2005– 9/4/2007 | (2) 9/5/2007– 10/31/2008 | (3) 11/3/2008– 8/5/2011 | (4) 8/8/2011– 10/1/2013 | (5) 10/2/2013– 5/8/2015 | (6) 5/11/2015– 2/28/2017 |
|---|---|---|---|---|---|---|
| U.S. $ | 0.450*** | 0.673*** | 0.456*** | 0.436*** | 0.431*** | 0.487*** |
| | (0.096) | (0.097) | (0.041) | (0.023) | (0.032) | (0.009) |
| Euro € | 0.298*** | 0.217*** | 0.357*** | 0.361*** | 0.356*** | 0.331*** |
| | (0.026) | (0.039) | (0.011) | (0.005) | (0.010) | (0.004) |
| Jpn Y | 0.065*** | 0.030 | 0.116*** | 0.095*** | 0.065*** | 0.080*** |
| | (0.019) | (0.023) | (0.007) | (0.004) | (0.009) | (0.003) |
| Cn Y | 0.096 | −0.019 | −0.006 | 0.000 | 0.027 | −0.009 |
| | (0.100) | (0.092) | (0.041) | (0.023) | (0.031) | (0.011) |
| ΔEMP | 0.768*** | 0.639*** | 0.935*** | 0.992*** | 0.963*** | 0.981*** |
| | (0.032) | (0.046) | (0.013) | (0.003) | (0.010) | (0.007) |
| Constant | −0.001*** | −0.001*** | −0.000*** | 0.000*** | −0.001*** | −0.000*** |
| | (0.000) | (0.000) | (0.000) | (0.000) | (0.000) | (0.000) |
| Observations | 523 | 292 | 692 | 540 | 400 | 451 |
| $R^2$ | 0.911 | 0.910 | 0.980 | 0.996 | 0.982 | 0.997 |
| GB£ | 0.091 | 0.100 | 0.078 | 0.108 | 0.120 | 0.110 |

***p<0.01, **p<0.05, *p<0.1. (Robust standard errors in parentheses.) $\Delta\, EMP \equiv \Delta\log H_t + (\Delta Res)/MB_t$ (daily interpolation).

Table 2.3 Singapore: Identifying break points in Singapore's exchange rate regime, daily M8:2005-M2:2017

| Variables | (1) 8/2/2005–11/9/2006 | (2) 11/10/2006–1/8/2008 | (3) 1/9/2008–3/2/2009 | (4) 3/3/2009–5/4/2010 | (5) 5/5/2010–8/19/2011 | (6) 8/22/2011–3/1/2013 | (7) 3/4/2013–2/28/2017 |
|---|---|---|---|---|---|---|---|
| U.S. $ | 0.468*** | 0.575*** | 0.154 | -0.293 | 0.376*** | 0.218* | 0.379*** |
| | (0.117) | (0.135) | (0.144) | (0.469) | (0.084) | (0.113) | (0.033) |
| Euro € | 0.137*** | 0.280*** | 0.294*** | 0.298*** | 0.324*** | 0.309*** | 0.316*** |
| | (0.034) | (0.041) | (0.026) | (0.028) | (0.019) | (0.029) | (0.011) |
| JP Y | 0.191*** | -0.032 | 0.009 | -0.002 | 0.048*** | 0.057** | 0.081*** |
| | (0.024) | (0.021) | (0.021) | (0.019) | (0.018) | (0.028) | (0.008) |
| CN Y | 0.118 | 0.095 | 0.465*** | 0.905* | 0.166** | 0.189* | 0.100*** |
| | (0.119) | (0.136) | (0.147) | (0.473) | (0.082) | (0.106) | (0.032) |
| $\Delta$EMP | 0.289*** | 0.181*** | 0.410*** | 0.121*** | 0.477*** | 0.314*** | 0.724*** |
| | (0.034) | (0.029) | (0.042) | (0.024) | (0.027) | (0.026) | (0.017) |
| Constant | -0.001*** | -0.001*** | -0.001*** | -0.000* | -0.001*** | -0.000*** | -0.000*** |
| | (0.000) | (0.000) | (0.000) | (0.000) | (0.000) | (0.000) | (0.000) |
| Observations | 319 | 289 | 289 | 295 | 325 | 383 | 998 |
| $R^2$ | 0.899 | 0.782 | 0.929 | 0.892 | 0.872 | 0.645 | 0.934 |
| GB£ | 0.086 | 0.082 | 0.077 | 0.092 | 0.085 | 0.227 | 0.124 |

***$p<0.01$, **$p<0.05$, *$p<0.1$. (Robust standard errors in parentheses.) $\Delta$ EMP $\equiv \Delta \log H_t + (\Delta Res)/MB_t$ (daily interpolation).

**Table 2.4** South Korea: Identifying break points in South Korea's exchange rate regime, daily M8:2005–M2:2013

| Variables | (1) 8/2/2005– 3/17/2008 | (2) 3/18/2008– 1/2/2009 | (3) 1/5/2009– 5/3/2010 | (4) 5/4/2010– 2/1/2013 |
|---|---|---|---|---|
| U.S. $ | 0.239** | 1.478*** | −0.636 | 0.307*** |
| | (0.099) | (0.444) | (0.411) | (0.050) |
| Euro € | 0.293*** | 0.443*** | 0.345*** | 0.384*** |
| | (0.030) | (0.118) | (0.030) | (0.012) |
| JP Y | 0.077*** | 0.063 | 0.083*** | 0.108*** |
| | (0.018) | (0.092) | (0.020) | (0.010) |
| CN Y | 0.310*** | −1.016** | 1.125*** | 0.122** |
| | (0.101) | (0.437) | (0.414) | (0.050) |
| ΔEMP | 0.661*** | 0.872*** | 0.858*** | 0.938*** |
| | (0.029) | (0.053) | (0.027) | (0.010) |
| Constant | −0.001*** | 0.004*** | −0.004*** | −0.001*** |
| | (0.000) | (0.001) | (0.000) | (0.000) |
| Observations | 657 | 199 | 335 | 690 |
| $R^2$ | 0.875 | 0.842 | 0.919 | 0.953 |
| GB£ | 0.082 | 0.032 | 0.084 | 0.080 |

***p<0.01, **p<0.05, *p<0.1. (Robust standard errors in parentheses.) $\Delta$ EMP $\equiv \Delta\log H_t$ + $(\Delta Res)/MB_t$ (daily interpolation).

The heavy weight on the euro and the smaller weight on the yen both remain undiminished.

The Korean won also has put significant weight on the RMB since August 2005. There is no sign of RMB influence for India, where the weights have been roughly steady: 0.5 on the dollar, 0.3 on the euro, and weights of 0.1 on both the Japanese yen and the British pound.

This research could be extended by incorporating estimation of a possible target zone, appropriate for a country that might be following a band or target zone, perhaps together with a basket. The target zone is incorporated into the equation by means of the Threshold Autoregression Technique.

c. How do these analyses depend on the use of intervention data versus reserve changes? The case of Turkey

It is easy enough to write down in theory that the magnitude of foreign exchange intervention equals the change in reserves. Many central banks do not report data on foreign exchange intervention operations, as opposed to data on reserves. For this reason, although empirical research on foreign exchange intervention per se usually focuses on the few countries and time samples where the data are available, the literature on exchange rate regimes often uses data on monthly changes in reserves, which are reported by almost all countries.

In practice, data on intervention, even when explicitly reported, tend to look very different from data on changes in foreign exchange reserves. In this section we seek to shed light on the question how much difference it makes whether one uses data on intervention or foreign exchange intervention, when assessing whether a country follows a systematically managed float.

There are two obvious reasons to expect the data on foreign exchange intervention to differ from the data on changes in foreign exchange reserves, reasons why reserves will change even if there has been no intervention. The first is that interest accrues on the central bank's holdings of U.S. treasury bills and other assets held as foreign exchange reserves. The second is the valuation effect: If the value of reserves is measured in terms of domestic currency, it will change every time the exchange rate changes.

Even when the monetary authority does not report the value of reserves in terms of foreign currency, if all the reserves are known to be held in U.S. treasury bills the researcher can use the monthly exchange rate to infer how much of a reported change in reserves is due to the pure valuation effect. But most central banks hold at least some of their reserves in other assets and few if any accommodate researchers by reporting the currency composition. Furthermore it has become more common in recent years for central banks to diversify out of U.S. treasury bills, not just into other non-U.S. currencies but also into other securities, such as longer-term bonds and even equities in some cases. This exacerbates each of the two measurement problems: earnings on the reserves are generally higher on these alternate assets than on U.S. treasury bills, and valuation effects now include capital gains and losses on securities beyond just exchange rate changes.

When one looks into the data one always finds a variety of further complications, some of which suggest that what counts as intervention is not just an issue of having access to the right data, but can be an issue of conceptual interpretation too. To take an example, some developing countries have official agencies that sell the country's commodity exports for dollars. If the agency chooses to hold the dollars (e.g., in a sovereign wealth fund), rather than exchange them for the local currency, does that count as foreign exchange intervention or as the absence of foreign exchange intervention? Something analogous apparently holds in the case of Turkey, a country to which we are about to turn: an official agency holds dollars for the purpose of importing oil.

We turn to Turkey because it is one of the only managed floaters that has also regularly made public its data on foreign exchange intervention. Most countries only publish monthly data on foreign exchange reserves.

We want to see how much difference it makes when studying the central bank's behavior with respect to the foreign exchange market whether one uses intervention data or reserve changes. We know that the two series will differ. But, in the context of classifying countries by exchange rate regime, we want to be able to distinguish within the broad class of floaters those that systematically manage their floats, versus those that float freely or only intervene unsystematically. To do that, we want to get an idea whether it makes a difference whether one uses the reserve data versus the intervention data.

It might be natural to think of the exercise as seeing whether the commonly available reserve data give the "right answer" represented by the more rarely available intervention data. But one could argue, in the context of classifying exchange rate regimes, that the foreign exchange reserves have at least as much a claim to being the right measure as intervention data. Recall the framework for thinking about the continuum of fixed versus flexible exchange rates that goes under the name of Exchange Market Pressure (EMP). EMP is defined as a weighted average of the percentage change in the foreign exchange value of the currency and the change in foreign exchange reserves (where the weight on foreign exchange reserves might variously be defined as the inverse of the monetary base, as the inverse relative standard deviation, or as an endogenously estimated parameter). EMP represents the increase in demand for domestic currency versus foreign currency. It is up to the central bank whether to allow EMP to show up entirely in the form an appreciation of the currency, which is floating; or entirely as an increase in foreign exchange reserves, which is fixing; or somewhere in between. If it consistently acts to absorb some share between zero and one in the exchange rate and the remainder in reserves, then we deem it to be a systematically-managed floater. For this purpose, it is the change in reserves that matters, not intervention normally defined. Again, if reserves rise because of interest earned on U.S. Treasury bills, that is not considered foreign exchange intervention, but may be relevant nonetheless.

Others have studied the Turkish intervention data. Basu and Varoudakis (2013) find a clear reaction function that shows systematic management of the floating lira: Turkish intervention responds to the level of the exchange rate (nominal effective), as is visible in Figure 4, borrowed from their paper. Frömmel and Midiliç (2016) similarly find statistically significant reaction of intervention to the level of the exchange rate relative to a trend (medium run moving average), but no reaction to the recent rate of change of the exchange rate. Their main focus is on an additional variable, the level of foreign exchange reserves relative to GDP. They find that it is a significant determinant of Turkish intervention. They also identify several significant structural breaks in the reaction function.

As they explain, the monetary authority, the Central Bank of the Republic of Turkey, undertakes two different modes of foreign exchange intervention: occasional auctions and regular market operations. On many days, the number for the auction is zero. We add the two together to get the measure of intervention. The series is still jagged because of

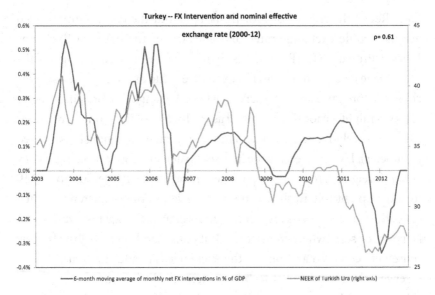

**Figure 4.** Turkey's systematic management of its float (Basu and Varoudakis 2013)
*Source*: IMF World Economic Outlook, Central Bank of the Republic of Turkey, and WB Global Economic Monitor.

the auctions. Thus we smooth out the data a bit, by looking at monthly averages or other moving averages, as other studies have done.

Figure 5 graphs the two different measures of intervention, along with various measures of the exchange rate. The two measures look quite different, as expected, but are highly correlated.

Several hypotheses are tested for the central bank reaction function. A particular sort of systematic behavior is flow intervention that seeks to drive the exchange rate in the direction of its long run equilibrium. This means buying foreign currency when the price of foreign currency, which is the exchange rate, is low (the value of the domestic currency is high), measured relative to either a long-run average or a long-run trend, and selling foreign currency when the price of foreign currency is high (the value of the domestic currency is low). But an alternative is "leaning against the wind," which is usually interpreted as intervention that opposes the most recent *direction of movement* of the exchange rate, as opposed to its *level*. A third relevant variable is the level of reserves.

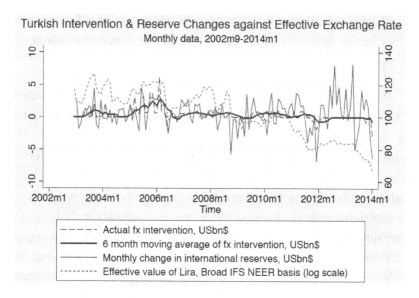

**Figure 5.** Foreign exchange actions by Turkey: Intervention data vs. reserve changes

Research on reserve holdings features the hypothesis that central banks have a target level of reserves,[31] held for precautionary purposes, and that the motivation for intervention behavior is not just to affect the exchange rate but also to move reserves in the direction of the target level. There has been some evidence in favor of this hypothesis, particularly since the currency crises of the 1990s and particularly in the case of Turkey (Frömmel and Midiliç 2016, as noted). A fourth relevant variable is the inflation rate, under the hypothesis that, in an inflation targeting country, central bank operations in the foreign exchange market are among the tools that are motivated by an effort to push the inflation rate in the direction of its target. The full equation is thus:

$$\text{FX acquisition} = \gamma + \alpha\,(s_t - s_{trend}) + \beta\,(s_t - s_{t-1}) + \delta\,(\text{Res}/\text{GDP})_t + \psi\,(\text{inflation} - \text{target})$$

---

[31] References on central bank's desired reserve holdings include Jeanne and Rancière (2011) and Rodrik (2006),

The dependent variable, "Acquisition of foreign exchange," is measured either by the data on foreign exchange intervention or by changes in foreign exchange reserves.

Regression results are reported in Table 3. Several conclusions emerge. When the rate of change variable is included on its own (Table 3.1), to test for "leaning against the wind," it is highly significant regardless whether the dependent variable is measured by intervention or changes in reserves. When the level of the exchange rate is included on its own (Table 3.2), it is highly significant for explaining Intervention and borderline-significant for explaining reserve changes. When both variables are included at the same time, there is evidence in favor of both (Table 3.3). When the central bank's behavior is judged by the intervention data, both the level and rate of change variables are significant. When it is judged by reserve changes, the rate of change variable is highly significant but the level variable is at best borderline-significant.

When the ratio of reserves/GDP is included to test the hypothesis of a target level (Table 3.3), the intervention data give strong support: the effect is negative and significant, thus suggesting that the authorities are more likely to add to their reserves when the level is low. The effect is not evident when central bank behavior is measured by the change in reserves, rather than the intervention data. Estimates for sub-periods are reported in the online appendix table (Sheets 7 and 8).[32]

We find no evidence for the inflation targeting hypothesis: Neither intervention nor changes in reserves appear to respond significantly to the level of inflation measured relative to its target. This finding is of interest since Turkey is supposedly an inflation-targeter. We omitted the inflation results from the equation estimates reported in Table 3, but they are included in the online appendix (Sheet 10).

To conclude, we get slightly different answers when we use intervention data to investigate the reaction function of the Central Bank

---

[32] Available at https://scholar.harvard.edu/frankel/exchange-rates-terms/fixed-vs-floating-exchange-rate-regimes.

**Table 3.** Estimating Foreign Exchange Reaction Function of Turkey's Central Bank monthly observations: 2003m1–2014m1

**Table 3.1** Regressing Turkish Intervention Measures Against Only $s_t - s_{t-1}$.

| Dependent Variable | Intervention | Δ Reserves |
|---|---|---|
| $s_t - s_{t-1}$ | 6.017** | 24.568*** |
| | (2.388) | (5.527) |
| Constant | 0.408*** | 0.645*** |
| | (0.098) | (0.200) |
| Observations | 133 | 133 |

**Table 3.2** Regressing Turkish Intervention Measures Against Only $s_t - s_{trend}$.

| Dependent Variable | Intervention | Δ Reserves |
|---|---|---|
| $s_t - s_{trend}$ | 3.240*** | 3.776* |
| | (0.871) | (2.034) |
| Constant | 0.390*** | 0.577*** |
| | (0.094) | (0.215) |
| Observations | 134 | 133 |

**Table 3.3.** Regressing Turkish Intervention Measures Against Both $(s_t - s_{t-1})$ and $(s_t - s_{trend})$.

| Dependent Variable | Intervention | Intervention | Intervention | Δ Reserves |
|---|---|---|---|---|
| $s_t - s_{t-1}$ | 4.403** | | 2.959 | 24.851*** |
| | (1.947) | | (1.816) | (5.497) |
| $s_t - s_{trend}$ | 3.017*** | 2.338*** | 2.264*** | 3.196* |
| | (0.831) | (0.867) | (0.855) | (1.754) |
| Reserves/GDP | Res/GDP | | −4.445*** | −4.070** |
| | | | (1.556) | (1.566) |
| Constant | 0.399*** | 2.256*** | 2.105*** | −1.203 |
| | (0.093) | (0.668) | (0.673) | (1.481) |
| Observations | 133 | 134 | 133 | 133 |

t-statistic significant at: *10 % level **5 % level ***1% level . (Newey-West standard errors.) Intervention is measured in $ billions. Exchange rates $s_t$ are in logs.

*Note*: A more complete set of results is reported in an on-line "Turkey Appendix" available at https://scholar.harvard.edu/frankel/exchange-rates-terms/fixed-vs-floating-exchange-rate-regimes. It includes, for example, tests for evidence that foreign exchange intervention is influenced by inflation relative to an inflation target. It also allows for three structural breaks, with the dates taken from Frömmel and Midiliç (2016): 2007m10–2011m7, 2011m8–2013m6, 2013m7–2014m1. Thanks to Shruti Lakhtakia.

of the Republic of Turkey from the answers when we use data on reserve changes. But in both cases, qualitatively, we find evidence of a systematic effort to dampen volatility of the exchange rate.

### Effects of external shocks

Do countries that systematically and aggressively manage their floats succeed in dampening fluctuations in the real exchange rate? Or is the exchange rate regime a mirage, as some claim?

Of course there is already quite a lot of evidence that exchange rate regimes make a difference, and that a regime that allows bigger changes in the nominal exchange rate will thereby allow bigger changes to the real exchange rate.[33]

A number of recent papers look at capital inflows to emerging markets, often gross capital inflows, and study the response of the local monetary authorities, including with respect to exchange rate flexibility.[34] We focus on the overall balance of payments instead of gross capital inflows. For one thing, the distinction between an increase in foreign assets in the domestic country and a decrease in foreign liabilities can be arbitrary, not just in an accounting sense but even conceptually, especially when it comes to banking flows. For another thing, a positive external commodity shock is often reflected in both a trade surplus and a capital account surplus.

The only way to solve the endogeneity problem is to use an exogenous variable like U.S. interest rates, the VIX, or dollar commodity prices. The severely endogenous nature of the capital inflows or overall balance of payments is widely recognized: If the authorities choose to respond to a positive shock by allowing the currency to appreciate, that may operate

---

[33] Convincing empirical results from different approaches include Mussa (1986), Taylor (2002), and Bahmani-Oskooee, Hegerty and Kutan (2008). The reasons why the exchange rate regime makes a difference can come from imperfect goods markets.

[34] Including Milesi-Ferretti and Tille (2011), Magud, Reinhart, and Vesperoni (2014), Blanchard, Adler, and de Carvalho Filho (2015), and Blanchard, Ostry, Ghosh, and Chamon (2016).

to shut off the inflow. If one can think of such an exogenous variable, then, there is a strong case for putting it directly on the right-hand side of an OLS equation. This is especially clear when the country is a pure floater, as Australia and New Zealand in our sample, in which case the comprehensive aggregate measure of inflows, i.e., the balance of payments, should be zero by definition of floating.

a.  Effects on the real exchange rate

The core exercise of the paper is to test the effects of exogenous external shocks on the real exchange rate, using time series for a select set of countries, and then to see if the sensitivity to shocks is different according to the country's exchange rate regime. The null hypothesis is that the regime makes no difference: that a shock will have the same effect on the real exchange rate regardless whether the nominal exchange rate is fixed, in which case it must show up in the price level, or floating, in which case it shows up directly in the nominal exchange rate. The alternative hypothesis is that shocks have a bigger effect on the real exchange rate under floating than under managed floating and a bigger effect under managed floating than under fixing.

It is crucial for this exercise that the measured shocks are truly and credibly exogenous on their face. We focus on two measures: dollar commodity prices and the VIX.[35] The VIX is a measure of market perceptions of near-term volatility extracted from put and call options on the U.S. S&P 500 stock index and traded on the Chicago Board of Exchange.

For the tests where commodity prices are taken to be the main exogenous variable, we restrict the sample to countries where a high

---

[35] Other possible measures of exogenous shocks include a broader measure of financial risk perceptions, US interest rates, and (for some countries) natural disasters. We tried the Global Economic Policy Uncertainty index, but it did not add any explanatory power beyond the VIX. We use dollar prices of the country's export commodities rather than a more comprehensive measure of its terms of trade because the former is plausibly exogenous (except perhaps for Saudi Arabia) as in the small open economy model, whereas measures of the terms of trade are in practice likely to be endogenous with respect to the nominal exchange rate.

percentage of exports is concentrated in a small number of commodities (energy, mineral or agricultural). For some, particularly oil exporters, that is a single commodity; for others it is several commodities. We construct a tailor-made monthly price index for each country by computing weights as the average commodity shares in exports during the sample period and then multiplying them by monthly dollar prices of the corresponding commodities.[36]

We do not want to attempt a comprehensive study of all countries. For one thing, we seek only those with compelling measures of exogenous external shocks [to be used either as instrumental variables or directly as independent variables In the real exchange rate regressions]. That narrows down the set of countries. We have good reason to think that commodity prices are important to commodity producing countries. Beyond the simple evidence of the share of the commodities in the countries' output, a number of empirical papers have confirmed that when the currencies of commodity-producing countries are allowed to float, they tend to rise and fall with the global prices of the commodities.[37]

A number of other studies have found that countries that export volatile-price commodities perform better with floating or managed floating exchange rates than with fixed rates,[38] which leads us to anticipate that the exchange rate regime will indeed make a difference.

Commodities are not as important for most Asian countries as for most in Latin America, Africa or the Middle East. (Commodities used to be very important in Southeast Asia, but have been substantially displaced by manufactures in most of the region.) For Asian countries we can use the VIX. Many studies have found that the VIX, reflecting the risk-sensitivity of global investors along the "risk-on" vs. "risk-off"

---

[36] Details are available from a data appendix at https://scholar.harvard.edu/frankel/exchange-rates-terms/fixed-vs-floating-exchange-rate-regimes.

[37] Including Cashin, Céspedes, and Sahay (2004), Chen and Rogoff (2003), and Frankel (2007).

[38] Including Broda (2004), Edwards and Levy-Yeyati (2005), Rafiq (2011), and Céspedes and Velasco (2012).

spectrum, is an important determinant of EM capital flows and, especially, of Emerging Market exchange rates and securities prices.[39]

Another dimension along which we seek deliberately to narrow down the set of countries is by the clarity of the exchange rate regime and the length of time that the country has maintained it. We are especially interested in those that have firm pegs and those that are good candidates for either systematically managed floating or free floating. (We recognize that very few fall in the latter category, among developing countries.) To make the first cut — identifying firm pegs and a group of floaters broadly defined — we rely on standard classification schemes, particularly the most recent from Ilzetzki, Reinhart, and Rogoff (2017). We deliberately drop those countries that change regimes every couple of years or have no clear regime at all, such as the free-fallers of Reinhart and Rogoff. But we wish to use our own criteria to distinguish countries that float freely (or virtually freely), such as New Zealand, and those that systematically manage their floats, such as Turkey. We want to omit those that intervene irregularly and unsystematically.

b.   Estimates for some Asian countries

We start with a set of eight Asian economies that are not primarily commodity-exporters for the period January 1997–December 2015. Regression results are reported in Appendix A. A few Asia/Pacific countries that *are* commodity producers will be considered below, where the sample will also have the advantage of several pure floaters and a number of firm fixers.

We start in Table A1 with an OLS regression of the real exchange rate directly against our external shock measure for the non-commodity countries: log (VIX). Because of the highly autoregressive nature of the real

---

[39] They include Di Giovanni, Kalemli-Ozcan, Ulu, and Baskaya (2018), Cerutti, Claessens, and Puy (2015), Forbes and Warnock, 2012) and Fratzscher (2012). Miranda-Agrippino and Rey (2015) and Rey (2015) trace these fluctuations in the global financial environment to changes in US monetary policy. Chari, Stedman and Lundblad (2017) find that the shocks do not show up in the quantity of capital flow so much as they drive EM asset *prices*.

exchange rate, we include a lagged endogenous variable, without which apparent significant levels would be spuriously high.[40] Even so, the VIX is statistically significant, with the hypothesized negative effect on the real exchange rate, defined here as the value of the local currency: An adverse shock in global financial market conditions causes a real depreciation. That is, we get the hypothesized negative effect for these 7 countries, all of which can be classified as systematic managed floaters: India, Korea, Malaysia, Philippines, Singapore, Thailand and Turkey. (The strongest effects are shown for Korea, followed by the Philippines, Thailand and Turkey.)

The one economy for which the coefficient is neither negative nor significant is precisely the one economy for which that is the hypothesis. Hong Kong, which has a firm peg to the dollar, shows no effect. To find no effect on the nominal exchange rate would tell us little. Finding zero effect on the *real* exchange rate confirms that regimes do matter for real variables, and that a peg prevents the real depreciation experienced by the seven flexible-rate currencies.

Table A2 regresses the Real Exchange Rate for the Asian countries against the balance of payments (measured as the change in foreign exchange reserves) as a ratio to GDP (expressed in common currency units).[41] We still think of log (VIX) as the driving exogenous shock, but

---

[40] The estimated coefficients on the lagged Real Exchange Rate are all high, as expected. Some appear statistically less than 1.0, some do not. A statistical failure to reject 1 is usually considered evidence of a unit root in the real exchange rate. If the real exchange rate truly has a unit root, then the equation should be estimated in first differences, or using more sophisticated time series techniques. Many studies have documented on long time samples that real exchange rates in truth have a tendency to regress slowly to an equilibrium level (represented by an average or trend), but that 20 years of data nevertheless do not have enough statistical power to reject a random walk. There is a tradeoff between the danger of spurious results on the one hand and the danger of throwing out perfectly good information on the other hand. Standard practice is that one should err on the side of rooting out unit roots (though the author is not aware of what research supports the general presumption that this is the greater danger). We hope in the future to refine the results in this paper with a more sophisticated time series approach.

[41] Now the lagged Real Exchange Rate shows estimated coefficients that are very close to 1.0. Thus one might think of the equation as essentially regressing the change in the real exchange rate against the change in reserves.

now it is the instrumental variable for the balance of payments. The estimated coefficients are now positive in every case, as they should be: a balance of payments surplus (resulting from a fall in the VIX) shows up in part as an appreciation of the local currency. However most of the coefficients now lose their statistical significance. Only in Korea and Turkey are the effects on the real exchange rate still highly significant statistically. The problem may lie in a weak first-stage instrument (especially in cases such as the Philippines and Thailand, judging by first-stage F-statistics).

c.   Estimates for commodity-exporting countries

Next we turn to estimates for a set of 21 commodity-exporting countries, reported in Appendix Table B. We have reason to hope that the exogenous variable will be a stronger instrument here, especially since we compute for each country an index of international commodity prices that is tailor-made to correspond to the commodity composition of its exports.

Table B1 reports the OLS regressions of the real exchange rate against the individual commodity price indices. The set of 21 includes three pure floaters: Australia, Canada and New Zealand. All three show highly significant effects on their real exchange rates, confirming their role as "commodity currencies." Chile also floated during much of this period, but not all, which may explain why its coefficient is only of borderline significance.

Of the countries that show no significant effect, four are firm fixers as one would expect: Ecuador, the UAE, Bahrain and Qatar (all pegged to the dollar). But South Africa also shows no significant effects here even though it is a systematic managed floaters by our criteria, while Brunei and Saudi Arabia show significant effects even though they are firm peggers (to the Singapore dollar and the U.S. dollar, respectively).[42]

----

[42] Brunei sometimes shows a significant positive effect, contrary to the hypothesis for a pegger. But this is probably because it is pegged to Singapore, which is a sort of managed floater.

For Indonesia, Papua New Guinea, Kazakhstan, Mongolia, and the rest of the 8 countries with managed floats or other intermediate regimes, the effect of the commodity price is statistically significant and positive.

Since many of these countries not only export commodities but also participate in international financial markets and thus qualify as emerging markets, Table B2 adds the VIX as an additional regressor. The results for the commodity price coefficient are similar. The VIX shows up with a significant RER effect for a few countries, all of them floaters. It is (just) significant for Colombia, one of the commodity-exporting intermediate-regime countries that did not show a significant responsiveness of the real exchange rate in Table B1.

Next we consider the regressions of the real exchange rate against the balance of payments, with both the country-specific commodity price index and the VIX as instrumental variables. We need a denominator for the balance of payments. We start with GDP in Table B3, which is perhaps the most obvious scale variable. But in Tables B4 and B5 we use M1 and the monetary base, respectively, as the denominator for the change in reserves, thereby linking up with the idea of Exchange Market Pressure.[43]

We want to distinguish the results for managed floaters as compared to firm fixers. The three free floaters (Australia, Canada and New Zealand) have been discarded, since floating implies by definition that the balance of payments is zero. Five managed floaters show significant effects on the real exchange rate in these three tables: Brazil, Chile, Colombia, Russia and South Africa. Two firm fixers show insignificant effects, again as hypothesized: Brunei and Ecuador.

Some show the anomalous result of a significant negative coefficient. In the case of a systematic managed floater like Peru, the result is indeed surprising.

---

[43] When a country is missing from a table, it is due to data availability. See online data appendix.

An explanation is available for why the coefficient estimates are negative for many of the Gulf countries and significantly so in the case of Saudi Arabia.[44] For these countries, the export commodity basket index consists simply of the dollar price of oil (or oil and natural gas). Even though oil and gas are priced and invoiced in dollars, the dollar price of oil falls quickly after an appreciation of the dollar against the euro, yen and other major currencies — as one would expect since Europe and Japan are major buyers of oil and gas. Bahrain, Qatar, the UAE and Saudi Arabia are all pegged specifically to the dollar. When the dollar appreciates against the euro, yen and other currencies, so do the dinar, dirham, and riyal. The implication is a negative correlation between the trade-weighted exchange rate, which is the one that goes into the regressions, and the dollar price of oil. This suggests that the dollar peg does *worse* than fail to accommodate terms of trade shocks; it actually tends to move in the wrong direction. (The Gulf countries might be better off pegging to a more sophisticated basket.)[45]

Perhaps something like this explanation also applies to Azerbaijan and Kazakhstan, since both are oil exporters. But these two are neither firm fixers nor managed floaters. Both of them have in recent years repeatedly tried to target their exchange rates and then been forced by alarming reserve losses into belated and large devaluations. In this paper we are concerned with the three special categories of firm fixers, free floaters and systematically-managed floaters. We have no hypothesis regarding those that fall outside these three categories.

d.  Summary of conclusions

A majority of countries follow exchange rate policies that can be designated as "intermediate," in that they are neither firm-fixers nor free-floaters. But this paper proposes the designation "systematically managed floater" only for those countries where the monetary

---

[44] There is a second possible explanation for anomalous results in the case of Saudi Arabia. It alone among all the commodity producers is large enough in the world market for its export commodity, oil, that we might want to question the assumption that the world price is exogenous. But the first reason seems a good enough explanation.

[45] Frankel (2019).

authorities tend consistently to react to exchange market pressure with some proportion of change in the exchange rate and some proportion of change in foreign exchange reserves. A sub-set of the intermediate regimes can be identified as meeting statistical criteria along the lines of this definition (Part 2, "What countries actually do").

In some theories, shocks will have the same effect on the real exchange rate regardless of regime, showing up in the exchange rate under floating but showing up in the price level if the exchange rate is fixed. A hypothesis of the paper is that exchange rate regimes do make a difference for the behavior of the real exchange rate. Specifically, an exogenous positive shock does not affect the real exchange rate in the short run if the nominal exchange rate is fixed, but will cause a real appreciation under a systematic managed float, with the magnitude of the real appreciation depending on how heavily managed is the float.

Our empirical tests focus on two kinds of shocks, measured by the VIX and export commodity prices. We have not attempted a comprehensive panel study. There are many reasons to view the various statistical results of this paper as rudimentary, particularly with respect to the familiar problems of causality and non-stationarity. But some of the results in Part 3 of the paper tend to support the hypothesis:

- Most EM economies with firmly fixed exchange rates do not experience real appreciation during periods of inflow arising from positive external shocks, such as 2003–2008 or 2010–2011, nor do they experience real depreciation during periods of outflow arising from negative external shocks such as 2008–2009 or 2014–2015. Of the firm-fixers, the case where the primary exogenous variable is the VIX is Hong Kong. The firm-fixers where it is the export commodity price include Ecuador and the Gulf countries.
- For our free-floating commodity exporters — Australia, Canada and New Zealand — positive shocks in their country-specific export commodity price index cause real appreciation of their currencies.

- For our systematic managed floaters in Asia, particularly Korea and Turkey, a fall in the VIX leads to real appreciation, regardless of whether observed directly (OLS) or indirectly via the balance of payments surplus (IV). For the others — India, Malaysia, the Philippines, Singapore and Thailand — the effect is statistically significant only when observed directly.

- For our commodity exporting managed floaters, the effects vary, but are significantly greater than zero more often than among the firm fixers and less often than among the free floaters.

In short, we reject the view that exchange rate regimes make no difference. We find that positive external shocks tend to cause real appreciation for most systematic managed-floaters; more strongly so for pure floaters; and not at all for most firm peggers.

## References

Adler, G, Lisack, N, and Mano, R (2015). Unveiling the effects of FX intervention: A panel approach. IMF Working Paper No. 15/130.

Adler, G and Tovar, CE (2011). FX intervention: A shield against appreciation winds? IMF Working Paper No. 11/165.

Aizenman, J, Chinn, M, and Ito, H (2010). The emerging global financial architecture: Tracing and evaluating new patterns of the trilemma configuration. *Journal of International Money and Finance*, 29(4), 615–641.

Aizenman, J, Chinn, M, and Ito, H (2011). Surfing the waves of globalization: Asia and financial globalization in the context of the trilemma. *Journal of the Japanese and International Economies*, 25(3), 290–320.

Avdjiev, S, Du, W, Koch, C, and Shin, HS (2019). The dollar, bank leverage and deviations from covered interest parity. *American Economic Review: Insights*, 1(2), 193–208.

Bahmani-Oskooee, M, Hegerty, S, and Kutan, A (2008). Do nominal devaluations lead to real devaluations? Evidence from 89 countries. *International Review of Economics and Finance*, 17, 644–670.

Bai, JS and Perron, P (2003). Computation and analysis of multiple structural change models. *Journal of Applied Econometrics*, 18(1), 1–22.

Basu, K and Varoudakis, A (2013). How to move the exchange rate if you must: The diverse practice of foreign exchange intervention by central banks and a proposal for doing it better. Policy RWP 6469, World Bank, May.

Beine, M, Bénassy-Quéré, A, and Lecourt, C (2002). Central bank intervention and foreign exchange rates: New evidence from FIGARCH estimation. *Journal of International Money and Finance,* 21(1), 115–144.

Bénassy-Quéré, A (1999). Exchange rate regimes and policies: an empirical analysis. In S Collignon, J Pisani-Ferry and YC Park (Eds.), *Exchange rate policies in emerging Asian countries* (pp.40–64). London: Routledge.

Bénassy-Quéré, A, Coeuré, B, and Mignon, V (2004). On the identification of de facto currency pegs. *Journal of the Japanese and International Economies,* 20(1), 112–127.

Blanchard, O, Adler, G and de Carvalho Filho, I (2015). Can foreign exchange intervention stem exchange rate pressures from global capital flow shocks? IMF Working Paper No. 15/159.

Blanchard, O, Ostry, J, Ghosh, AR, and Chamon, M (2016). Are capital inflows expansionary or contractionary? Theory, policy implications, and some evidence. NBER Working Paper No. 21619.

Broda, C (2004). Terms of trade and exchange rate regimes in developing countries. *Journal of International Economics,* 63(1), 31–58.

Bubula, A and Ötker-Robe, I (2002). The evolution of exchange rate regimes since 1990: evidence from de facto policies? IMF Working Paper 02/155.

Calvo, G and Reinhart, C (2002). Fear of floating. *Quarterly Journal of Economics,* 117(2), 379–408.

Cerutti, E, Claessens, S and Puy, D (2015). Push factors and capital flows to emerging markets: Why knowing your lender matters more than fundamentals. IMF Working Paper No. 15-127, June.

Cashin, P, Céspedes, LF and Sahay, R (2004). Commodity currencies and the real exchange rate. *Journal of Development Economics,* 75(1), 239–268.

Céspedes, LF and Velasco, A (2012). Macroeconomic performance during commodity price booms and busts. *IMF Economic Review,* 60(4), 570–599.

Chari, A, Stedman, CD, and Lundblad, C (2017). Taper tantrums: QE, its aftermath and emerging market capital flows. NBER Working Paper No. 23474, June.

Chen, Y-C and Rogoff, K (2003). Commodity currencies. *Journal of International Economics,* 60(1), 133–160.

Council on Foreign Relations (1999). *Safeguarding prosperity in a global financial system: the future international financial architecture.* Washington, DC: Institute for International Economics.

Crockett, A (1994). Monetary policy implications of increased capital flows. In *Changing Capital Markets: Implications for Monetary Policy*. Conference by Federal Reserve Bank of Kansas City, Jackson Hole, August.

Daude, C, Levy-Yeyati, E, and Nagengast, A (2016). On the effectiveness of exchange rate intervention in emerging markets. *Journal of International Money and Finance*, 64(June), 239–261.

Devereux, M and Engel, C (2002). Exchange rate pass-through, exchange rate volatility, and exchange rate disconnect. *Journal of Monetary Economics* 49(5), 913–940.

Devereux, M and Yetman, J (2014). Capital controls, global liquidity traps and the international policy trilemma. *The Scandinavian Journal of Economics*, 116(1), 158–189.

Di Giovanni, J, Kalemli-Ozcan, S, Ulu, MF, and Baskaya, YS (2018). International spillovers and local credit cycles. NBER Working Paper No. 2314. Barcelona: CREI, September.

Di Giovanni, J and Shambaugh, J (2008). The impact of foreign interest rates on the economy: the role of the exchange rate regime. *Journal of International Economics*, 74, 341–361.

Disyatat, P and Galati, G (2007). The effectiveness of foreign exchange intervention in emerging market countries: evidence from the Czech Koruna. *Journal of International Money and Finance*, 26(3), 383–402.

Dominguez, K (2006). When do central bank interventions influence intra-daily and longer-term exchange rate movements? *Journal of International Money and Finance*, 25, 1051–1071.

Dominguez, K, Fatum, R, and Vacek, P (2013). Do sales of foreign exchange reserves lead to currency appreciation? *Journal of Money, Credit and Banking*, 45(5), 867–890.

Dominguez, K and Frankel, J (1993a). Does foreign exchange intervention matter? The portfolio effect. *American Economic Review*, 83(5), 1356–1369.

Dominguez, K and Frankel, J (1993b). *Does foreign exchange intervention work?* Washington: Institute for International Economics.

Edison, H (1993). The effectiveness of central-bank intervention: A survey of the literature after 1982. Special Papers in International Economics No. 18. Princeton University Press: Princeton, NJ.

Edwards, S (2015). Monetary policy independence under flexible exchange rates: An illusion? *The World Economy*, 38 (5), 773–787. NBER Working Paper 20893.

Edwards, S and Levy Yeyati, E (2005). Flexible exchange rates as shock absorbers. *European Economic Review*, 49(8), 2079–2105.

Eichengreen, B (1994). *International monetary arrangements for the 21st century*. Washington, DC: Brookings Institution.

Eichengreen, B and Razo-Garcia, R (2013). How reliable are de facto exchange rate regime classifications? *International Journal of Finance & Economics*, 18(3), 216–239.

Farhi, E and Werning, I (2014). Dilemma not trilemma? Capital controls and exchange rates with volatile capital flows. *IMF Economic Review*, 62(4), pp. 569–605. NBER Working Paper No. 19854.

Fatum, R and Hutchison, MM (2003). Is sterilized FX intervention effective after all? An event study approach. *Economic Journal*, 113(487), 390–411.

Fatum, R and Hutchison, MM (2010). Evaluating FX market intervention: self-selection, counterfactuals and average treatment effects. *Journal of International Money and Finance*, 29(3), 570–584.

Fischer, S (2001). Exchange rate regimes: is the bipolar view correct? *Journal of Economic Perspectives*, 15(2), 3–24.

Flood, R and Rose, A (1999). Understanding exchange rate volatility without the contrivance of macroeconomics. *The Economic Journal*, 109(459), 660–672.

Forbes, K and Warnock, F (2012). Capital flow waves: surges stops, flight, and retrenchment. *Journal of International Economics*, 88(2), 235–251.

Frankel, J (2003). Experience of and lessons from exchange rate regimes in emerging economies. In Asian Development Bank (Ed.), *Monetary and Financial Cooperation in East Asia*. New York: Palgrave Macmillan.

Frankel, J (2009). New estimation of China's exchange rate regime. *Pacific Economic Review*, 13(3), 346–360.

Frankel, J (2016). The plaza accord, 30 years later. In CF Bergsten and R Green (Eds.), *Currency policy then and now: 30th anniversary of the plaza accord*. Washington DC: Peterson Institute for International Economics.

Frankel, J (2019). The currency-plus-commodity basket: A proposal for exchange rates in oil-exporting countries to accommodate trade shocks automatically. In H Selim, K Mohaddes, and J Nugent (Eds.), *Institutions and macroeconomic policies in resource-rich Arab economies* (pp. 149–182). Oxford: Oxford University Press.

Frankel, J, Fajnzylber, E, Schmukler, S, and Servén, L (2001). Verifying exchange rate regimes. *Journal of Development Economics*, 66(2), 351–386.

Frankel, J, Schmukler, S and Servén, L (2004). Global transmission of interest rates: monetary independence and the currency regime. *Journal of International Money and Finance*, 23(5), 701–734.

Frankel, J and Wei, S-J (1994). Yen bloc or dollar bloc? Exchange rate policies of the East Asian economies. In T Ito and A Krueger (Eds.), *Macroeconomic linkages: savings, exchange rates, and capital flows, NBER — East Asia seminar on economics, Vol. 3*. University of Chicago Press.

Frankel, J and Wei, S-J (2008). Estimation of de facto exchange rate regimes: synthesis of the techniques for inferring flexibility and basket weights. *IMF Staff Papers*, 55(3), 384–416.

Frankel, J and Xie, D (2010). Estimation of de facto flexibility parameter and basket weights in evolving exchange rate regimes. *American Economic Review*, 100(2), 568–572.

Fratzscher, M (2012). Capital flows, push versus pull factors and the global financial crisis. *Journal of International Economics*, 88, 341–356. NBER Working Paper No. 17357.

Fratzscher, M, Gloede, O, Menkhoff, L, Sarno, L, and Stöhr, T (2019). When is foreign exchange intervention effective? Evidence from 33 countries. *American Economic Journal: Macroeconomics*, 11(1), 132–156. Available at SSRN: https://ssrn.com/abstract=2686434 .

Friedman, M (1953). The case for flexible exchange rates. *Essays in Positive Economics*.

Frömmel, M and Midiliç, M (2016). Daily currency interventions in emerging markets: incorporating reserve accumulation. Proceedings of 25th International Academic Conference, OECD Headquarters. No. 4106590, International Institute of Social and Economic Sciences.

Ghosh, A, Gulde, A-M, and Wolf, H (2000). Currency boards: more than a quick fix? *Economic Policy*, 31(October), 270–335.

Ghosh, AR, Ostry, J, and Qureshi, M (2015). Exchange rate management and crisis susceptibility: A reassessment. *IMF Economic Review*, 63(1), 238–276.

Girton, L and Roper, D (1977). A monetary model of exchange market pressure applied to the postwar Canadian experience. *American Economic Review*, 67(4), 537–548.

Han, XW and Wei, S-J (2018). International transmissions of monetary shocks between a trilemma and a dilemma. *Journal of International Economics*, 110(January), 205–219. NBER Working Paper No. 22812.

Humpage, OF (1999). U.S. intervention: Assessing the probability of success. *Journal of Money, Credit and Banking*, 31(4), 732–747.

Ilzetzki, E, Reinhart, C, and Rogoff, K (2017). Exchange arrangements entering the 21st century: Which anchor will hold? NBER Working Paper No. 23134, February.

Ito, T (2001). Discussion of the case for a basket, band and crawl (BBC) regime for East Asia. In D Gruen and J Simon (Eds.), *Future directions for monetary policies in East Asia*. Sydney: Reserve Bank of Australia.

Ito, T (2003). Is foreign exchange intervention effective: the Japanese experience in the 1990s. In P Mizen (Ed.), *Monetary history, exchange rates and financial markets, essays in honour of Charles Goodhart, Vol. 2*. Cheltenham U.K.: Edward Elgar Publishers.

Jeanne, O and Rancière, R (2011). The optimal level of international reserves for emerging market countries: a new formula and some applications. *Economic Journal*, 121(555), 905–930.

Kearns, J and Rigobon, R (2005). Identifying the efficacy of central bank interventions: evidence from Australia and Japan. *Journal of International Economics*, 66(1), 31–48.

Klein, M and Marion, N (1997). Explaining the duration of exchange-rate pegs. *Journal of Development Economics*, 54(2), 387–404.

Klein, M and Shambaugh, J (2012). *Exchange rate regimes in the modern era*. Cambridge: MIT Press.

Klein, M and Shambaugh, J (2015). Rounding the corners of the policy trilemma: Sources of monetary policy autonomy. NBER Working Paper No. 19461, February.

Krugman, P (1991). Target zones and exchange rate dynamics. *Quarterly Journal of Economics*, 106, 669–682.

Levy Yeyati, E and Sturzenegger, F (2001). Exchange rate regimes and economic performance. *IMF Staff Papers*, 47, 62–98, February.

Levy-Yeyati, E and Sturzenegger, F (2003). To float or to trail: Evidence on the impact of exchange rate regimes on growth. *American Economic Review*, 93(4), 1173–1193.

Levy-Yeyati, E and Sturzenegger, F (2005). Classifying exchange rate regimes: Deeds vs. words. *European Economic Review*, 49(6), 1603–1635.

Magud, NE, Reinhart, CM, and Vesperoni, ER (2014). Capital inflows, exchange rate flexibility and credit booms. *Review of Development Economics*, 18(3), 415–430.

Meltzer, A (2000). *Report of the International Financial Institution Advisory Commission*. Submitted to the U.S. Congress and U.S. Department of the Treasury, 8 March.

Menkhoff, L (2010). High-frequency analysis of FX interventions: what do we learn? *Journal of Economic Surveys*, 24(1), 85–112.

Menkhoff, L (2013). Foreign exchange intervention in emerging markets: A survey of empirical studies. *World Economy,* 36(9), 1187–1208.

Milesi-Ferretti, G-M and Tille, C (2011). The great retrenchment: International capital flows during the global financial crisis. *Economic Policy,* 26(66), 289–346.

Miranda-Agrippino, S and Rey, H (2015). World asset markets and the global financial cycle. NBER Working Paper No. 21722.

Mohanty, MS (2013). Market volatility and foreign exchange intervention in EMEs: what has changed? An overview. BIS Papers No. 73, 1–10.

Mussa, M (1981) The role of official intervention. Group of Thirty Occasional Paper No. 6.

Mussa, M (1986). Nominal exchange rate regimes and the behavior of real exchange rates: Evidence and implications. *Carnegie-Rochester Conference Series on Public Policy No. 25,* 117-214.

Nelson, E (2018). The continuing validity of monetary policy autonomy under floating exchange rates. Federal Reserve Board, November.

Obstfeld, M and Rogoff, K (1995). The mirage of fixed exchange rates. *Journal of Economic Perspectives,* 9(4), 73–96.

Obstfeld, M (1990). The effectiveness of foreign-exchange intervention: Recent experience. In J. Frenkel, M Goldstein, and W Branson (Eds.), *International policy coordination and exchange rate fluctuations.* Chicago: University of Chicago Press.

Obstfeld, M (1997). Destabilizing effects of exchange-rate escape clauses. *Journal of International Economics,* 43(1), 61–77.

Obstfeld, M (2015). Trilemmas and tradeoffs: living with financial globalization. In C Raddatz, D Saravia and J Ventura (Eds.), *Global liquidity, spillovers to emerging markets and policy responses* (pp. 13–78). Santiago, Chile: Central Bank of Chile.

Obstfeld, M, Shambaugh, J, and Taylor, AM (2005). The trilemma in history: Tradeoffs among exchange rates, monetary policies, and capital mobility. *Review of Economics and Statistics,* 87(3), 423–438.

Ogawa, E (2006). The Chinese yuan after the Chinese exchange rate system reform. *China and World Economy,* 14(6), 39–57.

Rafiq, MS (2011). Sources of economic fluctuations in oil-exporting economies: implications for choice of exchange rate regimes. *International Journal of Economics and Finance,* 16(1), 70–91.

Reinhart, C (2000). The mirage of floating exchange rates. *American Economic Review,* 90(2), 65–70.

Reinhart, C and Rogoff, K (2004). The modern history of exchange rate arrangements: A reinterpretation. *Quarterly Journal of Economics,* 119(1), 1–48.

Rey, H (2014). Dilemma not trilemma: the global financial cycle and monetary policy independence. In *Global Dimensions of Unconventional Monetary Policy.* Proceedings of the 2013 Economic Policy Symposium at Jackson Hole, Federal Reserve Bank of Kansas City.

Rodrik, D (2006). The social cost of foreign exchange reserves. *International Economic Journal,* 20(3), 253–266.

Rose, A (2011). Exchange rate regimes in the modern era: fixed, floating, and flaky. *Journal of Economic Literature,* 49(3), 652–672.

Sarno, L and Taylor, MP (2001). Official intervention in the FX markets: Is it effective and, if so, how does it work? *Journal of Economic Literature,* 34(3), 839–868.

Shambaugh, J (2004). The effect of fixed exchange rates on monetary policy. *Quarterly Journal of Economics,* 119(1), 301–352.

Subramanian, A (2011a). Renminbi rules: the conditional imminence of the reserve currency transition. Working Paper Series No. 11–14. Washington, D.C.: Peterson Institute for International Economics, September.

Subramanian, A (2011b). *Eclipse: Living in the shadow of China's economic dominance.* Washington, DC: Peterson Institute for International Economics.

Summers, L (1999). Building an international financial architecture for the 21st century. *Cato Journal,* 18(3), 321–330.

Tavlas, G, Dellas, H, and Stockman, A (2008). The classification and performance of alternative exchange-rate systems. *European Economic Review,* 52(6), 941–963.

Taylor, AM (2002). A century of purchasing power parity. *Review of Economics and Statistics,* 84(February), 139–150.

Truman , E (2003). The limits of exchange market intervention. In CF Bergsten and J Williamson (Eds.), *Dollar overvaluation and the world economy* (pp. 247–265). Washington: Peterson Institute for International Economics.

Williamson, J (2001). The case for a basket, band and crawl (BBC) regime for East Asia. In D Gruen and J Simon (Eds.), *Future directions for monetary policies in East Asia* (pp. 97–111). Sydney: Reserve Bank of Australia.

**Appendix Tables 1 & 2: Estimation of weights and flexibility parameter**

**Appendix Table 1.** Identifying break points in Thailand's exchange rate regime (M1:1999–M5:2009)

| Variables | (1) 1/21/1999–8/5/2001 | (2) 8/12/2001–9/9/2006 | (3) 9/16/2006–3/25/2007 | (4) 4/1/2007–5/6/2009 |
|---|---|---|---|---|
| U.S. dollar | 0.62*** | 0.61*** | 0.80*** | 0.70*** |
| | (0.09) | (0.04) | (0.28) | (0.05) |
| Euro | 0.26*** | 0.17*** | −0.08 | 0.19*** |
| | (0.08) | (0.06) | (0.59) | (0.04) |
| Jpn yen | 0.15*** | 0.25*** | 0.16 | 0.04 |
| | (0.04) | (0.03) | (0.30) | (0.03) |
| $\Delta EMP$ | 0.20*** | 0.06*** | 0.50*** | 0.03** |
| | (0.05) | (0.02) | (0.17) | (0.01) |
| Constant | −0.00** | 0.00 | −0.01 | −0.00 |
| | (0.00) | (0.00) | (0.00) | (0.00) |
| Observations | 129 | 257 | 27 | 108 |
| $R^2$ | 0.66 | 0.76 | 0.64 | 0.90 |
| GB£ | −0.02 | −0.04 | 0.12 | 0.07 |

Appendix Table 2. Identifying break points in India's exchange rate regime (M1:2000–M5:2009)

| Variables | (1) 1/14/2000– 10/27/2000 | (2) 11/3/2000– 6/17/2001 | (3) 6/24/2001– 12/31/2001 | (4) 1/14/2002– 9/23/2003 | (5) 9/30/2003– 2/25/2007 | (6) 3/4/2007– 5/6/2009 |
|---|---|---|---|---|---|---|
| U.S. dollar | 0.77*** | 0.92*** | 0.66*** | 0.91*** | 0.72*** | 0.59*** |
|  | (0.06) | (0.04) | (0.08) | (0.04) | (0.06) | (0.10) |
| Euro | 0.12*** | 0.10*** | 0.23*** | 0.03 | 0.06 | 0.32*** |
|  | (0.03) | (0.03) | (0.07) | (0.03) | (0.05) | (0.07) |
| Jpn yen | 0.09*** | 0.04* | 0.05 | 0.03 | 0.24*** | 0.02 |
|  | (0.02) | (0.02) | (0.05) | (0.02) | (0.06) | (0.07) |
| $\Delta EMP$ | 0.44*** | 0.04 | 0.46*** | 0.06 | 0.15*** | 0.37*** |
|  | (0.06) | (0.04) | (0.10) | (0.04) | (0.05) | (0.07) |
| Observations | 42 | 32 | 28 | 88 | 172 | 109 |
| $R^2$ | 0.98 | 0.98 | 0.98 | 0.98 | 0.86 | 0.78 |
| GB£ | 0.02 | –0.06 | 0.06 | 0.03 | –0.01 | 0.08 |

Notes: $\Delta EMP$ is the exchange rate market pressure variable, which is defined as the percentage increase in the value of the local currency plus the increase in reserves (scaled by the monetary base) $\Delta EMP_t = \Delta \log H_t + \frac{[\text{Reserve}_t - \text{Reserve}_{t-1}]}{MB_{t-1}}$. All data are weekly. *** $p<0.01$, ** $p<0.05$, * $p<0.1$ (Robust standard errors in parentheses.)

Source: Frankel and Xie (2011).

## Appendix Tables A and B: Effect of shocks on real exchange rates

**Appendix Tables A:** Effect of shocks on real exchange rates among Asia non-commodity-exporters

A1) OLS: Log of REER on Log of VIX and lagged REER

| Variables | (1) HKG | (2) India | (3) Korea, R | (4) Malaysia | (5) Philippines | (6) Singapore | (7) Thailand | (8) Turkey |
|---|---|---|---|---|---|---|---|---|
| Log of VIX | 0.002 | −0.006* | −0.047*** | −0.009* | −0.011*** | −0.005*** | −0.011*** | −0.019*** |
| | (0.004) | (0.003) | (0.009) | (0.005) | (0.003) | (0.002) | (0.003) | (0.006) |
| REER Lag | 0.993*** | 0.987*** | 0.874*** | 0.935*** | 0.996*** | 0.997*** | 0.970*** | 0.955*** |
| | (0.008) | (0.012) | (0.027) | (0.028) | (0.007) | (0.005) | (0.024) | (0.016) |
| Constant | 0.027 | 0.080 | 0.703*** | 0.326** | 0.053 | 0.028 | 0.171 | 0.254*** |
| | (0.035) | (0.056) | (0.141) | (0.126) | (0.033) | (0.026) | (0.112) | (0.077) |
| Observations | 227 | 227 | 227 | 227 | 227 | 227 | 227 | 227 |
| R-squared | 0.990 | 0.968 | 0.928 | 0.904 | 0.986 | 0.992 | 0.954 | 0.956 |

A2) IV: Log of REER on ΔRes/GDP and lagged REER
Instrument: log of VIX

| Variables | (1) HKG | (2) India | (3) Korea, R. | (4) Malaysia | (5) Philippines | (6) Singapore | (7) Thailand | (8) Turkey |
|---|---|---|---|---|---|---|---|---|
| ΔRes/GDP | 0.074 | 0.396 | 1.754*** | 0.291 | 11.118 | 0.220 | −6.360 | 1.785*** |
| | (0.139) | (0.419) | (0.411) | (0.209) | (43.304) | (0.193) | (26.523) | (0.653) |
| REER Lag | 0.997*** | 0.993*** | 1.039*** | 0.979*** | 0.962*** | 1.029*** | 0.748 | 0.967*** |
| | (0.008) | (0.020) | (0.029) | (0.049) | (0.162) | (0.024) | (0.946) | (0.020) |
| Constant | 0.011 | 0.030 | −0.188 | 0.093 | 0.098 | −0.137 | 1.207 | 0.139 |
| | (0.042) | (0.092) | (0.131) | (0.227) | (0.493) | (0.116) | (4.551) | (0.090) |
| Observations | 227 | 144 | 227 | 227 | 227 | 219 | 225 | 225 |
| R-squared | 0.987 | 0.960 | 0.912 | 0.882 | | 0.975 | | 0.937 |

Robust standard errors in parentheses; ***p<0.01, **p<0.05, *p<0.1.

**Appendix Tables B:** Effect of shocks on real exchange rates among commodity-exporters

B1) OLS: Log of REER on a country-specific commodity price index and lagged REER

| Variables | (1) Austral. | (2) New Zea. | (3) S. Africa | (4) Brazil | (5) Chile | (6) Colombia | (7) Ecuador | (8) Peru | (9) UAE | (10) Indonesia | (11) Papua NG |
|---|---|---|---|---|---|---|---|---|---|---|---|
| Commodity Price Indices | 0.038*** | 0.086** | 0.000 | 0.144*** | 0.012* | 0.011 | 0.010 | 0.008** | −0.030 | 0.091*** | 0.025*** |
| | (0.015) | (0.042) | (0.010) | (0.052) | (0.006) | (0.008) | (0.010) | (0.004) | (0.020) | (0.033) | (0.006) |
| REER Lag | 0.944*** | 0.955*** | 0.970*** | 0.952*** | 0.960*** | 0.981*** | 0.965*** | 0.970*** | 0.942*** | 0.890*** | 0.963*** |
| | (0.019) | (0.022) | (0.021) | (0.017) | (0.014) | (0.016) | (0.036) | (0.013) | (0.049) | (0.041) | (0.013) |
| Constant | 0.269*** | 0.244** | 0.138 | 0.229*** | 0.170*** | 0.091 | 0.170 | 0.138** | 0.273 | 0.535*** | 0.187*** |
| | (0.092) | (0.114) | (0.095) | (0.079) | (0.064) | (0.077) | (0.170) | (0.059) | (0.233) | (0.197) | (0.062) |
| Observations | 226 | 226 | 227 | 227 | 227 | 227 | 227 | 227 | 107 | 227 | 227 |
| R-squared | 0.983 | 0.975 | 0.928 | 0.973 | 0.949 | 0.963 | 0.935 | 0.965 | 0.936 | 0.908 | 0.973 |

Robust standard errors in parentheses; *** $p<0.01$, ** $p<0.05$, * $p<0.1$

| Variables | (12) Azerbaij. | (13) Bahrain | (14) Brunei | (15) Canada | (16) Kazakhstan | (17) Kuwait | (18) Qatar | (19) Russia | (20) Saudi Arabia | (21) Mongolia |
|---|---|---|---|---|---|---|---|---|---|---|
| Commodity Price Indices | 0.011*** | −0.002 | 0.004*** | 0.013*** | 0.014*** | 0.003* | 0.002 | 0.033** | 0.004** | 0.044*** |
|  | (0.004) | (0.004) | (0.001) | (0.004) | (0.005) | (0.002) | (0.003) | (0.016) | (0.002) | (0.015) |
| REER Lag | 0.979*** | 0.979*** | 0.980*** | 0.939*** | 0.958*** | 0.996*** | 1.001*** | 0.926*** | 1.015*** | 0.946*** |
|  | (0.010) | (0.021) | (0.008) | (0.019) | (0.018) | (0.010) | (0.013) | (0.028) | (0.010) | (0.025) |
| Constant | 0.105** | 0.100 | 0.094** | 0.279*** | 0.198** | 0.022 | −0.003 | 0.349*** | −0.069 | 0.264** |
|  | (0.050) | (0.095) | (0.039) | (0.086) | (0.084) | (0.049) | (0.059) | (0.130) | (0.048) | (0.118) |
| Observations | 227 | 227 | 227 | 227 | 227 | 227 | 156 | 227 | 227 | 227 |
| R-squared | 0.988 | 0.979 | 0.982 | 0.984 | 0.965 | 0.976 | 0.978 | 0.974 | 0.980 | 0.968 |

Robust standard errors in parentheses; ***p<0.01, **p<0.05, *p<0.1

B2) OLS: Log of REER on a country-specific commodity price index, log of VIX and lagged REER

| Variables | (1) Austral | (2) New Zea. | (3) S. Africa | (4) Brazil | (5) Chile | (6) Colombia | (7) Ecuador | (8) Peru | (9) UAE | (10) Indonesia | (11) Papua NG |
|---|---|---|---|---|---|---|---|---|---|---|---|
| Commodity Price Indices | 0.039*** | 0.140*** | -0.003 | 0.100* | 0.007 | 0.005 | 0.012 | 0.010*** | -0.023 | 0.087*** | 0.027*** |
| | (0.014) | (0.043) | (0.011) | (0.054) | (0.007) | (0.009) | (0.010) | (0.004) | (0.019) | (0.033) | (0.006) |
| Log of VIX | -0.012 | -0.021*** | -0.008 | -0.021** | -0.008 | -0.013* | 0.005 | 0.005 | 0.006 | -0.006 | 0.009 |
| | (0.008) | (0.005) | (0.008) | (0.009) | (0.006) | (0.007) | (0.005) | (0.003) | (0.006) | (0.009) | (0.007) |
| REER Lag | 0.934*** | 0.905*** | 0.966*** | 0.959*** | 0.964*** | 0.985*** | 0.967*** | 0.969*** | 0.951*** | 0.890*** | 0.963*** |
| | (0.018) | (0.026) | (0.020) | (0.017) | (0.015) | (0.016) | (0.037) | (0.013) | (0.048) | (0.041) | (0.013) |
| Constant | 0.352*** | 0.554*** | 0.180* | 0.253*** | 0.181*** | 0.110 | 0.149 | 0.131** | 0.214 | 0.551*** | 0.158** |
| | (0.090) | (0.143) | (0.096) | (0.077) | (0.063) | (0.077) | (0.179) | (0.060) | (0.231) | (0.199) | (0.066) |
| Observations | 226 | 226 | 227 | 227 | 227 | 227 | 227 | 227 | 107 | 227 | 227 |
| R-squared | 0.984 | 0.977 | 0.929 | 0.974 | 0.950 | 0.964 | 0.935 | 0.966 | 0.937 | 0.908 | 0.973 |

| Variables | (12) Azerbaij | (13) Bahrain | (14) Brunei | (15) Canada | (16) Kazakhstan | (17) Kuwait | (18) Qatar | (19) Russia | (20) Saudi Arabia | (21) Mongolia |
|---|---|---|---|---|---|---|---|---|---|---|
| Commodity Price Indices | 0.014*** | -0.002 | 0.004*** | 0.011*** | 0.014** | 0.004* | 0.002 | 0.029** | 0.005** | 0.045*** |
|  | (0.005) | (0.004) | (0.001) | (0.004) | (0.005) | (0.002) | (0.003) | (0.014) | (0.002) | (0.017) |
| Log of VIX | 0.007 | 0.003 | 0.001 | -0.009* | -0.002 | 0.004 | 0.000 | -0.016 | 0.005 | 0.002 |
|  | (0.007) | (0.004) | (0.002) | (0.005) | (0.008) | (0.004) | (0.006) | (0.010) | (0.004) | (0.008) |
| REER Lag | 0.976*** | 0.979*** | 0.980*** | 0.937*** | 0.959*** | 0.994*** | 1.001*** | 0.928*** | 1.014*** | 0.945*** |
|  | (0.012) | (0.020) | (0.009) | (0.019) | (0.017) | (0.010) | (0.012) | (0.026) | (0.011) | (0.025) |
| Constant | 0.101** | 0.090 | 0.094** | 0.314*** | 0.201** | 0.022 | -0.003 | 0.385*** | -0.076 | 0.261** |
|  | (0.048) | (0.092) | (0.039) | (0.088) | (0.087) | (0.049) | (0.057) | (0.141) | (0.048) | (0.117) |
| Observations | 227 | 227 | 227 | 227 | 227 | 227 | 156 | 227 | 227 | 227 |
| R-squared | 0.988 | 0.980 | 0.982 | 0.985 | 0.965 | 0.976 | 0.978 | 0.974 | 0.980 | 0.968 |

Robust standard errors in parentheses; ***p<0.01, **p<0.05, *p<0.1

B3) IV: Log of REER on ΔRes/GDP and a time trend
Instruments: log of VIX and a country-specific commodity price index

| Variables | (1) S. Africa | (2) Brazil | (3) Chile | (4) Colombia | (5) Ecuador | (6) Peru | (7) Azerbaijan |
|---|---|---|---|---|---|---|---|
| ΔRes/GDP | −1.260 | 20.527*** | 14.315** | 23.670*** | 0.002 | −0.807* | 0.466 |
| | (3.837) | (6.402) | (5.900) | (8.312) | (0.006) | (0.458) | (0.632) |
| Time trend | −0.005*** | 0.001*** | 0.000 | 0.000 | −0.005 | 0.001*** | 0.004*** |
| | (0.000) | (0.000) | (0.000) | (0.000) | (0.012) | (0.000) | (0.000) |
| Constant | 5.484*** | 4.288*** | 4.559*** | 4.470*** | 5.009*** | 4.616*** | 4.097*** |
| | (0.093) | (0.073) | (0.046) | (0.039) | (0.774) | (0.010) | (0.034) |
| Observations | 70 | 227 | 227 | 227 | 130 | 227 | 180 |
| R-squared | 0.747 | | | | | 0.207 | 0.756 |

| Variables | (8) Bahrain | (9) Brunei | (10) Kazakhstan | (11) Qatar | (12) Russia | (13) Saudi Arabia |
|---|---|---|---|---|---|---|
| ΔRes/GDP | −1.269** | 2.004 | −2.562** | −1.670* | 3.071*** | −1.396*** |
| | (0.526) | (2.074) | (1.163) | (0.897) | (1.109) | (0.181) |
| Time trend | 0.006*** | 0.001*** | 0.002*** | 0.002*** | 0.003*** | 0.001*** |
| | (0.002) | (0.000) | (0.000) | (0.001) | (0.000) | (0.000) |
| Constant | 3.370*** | 4.439*** | 4.343*** | 4.250*** | 4.045*** | 4.555*** |
| | (0.386) | (0.020) | (0.026) | (0.114) | (0.042) | (0.054) |
| Observations | 19 | 142 | 225 | 72 | 227 | 72 |
| R-squared | 0.338 | | 0.249 | | 0.390 | 0.735 |

Robust standard errors in parentheses; ***p<0.01, **p<0.05, *p<0.1

B4) IV: Log of REER on ΔRes/M1 and a time trend
Instruments: log of VIX and a price index

| Variables | (1) S. Africa | (2) Brazil | (3) Chile | (4) Colombia | (5) Indonesia | (6) Mongolia |
|---|---|---|---|---|---|---|
| ΔRes/M1 | 36.876*** | 3.987*** | 6.470** | 7.770*** | 2.242 | 0.002 |
|  | (8.855) | (1.415) | (2.806) | (2.908) | (5.341) | (0.250) |
| Time trend | 0.000 | 0.001*** | 0.000 | 0.000 | 0.002*** | 0.002*** |
|  | (0.000) | (0.000) | (0.000) | (0.000) | (0.000) | (0.000) |
| Constant | 4.487*** | 4.294*** | 4.549*** | 4.465*** | 4.290*** | 4.402*** |
|  | (0.045) | (0.077) | (0.058) | (0.047) | (0.085) | (0.019) |
| Observations | 227 | 227 | 227 | 227 | 227 | 227 |
| R-squared |  |  |  |  | 0.128 | 0.529 |

| Variables | (7) Azerbaijan | (8) Bahrain | (9) Kazakhstan | (10) Kuwait | (11) Qatar | (12) Russia | (13) Saudi Arabia |
|---|---|---|---|---|---|---|---|
| ΔRes/M1 | -1.540*** | -15.274 | -2.016*** | -7.732 | 2.583 | 1.828** | -2.138*** |
|  | (0.595) | (24.278) | (0.698) | (7.227) | (5.855) | (0.912) | (0.267) |
| Time trend | 0.002*** | -0.001 | 0.001*** | 0.002** | 0.002** | -0.001 | -0.000* |
|  | (0.000) | (0.002) | (0.000) | (0.001) | (0.001) | (0.001) | (0.000) |
| Constant | 4.449*** | 4.937*** | 4.435*** | 4.490*** | 4.227*** | 4.752*** | 4.847*** |
|  | (0.044) | (0.425) | (0.076) | (0.106) | (0.236) | (0.116) | (0.014) |
| Observations | 227 | 141 | 145 | 169 | 157 | 97 | 227 |

Robust standard errors in parentheses; *** p<0.01, ** p<0.05, * p<0.1

B5) IV: Log of REER on ΔRes/MB and a time trend
Instruments: log of VIX and a price index

| Variables | (1) S. Africa | (2) Brazil | (3) Chile | (4) Colombia | (5) Peru | (6) UAE | (7) Indonesia | (8) Papua NG | (9) Azerbaijan |
|---|---|---|---|---|---|---|---|---|---|
| ΔRes/MB | 5.846*** | 6.750*** | 2.741*** | 5.419** | -0.461* | -0.568** | -8.107 | -0.231 | -1.468** |
|  | (1.389) | (2.053) | (0.814) | (2.131) | (0.247) | (0.253) | (18.714) | (0.207) | (0.579) |
| Time trend | 0.000 | 0.001*** | 0.000 | 0.001* | 0.001*** | 0.001*** | 0.002*** | 0.002*** | 0.002*** |
|  | (0.000) | (0.000) | (0.000) | (0.000) | (0.000) | (0.000) | (0.001) | (0.000) | (0.000) |
| Constant | 4.489*** | 4.287*** | 4.552*** | 4.455*** | 4.617*** | 4.547*** | 4.449*** | 4.446*** | 4.445*** |
|  | (0.045) | (0.064) | (0.037) | (0.046) | (0.010) | (0.039) | (0.277) | (0.019) | (0.043) |
| Observations | 227 | 227 | 227 | 227 | 227 | 105 | 227 | 227 | 227 |
| R-squared |  |  |  |  | 0.218 | 0.184 |  | 0.649 | 7.96 |

| Variables | (10) Bahrain | (11) Brunei | (12) Kazakhstan | (13) Kuwait | (14) Qatar | (15) Russia | (16) Saudi Arabia | (17) Mongolia |
|---|---|---|---|---|---|---|---|---|
| ΔRes/MB | -8.551 | 1.604 | -0.972** | -4.889 | -5.512 | 1.569*** | -0.678*** | -0.095 |
|  | (11.482) | (1.305) | (0.467) | (8.869) | (12.912) | (0.554) | (0.082) | (0.285) |
| Time trend | -0.001 | 0.001*** | 0.001*** | 0.000 | -0.000 | 0.003*** | -0.000* | 0.002*** |
|  | (0.001) | (0.000) | (0.000) | (0.001) | (0.005) | (0.000) | (0.000) | (0.000) |
| Constant | 4.981*** | 4.491*** | 4.363*** | 4.725*** | 4.800*** | 4.033*** | 4.845*** | 4.404*** |
|  | (0.197) | (0.024) | (0.031) | (0.276) | (1.236) | (0.047) | (0.013) | (0.019) |
| Observations | 222 | 168 | 227 | 227 | 157 | 227 | 227 | 227 |
| R-squared |  |  | 0.238 |  |  | 0.336 |  | 0.532 |

Robust standard errors in parentheses; *** p<0.01, ** p<0.05, * p<0.1

# CHAPTER 6

# Chapter 6

# Gauging Procyclicality and Financial Vulnerability in Asia through the BIS Banking and Financial Statistics*

Stefan Avdjiev, Bat-el Berger and Hyun Song Shin[1]

## Abstract

We look back at past episodes of financial stress in Asia with a forward-looking perspective. We put ourselves in the shoes of a contemporary observer with the data at hand and ask what evidence was available on the systematic build-up of vulnerabilities. We reconstruct a graphical narrative of banking and financial developments at the time. Our exercise aims to showcase the usefulness of the BIS international banking and financial statistics as a window on the financial system's procyclicality. We conclude with a real-time forward-looking exercise on financial vulnerabilities, focusing on the implications of the shift in the pattern of credit intermediation from banks to bond markets.

## Introduction

This year marks the 10th anniversary of the Great Financial Crisis (GFC) of 2008, and the 21st anniversary of the beginning of the 1997 Asian Financial Crisis (AFC). Given the time that has elapsed and with the benefit of the experience gained since, it is a good moment to reflect on the lessons learned.

---

[1] Stefan Avdjiev, Adviser for Financial Stability, Bank for International Settlements;
Bat-el Berger, Principal Data Scientist, Bank for International Settlements;
Hyun Song Shin, Economic Adviser and Head of Research, Bank for International Settlements.

One aim of our paper is to look back but with a forward-looking perspective. We put ourselves in the shoes of a contemporary observer with the data at hand and ask what evidence was available to observers on the systematic build-up of vulnerabilities. The spirit of the exercise is to reconstruct a graphical narrative of events through a chart pack of banking and financial developments at the time. Our exercise showcases the Bank for International Settlements (BIS) international banking statistics that were publicly available at the time. Finding a set of early warning indicators that can signal the vulnerability to financial turmoil has always been important for policymakers. However, there is a virtue in simplicity and in identifying common threads that can tie together episodes that span time periods and geographical distance.

A second goal of our paper is to engage in a "real-time" exercise on the assessment of vulnerabilities, taking into account the shift that has taken place in the pattern of credit intermediation from banks to the capital markets. Increasingly, credit to emerging market economy (EME) borrowers takes the form of debt securities with long maturities. We use the BIS international debt securities statistics to illustrate the pattern of financial intermediation, the lengthening maturities and the prevalence of dollar-denominated debt securities. While long maturities guard against rollover risk, market risk may be more relevant in the propagation of stress. Due to the higher duration of long maturity bonds, prices are more sensitive to changes in yields. Portfolio managers have limited appetite for losses, and longer-duration assets may be subject to the sharpest selling pressure when loss limits are triggered. We return to this issue in the concluding section, and also address the possible repercussions for the real economy.

Our study has two guiding themes. The first is that the build-up of vulnerabilities is reflected in the procyclicality and the slow-moving nature of balance sheet aggregates, especially of the banking sector. The second theme is the importance of the cross-border dimension of the procyclicality of the banking sector (Borio *et al.*, 2011; Avdjiev *et al.*, 2012; Lane and McQuade 2014). The fact that banking claims straddle the border is not important in itself. Nevertheless, the border is typically where measurements can be taken most reliably due to the reporting requirements imposed on supervised financial institutions. The external dimension, therefore, takes on great importance in the narrative of events, even if it may not have any special significance of itself.

The cross-border dimension also opens a window on the procyclical risk-taking propensity of financial intermediaries through the composition of liabilities. A bank that grants a loan marks up both sides of its balance sheet. The loan is booked as an asset and the bank grants a deposit to the borrower which the borrower can use to pay another party. In this way, deposit growth, as expressed in the growth of the money stock moves in tandem with the growth of lending, and the money stock tends to be procyclical. However, during periods of rapid growth in lending, the banking sector will avail itself of non-deposit sources of funding to feed its lending activity. Some of this non-deposit funding will be sourced in global capital markets, and hence will show up in the BIS banking and financial statistics.

Thus, the window provided by the BIS statistics proves to be useful for two reasons — first, as a consistent and readily available source of information and second, as a window on the procyclical nature of financial intermediation.

### *Two countries, two crises: The same, yet different*

To motivate our exercise, it is instructive to compare the experience of Spain and Korea during the GFC. The comparison illustrates both the similarities and the differences between boom-bust episodes. In both cases, the external dimension plays an important role in the narrative of events.

First, consider Spain. On the eve of the 1999 launch of the euro, total bank credit in Spain stood at €414 billion. Over the next 10 years, bank lending in Spain rose almost fivefold to €1.87 trillion. Loans unrelated to the property sector grew modestly, but property-related lending grew very rapidly (Figure 1).

How was the credit financed? Before the euro, domestic bank lending in Spain could be financed entirely from deposits of Spanish residents. Indeed, deposits exceeded lending, as shown by negative non-core

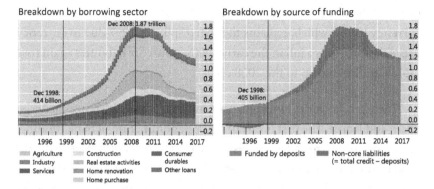

**Figure 1.** Spain: Banking sector credit composition and funding

*Total credit to domestic private non-financial resident sector, in trillions of euros*

*Source*: Bank of Spain.

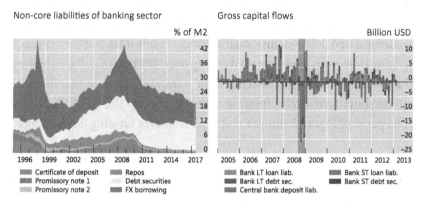

**Figure 2.** Korea: Non-core liabilities and capital flow

*Sources*: Bank of Korea; authors' calculations.

funding, defined as lending minus deposits, shown in the right-hand panel of Figure 1. However, as loan growth outpaced the growth of deposits, more funding came from investors outside Spain, for instance, through the issuance of long-term covered bonds that were bought by investors elsewhere in the euro area.

In the case of Korea, the rapid increase in non-core funding showed up as an increase in the foreign currency liabilities of the banking system. Figure 2 charts the most volatile components of bank liabilities, expressed as a percentage of M2, a proxy for core deposit liabilities. The first peak in non-core liabilities coincides with the AFC of 1997. The total is in local currency terms, which explains the sharp spike in 1997 due to currency depreciation. After a lull in the early 2000s, non-core liabilities again rose rapidly in the run-up to the 2008 crisis.

There are, however, two important and instructive differences between Spain and Korea. The first is on currency denomination of bank funding. Spanish banks borrowed in domestic currency (euros) while Korean banks had substantial dollar liabilities. Second, while Spanish banks borrowed long-term, by issuing covered bonds of several years' maturity, Korean banks borrowed short-term.

Korean banks had dollar claims on local corporate borrowers so that currency mismatch was limited, but there was an overall maturity mismatch when banks and corporates were taken together. Corporates had long-dated dollar claims, such as export receivables, but the currency hedging by Korean banks entailed rolling over short-term dollar liabilities. The overall maturity mismatch left the banking system vulnerable to a run on short-term dollar funding with the onset of the GFC. The right-hand panel of Figure 2 shows the sharp reversal of funding flows in 2008.

Comparing the respective experiences of Spain and Korea reveals some common themes — especially the growth of banking sector balance sheet aggregates — but it also shines a light on the differences, such as the currency denomination of bank liabilities and the maturity of those liabilities. We will explore each of these dimensions in our review of the events of the AFC.

### Leverage in the small and large

Before we launch into the details, it is important to establish a few basic principles of balance sheet management by banks. Familiarity with these principles will allow us to more clearly interpret the contemporaneous evidence.

Systemic risk is about the system as a whole. One popular approach to gauging systemic risk is to drill down to detailed micro evidence on how financial institutions are intertwined.[2] There is much to be learned through this approach, as we delve into the complex web of interconnections.

The other way to go is to "drill up", to the macro, and indeed, global aggregates. It turns out that drilling up is often more informative, as it delivers the all-important time dimension of systemic risk — how it builds up over time and how it unwinds. We can draw a distinction between leverage in the small (leverage of individual institutions) from leverage in the large (leverage of the financial system as a whole).[3]

Mitigating complexity is mostly about taming leverage in the small. The motto is: if you take care of leverage in the small, complexity will take care of itself.

However, taming complexity may not be sufficient to ward off vulnerability to a reversal with macro consequences. Vulnerability in this sense has more to do with leverage in the large, and identifying the build-up of risks entails taking a macro and global perspective.

Banks are intermediaries; they borrow from other lenders, combine the borrowed funds with their own funds, and then lend the combined total to ultimate borrowers. Equity is the bank's own funds. The more equity a bank has, the more own funds it has to lend out. As well as lending out its own funds, a bank can borrow and lend out the proceeds. Imagine a bank's total lending as the capacity of a building. Then the bank's equity is like the size of the building's foundations, and its leverage is the height of the building. Increasing leverage expands lending by building a taller building on the same foundations. During boom times, the bank increases lending by adding floors to the building. When the downturn arrives, the bank has to remove some floors, in a painful adjustment.

---

[2] See Brunnermeier *et al.* (2012) and the references therein.
[3] See Shin (2017).

What about the system as a whole? In principle, leverage in the small (leverage of the individual bank) can vary a lot, even if leverage in the large does not. A deposit-taking bank draws on savers' deposits to finance its lending, but it can also borrow from other banks. The leverage of the banking sector as a whole (leverage in the large) depends on how much lending is being done by the banking sector as a whole compared with its total equity base.

In theory, leverage in the small can diverge from leverage in the large. Indeed, it is a theorem[4] that any level of leverage for the financial system is consistent with (almost) any leverage profile for individual banks. In practice, however, aggregate leverage is closely tied to the leverage of individual institutions.

### Related literature

The causes and consequences of EME financial crises have been extensively studied. Our work is most closely related to the strand of the literature that examines the role of international capital flows in EME financial crises (see Koepke 2015) for a comprehensive review of the literature).

The literature on the importance on international capital flows started to emerge during the early-1990s, after the Latin American crisis. While Latin American countries were going through reforms to strengthen their economies after the crisis, the United States went through a recession, which led to very low interest rates there. International capital flows to Latin America increased and most of the literature at the time focused on whether this was due to domestic (pull) factors such as borrowing countries' economic growth and country risk, or external (push) factors such as advanced economies' economic growth, interest rates and global risk aversion (Ghosh and Ostry 1994; Taylor and Sarno 1997 and Chuhan *et al.*, 1998).

---

[4] See Proposition 1 in H S Shin, "Securitisation and financial stability", *Economic Journal*, vol 119, 2009, pp 309–332. The relationship is: $L = 1 + \left( \Sigma_{i=1}^{n} e_i z_i (\lambda_i - 1) \right) / \left( \Sigma_{i=1}^{n} e_i \right)$, where $L$ is the leverage of the banking system, $e_i$ is the equity of bank $i$, $\lambda_i$ is leverage of $i$ and $z_i$ is $i$'s funding that comes from outside the banking system.

During the 2000s, the empirical literature started to focus on balance of payments components, such as portfolio equity, portfolio debt and FDI, and by looking at different EME regions, such Asia, separately instead of as one EME country group (Filardo *et al.,* 2010). Goldberg (2002) examines the difference in exposure that big and small U.S. banks have vis-à-vis advanced economies, Latin America and emerging Asia. Baek (2006) finds that external (push) factors tend to be more important for portfolio flows to emerging Asia compared with those to Latin America.

The 2008 GFC caused large retrenchments of capital flows directed to EMEs. This shifted the focus of the literature from looking at the impact of net flows to gross flows (e.g., Lane and Milesi-Ferretti (2001; 2007)). Net flows had been relatively stable in the run-up to the GFC, whereas gross flows turned out to be more volatile. Moreover, Broner *et al.* (2013) show that gross flows are highly procyclical, specifically in the context of business cycles and crises. Forbes and Warnock (2012) present a systematic framework for analysing capital flows, splitting gross inflows into surges (increases) and stops (decreases) and gross outflows into flights (increases) and retrenchments (decreases). This paper shows how the most extreme capital flows episodes are driven by global factors, notably global risk aversion. Looking at the different components of international capital flows, Milesi-Ferretti and Tille (2011) find differences in the behavior of these components during the GFC, showing that international banking flows are hit hardest while foreign direct investment remains relatively stable. Cetorelli and Goldberg (2011) demonstrate that global banks played a significant role in the transmission of the 2007–2009 crisis to EMEs and that the main propagation vehicle was exposure to international funding from source country banking systems that were ex-ante more likely to suffer from the GFC liquidity shock.

During the post-crisis period, with advanced economies conducting loose monetary policy for extended periods, attention has turned to how monetary policy conditions in those economies have impacted capital flows to EMEs. Many papers identify two main global factors: global risk aversion (often proxied by the VIX) and the U.S. monetary policy stance.

Before the GFC, there used to be a wide consensus in the literature that global risk aversion has a negative effect on capital flows. Nevertheless, there is now growing evidence that the sensitivity of capital flows to global risk aversion has declined considerably after the GFC (Avdjiev *et al.*, 2017; Krogstrup and Tille 2018; Shin 2016). In a recent related paper, Goldberg and Krogstrup (2018) use their newly-proposed Exchange Market Pressure index to construct a Global Risk Response Index, which reflects the country-specific sensitivity of capital flow pressures to measures of global risk aversion.

At the same time, the effect of U.S. monetary policy on capital flows is not so clear-cut. While some studies have concluded that the impact is negative (e.g., Ghosh *et al.*, 2014; Bruno and Shin 2015a), others have found a positive relationship or mixed results (e.g., Goldberg 2002 and Cerutti *et al.*, 2017). Avdjiev and Hale (2018) reconcile those seemingly contradictory findings by presenting evidence that the impact of U.S. monetary policy on cross-border bank lending depends on the prevailing capital flow regime (expansion versus contraction) and on the level of the two main federal funds rate components (macroeconomic fundamentals versus monetary policy stance). Taking a different perspective, Cetorelli and Goldberg (2012) find that global banks use their global network to manage local shocks by using internal cross-border funding, making them less susceptible to changes in monetary policy.

There are also a number of important contributions on the theoretical side of the literature. Calvo *et al.* (1992) and Fernandez-Arias (1996) were the first to distinguish between country-specific "pull" factors and external "push" factors. Their work provided the theoretical framework for the subsequent empirical studies on the topic. In more recent work, Mendoza (2010) and Bianchi (2011), have modelled sudden stops using occasionally binding collateral constraints. In related work, Brunnermeier and Sannikov (2015) propose a unified theoretical framework to analyse the macroeconomic consequences of capital controls. Finally, Bruno and Shin (2015b) formulate a model of the international banking system that highlights the bank leverage cycle as the determinant of the transmission of financial conditions across borders through banking sector capital flows. A key prediction of the model is that local currency appreciation is associated with higher leverage of the banking sector. We discuss this theoretical prediction in more detail and provide empirical evidence to support it in Section 2 ("International Bank Lending Over the Past Four Decades").

The rest of this paper is organised as follows. In the next section, we take a longer-term perspective and trace the evolution of international banking over the past four decades. In Section 3 ("The Asian Financial Crisis Through the Lens of The BIS International Banking Statistics"), we study the AFC through the lens of the BIS international banking statistics. We then examine the broader global international financial landscape in Section 4 ("The Global Picture"). In Section 5 ("Where Do We Stand Now?"), we take stock of the latest developments in the global financial system, with a particular emphasis on the post-crisis shift from bank-based to market-based international financial intermediation. We conclude in Section 6 ("Concluding Remarks").

## International Bank Lending Over the Past Four Decades

With the benefit of the experience gained since the AFC, we can look back on the events at the time through the lenses of procyclicality and financial vulnerability. As part of our exercise, we shine a light both on the borrowers and the lenders. The two-way investigation of the banking balance sheet is made possible by the comprehensiveness of the BIS international banking statistics (IBS). We examine the evolution of international banking over the past four decades and pose the following questions. Who were the most important lenders? Who were the largest borrowers? How has the broad international banking landscape evolved?

The BIS international banking statistics (IBS) consist of two main data sets: the locational banking statistics (LBS) and the consolidated banking statistics (CBS).

The locational banking statistics (LBS), as the name suggests, organise their information according to the *residence* of reporting banks — i.e., their place of business. Compilation of the LBS is consistent with balance of payments principles. Under this broad heading, this data set offers two main perspectives: positions by *residence* of reporting bank and by *nationality* of reporting bank, meaning the jurisdiction of the bank's headquarters. So, for instance, the locational banking statistics by residence would shed light on the cross-border claims of banks doing business in Japan on borrowers in the rest of the world. An example of the locational banking statistics by nationality is the cross-border claims of *Japanese banks* (i.e., banks whose headquarters are in Japan), located anywhere in the world, on borrowers in the rest of the world. In both cases, LBS by residence and by nationality, positions are unconsolidated in the sense that the claims between offices of the same banking organisation (intrabank positions) are not netted out.

By contrast, the intragroup positions in the BIS consolidated banking statistics (CBS) are netted out. This is closer to the principles used by banking supervisors. The CBS also have a breakdown in two main perspectives: claims on an immediate counterparty (IC) basis, or on an ultimate risk (UR) basis. To illustrate the difference between the two (IC and UR) statistical perspectives, consider an example in which a Korean bank extends a loan to a borrower in China, and the loan is guaranteed by a Japanese bank. On an IC basis, the loan will be recorded as a claim of Korean banks on China. On an UR basis, the loans will be reported as a claim of Korean banks on Japan.

In this paper, we will look mainly at cross-border claims from the LBS and international claims from the CBS. Cross-border claims are claims between residents and non-residents in the sense of the balance of payments accounts. For example, a claim booked by a bank in Japan on a counterparty residing outside Japan would be classified as a cross-border claim. International claims are the sum of cross-border claims and local claims in foreign currency. For example, the international claims of Japanese banks on counterparties in Korea include cross-border claims from Japanese banks outside Korea to parties in Korea, plus local lending in Korea by Japanese banks in any currency other than the Korean won.

Together, the LBS and CBS can offer complementary views on banking trends. When they are combined in a judicious manner, the two sets of statistics can be very informative. We will have many opportunities to illustrate this throughout the paper.

Nevertheless, there are also some caveats. Numbers from LBS and CBS cannot be compared one-to-one. This is due mainly to three wedges. Two of those wedges have already been mentioned above: (1) whereas the positions reported in the CBS are consolidated, those reported in the LBS are not, and (2) the cross-border claims available in the LBS are defined differently from the international claims in the CBS. Finally, more countries report LBS than CBS.[5] It is important to keep these three distinctions in mind, especially when comparing data from the same lender or on the same borrower.

### Main lenders

In the early 1980s, U.S. banks were the biggest international lenders. Their international claims stood at $375 billion, equivalent to 3.3% of world GDP at the time (Figure 3). Nevertheless, the leadership of global banking began to switch almost immediately after the start of the sample. Heavily affected by the Latin American debt crisis, U.S. banks began a long period of relative decline, handing the baton of global banking leadership to European banks. European banks' share stayed relatively stable over the next five years, hovering at just below 50% of aggregate global international claims.

In the meantime, the share of lending by Japanese banks increased from 2.6% of world GDP in Q2 1983 to a peak of 6.4% in Q3 1989. This is notable in two regards. First, this turned out to be the peak of the relative heft of Japanese banks for the whole sample to this day. Second, this peak occurred eight years before the onset of the AFC.

---

[5] The full lists of reporting countries for the BIS LBS and the BIS CBS are available at: https://www.bis.org/statistics/rep_countries.htm

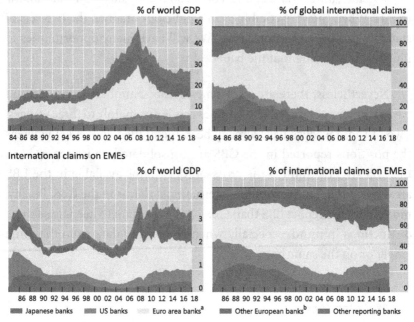

Global international claims

International claims on EMEs

Japanese banks    US banks    Euro area banks[a]    Other European banks[b]    Other reporting banks

**Figure 3.** Broad trends in international bank lending, By lender nationality

*International claims*

[a]Austria, Belgium, Finland, France, Germany, Greece, Ireland, Italy, the Netherlands, Portugal and Spain.

[b]Denmark, Sweden, Switzerland, United Kingdom.

*Sources*: IMF, *World Economic Outlook*; BIS locational banking statistics and consolidated banking statistics on IC basis.

As lending by Japanese and U.S. banks subsided in the 1990s, lending by European banks picked up. Whereas during the run-up to the 2008 GFC, lending by Japanese, U.S. and other banks stayed below 5% of world GDP, lending by European banks surged, reaching a peak of 36% of world GDP ($21 trillion) in Q1 2008. The sharp decline that followed took the outstanding lending stock back to its 2004 level (around $11 trillion) as of end-2017.

### Main borrowers

Lending to EMEs has grown considerably over the last four decades, growing from less than $350 billion (3% of world GDP) in Q4 1980 to almost \$4 trillion (5% of world GDP) in Q4 2017. Remarkable as this may sound, it still pales in comparison with lending to advanced economies (AEs), which went from a little under \$800 billion (7% of world GDP) to \$20 trillion (25% of world GDP) over the same period, a 25-fold increase in less than 40 years.

Compared with the overwhelming volume of borrowing by advanced economies, it might appear that borrowing by EMEs is relatively stable. However, when we zoom in and only look at borrowing by EME regions, we see some interesting shifts among EME regions.

In the mid-1980s, when U.S. banks were still the world's largest lenders, the biggest EME borrowers were located in Latin America. Figure 4 clearly illustrates the build-up and the deleveraging of the Latin American debt crisis. In the early 1990s, right around the time that borrowing by Latin

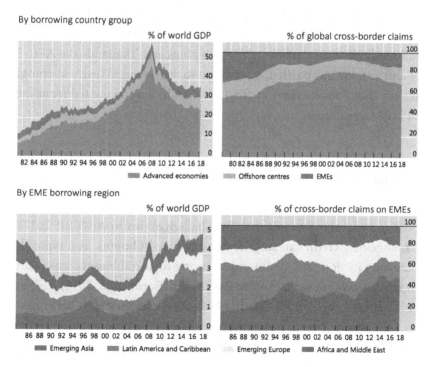

**Figure 4.** Broad trends in international bank lending, by borrower location
*Cross-border claims*
Sources: IMF, *World Economic Outlook*; BIS locational banking statistics.

America stabilised, bank lending to emerging Asia increased rapidly. This continued until the start of the AFC in 1997.

In the run-up to the GFC of 2008, bank lending to emerging Europe and emerging Asia really picked up. Both regions saw a sharp deleveraging after the GFC. Nevertheless, while lending to emerging Europe has not increased again, lending to emerging Asia has surpassed its pre-GFC peak and currently accounts for roughly half of all bank lending to EMEs. China alone accounted for 24% of all EME borrowing as of end-2017.

## The Asian Financial Crisis Through the Lens of The BIS International Banking Statistics

The previous section provided a broad overview of global banking trends to help put the AFC into perspective. In this section, we take a closer look at what happened to international bank lending during the AFC. More concretely, we focus on bank lending to the hardest-hit countries: Indonesia, Korea, Malaysia, the Philippines and Thailand (the AFC-5 countries). We pay particular attention to the potential (early warning) signals that policymakers in the 1990s could have extracted from the BIS IBS in real time.

### Aggregate cross-border bank lending

The close link between cross-border credit and domestic credit tends to pose considerable financial stability challenges (Borio 2016; BIS 2017). Cross-border credit can amplify domestic credit booms, as it typically outgrows its domestic counterpart during financial booms, especially those that precede serious financial strains (Borio *et al.*, 2011; Avdjiev *et al.*, 2012; Lane and McQuade 2014). As Aldasoro *et al.* (2018) have recently shown, the 12-quarter growth rate of the ratio of cross-border claims on a given country to its GDP is a useful early warning indicator for systemic banking crises.

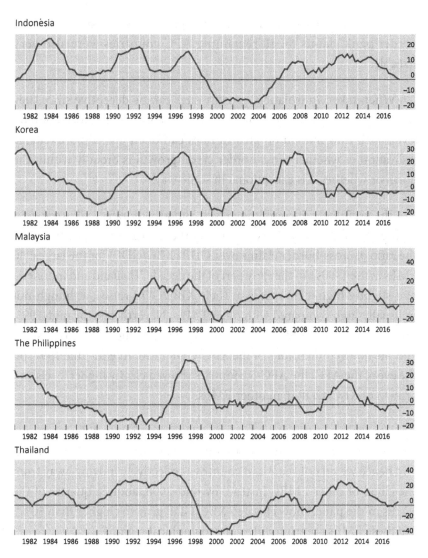

**Figure 5.** Growth of cross-border claims on the AFC-5 countries

*Break- and exchange rate-adjusted quarterly growth, 12Q moving average, in per cent*

*Source*: BIS locational banking statistics.

All the AFC-5 countries experienced a rapid expansion of cross-border credit ahead of the AFC (Figure 5). The most notable example is Thailand, whose external bank borrowing reached an unprecedented quarterly growth rate of 42% at end-March 1996. Although not as dramatic as in the case of Thailand, the pre-AFC expansions in cross-border bank claims on all remaining AFC countries were also very sizeable.

When taken in isolation, growth rates can be deceptive since they could be derived from a low base. Therefore, combining information on levels with information on growth rates can often give a more reliable indication of whether cross-border credit growth is broadly within the norm or whether it is exceptional in some way.

The usefulness of combining levels and growth rates is illustrated in Figure 6a, which shows the evolution of the level and the growth rate of the ratio of cross-border claims over GDP (XBC/GDP) for the largest 40 EMEs in the 1990s.[6] In the early part of the decade, Thailand and Indonesia had slightly higher increases in their XBC/GDP ratios, although not unusually high compared with other EMEs. Nevertheless, by mid-1995, Thailand had separated from the "rest of the pack" along both (the stock and the flows) dimensions of the XBC/GDP ratio. At end-June 1997, on the eve of the AFC, the AFC-5 countries showed clearly higher levels and growth of XBC/GDP than other EMEs.[7]

Doing the same exercise for the GFC shows slightly different results (Figure 6b). Here the shock hitting the system was not region-specific, and hence we do not see Asian countries collectively moving away from the cloud of other EMEs. Instead, by mid-2008, about a quarter of the EMEs in the panel show elevated XBC/GDP growth (higher than 50%), but these EMEs are from different geographical regions.

---

[6] The growth rate of the ratio of cross-border claims over GDP is defined in a similar (but not identical) fashion to the respective early warning indicator of Aldasoro *et al.* (2018). See footnote 1 in Figures 6a and 6b for the exact definition.

[7] In addition to the above "growth rate" measure for cross border claims, we have also explored several alternative "flow" metrics — (i) the growth rate of the ratio of unadjusted cross-border claims to GDP; (ii) the adjusted growth rate of cross-border claims; (iii) the unadjusted growth rate of cross-border claims; and (iv) the compounded adjusted growth rate of cross-border claims. The key takeaways that emerge from the scatter plots associated with each of those alternative measures are very similar to the ones revealed by Figure 6a. All of these alternative scatter plots are available upon request.

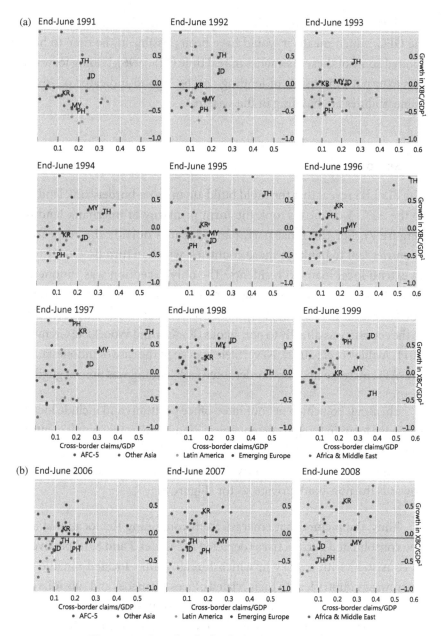

**Figure 6.** Cross-border bank claims as share of GDP

*Stocks and 12-quarter growth rates, at selected points in time*

[a]Twelve-quarter growth in cross-border claims over GDP, adjusted for breaks and exchange rate movements as follows: $\frac{XBCS_t}{GDP_t} \bigg/ \frac{XBCS_t - \sum_{i=0}^{11} XBCF_{t-i}}{GDP_{t-12}}$, where XBCS = cross-border claim amounts outstanding; XBCF = break- and exchange rate-adjusted cross-border flows.

*Sources*: IMF, *World Economic Outlook*; national data; BIS locational banking statistics.

These statistics were available to policymakers before the AFC and the GFC, which means it would have been possible at the time to have spotted some of these anomalies in real time (BIS 1996).[8] Going forward, this external dimension of lending can be a good indicator of where vulnerabilities are building in the system.

### Sector breakdowns

The BIS LBS reveal that the rapid build-up in cross-border bank lending to the AFC-5 countries took the form primarily of interbank lending (Figure 7). For the most part, banks located outside the respective countries lent to banks in those countries, which in turn used the funds to extend local loans to residents. The only exception was Indonesia, which had regulations restricting the ability of local banks to make foreign currency loans to residents. Largely as a result, most cross-border lending to the country was directly to non-banks (Radelet and Woo 2000; Grenville 2011, Avdjiev *et al.*, 2012). Nevertheless, even in the case of Indonesia, the pre-AFC increase in cross-border interbank lending was non-negligible.

The BIS CBS, which net out inter-office positions and include locally extended loans in foreign currency, provide an important complementary perspective. The sectoral breakdown available for international claims in the CBS reveals that the majority of foreign banks' lending was directed towards the non-bank private sector (Figure 8).

Thus, the picture that emerges from combining the locational and the consolidated perspectives (depicted in Figures 7 and 8, respectively) is consistent with a story in which foreign banks located outside the borrowing country lent to their related offices (branches and subsidiaries) inside the country, which in turn extended local loans (denominated in foreign currency) to the non-bank private sector. This largely explains why the share of lending to the non-bank private sector in Figure 8 is

---

[8] Strictly speaking, the BIS IBS are published with a lag of four months. Against the backdrop of the typically much longer time horizon over which financial vulnerabilities tend to accumulate, it can be reasonably argued that the BIS IBS data still provide "de facto" real-time information.

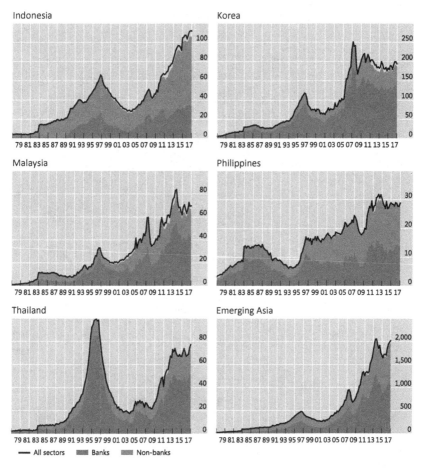

**Figure 7.** Cross-border claims by counterparty sector

*In billions of U.S. dollars*

Source: BIS locational banking statistics.

substantially higher than the share of lending to non-banks in Figure 7.[9] It also reflects the importance of the distinction between direct and indirect cross-border credit, highlighted in Avdjiev *et al.* (2012).

---

[9] An additional potential wedge between the amounts reported in the above two data sets is related to the respective reporting populations. The LBS cover the positions of all internationally active banking units *located* in LBS reporting countries (regardless of the nationality of the banking unit). By contrast, the CBS cover the positions of all banking units whose controlling *parents are from* CBS reporting countries (regardless of the residence of the banking unit). The full lists of reporting countries for the BIS LBS and the BIS CBS are available at: https://www.bis.org/statistics/rep_countries.htm.

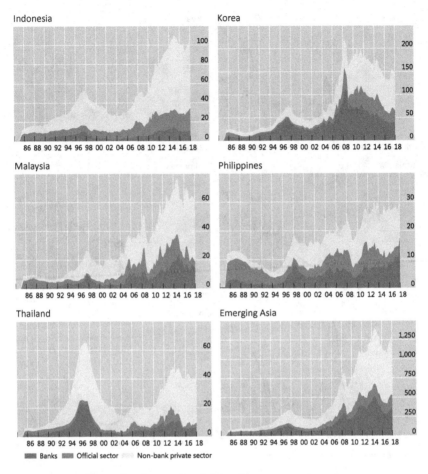

**Figure 8.** International claims by counterparty sector

*In billions of U.S. dollars*

Source: BIS consolidated banking statistics on IC basis.

### *Maturity breakdowns*

The BIS consolidated banking statistics (CBS) provide a breakdown into the short and long maturities of claims. When looking at the maturity composition of international claims in Asia, most of the international bank lending to the AFC-5 countries during the run-up to the AFC represented "hot money" (i.e., claims with a maturity of less than one year).

Such short-term claims were the main drivers of the rapid pre-AFC increases not only for the entire region, but also for each of the five

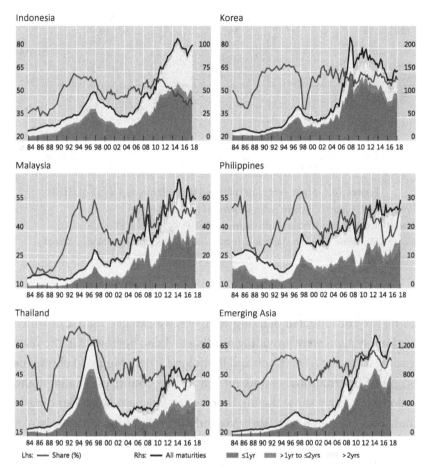

**Figure 9.** International claims by maturity

*In billions of U.S. dollars*

Source: BIS consolidated banking statistics on an IC basis.

individual AFC countries (Figure 9). During the run-up to the GFC, short-term borrowing also took off in Indonesia, Korea and Malaysia. After the GFC, the proportion of long-term borrowing has increased for some countries in the region, such as Indonesia and Thailand.

As in Section 3(a), we can plot the ratio of short-term international claims to GDP (STC/GDP) on one axis and compare that with the growth of this ratio, as in Figure 10. Here too we see the AFC-5 countries leaving the other EMEs behind, as both stocks of and growth in STC/GDP increase for the AFC-5 countries, but less so for most other EMEs.

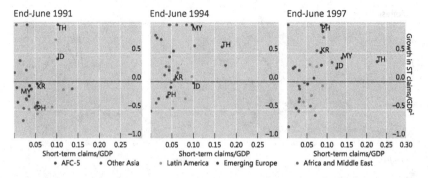

**Figure 10.** Short-term international bank claims as a share of GDP

*Stocks and 12-quarter growth rates, at selected points in time*

[a]Twelve-quarter growth in short-term claims over GDP: $\frac{ST\,claims_t}{GDP_t} \Big/ \frac{ST\,claims_{t-12}}{GDP_{t-12}}$.

*Sources*: IMF, *World Economic Outlook*; national data; BIS consolidated banking statistics.

### *Lender breakdowns*

Using the consolidated banking statistics, we can get a sense of which banking systems were providing funding to Asian borrowers in the years leading up to the AFC (Koch and Remolona 2018). Figure 11 shows the origin of international claims on the AFC-5 countries. Thailand and Indonesia clearly show the big increase in Japanese banks' lending to these countries. In Korea, Malaysia and the Philippines, Japanese banks' involvement also increased, although not as much as European banks' lending to these countries. U.S. banks on the other hand were not very active in the region during the AFC, but have increased their lending in the last decade (especially to Korea). Since the GFC, the gap between total lending to emerging Asia (Figure 11, black line) and lending by advanced economies (Figure 11, stacked areas) has been filled largely by banks from within the Asia-Pacific region itself (Remolona and Shim 2015; Ehlers and Wooldridge 2015).

The BIS IBS also reveal that virtually all major national banking systems were rapidly increasing the shares in their international lending portfolios that were allocated to the AFC-5 countries (Figure 12). The steep increase for Japanese banks is particularly notable, although U.K. and euro area banks also had fairly sharp increases. By contrast, most

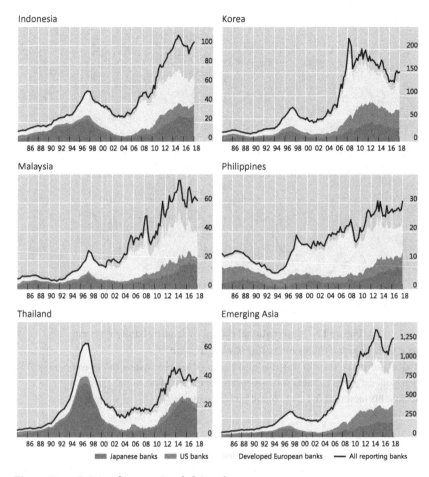

**Figure 11.** Origin of international claims, by counterparty country
*In billions of U.S. dollars*
Source: BIS consolidated banking statistics on an IC basis.

banking systems were simultaneously reducing their lending shares in Latin America (in line with the global trends discussed in Section 2).

In the years after the GFC, lending to Asian countries other than the AFC-5, such as China and India, has increased significantly for all four major banking systems. For U.S. banks, which for most of the sample lent primarily to Latin America, these other Asian borrowers have become the most important EME borrowing region in the last couple of years.

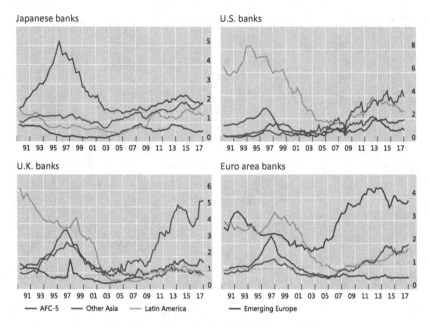

**Figure 12.** International claims, by lending banking system

*As a share of global claims by lending banking system*[a]

[a]Calculated as the share of (international claims of banking system *i* to country group *j*) to (international claims by banks with nationality *i* to the rest of the world).

*Sources*: BIS locational and consolidated banking statistics.

### Currency breakdowns

The locational banking statistics include information on the currency denomination of claims. This allows for a detailed breakdown of foreign currency denominated lending in the region. Figure 13 provides this breakdown for the AFC-5 countries and emerging Asia as a whole.

The U.S. dollar played a prominent role in the AFC. It was the main currency in which most cross-border claims on the AFC-5 countries were denominated. This was another manifestation of the lack of triple coincidence in international finance (Avdjiev *et al.*, 2016): most of the cross-border lending in the run-up to the AFC was denominated in U.S. dollars, despite the fact that neither the lending banks, nor the borrowers were located in the United States.

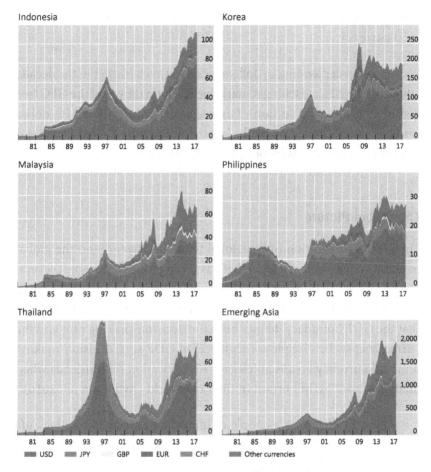

**Figure 13.** Currency breakdown of cross-border Claims

*In billions of U.S. dollars*

Source: BIS locational banking statistics

At the height of the AFC, lending in Japanese yen became very significant for Thailand, but less so for the other AFC-5 countries. Even though much of the funding in emerging Asia comes from euro area banks (see Figure 11), borrowing in euro was and still is only a small percentage of total foreign currency borrowing.

The local currency of borrowing countries is included in the category "other currencies". Up until the early 2000s, this category was negligible for most countries in the region, indicating that virtually all cross-border lending was done in currencies other than the borrower's local currency.

Cross-border lending in dollars increased even further in the decade following the AFC, reaching remarkable levels on the eve of the GFC (see Figure 15 in the next section). Once again, the majority of U.S. dollar lending was originated by banks located outside the United States and was provided to borrowers outside the United States.

## The Global Picture

The greater integration of the global financial system (and the global banking system, in particular) that has taken place over the past several decades has profound implications about the way we study and analyse international finance. The traditional approach has been to assume that the GDP boundary defines both the decision-making unit and the currency area. This "triple coincidence" of GDP area, decision-making unit and currency area is an elegant simplification but misleads when financial flows are important in their own right (Avdjiev *et al.*, 2016).

Figure 14 illustrates a couple of important aspects of the (lack of) triple coincidence in international finance. First, the currency area tends to be much broader than the GDP area, especially in the case of major international funding currencies, such as the U.S. dollar and the euro. More specifically, the majority of U.S. dollar- and euro-denominated cross-border bank claims are booked by banks located outside the respective currency issuing jurisdictions (Figure 14, left-hand panels).

Second, the overlap between decision-making units and GDP areas is (very) far from perfect. More concretely, the country in which banks book their cross-border claims is very often different from the country of their headquarters (i.e., their nationality), which represents a much closer empirical counterpart to the theoretical concept of "decision-making unit".

Before the GFC, commentators pointed to the large U.S. current account deficit and raised concerns about a depreciation of the U.S. dollar,

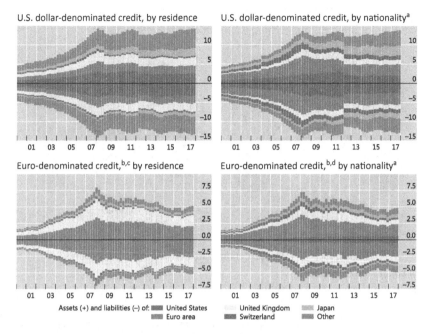

U.S. dollar-denominated credit, by residence

U.S. dollar-denominated credit, by nationality[a]

Euro-denominated credit,[b,c] by residence

Euro-denominated credit,[b,d] by nationality[a]

Assets (+) and liabilities (−) of: United States, Euro area, United Kingdom, Switzerland, Japan, Other

**Figure 14.** Cross-border credit, all sectors, in USD trillion

[a]The break in series between Q1 2012 and Q2 2012 is due to the Q2 2012 introduction of a more comprehensive reporting of cross-border positions (for more details, see www.bis.org/publ/qtrpdf/r_ qt1212v.htm).

[b]Excludes intra-euro area cross-border assets and liabilities.

[c]Euro-denominated assets and liabilities of banks located in the United States are estimated between Q1 2000 and Q1 2012.

[d]Before Q2 2012: an estimate of intra-euro area cross-border assets and liabilities is obtained by applying the average share between Q2 2012 and Q3 2017 of intra-euro area assets and liabilities to all asset and liabilities of euro area banks.

*Source*: BIS locational banking statistics, Tables A5 (by residence) and A7 (by nationality).

drawing parallels with the experience of EMEs that suffer a "sudden stop" in capital flows.

Instead of crashing, the dollar actually soared during the crisis. The main reason was that European banks had used short-term dollar funding to invest in long-term dollar assets in the U.S. (McGuire and von Peter 2012). As asset prices fell and dollar debts became due, borrowers sought dollars to repay their maturing debts. Dollar appreciation fed on itself, as the stronger dollar piled further pressure onto these banks' balance sheets.

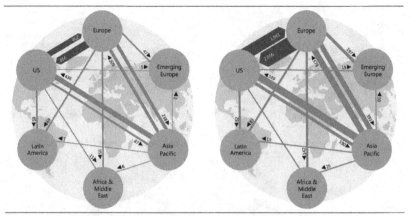

**Figure 15.** U.S. Dollar-denominated cross-border bank claims
*In billions of U.S. dollars*
*Source*: BIS locational banking statistics.

Figure 15, which displays two snapshots (as of 2002 and 2017) of cross-border bank claims in U.S. dollars, provides an important complementary perspective to the global picture presented in Figure 14. European banks had claims of $856 billion on U.S. borrowers in 2002, but this grew to over $2 trillion by 2007. This increase was associated with the rapid growth of the asset-backed securities issuer sector, which grew from modest beginnings in the early 2000s to well over $2 trillion by 2007. Subprime mortgage securitisation reflected the activity of European banks (Bertaut *et al.,* 2011). Some of the short-term dollar funding came from U.S. money market funds, but a substantial amount came from the currency swap market, where European banks borrowed dollars by pledging other currencies (euros, for instance) as collateral.

## Where Do We Stand Now?

How far does the history help us to understand current vulnerabilities? The lessons of past crises are extremely important and should undoubtedly be heeded going forward. Nevertheless, this does not automatically imply that future bouts of financial disruption must follow the same mechanism as those of the past.

In order to gauge ease of financing in the world, the BIS calculates global liquidity indicators by combining the BIS LBS with the BIS international debt securities statistics. A popular global liquidity number is the total amount of U.S. dollar-denominated credit to non-banks located outside the United States. This indicator is the sum of all USD-denominated cross-border lending to non-residents, USD-denominated local loans outside the U.S. and USD-denominated debt securities issued by non-residents.

Two developments are important in assessing current risks to financial stability. The first development is the "second phase of global liquidity" — the shift in financial intermediation from banks to capital markets, especially through the issuance of fixed income instruments (Shin 2013). The second is the fluctuation in risk-taking attitudes over time. As credit intermediation migrates from banks to capital markets, drivers of risk-taking also change.

Regarding the shifts in credit intermediation, banking sector retrenchment after the crisis resulted in a long period of subdued cross-border bank flows. For advanced economies, cross-border banking has been subdued for much of the post-crisis period. The annual growth rate of aggregate cross-border lending to advanced economies turned consistently positive only in early 2016. For EMEs, U.S. dollar bank loans were shrinking at an annual rate of 8% as recently as the middle of 2016, but have now levelled out and are growing again in most regions (Figure 16).

The most notable recent development is the very rapid growth in U.S. dollar-denominated debt securities issued by EME borrowers. The outstanding amount has been growing at an annual rate of 17% since late last year.

The growth in U.S. dollar-denominated international bond issuance by EME borrowers has been very broad-based. The global wave has swept across all major EME regions (Figure 17). The post-GFC surge has been especially notable for several major EMEs — China, Brazil, Chile and

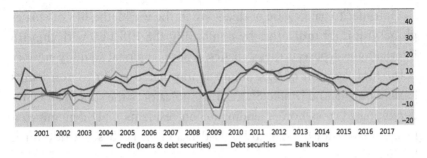

**Figure 16.**   U.S. Dollar-denominated credit to EME non-banks
*Annual growth in percentage*
Source: BIS global liquidity indicators.

Turkey. In the case of the former two countries, a very large portion of the increase has been due to offshore issuance (Figure 17).

As intermediation migrates from banks to bond markets, credit conditions are more vulnerable to a snapback of long-term interest rates and increased volatilities than before. A snapback could be accompanied by reversals of cross-border portfolio flows, threatening the sustainability of the high debt levels in many sectors.

A snapback could have several potential triggers, including an inflation surprise, but the key is a sudden shift in risk assessments. Long-term investors are thought to be a stabilising influence in financial markets, absorbing losses without triggering insolvency. However, we are reminded from time to time that such investors can have limited appetite for losses, and they can join in a selling spree. We saw an example in February 2018, although the disturbance was mainly in the equities market.

In spite of the large stock of dollar-denominated debt securities outstanding issued by EME borrowers, there are some mitigating factors. First, the international debt securities issued by EME corporates have long maturities, and the maturities have been getting longer, as seen in Figure 18. Borrowers with long-maturity debt are less vulnerable to runs and rollover risk. Second, many EMEs hold substantial foreign exchange reserves, in contrast to their situation in past crises. And third, many of the EME issuers are global firms with revenues in foreign currency.

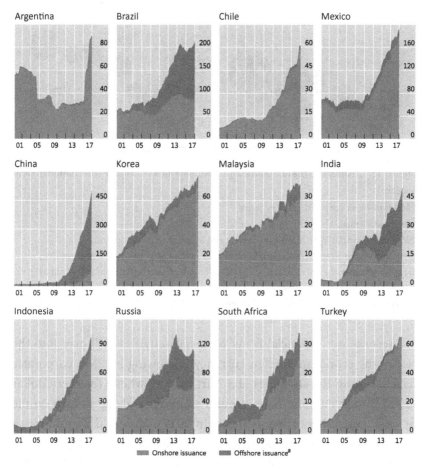

**Figure 17.** U.S. Dollar-denominated debt securities issued by EME non-banks

*In billions of U.S. dollars*

[a]Offshore bond issuance is defined as outstanding U.S. dollar-denominated bonds issued offshore (i.e., outside the country listed in the panel title) by non-banks with the nationality listed in the panel title.

*Sources*: Dealogic; Euroclear; Thomson Reuters; TRAX; BIS calculations.

But, even here, we need to bear in mind some important qualifications.

First, bonds with long maturities protect against runs, but they are vulnerable to market risk. They have longer duration, so that their prices are more sensitive to yield changes. If bond investors have limited appetite for losses and cut their positions in the face of a sharp decline in their values, the selling pressure will exacerbate the snapback in yields.

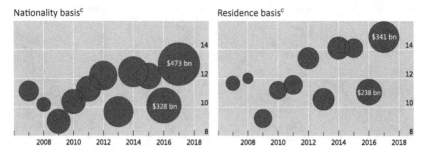

**Figure 18.** Annual Gross Issuance and Maturity[a] of U.S. Dollar International Debt Securities

*EME non-bank corporations,[b] in years*

[a]Weighted average.

[b]Non-bank financial institutions, government and non-financial institutions.

[c]Nationality basis refers to firms with headquarters in the EME countries. Residence basis refers to firms resident in the EME countries. The size of bubbles reflects relative volume of annual gross issuance of long-term securities.

*Sources*: Dealogic; Euroclear; Thomson Reuters; Trax (Xtrakter Ltd); BIS calculations.

Second, non-financial firms' financial activities spill over into the rest of the economy. Foreign currency borrowing by EME corporates have taken on the attributes of a "carry trade" where, for every dollar raised through a bond issue, around a quarter ends up as cash on the firm's balance sheet (Bruno and Shin 2017). Here, cash could mean a domestic currency bank deposit or a claim on the shadow banking system, or indeed a financial instrument issued by another firm. So, dollar borrowing will spill over into the rest of the economy in the form of easier credit conditions. When the dollar borrowing is reversed, these easier domestic financial conditions will be reversed. A broad-based rise in the dollar could usher in a period of tighter global financial conditions.

Third, even if the monetary authorities of a country hold large foreign exchange reserves, there is a sectoral disparity within the country, as it is the corporate sector which has done much of the borrowing. So, even if the country in aggregate has sufficient FX reserves to meet FX liabilities, there is an uneven distribution within the economy. The corporate sector itself may find itself short of financial resources and may cut investment and curtail operations, resulting in a slowdown of growth.

So, even a central bank that holds a large stock of foreign exchange reserves may find it difficult to head off a slowdown in the real economy when global financial conditions tighten.

Central bank FX reserves can cushion the blow by supporting commercial banks so that they can continue lending to domestic firms. FX reserves can also be deployed to support intervention in the swap or forward markets. In both cases, additional resources from the Global Financial Safety Net will prove useful. Nevertheless, the interventions in a bond-dominated setting will be more challenging than in a traditional bank-dominated setting, as seen in the example of Korea that we opened with.

For EMEs, an important aspect is the role of the U.S. dollar as a barometer of risk appetite. When the dollar is weak, there tends to be greater appetite for risk, but a stronger dollar often goes hand in hand with the reversal of risk attitudes. There is accumulating evidence that cross-border bank lending and international portfolio flows tend to increase as the dollar weakens and vice versa (Figure 19).

The above empirical relationship appears to be driven by the financial channel of exchange rate fluctuations (Shin 2016; Avdjiev et al., 2018). This channel has several drivers, both on the demand side and on the supply side of dollar credit.

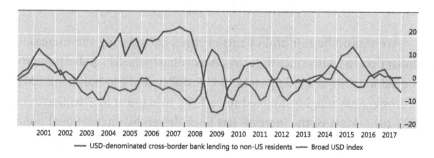

**Figure 19.** Growth of USD-denominated Cross-border Bank Lending and the Broad USD Index

*Annual change, in percentage*

Sources: BIS locational banking statistics and nominal effective exchange rate indices.

In terms of the demand for dollar credit, a borrower who has dollar-denominated liabilities and domestic currency assets would see a strengthening of its balance sheet as a result of a dollar depreciation. Furthermore, an exporting firm with dollar receivables or an asset manager with dollar denominated assets — but with domestic currency obligations — would hedge currency risk more aggressively when the dollar is expected to depreciate further. Notably, this was the main driver of the large build-up of foreign currency credit in Korea during the period preceding the GFC (Chung *et al.*, 2012). Incurring dollar liabilities, or an equivalent off-balance sheet transaction, would be the way to hedge currency risk in such instances.

The link between dollar depreciation and greater borrowing in dollars by non-residents may also operate through the supply of dollar credit, and has been dubbed the risk-taking channel by Bruno and Shin (2015b). When the potential for valuation mismatches on borrowers' balance sheets arises from exchange rate changes, a weaker dollar flatters the balance sheets of dollar borrowers, whose liabilities fall relative to assets. From the standpoint of creditors, the stronger credit position of the borrowers reduces tail risk in the credit portfolio and creates spare capacity for additional credit extension even with a fixed exposure limit through a value-at-risk (VaR) constraint or economic capital (EC) constraint. This is why, for an EME, a depreciation of the local currency against the dollar tends to be associated with an economic contraction rather than an expansion, as the textbook would suggest.

We should be mindful of this channel considering the increased dollar debt in EMEs since the crisis. According to the BIS global liquidity indicators, the outstanding stock of U.S. dollar credit to non-bank EME borrowers has roughly doubled since 2008, to stand at $3.7 trillion as of end-2017. Most of the increase has been driven by international bond issuance. And, while governments have issued bonds mainly in domestic currency, a tightening of global conditions still impacts domestic interest rates (Hofmann *et al.*, 2016).

## Concluding Remarks

Our study has been guided by two themes. The first is that the build-up of vulnerabilities is reflected in the procyclicality and the slow-moving nature of balance sheet aggregates, especially of the banking sector. The second theme is the importance of the cross-border dimension of the procyclicality of the financial system.

The bare fact that the lending relationship crosses a border is not important in itself, but the border is where measurements have most often been taken. Cross-border activity therefore provides a window on the trends taking place globally. Often, the window is a narrow one, and as observers we look to alternative measures as necessary. However, the external dimension of banking and financial activity provides an opportunity to piece together a more complete and informative picture. In this endeavour, our study has showcased the usefulness of the BIS international banking and financial statistics.

## References

Aldasoro, I, Borio, C, and Drehmann, M (2018). Early warning indicators of banking crises: expanding the family. *BIS Quarterly Review*, (March), 29–45.

Avdjiev, S, Bruno, V, Koch, C, and Shin, HS (2018). The dollar exchange rate as a global risk factor: evidence from investment. BIS Working Papers No. 695, January.

Avdjiev, S, Gambacorta, L, Goldberg, L, and Schiaffi, S (2017). The shifting drivers of global liquidity. BIS Working Papers No. 644, June.

Avdjiev, S and Hale, G (2018). U.S. monetary policy and fluctuations of international bank lending. BIS Working Papers No. 730, June.

Avdjiev, S, McCauley, R, and McGuire, P (2012). Rapid credit growth and international credit: challenges for Asia. BIS Working Papers No. 377, April.

Avdjiev, S, McCauley, R, and Shin, HS (2016). Breaking free of the triple coincidence in international finance. *Economic Policy*, 31(87), 409–451.

Baek, I (2006). Portfolio investment flows to Asia and Latin America: pull, push or market sentiment? *Journal of Asian Economics*, 17(2), 363–373.

Bank for International Settlements (1996). *66th Annual Report*, June.

Bank for International Settlements (2017). *87th Annual Report*, Chapter VI, June.

Bertaut, C, DeMarco, L, Kamin, S, and Tryon, R (2011). ABS inflows to the United States and the global financial crisis. Board of the Federal Reserve System, International Finance Discussion Papers No. 2011–1028.

Bianchi, J (2011). Overborrowing and systemic externalities in the business cycle. *American Economic Review*, 101(7), 3400–3426.

Borio, C (2016). More pluralism, more stability? Presentation at the Seventh High-level Swiss National Bank–International Monetary Fund Conference on the International Monetary System, Zurich, 10 May.

Borio, C, McCauley, R, and McGuire, P (2011). Global credit and domestic credit booms. *BIS Quarterly Review*, (September), 43–57.

Broner, F, Didier, T, Erce, A, and Schmukler, S (2013). Gross capital flows: Dynamics and crises. *Journal of Monetary Economics*, 60(1), 113–133.

Brunnermeier, M, Gorton, G and Krishnamurthy, A (2012). Risk topography. *NBER Macroeconomics Annual 2011*, (26), 149–176.

Brunnermeier, M and Sannikov, Y (2015). International credit flows and pecuniary externalities. *American Economic Journal: Macroeconomics*, 7(1), 297–338.

Bruno, V and Shin, HS (2015a). Cross-border banking and global liquidity. *Review of Economic Studies*, 82(2), 535–564.

Bruno, V and Shin, HS (2015b). Capital flows and the risk-taking channel of monetary policy. *Journal of Monetary Economics*, 71, 119–32.

Bruno, V and Shin, HS (2017). Global dollar credit and carry trades: a firm-level analysis. *Review of Financial Studies*, 30, 703–749.

Calvo, G, Leiderman, K, and Reinhart, C (1992). Capital inflows and real exchange rate appreciation in Latin America: the role of external factors. IMF Working Paper No. 62.

Cerutti, E, Claessens, S, and Laeven, L (2017). The use and effectiveness of macroprudential policies: new evidence. *Journal of Financial Stability*, 28, 203–224.

Cetorelli, N and Goldberg, L (2011). Global banks and international shock transmission: Evidence from the crisis. *IMF Economic Review*, 59(1), 41–76.

Cetorelli, N and Goldberg, L (2012). Liquidity management of U.S. global banks: internal capital markets in the great recession. *Journal of International Economics*, 88(2), 299–311.

Chuhan, P, Claessens, S, and Mamingi, N (1998). Equity and bond flows to Latin America and Asia: The role of global and country factors. *Journal of Development Economics*, 55(2), 439–463.

Chung, K, Park, H, and Shin, HS (2012). Mitigating systemic spillovers from currency hedging. *National Institute Economic Review*, 221(1), R44–R56.

Ehlers, T and Wooldridge, P (2015). Channels and determinants of foreign bank lending. BIS Papers No. 82, October.

Fernandez-Arias, E (1996). The new wave of private capital inflows: Push or pull? *Journal of Development Economics*, 48(2), 389–418.

Filardo, A, George, J, Loretan, M, Ma, G, Munro, A, Shim, I, Wooldridge, P, Yetman, J, and Zhu, H (2010). The international financial crisis: Timeline, impact and policy responses in Asia and the Pacific. BIS Working Papers No. 52, July.

Forbes, K and Warnock, F (2012). Debt- and equity-led capital flow episodes. NBER Working Paper No. 18329.

Ghosh, A and Ostry, J (1994). Export instability and the external balance in developing countries. *IMF Staff Papers*, 41(2), 214–235.

Ghosh, A, Qureshi, M, Kim, JI, and Zalduando, J (2014). Surges. *Journal of International Economics*, 92(2), 266–285.

Goldberg, L (2002). When is U.S. bank lending to emerging markets volatile? *In* S Edwards and J Frankel (Eds.), *Preventing currency crises in emerging markets* (pp. 171–196), NBER and University of Chicago Press.

Goldberg, L and Krogstrup, S (2018). International capital flow pressures. Federal Reserve Bank of New York Staff Report No. 834.

Grenville, S (2011). Rethinking capital flows for emerging East Asia. Presentation at the Asian Development Bank Institute Annual Conference, Tokyo, December.

Hofmann, B, Shim, I, and Shin, HS (2016). Sovereign yields and the risk-taking channel of currency appreciation. BIS Working Papers No. 538, revised May 2017.

Koch, C and Remolona, E (2018). Common lenders in emerging Asia: Their changing roles in three crises. *BIS Quarterly Review*, (March), 17–28.

Koepke, R (2015). What drives capital flows to emerging markets? A survey of the empirical literature. IIF Working Papers.

Krogstrup, S and Tille, C (2018). Foreign currency bank funding and global factors. IMF Working Paper 18/97, January.

Lane, P and McQuade, P (2014). Domestic credit growth and international capital flows. *Scandinavian Journal of Economics*, 116(1), 218–252.

Lane, P and Milesi-Ferretti, G (2001). The external wealth of nations: measures of foreign assets and liabilities for industrial and developing countries. *Journal of International Economics*, 55(2), 263–294.

Lane, P and Milesi-Ferretti, G (2007). The external wealth of nations mark II: Revised and extended estimates of foreign assets and liabilities, 1970–2004. *Journal of international Economics*, 73(2), 223–250.

McGuire, P and von Peter, G (2012). The dollar shortage in global banking and the international policy response. *International Finance*, 15(2), 155–178.

Mendoza, E (2010). Sudden stops, financial crises and leverage. *American Economic Review*, 100(5), 1941–1966.

Milesi-Ferretti, G and Tille, C (2011). The great retrenchment: international capital flows during the global financial crisis. *Economic Policy*, 26(66), 289–346.

Radelet, S and Woo, WT (2000). Indonesia: A troubled beginning. In J Sachs, K Schwab and WT Woo (Eds.), *The Asian financial crisis: Lessons for a resilient Asia* (pp. 167–184). MIT Press.

Remolona, E and Shim, I (2015). The rise of regional banking in Asia and the Pacific. *BIS Quarterly Review*, (September), 119–134.

Shin, HS (2009). Securitisation and financial stability. *Economic Journal*, 119, 309–332.

Shin, HS (2013). The second phase of global liquidity and its impact on emerging economies. Keynote address at the Federal Reserve Bank of San Francisco Asia Economic Policy Conference, 3–5 November.

Shin, HS (2016). The bank/capital markets nexus goes global. Speech delivered to the London School of Economics and Political Science, London, 15 November.

Shin, HS (2017). Leverage in the small and in the large. Panel remarks at the IMF conference on Systemic Risk and Macroprudential Stress Testing, Washington DC, 10 October.

Taylor, M and Sarno, L (1997). Capital flows to developing countries: Long- and short-term determinants. *The World Bank Economic Review*, 11(3), 451–470.

# CHAPTER 7

# Chapter 7

# The Dollar Hegemon?
# Evidence and Implications for
# Policymakers[*]

Pierre-Olivier Gourinchas[1]

## Abstract

This paper reviews the central role of the U.S. dollar in the global trade, financial and monetary systems. The dominance of the U.S. dollar as an invoicing, issuance, anchor and reserve currency has increased over time, especially so and somewhat paradoxically since the end of the Bretton Woods system. The dollar is now the 'hegemon' currency. I propose an explanation based on the growing complementarities between the role of the dollar for international trade and for international financial transactions. I also discuss the implications for policymakers of living in a 'dollar world.' The paper concludes with a discussion of some possible challenges to the dollar's hegemony.

## Introduction

In his insightful account of the Great Depression, Charles P. Kindleberger spelled out the elements of a theory of 'hegemonic stability' for the international monetary system (Kindleberger 1973).[2] Writing in 1981, he summarized his view as follows:

---

[*] Prepared for the 6th Asian Monetary Policy Forum held on May 31, 2019 in Singapore.
[1] S.K. and Angela Chan Professor of Global Management, Haas School of Business; Director, Clausen Centre for International Business and Policy; University of California, Berkeley; Program director, International Macroeconomics & Finance, National Bureau of Economic Research (NBER).
[2] Kindleberger himself never used the term 'hegemonic stability.' The label was later coined by international relation specialists, in part inspired by his work. According to

I argue(d) that for the world economy to be stable, it needs a stabilizer, some country that would undertake to provide a market for distress goods, a steady if not countercyclical flow of capital, and a rediscount mechanism for providing liquidity when the monetary system is frozen in panic. [...] Britain, with frequent assistance from France, furnished coherence to the world economy along these lines during the nineteenth century and through the "belle époque." The United States did so from 1945 (or perhaps 1936) to 1968 (or 1963 or 1971).

Kindleberger (1981, p. 247)

According to Kindleberger, the benevolent leader or 'hegemon' actively stabilizes the global system by supporting free trade and open capital markets, by coordinating macroeconomic and financial policies, and by acting as a lender of last resort providing much needed international liquidity in times of crisis.[3] The currency issued by the center country plays a critical role for each of these different functions. Since at least 1945, that currency is the U.S. dollar.

First, the dollar is the currency of choice for trade invoicing, international security issuance, or cross-border banking (Gourinchas, Rey, and Sauzet 2019). Over the last half century, this has greatly helped promote an open global environment for international trade and financial transactions, facilitating international trade and exchange.

Second, in part because of its prominence in trade and financial transactions, the dollar is also the main currency of intervention for central banks, as well as the currency in which they accumulate the largest share of their official reserves. Not surprisingly, it is also the dominant anchor currency, i.e., the currency against which central banks aim to stabilize their own (Calvo and Reinhart 2002; Ilzetzki, Reinhart, and

---

Keohane (1980), hegemonic stability postulates that "hegemonic structures of power, dominated by a single country, are most conducive to the development of strong international regimes whose rules are relatively precise and well obeyed."

[3] Historians of Greek antiquity establish a distinction between 'hegemonia', i.e., leadership via persuasion and trust, and 'arkhe', i.e., leadership via force and power. See Coeuré (2018) for a recent analysis emphasizing this distinction in monetary affairs.

Rogoff 2019). This role of the dollar as both an intervention currency and an anchor currency helps propagate U.S. monetary policy impulses from the center to the periphery, and provides a common component to the global monetary environment. The spillovers of U.S. monetary policy to the rest of the world are further strengthened by the importance of dollar funding for global banks' balance sheet, as well as the increasing length and complexity of global supply chains (Bruno and Shin 2015; Bruno, Kim, and Shin 2018; Kalemli-Özcan *et al.* 2014).

Lastly, because the dollar is also viewed as the safest currency, it is a key determinant of private investors' demand for stores of value. In times of crisis, markets freeze and the demand for dollar safe assets spikes. Preventing a full market collapse requires aggressive provision of dollar liquidity. This can only be provided by the U.S. Federal Reserve, either directly to domestic banks and the foreign subsidiaries of global banks via its discount or repo windows, or indirectly via central bank swap lines (Farhi, Gourinchas, and Rey 2011). It follows that a proper analysis of the U.S. hegemon is an analysis of the dollar dominance in international trade, finance and monetary affairs: the U.S. hegemon is a dollar hegemon.

The simple reality is that we live in a dollar world: on the real side, where dollar invoicing is dominant; on the financial side, where dollar funding is essential to global banks and non-financial corporations; and on the policy side, where dollar anchoring and dollar reserves are prevalent. If anything, this dominance of the dollar has increased over time. Section 2 ("The Emergence of the Dollar Hegemon") starts by reviewing the key historical developments that help us understand the emergence of this dollar hegemon while Section 3 ("The Dollar Hegemon Today") analyzes the current roles of the dollar as an international currency. The dominance of the dollar has important implications for policymakers which we discuss in Section 4 ("Implications for Policymakers"). The dominance of the dollar matters for the transmission of various shocks to local economies. It matters for the way in which monetary policy operates, and the choice of exchange rate regime. It matters for the exposure to global financial shocks, and last but not least, it matters for the global stability of the international financial system. Section 5 ("Where Do We Go

From Here? New Triffin Dilemma and Shadow RMB Anchor") explores, speculatively, how the system might evolve and concludes.

## The Emergence of the Dollar Hegemon

The introductory quote from Kindleberger makes it clear that he viewed the suspension of gold convertibility, first in 1968 for the private market, then in 1971 for foreign central banks, as the beginning of the end of the era of uncontested U.S. monetary leadership. Figure 1 reports the value of the U.S. dollar against the German Deutsche Mark, the Japanese Yen, the Swiss Franc and the British pound between 1969 and 1989, rebased to 100 in January 1969. The dollar depreciated nominally between 20 and 40% against the first three currencies between 1971 and 1974. Figure 2 reports the U.S. share of world output between 1950 and 2016. It declined from 25% in 1950 to 18% in 1971, mostly as Western

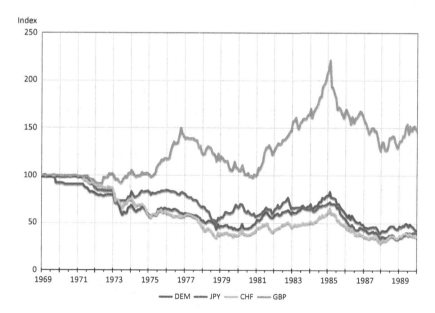

**Figure 1.**   Major exchange rates

The figure reports the value of the U.S. dollar in terms of the german Deutsche Mark (DEM), Japanese Yen (SPY), Swiss Franc (CHF) and British pound (GBP). Exchange rates are normalized at 100 in Jan. 1969. A decrease in the index is a depreciation of the dollar.

*Source*: Global Financial Database.

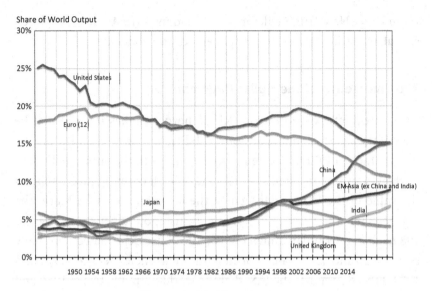

Share of World Output

**Figure 2.** World output shares

Output is measured in constant 2011 U.S.$. EM-Asia ex China and India consists of Bangladesh, Cambodia, Hong Kong, Indonesia, Korea, Malaysia, Pakistan, Philippines, Singapore, Thailand and Vietnam. Euro12 consists of: Austria, Belgium, Finland, France, Germany, Greece, Ireland, Italy, Luxembourg, the Netherlands, Portugal and Spain.

*Source*: Maddison Project Database, version 2018, Bolt *et al.* (2018).

Europe and Japan, devastated by the destructions of the Second World War, rebuilt their economies. Many contemporary observers shared similar worries: foreign exchange volatility, coupled with a substantial decline in the value of the dollar against other potential international currencies, rising U.S. inflation in the 1970s and a decline in the share of the U.S. in world output could undermine confidence in the dollar as an international currency (Aliber 1973; McKinnon 1974; Rueff 1971).

Quite the opposite happened. As a number of scholars observed early on, the transition to floating exchange rates had little impact on the use of the dollar as an international currency (see Cooper 1973, McKinnon 1979, Mundell 1973, Whitman 1974, and Kenen 1983). Astonishingly, while the end of the Bretton Woods era was triggered by a run on the dollar, it ushered in the era of the global dollar standard, of the dollar hegemon, that is still with us to this day. Put simply, since 1971, the centrality and dominance of the dollar has increased in all dimensions. In the words of

**Table 1.** Asian economies and the dollar anchor

| Country | Start of the dollar anchor |
| --- | --- |
| Philippines | 1945 |
| Japan | July 1947 |
| Korea | February 1953 |
| Indonesia | April 1969 |
| Pakistan | January 1971 |
| Singapore | June 1972 |
| Hong Kong | July 1972 |
| China (Mainland) | January 1974 |
| Malaysia | September 1975 |
| India | August 1979 |
| Vietnam | January 1992 |
| Cambodia | January 1994 |

The table reports the date at which dollar anchoring begins, according to Ilzetzki, Reinhart and Rogoff (2019).
*Source*: Ilzetzki, Reinhart and Rogoff (2017).

Mundell (1973, p. 390), "the dollar assumed greater monetary importance than gold."

Part of the increased importance of the dollar reflects somewhat mechanically the collapse of the Soviet bloc in the late 1980s, and more generally, the transition of centrally planned economies to market principles, with accompanying trade and financial liberalizations. Yet, it also goes beyond this simple accounting. As an illustration, consider the choice of anchor currency of Asian countries. Table 1 reports the start date of the most recent episode of dollar anchoring for various Asian countries, according to the detailed country narratives compiled by Ilzetzki, Reinhart and Rogoff (2019). China, Hong Kong, Indonesia, Pakistan, Singapore anchored their currency to the U.S. dollar during or in the immediate aftermath of the Bretton Woods collapse, between 1969 and 1974. Malaysia, India, Cambodia and Vietnam followed between 1975 and 1994.[4]

---

[4] Only three Asian countries were anchoring to the dollar prior to 1969, all with close historical and military ties to the U.S.: the Philippines (since 1945), Japan (since 1947)

A number of interesting observations arises from this table: in the case of Hong Kong, India, Malaysia, Pakistan and Singapore, the dollar anchor replaced a sterling anchor. The latter naturally reflected the strong historical and colonial ties that each of these countries had with the United Kingdom (U.K.). They maintained a sterling anchor long after the U.K. had lost most of its lustre: by 1970, its economy accounted for only 3.5% of world output, down from 5.9% in 1950 (see Figure 1). Such path-dependence could be the consequence of strong network effects and strategic complementarities.

Another interpretation is that anchoring to the sterling may have been largely illusory. During the Bretton Woods era, most currencies, including the sterling, were fixed against the dollar. Very few changes in par values of the major currencies occurred between 1955 and 1969: France devalued three times, in 1957, 1958 and 1969; Britain devalued in 1967; and Germany revalued in 1961 and 1969. It follows that anchoring to the dollar, to the sterling or to any other currency pegged to the former must have been economically roughly equivalent, and quasi impossible to detect empirically. In other words, it is quite plausible that emerging Asian economies were already shadow anchoring to the dollar, and that the collapse of the Bretton Woods system only brought to light what had been an economic reality for some time. This last observation is especially relevant as we look ahead and consider possible paths for the internationalization of the renminbi. As long as the dollar-yuan exchange rate remains stable, a similar form of shadow renminbi anchoring may be at work, masquerading as a dollar anchoring. If, and when, the global economy is ready for a competing renminbi standard, the latter may unveil itself suddenly and precisely at a time of monetary instability between the U.S. and China.

The concept of 'shadow anchoring' also helps us understand how the dollar could prove so resilient to the collapse of the Bretton Woods system. The traditional interpretation emphasizes the lack of an alternative. For instance, Mundell writes:

---

and Korea (since 1953). See Eichengreen, Mehl, and Chitu (2017) for an analysis of the geopolitics of international currency choice.

[T]he 1971 float of the dollar led to a brief period of confusion that exaggerated the weakness of the dollar. [...] By December 1971, however, when the Smithsonian agreement was signed, there was a tacit (and reluctant) acceptance of a dollar standard. That the dollar could survive the crisis of 1971 as it did proved its growing secular strength despite its short-term weakness. [...] [W]hen the United States suspended convertibility, the dollar was still the world unit of account. That is why the system did not collapse in 1971 or, to be more exact, why countries went back to the dollar. There was no alternative ready.

Mundell (1973, p. 390)

Yet this interpretation does not explain why the role of the dollar expanded as dramatically as it did in subsequent years. After all, between December 1971 and February 1973 when the Smithsonian agreement collapsed, the dollar depreciated by 14% against the DEM, 17% against the Yen and 22% against the Swiss franc (see Figure 1). There is little doubt that the transition to floating rates initially weakened the dollar as an international currency. But deeper forces were at play. In particular, one must consider the key role that the center country plays in providing safe stores of value to the rest of the world. This global provision of safe assets is one of the central aspects underpinning the architecture of the international monetary and financial system. What defines the center country is precisely that it is a net producer of safe assets, i.e. assets that deliver superior returns during global downturns.[5] The provision of safe assets is intimately tied to the level of development of financial markets, the fiscal capacity of the sovereign, as well as the stability of its macroeconomic policies. A key insight from my work with Hélène Rey, Ricardo Caballero and Emmanuel Farhi is that regardless of the formal 'rules of the game' or formal exchange rate arrangements, the international monetary system naturally evolves in an asymmetrical way, with large net global safe asset producers at its center (see Gourinchas 2017; Gourinchas, Rey, and Sauzet 2019; and Caballero, Farhi, and Gourinchas 2017b).

---

[5] Note that this definition is relative: all assets returns may decline in a global downturn. Safe assets are those providing the strongest level of protection.

The architects of the Bretton Woods system attempted to deal with this fundamental asymmetry in two ways, one that proved fatal and one that helped, albeit only temporarily. First, by fixing the value of the dollar in terms of gold at $35/oz, the Bretton Woods architects aimed to restore some symmetry in the system. The explicit aim was to introduce an external constraint on U.S. policymakers, just as foreign policymakers faced the external constraint of maintaining the par value of their currency against the dollar. As Robert Triffin brilliantly observed in 1961 in what came to be known as the 'Triffin dilemma,' the U.S. would ultimately be unable to simultaneously increase the supply of dollars needed to meet the demand of a growing global economy, and maintain the dollar price of gold.

Second, for most of its existence, the Bretton Woods system of fixed parities operated with severely limited capital mobility. Limited capital mobility helped curtail direct demand for U.S. safe assets originating with private foreign investors. Fixed parities meant that a local alternative, almost as good as dollars, existed in the form of domestic central bank liabilities and their substitutes, such as local short-term government debt. As long as the fixed parities remained credible and capital was not allowed to flow freely between the center and the periphery, this allowed an elastic supply of local 'quasi-safe' assets by foreign central banks, partly backed by dollar reserve holdings. In other words, while local financial institutions had little choice but to hold local assets instead of true U.S. dollar safe assets, the two were largely equivalent: local safe assets 'shadowed' dollar safe assets.

As long as dollars were scarce — acutely so in the immediate post-war period — this allowed the global economy to 'economize' on dollar safe assets, alleviating their underlying scarcity and letting the financial system operate smoothly. By the late 1960s, however, the world economy faced instead a dollar glut, largely as a consequence of years of loose U.S. monetary policy. Under a fixed exchange rate system, this required foreign central banks to accumulate dollar reserves, which propagated the glut to their local financial system. This state of affairs was in some ways an inverted mirror image of the environment preceding the Global

Financial Crisis (GFC) of 2008. In the 2000s, a global scarcity of safe assets triggered the endogenous creation of public and private sector alternatives: 'quasi-safe' assets that helped prop up the global economy in the years 2000–2007 (Bernanke *et al.* 2011; Caballero, Farhi, and Gourinchas 2008). The vulnerability was the lack of a proper backstop for quasi-safe assets: these would ultimately buckle under stress and be vulnerable to runs, as their holders quickly tried to convert them into true dollar safe assets (Gorton and Metrick 2012). In the late 1960s and early 1970s instead, an excessive supply of dollar assets was forced onto the global economy via the fixed exchange rate system. The initial depreciation of the dollar between 1968 and 1973 was a corrective mechanism that reduced the market value of dollar safe assets and equilibrated the market.

Interpreted in this light, the collapse of Bretton Woods first severed the link between dollar and gold in 1969, resolving the original Triffin dilemma. The failure of the Smithsonian agreement in 1973 then officially severed the link between the dollar and other currencies, in an environment marked by increasingly porous capital controls and the emergence of offshore dollar markets. Ultimately, Triffin correctly analyzed the first contradiction built into the Bretton Woods system, but did not address the second one. From 1973 onwards, the demand for safe assets relocated narrowly on dollar assets since the U.S. remained the sole provider of global safe assets. Increased capital mobility, currency volatility and growth in the rest of the world, especially in emerging Asia which embarked on an astonishingly rapid path of industrialization, further increased the demand for dollar safe assets in subsequent years.[6]


## The Dollar Hegemon Today

What is the current status of the dollar as an international currency? The short answer is that we live in a dollar world! Figure 3, compiled by

---

[6] Coincidentally, the first oil price shock of October 1973 also contributed to stabilize the demand for dollar-denominated stores of value. The offset of the large current account surpluses of OPEC countries, the so-called 'petrodollars', was a surge in direct foreign holdings of U.S. Treasuries as well as offshore bank deposits and short-term instruments.

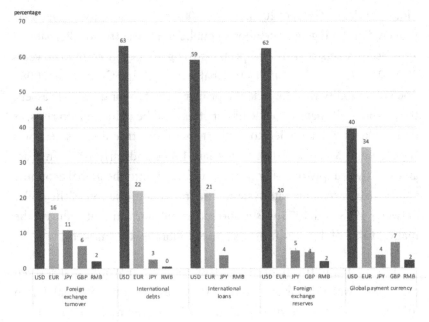

**Figure 3.** The dominance of the dollar

*Source*: Eichengreen and Xia (2019).

Eichengreen and Xia (2019), updating data from European Central Bank (2018)'s annual report on the international role of the Euro, documents the dominance of the dollar in all domains of the international financial system: international debt issuance, cross border loans, FX turnover or reserve accumulation. All other international currencies are far behind.

To go further, we briefly review the empirical evidence on the main functions of the dollar as an international currency, building from the useful typology introduced by Kenen (1983) and reproduced in Table 2.[7] It separates the traditional roles of the international currency as a medium of exchange, a store of value and a unit of account for the private and official sectors.

### The dollar as a unit of account

---

[7] This section borrows heavily from Gourinchas, Rey and Sauzet (2019).

**Table 2.**  International currrency

|  | Roles | | |
|---|---|---|---|
|  | **Medium of exchange** | **Store of value** | **Unit of account** |
| Private sector | Vehicle currency | Nominal securities | Denomination |
|  | Liquid & safe asset | issuance | of securities |
|  | markets | Banking, cash hoarding | Trade invoicing |
| Official sector | Intervention currency | Reserves | Exchange rate pegs |
|  | Lender of last resort | | Anchor currency |

*Note*: Adapted from Kenen (1983).

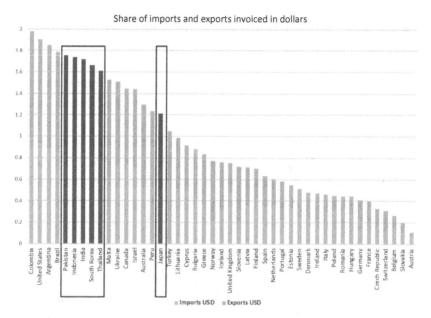

**Figure 4.**  Share of invoice of imports and exports in U.S. dollars
We keep all the countries for which data on exports and imports are both available.
*Source*: Gopinath (2016).

We begin with the dollar's role as a unit of account. Thanks to the work of Goldberg and Tille (2009) and Gopinath (2016), we have ample evidence on the extensive use of the dollar for trade invoicing.[8] Gopinath (2016) reports that the dollar's share as an invoicing currency is approximately

---

[8] See also Kamps (2006) and Ito and Chinn (2015).

4.7 times the share of the U.S. in goods in worlds imports and 3.1 times its share in world exports. Figure 4 reports the combined share of exports and imports invoiced in U.S. dollars, as a share of total exports and imports respectively. A sum equal to 2 means that all exports and imports are invoiced in dollars. The figure also singles out the Asian economies in the sample.[9] The average across Asian economies, at 1.61 is very high (the average across all countries is 0.94), placing Asian economies only slightly behind Latin America (1.71).

From a theoretical perspective, the dominance of dollar invoicing arises naturally the stronger the strategic complementarities between exporters, the more open the economy is and the lower volatility of the dollar (Gopinath *et al.* 2018; Mukhin 2017).

Turning to the official sector, Figure 5, based on the important work of Ilzetzki, Reinhart and Rogoff (2019), documents the dramatic rise of the dollar zone between 1950 and 2015. According to these authors, until 1970, about 30% of countries were anchored to the dollar, with the rest split between the U.K. pound, the French franc and the Soviet rouble. By 2015, the dollar zone has expanded considerably, including not only the former Soviet bloc, but also communist China, large parts of Asia, Africa and all of Latin America.

The dominant role of the dollar anchor reflects its importance both on the real and financial side. On the real side, the dominance of dollar invoicing generates asymmetric international spillovers that make it desirable to stabilize the dollar exchange rate (Egorov and Mukhin 2019). The intuition for this result is quite straightforward: In a world with dollar pricing, domestic monetary policy cannot affect the demand for exports (whose price in dollars

---

[9] An important omission from Figure 4 is China. Lai and Yu (2015) report that, while the share of China's cross border trade settled in renminbi increased rapidly from 0 in 2009 to 16.6% in 2013, the share invoiced in the Chinese currency remains minimal. For our purpose, what matters is the currency of invoicing, not that of settlement. The empirical evidence strongly suggests that prices are sticky in the currency of invoicing. We conjecture that China's cross border trade is similar to other Asian economies and predominantly invoiced in dollars.

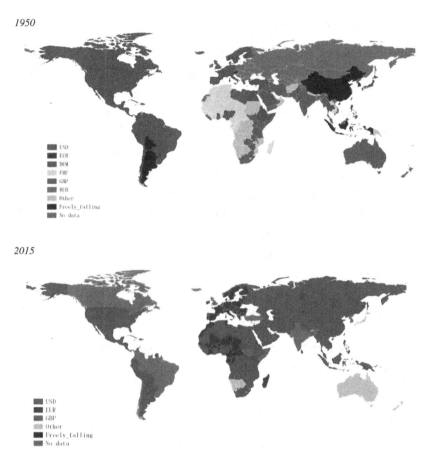

*1950*

*2015*

**Figure 5.** The geography of anchor currencies, 1950 and 2015
The figure reports the geographic distribution of anchor currencies.
*Source*: Ilzetzki, Reinhart and Rogoff (2019).

is independent from the exchange rate). Instead, the monetary authority will aim to stabilize the price of domestic goods. With imported intermediate inputs also invoiced in dollars, this requires 'leaning against the wind' and stabilizing the dollar exchange rate. On the financial side, another strand of the literature emphasizes the spillovers of U.S. monetary policy via asset markets. Dollar dominance in banking and the dollarization of cross border claims imply that U.S. monetary policy impulses get transmitted beyond U.S. borders in international financial markets, contributing to a global financial cycle (Avdjiev, McCauley, and Shin 2015; Avdjiev, *et al.* 2016; Miranda-Agrippino and Rey 2018; Rey 2013).

### The dollar as a means of payment

Due to network externalities, few currencies emerge as vehicle currencies, that is, as international means of payments. This vehicle currency role is closely tied to the liquidity properties of the currency. Private investors around the world use dollars for their transactions because they value the ability to conduct large transactions with minimum adverse price impact. The depth and development of the dollar markets — not necessarily located in the U.S. since most of the foreign exchange transactions are conducted in London — is unparalleled. They are also more likely to use dollars if this is the currency in which transactions are invoiced in the first place: currency of settlement and currency of invoicing are often closely tied. As Figure 3 documents, the dollar serves as the undisputed vehicle currency.

Naturally, since the vehicle currency is used by most market participants, and is the currency they need to obtain for emergency funding, it tends to be the intervention currency, i.e., the currency used by central banks for their official interventions.

### The dollar as a store of value

International currencies also serve as store of value. Safety is a key attribute and the demand for safe assets undergirds large parts of the international financial system. Private investors use dollars for their short-term investment needs as they are considered among the safest instruments.

It follows that the currency of issuance of international assets is a key determinant of the private sector's portfolios. This was demonstrated recently by Maggiori, Neiman and Schreger (2018). Using finely disaggregated data on international mutual fund positions, these authors demonstrate that investor's holdings are strongly biased towards instruments issued in their own currency, with the exception of securities issued in U.S. dollar. Figure 6 illustrates this point. Consider the case of Canada (second from top). While Canadian investors' holding of

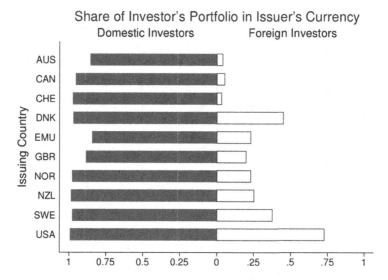

**Figure 6.** Share of corporate bond investment denominated in the issuer's local currency

The full bar reports for each issuing country, the share of bonds denominated in the issuer's local currency out of all domestic investment in its corporate bonds. The hollow bars show, for each issuing country, the share of bonds denominated in the issuer's local currency out of all foreign investment in its corporate bonds.

*Source:* Maggiori, Neiman, and Schreger (2018).

Canadian bonds are mostly in Canadian dollars, foreign investors holdings of Canadian bonds are mostly in foreign currency, i.e., in dollars.

Recent years have also witnessed a sharp increase in the amount of non-U.S. resident dollar borrowing. Figure 7 reports bank loans and international debt securities issued by non-residents for the U.S. dollar, the Euro and the Japanese Yen, as a share of global output. As the figure shows, in recent years, the bulk of the increase reflects the growing issuance of dollar debt by non-U.S. residents. As of 2018, dollar credit to non-U.S. residents represented close to 14% of global output.

Lastly, the currency of intervention, and the anchor currency naturally determine the reserve currency, i.e., the currency in which most official reserves are held. Figure 8 reports the distribution of Central Bank reserves by currency and its evolution over time. U.S. dollar reserves vastly outweigh the Euro or other currencies.

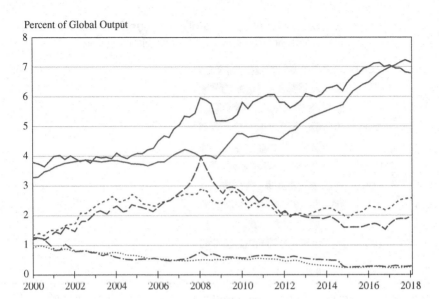

Percent of Global Output

| Bank Loans | USD | EUR | JPY |
| International Debt Securities | USD | EUR | JPY |

**Figure 7.** International credit to non-resident by currency and instrument, percent of global GDP

*Source*: BIS Global Liquidity Indicators.

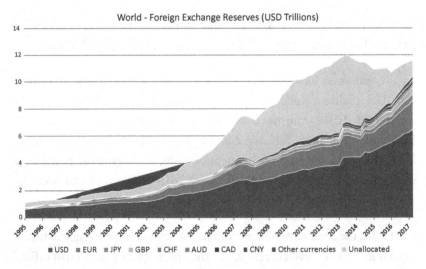

World - Foreign Exchange Reserves (USD Trillions)

USD ■ EUR ■ JPY ■ GBP ■ CHF ■ AUD ■ CAD ■ CNY ■ Other currencies ■ Unallocated

**Figure 8.** Currency composition of foreign exchange reserves for the world

The date indicates the last quarter of each year.

*Source*: IMF COFER as compiled by Gourinchas, Rey, and Sauzet (2019). The date indicates the last quarter of each year.

These are important complementarities between the different roles of an international currency. For instance, more dollar invoicing, or longer supply chains involving dollar invoiced imported intermediates, are likely to increase the demand for dollar safe assets. As analyzed by Gopinath and Stein (2018a), financial institutions are then likely to intermediate these dollar assets into local dollar liabilities. In turn, more dollar debt issuance by the non-financial corporate sector, or more dollar funding for local banks make it more likely that the domestic central bank will monitor carefully the dollar exchange rate, intervene on currency markets, or accumulate more dollar reserves (Gopinath and Stein 2018b). Conversely, a more stable dollar exchange rate, or a larger stock of dollar reserves can make it more appealing to invoice in dollars, to borrow in foreign currency for banks or nonbanks, or to lengthen the global supply chain by relying more on dollar-invoiced foreign imported inputs.

## Implications for Policymakers

This section explores the implications of the dollar dominance for policymakers. We begin by discussing how dollar invoicing matters for the pass-through of exchange rates to local prices and terms of trade. We then discuss how monetary policy transmission is affected and how the value of the dollar affects global trade.[10] Next, we consider how fluctuations in the dollar may affect domestic financial frictions and the transmission of local and U.S. monetary policy. In this context, we revisit Rey (2013)'s argument that countries face a dilemma, not a trilemma. Lastly, we consider the global implications of the dollar standard for the scarcity of safe assets and the global stability of the international financial system.

### Exchange rate pass-through, expenditure switching and the effectiveness of flexible exchange rates

The combination of dollar invoicing, strategic complementarities in pricing and imported intermediate inputs gives rise to a Dominant

---

[10] This discussion builds on Gopinath *et al.* (2018).

Currency Paradigm (DCP), explored in detail empirically and theoretically in Gopinath *et al.* (2018). This paradigm forces us to rethink a number of key predictions arising from standard models. For instance, in the traditional New Keynesian framework prices are assumed to be set — and sticky — in the producer's currency (producer currency pricing or PCP). Under that assumption, a depreciation of the local currency raises the price of imports relative to exports, a depreciation of the terms of trade that shifts demand towards domestic produced goods and away from foreign produced ones. This 'expenditure switching effect' of exchange rate movements is a key argument in favor of flexible exchange rates. If all prices were set in the producer's currency, a 1% depreciation of the nominal exchange rate would depreciate the terms of trade — defined as the ratio of the price of imports to the price of exports by 1% in the short term. Instead, under DCP, both imports and export prices are set in dollar and a depreciation of the bilateral exchange rate has no effect on the terms of trade.

Empirically, Gopinath *et al.* (2018) put together aggregate data on harmonized annual bilateral import and export unit values for a large number of countries pairs that covers 91% of world trade. They confirm that non-commodities terms of trade are largely uncorrelated with bilateral exchange rate movements (Table 3).

A second key implication of DCP is that the dollar exchange rate dominates bilateral exchange rates in price pass-through and trade elasticity regressions. The first two columns of Table 4 shows that the explanatory power of the the bilateral exchange rate for import prices disappears once we control for the dollar exchange rate. The last two columns of Table 4 show a similar result for trade volumes. Gopinath *et al.* (2018) also document similar results using finely disaggregated product-firm level prices and quantities for Colombian exports and imports. This result indicates that some expenditure switching still operates, but only in response to the dollar exchange rate, and only on the import margin.[11]

---

[11] Exports will respond to movements in the destination country dollar exchange rate.

**Table 3.** Terms of trade and exchange rates

|  | (1)<br>$\Delta tot_{ij,t}$ | (2)<br>$\Delta tot_{ij,t}$ |
|---|---|---|
| $\Delta e_{ij,t}$ | −0.00938 | 0.0218 |
|  | (0.0130) | (0.0317) |
| trade-weighted | no | yes |
| R-squared | 0.011 | 0.042 |
| Observations | 19,847 | 19,847 |
| Dyads | 1,200 | 1,200 |

*Source*: Gopinath *et al.* (2018). The table reports regressions of the change in the (log) bilateral terms of trade between countries $i$ and $j$, $\Delta tot_{ij}$, on the change in the (log) bilateral nominal exchange rate between $i$ and $j$, $\Delta e_{ij}$. All regressions include two lags of $\Delta$ER, $\Delta$PPI and time fixed effects. S.e. clustered by dyad. ***p < 0.01, **p < 0.05, *p < 0.1.

**Table 4.** Exchange rate price pass-through and trade elasticity

|  | Import prices | | Import quantities | |
|---|---|---|---|---|
|  | (1)<br>$\Delta p_{ij,t}$ | (2)<br>$\Delta p_{ij,t}$ | (3)<br>$\Delta y_{ij,t}$ | (4)<br>$\Delta y_{ij,t}$ |
| $\Delta e_{ij,t}$ | 0.757*** | 0.164*** | −0.119*** | −0.0310* |
|  | (0.0132) | (0.0126) | (0.0139) | (0.0160) |
| $\Delta e\$_{j,t}$ |  | 0.781*** |  | −0.186*** |
|  |  | (0.0143) |  | (0.0250) |
| R-squared | 0.356 | 0.398 | 0.069 | 0.071 |
| Observations | 46,820 | 46,820 | 52,272 | 52,272 |
| Dyads | 2,647 | 2,647 | 2,807 | 2,807 |

*Source*: Gopinath *et al.* (2018). The first (resp., last) two columns use import prices (resp. import quantities). All regressions are unweighted, include two $\Delta$ER lags, lags 0–2 of exporter $\Delta$PPI (resp. $\Delta$GDP), and time FE. S.e. clustered by dyad. ***p < 0.01, **p < 0.05, *p < 0.1.

These findings suggest that flexible exchange rates will be less effective under DCP than in standard New Keynesian models. Everything else equal, a unilateral depreciation of the domestic currency against all currencies (including the dollar) will quickly pass through into the price

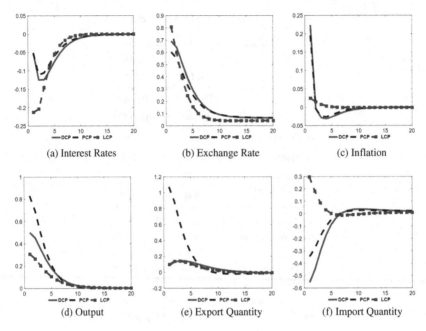

(a) Interest Rates  (b) Exchange Rate  (c) Inflation

(d) Output  (e) Export Quantity  (f) Import Quantity

**Figure 9.** Impulse response to a 25bps domestic monetary policy easing in a Small Open Economy under different invoicing regimes: Producer Currency Pricing (PCP, dashed), Local Currency Pricing (LCP, dashed with square end-blocks) and Dominant Currency Pricing (DCP, solid)
*Source*: Gopinath *et al.* (2018).

of imported goods, but have a very limited impact on exports, improving the trade balance mostly via a reduction in imports. It follows that local monetary authorities will face a more adverse inflation-output tradeoff.

Figure 9 illustrates this finding. It reports the theoretical responses of local interest rates, the nominal exchange rate, consumer price inflation, output, export and import quantities to a 25bps surprise reduction in the domestic policy rate, in a New Keynesian model calibrated under three different pricing regimes: Producer Currency Pricing (PCP), Local Currency Pricing (LCP) where the prices are invoiced and sticky in the destination currency, and dollar pricing (DCP). This monetary impulse translates into roughly similar depreciation under the three pricing regimes (panel (b)). However, the implications for inflation (panel (c)) and output (panel (d)) dynamics are vastly different. Under PCP and DCP, the depreciation increases the price of imports, increasing consumer price inflation. However, the depreciation does not stimulate exports under DCP (panel (e)), hence the increase in output remains more limited.[12]

To summarize, in a world of dollar invoicing, the gains to exchange flexibility are more limited. As discussed by Egorov and Mukhin (2019) this also makes it more desirable to stabilize the dollar exchange rate.

### *Dollar factor and global trade*

The converse is also true: when most trade is invoiced in dollars, U.S. monetary policy has a global reach. To illustrate this point,

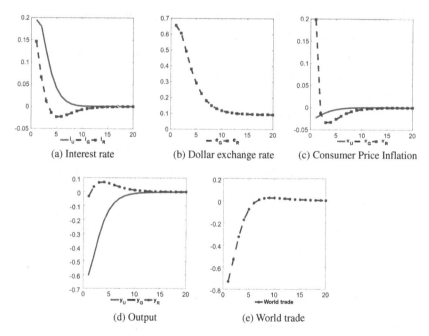

(a) Interest rate     (b) Dollar exchange rate     (c) Consumer Price Inflation

(d) Output     (e) World trade

**Figure 10.** Impulse response to a 25bps monetary tightening in the U.S. ($U$) in the threecountry version of the model under dollar pricing. The three countries are labeled $U$, $G$ and $R$. $G$ and $R$ are symmetric in this simulation so their responses are identical. World trade is defined as the sum of export quantities from all countries
*Source*: Gopinath *et al.* (2018).

---

[12] The model assumes a Taylor type rule for monetary policy, responding to consumer price inflation and the output gap. This is why the behavior of policy rates in panel (a) is different under the three different pricing regimes.

Figure 10 reports the simulated impact of a 25bps U.S. monetary policy contraction in a stylized three-country version of a Gali and Monacelli (2005) model with dollar pricing. As expected, a monetary tightening in the U.S. appreciates the dollar (panel (b)), reduces U.S. output (panel (d)) and lowers U.S. inflation (panel (c)). However, under dollar pricing, U.S. monetary policy has a very different impact on the rest of the world than under standard models. First, under dollar pricing, the appreciation of the dollar has only limited effects on U.S. inflation: dollar pricing insulates U.S. inflation from movements in the dollar. Instead, the appreciation of the dollar raises foreign import prices (and consumer price inflation) (panel (c)). Foreign central banks aiming to stabilize inflation are then forced to raise their own policy rate (panel (a)). Hence, a contractionary monetary impulse in the U.S. triggers a contractionary monetary impulse more globally. As a result, the appreciation of the dollar — which is typically expected to expand output abroad via expenditure switching effects — fails to stimulate foreign output (panel (d)). Instead, the dollar appreciation reduces exports for all countries, decreasing world trade (panel (e)).

It follows that under dollar pricing, U.S. monetary policy turns the dollar into an important driver for global trade: as the dollar appreciates, trade volumes between nondollarized economies declines. Gopinath *et al.* (2018) explore this implication. Figure 11 shows that a 1% appreciation of the dollar leads, ceteris paribus, to a 0.6% contraction in trade volume in the rest of the world.

### Financial frictions, the dollar and the trilemma

While dollar pricing creates a link between global trade and the dollar, it is not the only channel. Other factors could also explain why a dollar appreciation might cause global trade to decline. One such factor is the currency of debt issuance. A dollar appreciation mechanically increases the real debt burden of dollar borrowers. This could cause foreign banks reliant on dollar funding to curtail domestic lending, or force nonfinancial dollar borrowers to raise prices. A dollar appreciation tightens local financial conditions, curtailing economic growth, and trade.

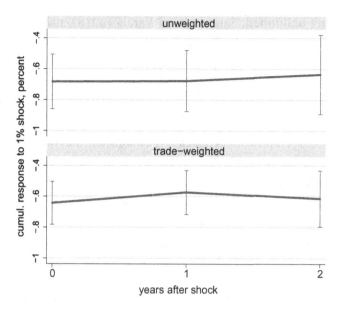

**Figure 11.** Response of rest-of-world aggregate trade to USD appreciation, 2002–2015
*Source*: Gopinath *et al.* (2018). Impulse responses of rest-of-world aggregate trade volume to a 1% U.S. dollar appreciation against all other currencies, holding constant all other exchange rates and the global business cycle. Top row: unweighted regression, bottom row: trade-weighted. Error bars: 95% confidence intervals, clustering by dyad.

An important question attracting substantial attention is that of the optimality of dollar borrowing for foreign non-financial corporates. It shares many similarities and interacts with the question of the optimality of dollar invoicing: dollar borrowing is optimal if it reduces the variability of profits, given the currency of invoicing, just like dollar invoicing is optimal it it reduces the variability of profits, given the currency composition of debt. Not surprisingly, the two decisions feed on each other: dollar borrowing makes dollar invoicing more desirable, and vice versa.

While there is a long and distinguished literature on the 'original sin', i.e. the extent to which sovereigns borrow in foreign currency (Eichengreen and Hausmann 1999), there has been comparatively less work on the currency of borrowing of the private sector. In recent years many emerging market (EM) sovereigns switched from foreign currency to local currency debt. Yet over the same period, private sector dollar borrowing ballooned. Salomao and Varela (2018), using data from Hungarian firms, emphasize that in an environment with financial frictions, firms with higher growth prospects are more likely to resort to Euro borrowing. Eren and Malamud (2018) argue that firms may prefer to borrow in dollars if the U.S. pursues expansionary monetary policy that lowers the real burden of debt in times of global stress. Whether this is the case empirically is not clearly established. Stavrakeva and Tang (2018) show convincingly that in times of global stress, U.S. monetary easing leads to an appreciation of the dollar, not a depreciation, thus generating the pattern of valuation losses as documented in Gourinchas, Rey and Govillot (2017). Undoubtedly, these questions will attract further empirical and theoretical research.

More broadly, dollar dominance in banking and the dollarization of cross-border claims also imply that U.S. monetary policy impulses get transmitted to the broader economy. In a celebrated contribution, Rey (2013) argued that the induced global financial cycle reduced the desirability of flexible exchange rates, turning the classic Trilemma into a Dilemma. Yet, in Gourinchas (2018), I argued that in an environment with financial spillovers, flexible exchange rates may become more, not less, desirable (see also Akinci and Queralto 2018).

To see why this might be the case, suppose that it is indeed the case that a U.S. monetary policy tightening is contractionary abroad, for instance because the incipient appreciation of the dollar tightens local financial conditions for dollar borrowers. How local monetary authorities should respond depends, in turn, on how local monetary policy transmits to their own economy. It is a simple matter of logic to observe that, if a local monetary policy easing is expansionary, as is usually assumed, then the optimal response to the contractionary impulse originating from the center remains a local monetary easing. It follows immediately that the local currency must be allowed to depreciate against the dollar.

Stabilizing the exchange rate would be desirable if local monetary policy tightenings were 'perversely' expansionary locally, instead of contractionary. Many EM policymakers seem to think this is indeed the case. The resulting monetary policy dilemma is sometimes called the 'Tošovský dilemma', in reference to Josef Tošovský, governor of the Czech National Bank in the mid 1990s when capital inflows to Eastern European countries surged (see Na 2019). Similar arguments have been made more recently by the central banks of Iceland and Turkey (see Gudmundsson 2017 and Başçı, Özel and Sarıkaya 2008): a local monetary tightening can become expansionary if the higher yields attract a massive amount of foreign capital, and the appreciation of the local currency relaxes collateral constraints in the local economy. In that case, the contractionary impulse from the U.S. should be countered by tightening domestic monetary conditions, leaving the exchange rate more or less unchanged. Obviously, this requires that financial spillovers are sufficiently strong: the direct expansionary effects of an appreciation become so large that they overwhelm the other and more usual contractionary channels of transmission of monetary policy.

To illustrate this possibility, Figure 12 reports the impulse response of EM output for a U.S. monetary policy tightening, in a New Keynesian model calibrated to Chile, with dominant currency pricing and financial spillovers from the exchange rate.[13] For low levels of financial spillovers (panel (a)),

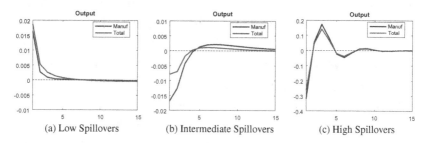

**Figure 12.** Impulse response of emerging market economies output to a U.S. monetary policy tightening for various degrees of financial spillovers
*Source*: Gourinchas (2018). The figure reports the effect of a U.S. monetary tightening on EM's output with various degrees of financial spillovers.

[13] The financial spillovers are modeled simply by assuming that some households are borrowing constrained and that their borrowing limit increases as the currency appreciates.

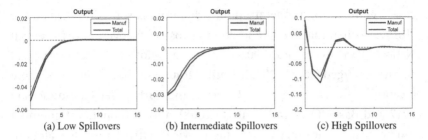

**Figure 13.** Impulse response of EME output to an EME monetary policy tightening for various degrees of financial spillovers

*Source*: Gourinchas (2018). The figure reports the effect of a domestic monetary tightening on domestic output for various degrees of financial spillovers.

the model operates as a standard Mundell-Fleming or Gali and Monacelli (2005) model: a monetary policy tightening in the U.S. is expansionary abroad, thanks to the depreciation of the local currency against the dollar. As we increase the degree of financial spillovers, the depreciation tightens the financial constraints, hurting the local economy. For moderate or high levels of financial spillovers, a U.S. tightening contracts the local economy (panels (b) and (c)). Figure 13 reports the calibrated impulse responses to a domestic monetary policy tightening. The case of low financial spillovers, as before, corresponds to the Mundell-Fleming case where a monetary tightening is contractionary (panel (a)). For moderate levels of spillovers, a domestic tightening remains contractionary, but less so: the appreciation of the local currency against the dollar relaxes borrowing constraints (panel (b)). Overall, though even if local monetary policy has become less effective, the optimal response to a U.S. tightening — which contracts the EM economy — is to ease monetary policy. Finally, panel (c) considers the case of high financial spillovers. In that case, the balance sheet effects of an appreciating currency are so strong that the economy expands when the domestic policy rate is increased. A tightening of domestic monetary policy becomes desirable precisely because it is expansionary.

The upshot is that, while financial spillovers and dollar invoicing reduce the effectiveness of flexible exchange rates, they do not necessarily make flexible exchange rates less desirable for emerging market economies. In other words, the Trilemma may be reinforced, not weakened, by the global financial cycle. Whether this is the case or not depends, crucially, on the strength of financial spillovers from the exchange rate, and on the transmission of U.S. and local monetary policy. These are empirical questions of the first importance to which we have, so far, few definitive answers.

### Safe asset scarcity, safety traps and currency wars

The transition to a dollar standard limited the supply of global safe assets to dollar safe assets. While dollar safe assets may have initially been in abundant supply, increases in capital mobility, rapid economic growth in emerging markets ahead of their level of financial development, and new regulations in the wake of the global financial crisis have created and perpetuated a global scarcity of safe assets (Caballero *et al.* 2017b). This scarcity is one of the defining characteristics of our economic environment. It is consistent with the secular decline in global real interest rates since the early 1980s. It is also consistent with the observed divergence between the average real return to physical capital and the risk free real rate.[14]

Caballero, Farhi and Gourinchas (2016) argue that the scarcity of safe assets mutates once the economy reaches the Effective Lower Bound (ELB) on the policy rate. Above the ELB, the scarcity is benign: countries with a scarcity of safe assets run a current account surplus vis-à-vis safe asset providers, and these surpluses push the global safe real rate downwards. At the ELB, the scarcity becomes malign: since the equilibrium real rate cannot fall sufficiently to equilibrate the market for safe assets, aggregate demand falls short of potential output and the global economy experiences a recession. In that environment, countries face a strong incentive to reflate their economy at the expense of their neighbor, for instance by depreciating their currency. In other words,

---

[14] The increased spread between the economic return to productive capital and the risk free rate is also consistent with increased rents in the economy. Caballero, Farhi and Gourinchas (2017a) proposes a macro decomposition that allows for increased rents as well as increased risk premia or factor-augmenting technological progress. It finds that increased rents or technological progress cannot alone explain the decline in the labor share and observed trends in returns. See also Farhi and Gourio (2019).

there is a potential for currency wars. More generally, there are strong gains from coordinating macroeconomic policies. In the extreme, policies that seem to be appropriate locally, such as increasing price flexibility, or building safety nets by accumulating reserves, or implementing stricter liquidity requirement on the banking sector as envisioned under Basel III, may be self-defeating globally: by accentuating the scarcity of safe assets, they may push the global economy further into a recession (Fornaro and Romei 2018).

### Where Do We Go from There? New Triffin Dilemma and Shadow RMB Anchor

In conclusion, I would like to offer a few prospective remarks. First, Figure 14 extends Figure 2, using World Economic Outlook data. It reports output shares between 1980 and 2024 as predicted by the International Monetary Fund, for the same countries and regions.[15] The message is very clear: the share of U.S. output in world output is expected to decline further, from 15.5% in 2016 to 13.7% in 2024. Much of the growth is expected to come from India (7.3% to 9.8%) and China (17.6% to 21.4%). This secular decline in the relative size of the U.S. raises important questions for the continued primacy of the dollar.

To begin with, in the near future, the U.S. is bound to remain the primary issuer of global safe assets. All other candidate international currencies lag far behind the dollar along almost all dimensions (see Figure 3). The immediate implication is that, unless the supply of dollar safe assets rises in line with global demand, the global scarcity of safe assets is bound to increase, pushing global real safe rates uncomfortably close to the ELB. The macroeconomic risks of such an environment are quite easy to grasp: at the ELB, the global economy tips over into a recession. The increasing scarcity of safe assets keeps the economy in the danger zone. Furthermore, as I've argued above, self-oriented policies such as fiscal austerity, reserve accumulation or stricter liquidity requirement in

---

[15] There are small but non-negligible differences between Figure 2 and Figure 14. These are not important for our purpose and I will ignore them.

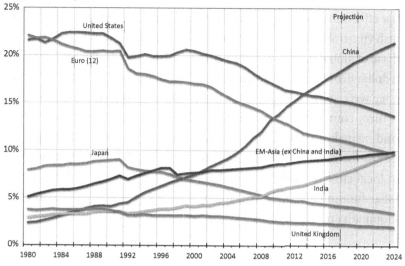

**Figure 14.** World output shares — 2

*Output shares based on PPP. EM-Asia ex China and India consists of Bangladesh, Cambodia, Hong Kong, Indonesia, Korea, Malaysia, Pakistan, Philippines, Singapore, Thailand and Vietnam. Euro12 consists of: Austria, Belgium, Finland, France, Germany, Greece, Ireland, Italy, Luxembourg, the Netherlands, Portugal and Spain.*

*Source*: World Economic Outlook, April 2019.

the banking sector, that may look appropriate at the country level, could well be self-defeating globally as they further increase global demand for safe assets or reduce its supply.

Other dangers lurk in the corners. Low safe real rates, below the growth rate of the economy, send a strong market signal that debt sustainability is not an issue. This is the case whether the issuers have sufficient borrowing capacity or not. For the former, more debt issuance increases the supply of safe assets and helps move the global economy away from safety traps (Caballero *et al.* 2016, 2017b). For the latter, whether private or public, a key question is whether markets have the ability to correctly price credit risk. The experience of the latest global financial crisis is not encouraging. Caballero *et al.* (2008) argued that environments with a scarcity of safe assets are prone to bubbles. One way to think about these bubbles is that they increase the supply of 'quasi-safe' assets. While this may temporarily alleviate the problem, it also makes the global economy more risky since these are not truly safe assets: bubble are rarely safe. The danger, then, is that efforts to make some parts of the financial system safer only help to push vulnerabilities to other corners.[16] As argued by Shin (2014), a second phase of global liquidity started around 2010, with a substantial increase in dollar debt issuance substituting for crossborder dollar loans, since the latter were subject to a stricter regulatory environment (see Figure 7). In turn, continued or even increased private sector reliance on dollar funding makes local authorities reluctant to let their currency depreciate against the dollar, and potentially increases sovereign default risk, even on local currency debt (Du and Schreger 2016). Increased reliance on dollar funding also increases the desirability of holding dollar reserves (Gopinath and Stein 2018b).

Core safe asset providers such as the U.S. face a problem of a different nature: a modern version of the old Triffin dilemma. Expanding public debt in line with a growing global demand is tempting: yields remain low, so that debt sustainability does not appear to be an issue. Furthermore, to the extent that the global economy is close to the effective lower bound, fiscal policy is likely to be quite stimulative. The alternative, with an unchanged supply of safe assets and real rates at the ELB, is a secular appreciation of the dollar which restores equilibrium on the market for safe assets by reducing foreign demand (in dollars) (Caballero *et al.* 2017b). However, since the share of the U.S. economy will continue to decline, expanding U.S. public debt in line with the growth of the world economy must eventually exhaust the fiscal capacity of the U.S., and before that, runs the risk of coordination failure type run on its debt (Farhi and Maggiori 2018).

To put it differently, while the dollar hegemon is locally stable, it is not sustainable. The global economy will have to transition, at some

---

[16] Carstens and Shin (2019) make a similar argument in relation to the original sin debate: the development of local currency bond markets for sovereign debt may look like it is insulating sovereigns from fluctuations in the dollar exchange rate. Yet it simply pushes the currency risk onto the marginal (and foreign) lender. In the end, local currency bond markets may simply substitute currency risk for default risk without substantially improving risk sharing.

point in the future, either to another single anchor, or to a multipolar environment. The former scenario is much less likely than the latter since no-one anticipates a full displacement of the dollar. The most likely path is one where the dollar co-exists with one or two other global international currencies: the renminbi (RMB) and possibly the euro.

While that transition will not be completed anytime soon, it is already partially under way. First, RMB internationalization has started, both by design, and as a consequence of the increased size of the Chinese economy and the explosion in the volume of trade between China and the rest of the world. The use of RMB for trade invoicing, trade settlement, cross-border financial transactions, or official use, has soared in the last ten years, in part due to a number of policy initiatives implemented by the Chinese authorities, including trade settlement programs, RMB offshore clearing banks, off-shore RMB denominated bond market in Hong Kong (so called 'dim sum' bonds), and a network of central bank RMB swap lines.[17] These initial efforts culminated in October 2016 with the addition of the RMB to the basket making up the International Monetary Fund's Special Drawing Rights. More recently, China introduced an RMB denominated oil future contract ('petroyuan') and allowed the inclusion of Chinese local bonds in the Bloomberg global bond index. As in the case of the dollar, we ought to expect that the use of the renminbi for trade invoicing and settlement will increase the private sector demand for renminbi funding, and vice versa; that increased renminbi invoicing and borrowing will increase the desirability of anchoring one's currency to the RMB, and to hold RMB reserves; and conversely that stability in the RMB-local exchange rate and abundant RMB reserves will make it more desirable to invoice and borrow in RMB.

These complementarities also suggest that the transition could gather speed once it gets seriously under way. Consider, for instance, the question of RMB anchoring. No country is currently anchoring to the RMB. In part this is because, while the currency is technically deemed 'freely usable,' it still faces significant restrictions.[18] Another reason is that, as long as the

---

[17] See Eichengreen and Kawai (2015) for a detailed description of each policy initiative.
[18] The IMF criterion for a 'freely usable' currency does not require that all capital controls be dismantled.

dollar-RMB exchange rate remains reasonably stable, anchoring to the dollar indirectly also anchors to the RMB. The argument is similar to that of sterling anchoring during the Bretton Woods era and described above: for all intents and purposes, sterling anchors were shadow dollar anchors. Once currencies started floating, countries — especially in Asia — had to choose whether to remain anchored to the sterling or the dollar. All of them chose the dollar. Similarly, for some countries, a dollar anchor may already be a 'shadow RMB anchor.' A switch to RMB anchoring would occur, should significant monetary instability between the two countries arise. This could force a rapid realignment with the emergence of a RMB zone.

## References

Akinci, O and Queralto, A (2018). Balance sheets, exchange rates, and international monetary spillovers. FRB of New York Staff Report No. 849, June.

Aliber, RZ (1973). National preferences and the scope for international monetary reform. Paper No. 101, International Finance Section, Princeton University.

Avdjiev, S, McCauley, RN, and Shin, HS (2015). Breaking free of the triple coincidence in international finance. BIS Working Papers No. 524.

Avdjiev, S, Du, WX, Koch, C, and Shin, HS (2016). Exchange rates, currency hedging and the cross-currency basis. BIS Working Papers No. 592.

Başçı, E, Özel, O, and Sarıkaya, C (2008). The monetary transmission mechanism in Turkey: New developments. BIS Working Papers No. 35.

Bernanke, BS, Bertaut, C, DeMarco, LP, and Kamin, S (2011). International capital flows and the returns to safe assets in the United States, 2003–2007. International Finance Discussion Papers 1014, Board of Governors of the Federal Reserve System.

Bolt, J, Inklaar, R, de Jong, H, and van Zanden, JL (2018). Rebasing 'Maddison': New income comparisons and the shape of long-run economic development. GGDC Research Memorandum, 174.

Bruno, V and Shin, HS (2015). Capital flows and the risk-taking channel of monetary policy. *Journal of Monetary Economics*, 71, 119–132.

Bruno, V , Kim, S-J, and Shin, HS (2018). Exchange rates and the working capital channel of trade fluctuations. *AEA Papers and Proceedings*, 108, 531–536.

Caballero, RJ, Farhi, E, and Gourinchas, P-O (2008). Financial crash, commodity prices and global imbalances. *Brookings Papers on Economic Activity*, 2, 1–55.

Caballero, RJ, Farhi, E, and Gourinchas, P-O (2016). Global imbalances and currency wars at the ZLB. NBER Working Paper No. 21670, March.

Caballero, RJ, Farhi, E, and Gourinchas, P-O (2017a). Rents, technical change, and risk premia accounting for secular trends in interest rates, returns on capital, earning yields, and factor shares. *American Economic Review*, 107(5), 614–620.

Caballero, RJ, Farhi, E, and Gourinchas, P-O (2017b). The safe assets shortage conundrum. *Journal of Economic Perspectives*, 31(3), 29–46.

Calvo, GA and Reinhart, CM (2002). Fear of floating. *The Quarterly Journal of Economics*, 117(2), 379–408.

Carstens, A and Shin, HS (2019). Emerging markets aren't out of the woods yet. *Foreign Affairs*, 15 March.

Coeuré, B (2018). Asserting Europe's leadership," Panel remarks, Les rencontres économiques d'Aix-en-Provence, July.

Cooper, RN (1973). The future of the dollar. *Foreign Policy*, (11), 3–32.

Du, WX and Schreger, J (2016). Sovereign risk, currency risk, and corporate balance sheets. Harvard Business School Working Papers 17-024, 2016.

Egorov, K and Mukhin, D (2019). Optimal monetary policy under dollar pricing. Yale University, March (mimeo).

Eichengreen, B and Xia, GT (2019). China and the SDR: Financial liberalization through the back door. *Quarterly Journal of Finance*, 9(3).

Eichengreen, B and Kawai, M (2015). Renminbi internationalization: Achievements, prospects, and challenges. Brookings Institution Press.

Eichengreen, B and Hausmann, R. (1999). Exchange rates and financial fragility. Presented at the 1999 Economic Policy Symposium, Federal Reserve Bank of Kansas City.

Eichengreen, B, Mehl, AJ, and Chitu, L (2017). Mars or Mercury? The geopolitics of international currency choice. NBER Working Paper No. 24145, December.

Eren, E and Malamud, S (2018). Dominant currency debt. CEPR Discussion Paper No. DP13391, November.

European Central Bank (2018). The international role of the euro. Interim report, June.

Farhi, E and Gourio, F (2019). Accounting for macro-finance trends: Market power, intangibles, and risk premia. NBER Working Paper No. 2582, February.

Farhi, E and Maggiori, M (2018). A model of the international monetary system. *Quarterly Journal of Economics*, 133(1), 295–355.

Farhi, E, Gourinchas, P-O, and Rey, H (2011). Reforming the international monetary system, CEPR eBook.

Fornaro, L and Federica Romei, F (2018). The paradox of global thrift. Banco de Espana Working Paper No. 1845, December.

Gali, J and Monacelli, T (2005). Monetary policy and exchange rate volatility in a small open economy. *The Review of Economic Studies*, 72(3), 707–734.

Goldberg, L and Tille, C (2009). Macroeconomic interdependence and the international role of the dollar. *Journal of Monetary Economics*, 56(7), 990–1003.

Gopinath, G (2016). The international price system. Presented at 2016 Economic Policy Symposium at Jackson Hole, Federal Reserve Bank of Kansas City.

Gopinath, G and Stein, JC (2018a). Banking, trade, and the making of a dominant currency. Technical Report, NBER Working Paper No. w24485, April.

Gopinath, G and Stein, JC (2018b). Trade invoicing, bank funding, and central bank reserve holdings. *AEA Papers and Proceedings*, 108, 542–546.

Gopinath, G, Boz, E, Casas, C, Diez, F, Gourinchas, P-O, and Plagborg-Møller, M (2018). Dominant currency paradigm. NBER Working Paper No. 22943, December.

Gorton, G and Metrick, A (2012). Securitized banking and the run on repo. *Journal of Financial Economics*, 104(3), 425–451.

Gourinchas, P-O (2017). The fundamental structure of the international monetary system, In MD Bordo and JB Taylor (Eds.), *Rules for International Monetary Stability: Past, Present and Future* (pp. 169–203). Hoover Institution Press.

Gourinchas, P-O (2018). Monetary policy transmission in emerging markets: An application to Chile. In E Pastén, E Mendoza and D Saravia (Eds.), *Monetary Policy and Global Spillovers: Mechanisms, Effects and Policy Measures*, Vol. 25 (pp. 279–324). Santiago: Banco Central de Chile.

Gourinchas, P-O, Rey, H, and Sauzet, M (2019). The international monetary and financial system. *Annual Review of Economics*, 11, 859–893.

Gourinchas, P-O, Rey, H, and Govillot, N (2017). Exorbitant privilege and exorbitant duty. UC Berkeley (mimeo).

Gudmundsson, M (2017). Global financial integration and central bank policies in small, open economies. *The Singapore Economic Review*, 62(1), 135–146.

Ilzetzki, E, Reinhart, CM, and Rogoff, KS (2017). The country chronologies to exchange rate arrangements into the 21st century: Will the anchor currency hold? Technical Report No. 23135, National Bureau of Economic Research, February.

Ilzetzki, E, Reinhart, C, and Rogoff, R (2019). Exchange arrangements entering the 21st century: Which anchor will hold? *Quarterly Journal of Economics*, 134(2), 599–646.

Ito, H and Chinn, MD (2015). The rise of the 'redback' and the People's Republic of China's capital account liberalization: An empirical analysis of the determinants of invoicing currencies. In B. Eichengreen and M. Kawai (Eds.), *Renminbi Internationalization: Achievements, Prospects, and Challenges*. Asian Development Bank Institute and Brookings Institution Press.

Kalemli-Özcan, Ş, Kim, S-J, Shin, HS, Sørensen, BE, and Sevcan Yesiltas, S (2014). Financial shocks in production chains. University of Maryland (mimeo).

Kamps, A (2006). The Euro as invoicing currency in international trade. ECB Working Paper Series, August.

Kenen, PB (1983). The role of the dollar as an international currency. Occasional Paper No. 13.

Keohane, RO (1980). The theory of hegemonic stability and changes in international economic regimes, 1967–1977. Center for International and Strategic Affairs, University of California.

Kindleberger, CP (1973). *The World in Depression, 1929–1939*. University of California Press.

Kindleberger, CP (1981). Dominance and leadership in the international economy: Exploitation, public goods, and free rides. *International Studies Quarterly*, 25(2), 242–254.

Lai, EL-C and Yu, XR (2015). Invoicing currency in international trade: An empirical investigation and some implications for the renminbi. *The World Economy*, 38(1), 193–229.

Maggiori, M, Neiman, B, and Schreger, J (2018). International currencies and capital allocation. Working Paper, Harvard University.

McKinnon, R (1974). A new tripartite monetary agreement or a limping dollar standard? Paper No. 106, International Finance Section, Princeton University.

McKinnon, R (1979). *Money in International Exchange: The Convertible Currency System*. Oxford: Oxford University Press.

Miranda-Agrippino, S and Rey, H (2018). U.S. monetary policy and the global financial cycle. Technical Report, NBER Working Paper No. 21722, issued in November 2015, revised in February 2018.

Mukhin, D (2017). An equilibrium model of the international price system. Princeton University (mimeo).

Mundell, RA (1973). The monetary consequences of Jacques Rueff. *Journal of Business*, 46(3), 384–395.

Na, SH (2019). The monetary policy dilemma of emerging economies. Purdue University, April (mimeo).

Rey, H (2013). Dilemma not trilemma: The global financial cycle and monetary policy independence. In *Global Dimensions of Unconventional Monetary Policy*. Proceedings of the Economic Policy Symposium at Jackson Hole, Federal Reserve Bank of Kansas City.

Rueff, J (1971). Le péché monétaire de l'Occident, Paris: Plon.

Salomao, J and Liliana Varela, L (2018). Exchange rate exposure and firm dynamics. C.E.P.R. Discussion Papers No. 12654, January.

Shin, HS (2014). The second phase of global liquidity and its impact on emerging economies. In KI Chung, SY Kim, HI Park, CH Choi, HS Shin (Eds.), *Volatile Capital Flows in Korea* (pp. 247–257) New York: Palgrave-MacMillan.

Stavrakeva, V and Tang, J (2018). The dollar during the global recession: U.S. monetary policy and the exorbitant duty. Federal Reserve Bank of Boston Working Paper No. 18–10.

Triffin, R (1961). *Gold and the Dollar Crisis; the Future of Convertibility*. New Haven, Connecticut: Yale University Press.

Whitman, MVN (1974). The current and future role of the dollar: How much symmetry? *Brookings Papers on Economic Activity*, 3, 539–591.

# CHAPTER 8

# Chapter 8

# A Safe-Asset Perspective for an Integrated Policy Framework[*]

Markus K. Brunnermeier, Sebastian Merkel and Yuliy Sannikov[1]

## Abstract

Borrowing from Brunnermeier and Sannikov (2016a; 2019) this policy paper sketches a policy framework for emerging market economies by mapping out the roles and interactions of monetary policy, macroprudential policies, foreign exchange interventions, and capital controls. Safe assets are central in a world in which financial frictions, distribution of risk, and risk premia are important elements. The paper also proposes a global safe asset for a more self-stabilizing global financial architecture.

## Introduction

International monetary and financial systems have become inextricably entwined over the past decades, leading to strong and volatile cross-border capital flows as well as powerful monetary policy spillovers. The Integrated Policy Framework (IPF) proposed by the International Monetary Fund (IMF) seeks to address these issues by developing a unified framework to study optimal monetary policy, macroprudential

[*] This paper was prepared for the 7th Asian Monetary Policy Forum. We especially thank Joseph Abadi.
[1] Markus K. Brunnermeier, Edwards S. Sanford Professor of Economics, Director of the Bendheim Center for Finance, Princeton University; Sebastian Merkel, Postdoctoral Research Associate Princeton University; Yuliy Sannikov, The Jack Steele Parker Professor of Economics, Stanford University.

policies, foreign exchange interventions, and capital controls in an interconnected global financial system.

In that framework, the key friction that gives rise to a role for monetary policy is price stickiness: monetary policy primarily serves to stabilize demand, and international capital market imperfections force central banks to tradeoff domestic demand against financial stability. Basu *et al.* (2020) and Adrian *et al.* (2020) present models of the current IMF New Keynesian approach. This paper will instead emphasize that certain assets serve as safe harbors to hedge risk and deliberately ignores any form of price rigidities, complementing the IPF's Keynesian view. Domestic money and government debt can possibly take on the role of safe assets, but they compete with other reserve assets like the U.S. Treasury bond, the German Bund, and Japanese Government Bonds. Monetary policy, foreign exchange interventions, capital control policy, and macroprudential regulation will shape the international competition among safe assets and global risk appetites. These have first-order importance for emerging countries' integrated policy framework.

In this policy paper we combine insights from academic analysis in Brunnermeier and Sannikov (2016a; 2019). We first outline what determines monetary sovereignty and then argue that the two key characteristics of a safe asset are the good-friend analogy and the safe-asset tautology.

Importantly, we rely on a broader perspective of asset pricing. Not only are asset prices derived as a discounted stream of cash flows, but service flows also contribute to the value of assets. For example, they might relax collateral constraints, a safe asset can provide some better insurance through re-trading, and money assets relax in addition to the double-coincidence of wants constraint. These additional service flows push the prices of assets beyond their fundamental values. A bubble component emerges that results in a lower expected cash flow return. When risk in the economy rises, the safe-asset bubble component increases in value. To understand the important role that safe assets play, we go through the three key phases of the global financial cycle. Starting with a high U.S.

dollar interest rate phase (or risk-off phase), followed by a phase with low U.S. interest rates dropping (or low perceived risk) in which emerging markets and development economies (EMDEs) are tempted to create their own bubbly safe asset for which the government's interest burden is lower. During that phase domestic citizens and firms hold the domestic bonds as safe assets to hedge their idiosyncratic risk and borrow at the low U.S. interest rate in U.S. dollars. The cheap U.S. dollar borrowing rate boosts economic growth, making the safe-asset bubble sustainable. When fear of a possible subsequent U.S. interest hike kicks in, the bubble becomes wobbly. A sudden stop might occur, and suddenly domestic citizens want to save in U.S. Treasuries instead of borrowing in dollars and holding the EMDEs' bond for precautionary savings. Economic growth collapses, which further undermines the sustainability of the bubble.

The integrated policy framework has to take into account the interaction across various policy instruments. To protect the safe-asset status of a country, one can either boost the fundamentals or support the bubble component. Higher domestic interest rates supported with accompanying fiscal austerity measures typically improve the fundamentals if they don't stall growth. Bubble-supporting measures come in three flavors: (i) improving market liquidity of the government bond to facilitate re-trading, (ii) foreign exchange interventions, and (iii) importantly as an ultima ratio, imposing capital controls to prevent the competition with U.S. Treasuries. Ex ante measures include limits on foreign capital inflows, the buildup of reserve buffers, and tighter overall borrowing limits.

To study macroprudential regulation one has to include a financial sector. As outlined in Brunnermeier and Sannikov's (2016a) I Theory of Money, banks are good at diversifying away idiosyncratic risk. After an adverse shock, they scale back and push idiosyncratic risk on to the domestic citizens and firms, who then tilt their portfolios more toward the safe asset. When capital controls are in place, the domestic bond is the only safe asset and it rises in value during crisis times. That is, disinflationary pressures kick in. In contrast, when capital outflows into U.S. Treasuries are possible, inflationary pressures are present, potentially killing the safe-asset status of the EMDE. Macroprudential measures and banks' capital requirements lower these forces. Hence, capital controls and bank capital requirements are substitute policy instruments. In contrast, both instruments are complementary to monetary policy: more stringent implementation of international capital controls and bank capital requirements creates a bigger space for monetary policy.

Our approach also provides a coherent framework for why the Mundell-Fleming trilemma collapses to a dilemma, as proposed in Rey (2013). Monetary policy might face a Catch-22 problem even when the exchange rate is freely floating, if it is not supported ex-ante with macroprudential regulation or capital control.

The final section argues that tranching sovereign debt into a senior and a junior bond makes it easier for EMDEs to preserve their safe-asset status. To overcome commitment problems, the tranching should be done by establishing an international special-purpose vehicle that pools sovereign debt from several EMDEs and tranches the pool in a junior bond that protects the senior bond. The latter will enjoy the safe-asset status, which lowers overall funding costs for the EMDEs.

## Safe Asset Definition and Assets' Value

Before going into details, it is necessary to define a safe asset in order to understand its particular role and why money is a special form of safe asset. A safe asset can be characterized by two distinguishing features:

- The "good-friend analogy": A safe asset is like a good friend in that it is there when one needs it, in times of market stress. This definition is in contrast to a risk-free asset, which pays a specified amount at a certain maturity but may fluctuate in value before it matures.
- The "safe-asset tautology": A safe asset is safe because others perceive it to be safe. In times of financial distress, agents coordinate on investment in safe assets.

This definition of money appeals to some notion of multiple equilibria or "money as a bubble." Henceforth, "money" can be thought of as a safe asset denominated in a particular unit of account. As such, this definition of safe assets can be viewed as a definition of broad money: it includes a wide array of government-issued paper of different maturities as well as privately issued inside money.

Risk plays a central role in modern asset pricing. However, the focus is primarily on cash flow payoffs of assets and claims. The fundamental value of an asset is indeed derived from the discounted stream of future risky payoffs. However, in a world with financial frictions, several other aspects can boost the value of an asset (and hence lower its expected return).

First, an asset has an additional benefit if it can be used as a safe store-of-value that can be sold at a relatively stable price after an adverse shock. This "safe asset" component can significantly boost its value. For this benefit to arise, the asset must enjoy high market liquidity, i.e., it can be sold without a large discount, when one needs funds. Like a good friend, it is there when you need it. Safe assets provide an "insurance service" in a world when explicit insurance contracts are missing. Investors are willing to hold safe assets for precautionary reasons. Keynes (1936) referred to it as a speculative or bubble component of an asset's value. Interestingly, an asset can be valuable even if it never pays any dividends or interest payments. Typically, government bonds take on this role within a country; and global reserve assets, like the U.S. Treasury bond, German Bund, and Japanese Government Bonds, take on this role for international finance. Not surprisingly, countries are eager to issue safe assets since their low required return makes them a very cheap source of funding.

The extra safe-asset value derives from the fact that (i) the asset holds its value or even appreciates in times of need and (ii) it enjoys high market liquidity, i.e., it can be traded and re-traded with a low bid-ask spread. The former is self-fulfilling. In times of crisis, safe assets gain in value, which makes it easier for governments, which can issue a safe asset, to finance various stimulus measures in order to stabilize their economies. This, in turn, makes the country's government bond more resilient against the macro shock. Viewing government debt as a safe asset that takes the form of a possibly "wobbly" bubble is the key novel element in our integrated policy framework. Of course, a country's debt may lose its safe-asset status if, for example, a debt restructuring is seen as becoming increasingly likely. The competition among governments to issue bubbly safe assets delivers a different perspective on how to manage the macroeconomy.

Second, when an asset can be used as collateral, it loosens a borrower's borrowing constraints, which is an additional service of the asset besides its payoffs.[2] A government bond that can be used to relax borrowing constraints, e.g., because it is the most common collateral for repo transactions, is valuable even if its cash flow payoff is negligible.

Third, if an asset serves as a medium-of-exchange to overcome the double-coincidence of wants that plagues barter economies, it takes on an even higher value (i.e., its expected real cash flow return is even lower). Formally, this is modeled in monetary theory through cash-in-advance constraints, money in the utility function, shopping time models etc.[3] In theory, many assets and objects can take on the role as a medium of exchange. Governments encourage coordination on a particular piece of paper, the domestic currency, which we refer to as narrow money.

The fact that narrow money is a bubble is well understood since it takes on positive value even if the cash flow payoff is negative due to inflation. When dollarization occurs, the domestic safe asset is stripped of this characteristic.[4]

This (narrower) form of money is largely provided by the banking sector in the form of deposits (inside money). Indeed, banks are profitable since they bundle and diversify a portfolio of typically illiquid (non-safe) assets and transfer them into liquid inside money.

Of course, the liquidity transformation process works only as long as the bank is regarded as solvent and shielded against liquidity runs. As soon as depositors doubt the solvency of a bank, the bank loses its

---

[2] The extra value is given by the Lagrange multiplier on the collateral constraint.
[3] See, e.g., Brunnermeier and Niepelt (2019).
[4] For the digital dollarization concept see Brunnermeier *et al.* (2019).

transformative power, depriving it of profit opportunities, which justifies the initial solvency doubts. The self-fulfilling nature of insolvency illustrates the fragility of banking (even absent any maturity mismatch).

While a large part of monetary theory focuses on (the narrow form of) money, our proposed Integrated Policy Framework focuses on the safe-asset perspective. We have in mind a broader asset class than the narrow definition of money that primarily focuses on overcoming limitations due to barter. In sum, an asset value is given by the discounted stream of future cash flows in the form of dividends and interest payments. Insurance service operated through the safe-asset mechanism "relaxation of collateral" constraints "medium-of-exchange" service. The additional "service payoffs" explain what is often referred to as the liquidity premium or convenience yield of certain assets. The medium-of-exchange service depends on the degree of moneyness of an asset. Central bank reserves have a high degree of moneyness, while private bank deposits might lose it if the solvency of the bank is in doubt. Money is a special form of safe asset as it also acts as a medium of exchange. Government debt is typically a safe asset if it is considered to be default-free since people might simply hold it to be able to sell it (in times of need), i.e., for speculative reasons. In other words, a safe asset can contain a bubble component. Importantly, bubbles can burst and jump to another asset, leading to large price swings and excess volatility. Figure 1 illustrates the set of assets graphically.

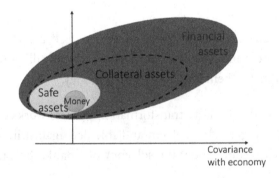

**Figure 1.** Various asset classes with different "service flows"

The price level, whose log-change determines inflation, can also be seen as an asset-pricing equation. We refer to it in this document as the Fiscal Theory of the Price Level (FTPL) equation.

Total real value of all government debt + money = E[PV of primary surpluses] + E[PV of future transaction services from narrow money] + E[PV collateral services] + E[PV insurances services],

where the last three terms are bubble terms as they do not reflect a cash flow payoff. For details, see Brunnermeier *et al.* (2020). That is, if one owns all government debt, one would receive from the government as cash flow only the future stream of primary surpluses.[5] Note that the present value (PV) cash and service flows are discounted with the stochastic discount factor (SDF). For example, if the insurance service of an asset primarily arises in states of crisis, then these services are discounted at a lower rate. In other words, the risk premium is negative, which makes the bubble term larger.

Keeping in mind that the bubble component can jump from one government safe asset to another, possibly to a foreign safe asset, the expectations operator in the FTPL equation is important.

## Monetary Sovereignty

In order to understand the role of monetary policy, it is necessary to understand when it will be desirable for the national monetary authority to affect the real macroeconomy. In particular, the focus here will be on the conduct of optimal monetary and other policies in EMDEs when faced with spillovers from policy actions in a large developed economy (i.e., a dollar monetary policy). If an EMDE's optimal monetary policy is the same as the U.S. dollar monetary policy, the central bank does not face a meaningful tradeoff: it can achieve the optimum by implementing

---

[5] Money can relax the double-coincidence of wants constraint and government can relax the collateral constraint. Its value is reflected by the corresponding Lagrange multiplier.

a currency board, which neutralizes all undesirable spillovers. Also, dollarization is not so costly aside from some forgone seigniorage profits. Therefore, going forward, we will assume that the EMDE faces shocks different from the U.S. and that the EMDE's optimal policy is not the same as U.S. monetary policy. In addition, domestic financial stability may be affected by U.S. policy.

The role of domestic safe assets in this risk-based framework allows citizens to hedge the idiosyncratic risks they face. Hence, in addition to whatever value money has as a medium of exchange, the value of the domestic safe asset will stem from its store-of-value properties.

In Brunnermeier and Sannikov (2016b)'s I Theory of Money, monetary policy can have real effects through the revaluation of these safe assets when markets are incomplete: if citizens hold some long-term bonds in domestic safe assets, a change in interest rates will affect their net worth and risk-taking decisions. Monetary sovereignty is desirable to the extent that the central bank would like to redistribute risk and affect risk premia. Importantly, risk consists of unavoidable exogenous risk and endogenous risk that is generated by the economic system itself due to amplification effects, spirals, and adverse feedback loops. The central bank can moderate domestic financial stability and lower the amount of endogenous risk in the domestic economy, which then, in turn, lowers the price of risk and risk premia, as reflected by the equation:

Risk premium = price of risk * (exogenous risk + endogenous risk)

Real risk-free rate, $r$ = time preference rate + E[consumption growth rate]

– Consumption volatility

– Collateral interest rate differential

The real return on narrow money is even lower as one has to subtract the advantage it yields from being able to serve as a medium of exchange. Note that a safe asset is typically not risk-free. Hence, the expected return on the safe asset can be higher (lower) because it contains an additional (negative) risk premium. We deliberately mention the risk premia before the risk-free rate since monetary policy can work via the redistribution of risk and risk-bearing capacity/wealth and it has a larger impact by reducing the risk premium. In our view, the current emphasis on the risk-free rate and the step-child treatment of risk premia is lopsided. Note that collateral shortage due to the lack of other good collateral assets will lower the real risk-free asset if the risk-free asset — say, the government bond — can be used as collateral. Broadening the collateral set therefore increases the real risk-free rate.

## Safe Asset Competition Through the Global Financial Cycle

So far, we have ignored the fact that the domestic safe asset is in competition with global safe assets, for which we use U.S. Treasury bonds as a stand-in. Hence, U.S. monetary policy complicates an EMDE's goal of providing a safe asset. For simplicity, we ignore narrow-money currency competition in this paper and simply assume that the domestic currency will always be used as a medium of exchange. That is, we assume that dollarization and digital dollarization do not threaten the domestic currency.[6]

It is instructive to analyze the competition among safe assets through the global financial cycle. Here we focus on the U.S. monetary policy cycle, starting with a high U.S. interest rate environment in phase 1. Phase 2 is characterized by a low U.S. interest rate, while phase 3 leads us back to a higher U.S. interest rate.

Note that we could have alternatively focused on a global financial cycle that is driven by shifts in risk (perceptions), which leads to associated movements in the price of risk. Phase 1 is characterized by a low (idiosyncratic) risk environment, and consequently the price of risk is also low. In phase 2 the risk is elevated, and in phase 3 it returns to the initial level. Finally, the global financial cycle and the associated price of risk could also be driven by shifts in risk aversion. Since the latter two scenarios lead to overall similar implications, we focus here primarily on the U.S. monetary policy cycle.

---

[6] For a detailed discussion on digital dollarization, see Brunnermeier *et al.* (2019).

The switch from one phase to the next is typically associated with large swings and excessive volatility in capital flows in and out of EMDEs. Let us illustrate the three phases and their potential disruptions in the context of U.S. monetary policy movements. We label the three phases as the initial phase for a high-interest-rate environment, followed by the "temptation phase," which ultimately leads to the "wobbly bubble" phase in which the EMDE's safe asset might collapse when financial markets foresee a tightening of U.S. monetary policy.

### Initial phase

In the first phase, when U.S. monetary policy is tight, agents in the EMDE view dollars as an attractive investment. When the U.S. dollar interest rate is high, domestic government bonds face fierce competition from U.S. Treasuries, which can also be used to hedge idiosyncratic risks. The competition between dollars and the domestic safe assets mitigates the bubbly store-of-value role of the domestic safe asset, so the value of government liabilities stems mostly from the expected fiscal primary surpluses. That is, the traditional FTPL equation holds without a bubble term. The bubble term is absent since the domestic interest rate $r$ is too high.

### Temptation phase

The "temptation phase" begins when the U.S. lowers rates. Lower dollar rates make domestic safe-asset debt more attractive compared to the U.S. Treasury bond as a safe asset. Citizens in the EMDE now facing a low dollar interest rate instead borrow in U.S. dollars up to their collateral constraints (or a limit set by macroprudential policy) and use the domestic safe asset, say peso asset, as a hedge for their (idiosyncratic and other) risk. Cheap dollar funding leads to an investment boom, increasing the growth rate of the economy and, with it, the growth rate of the (insurance) services provided by the safe asset. As soon as this growth rate, $g$, exceeds the real discount rate, $r$ + safe asset risk premium, the safe asset can take on a bubble component. Hence, in general the (safe-asset) bubble condition is

$$r + \text{safe asset risk premium} < g.$$

Note that any bubble has to grow in expectations $r$ + safe asset risk premium. If this were larger than $g$, then the bubble had to outgrow the economy, which is unsustainable. Four important remarks are in order: First, an increase in idiosyncratic risk depresses the real risk-free rate $r$, as discussed above. Second, the safe-asset risk premium can be negative if the safe asset appreciates in bad times. Both effects make it easier to satisfy the bubble condition. Third, the safe-asset risk premium reflects various risks, including bubble-bursting risk, default risk, and inflation risk.[7] The growth rate $g$ reflects a weighted average of economic, collateral service, insurance service, and transaction volume growth. Economic growth is often a good proxy for this weighted average. Strictly speaking, if the growth rate of the aggregate economy is stochastic, $g$ is the expected growth rate minus some 'growth risk premium'.

The bubbly value of government liabilities tempts the EMDE's government into expanding the supply of debt, thereby "mining" the bubble. The government can mine the bubble by using its outstanding government debt to run an **ever-expanding Ponzi scheme**: letting the stock of government debt grow generates a steady revenue flow that does not have to be paid for by future taxes as long as a bubble term is present.

Figure 2 shows the balance sheet structure. Note that government debt is only partially backed by future primary surpluses and U.S. dollar reserve holdings, since part of it can be attributed to the "bubble" component.

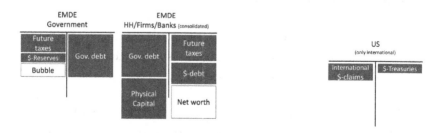

**Figure 2.**   Balance sheets in temptation phase

---

[7] The size of the bubble is determined in equilibrium since the bubble's wealth effect creates extra goods demand, which has to equal goods supply.

### *"Wobbly bubble" phase*

The EMDE enters the final "wobbly bubble" phase when news arrives that dollar interest rates might rise. The prospect of increased rates raises the possibility of a depreciation of the domestic safe asset, again making the domestic safe asset a less desirable store of value. An increase in dollar interest rates will make domestic agents rush out of the domestic safe asset and into dollars, causing a depreciation. This threatens the bubble value of government debt because, in order for a bubble to be possible, the expected return on the domestic safe asset, including the safe-asset risk premium, must be less than the growth rate of the economy. During this phase we focus on the component of the safe-asset risk premium that is due to the possible bursting of the bubble. Ignoring other risks, the bubble condition is simply

$$r + \text{(bursting bubble) safe asset risk premium} < g.$$

When dollar interest rates are expected to rise, $r$ of the EMDE bond has to rise to stay competitive with the U.S. Treasuries, which makes it more difficult for the domestic safe asset to sustain a bubble, so the bubble begins to "wobble." The pure possibility of bursting requires a risk premium, which again makes it tougher to satisfy the bubble condition. When the bubble bursts, the value of the safe asset falls back down to the fundamental, reducing risk-sharing between domestic agents. This, in turn, reduces domestic investment and asset prices, causing fire sales of capital in the EMDE and a recession. In other words, the growth rate $g$ in the EMDE will also decline.

Note that with flexible prices there is perfect pass-through of exchange rate movements. That is, any depreciation is associated with domestic inflation as the price of imported goods rises.[8]

In fact, this argument suggests that expectations of a future depreciation can cause the bubble to wobble and can therefore be

---

[8] With price stickiness, exchange rate pass-through is not 100% and the inflationary effect is delayed.

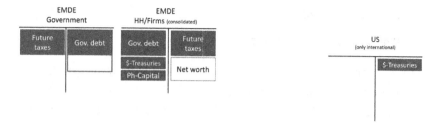

**Figure 3.**   Balance sheets after sudden stop

self-fulfilling. Hence, the bubble that emerges during the temptation phase may become wobbly not only when foreign monetary policy is expected to tighten, but also during risk-off episodes when global investors are expected to rush out of EM currencies. Our framework shares some features of Calvo (1988) and also with the second-generation currency attack models initially pioneered by Obstfeld (1996), though with the difference that it builds on bursting bubbles.

When the EMDE loses its safe-asset status — i.e., the bubble burst, the government used up its foreign reserves, and firms sold part of their physical capital — the balance sheet structure ends up as depicted in Figure 3.

## Policies

The policy space is characterized by a set of various policy measures. Ex-post policy instruments are employed in crisis times and include monetary policy, capital outflow controls, market liquidity support, or foreign exchange interventions. Ex-ante policy measures are often commitment strategies, such as capital inflow controls, or signaling strategies, like the buildup of foreign reserves, that do not reduce the likelihood of a crisis as much. Domestic macroprudential policy measures that target the financial sector are discussed in the next section, in which we introduce the financial sector to the analysis.

The key to an integrated policy framework is to clearly spell out the interaction between the various policy instruments and highlight which measures are substitutes and which are complements.

### Ex post crisis management

*Propping up fundamentals: Future tax hikes*

The government can choose to support the safe asset directly by implementing traditional policies to prop up fundamentals of the government debt. For instance, the government could try to support the safe asset by raising the nominal interest rate. In an environment without price stickiness or heterogeneity among agents, though, this policy is ineffective without the supporting fiscal measures — nominal interest rate hikes without changes in fiscal policy are passed through one-to-one to inflation. By itself, this sort of policy can be useful only if there is heterogeneity in domestic agents' exposures to the safe asset. For instance, if systemically important domestic banks are exposed to deflation, the central bank can shore up the economy by changing rates and engineering an inflation. The government can also support the safe asset's fundamental value by increasing the present value of expected fiscal surpluses. In order to do so, the government must increase taxes, and it faces two potential problems. For one, distortion-free lump-sum taxation is typically politically infeasible. Hence, the government must resort to increasing distortionary taxes, which lower the growth rate of the economy. This, in turn, makes it more difficult for domestic safe assets to maintain their bubbly value. (Recall that the domestic interest rate must fall below the economy's growth rate, i.e., $r < g$.)

Furthermore, a strategy that maintains the bubble's value by increasing taxes inevitably involves a great deal of commitment on the fiscal authority's behalf, which may not be credible. Indeed, a government with commitment power would usually be unconcerned with the possibility of self-fulfilling depreciations of its domestic safe asset.

*Supporting the bubble: Capital outflow controls and FX interventions*

The government may choose to implement ex-post measures that support the safe asset's bubbly value rather than its fundamental value. For example, it may impose **capital outflow controls** to restrict outflows during crises. These policies do not involve taxation and thus avoid the drawbacks discussed above. Capital control policies can prevent domestic citizens from purchasing U.S. dollar safe assets and prevent foreigners from withdrawing funding. Capital controls support the value of the domestic safe asset in a straightforward way: they restrict access to dollars for domestic agents, so the domestic safe asset (and money) remains the only available hedge against the idiosyncratic risk faced by domestic citizens. The source of the bubble is precisely the safe asset's value as a hedge against idiosyncratic risk, so the value of the bubble can be sustained through the global financial policy cycle.

Ex-post capital controls also increase the bubble's value (as well as incentives for investment) from an ex-ante perspective: if agents foresee that the bubble will remain even after the U.S. raises rates, they will be more willing to hold the domestic safe asset beforehand as well. It may be especially valuable to commit to a conditional capital control policy that binds when U.S. monetary policy is expected to tighten but then loosens over time. Such a policy can allow the government to support the bubble underlying its safe asset by precluding the possibility of a large devaluation. Nevertheless, this policy does encourage overaccumulation of domestic capital in the short run: if dollar interest rates rise, then some domestic divestment is, in fact, efficient.

Another way to support the bubble on the domestic safe asset is to ensure that it enjoys high market liquidity. Recall, the bubble's value relies on the fact that the asset can be easily traded with only a small bid-ask spread. It is therefore not surprising that central banks often act as the **'market maker of last resort'** to ensure the smooth functioning of government debt markets. Historically, many central banks, most prominently the Bank of England, were founded to take on the role of government debt managers. Most recently, the Fed intervened in order to improve market liquidity in the long-dated U.S. Treasury market.

**Foreign exchange interventions** can also be used to maintain the value of the bubble ex-post, but they do so through different channels. The main idea behind these policies is that U.S. dollar reserves can be used to purchase domestic safe assets and fight outflows during the wobbly bubble phase. These reserves can also be managed over the global financial cycle in order to buffer smaller shocks to the domestic safe asset's value that, perhaps, do not merit the imposition of capital controls.

EMDEs are often subject to self-fulfilling speculative attacks on their currencies. By and large, the consensus in the literature is that such attacks are facilitated by coordination through price movements: when speculators are able to see a drop in the value of a safe asset that reveals an attack is occurring, they are more likely to attack the safe asset as well. Experimental evidence from "clock games" shows that markets in which speculative attacks are possible behave in a radically different way when participants are unable to observe price signals of how others are behaving.[9] By the same token, if the central bank manages to support the value of its safe asset when some speculators attack, it prevents other speculators from joining the attack. Employing reserves, then, is an ideal tool to ward off sudden devaluations as it makes it more difficult for speculators to attack the safe-asset-status.

### Ex-ante crisis prevention policies

Good policy is forward-looking policy. Many of the problems in the 'wobbly' phase can be avoided by implementing ex-ante safety measures that are expected to automatically spring into action should a crisis emerge. The emphasis is hereby on "are expected" since the pure expectation reduces the probability of a crisis.

#### Ex-ante commitment to ex-post crisis policies: Capital inflow controls and reserve holdings

All the crisis policies discussed above are more effective if the government can credibly commit itself to them in advance.

**Capital inflow controls** during times when U.S. interest rates are very low are very credible, but also costly since one deprives the economy of

---

[9] See Abreu and Brunnermeier (2003) and Brunnermeier and Morgan (2010).

a possibly faster growth rate. The solution to allow only stickier FDI or foreign equity portfolio investors into the country is often regarded as an intermediate solution.

Holding international **reserves** to defend the domestic safe-asset bubble is the most prominent solution, which many EMDE countries adopted after the Southeast Asian crisis in the late 1990s. Having reserves enables a country to credibly signal its commitment to fend off a possible attack on its safe asset and to preserve its bubble component. Note that it is often worthwhile for the EMDE to hold large international reserves even when they are badly remunerated — the dollar interest rate is lower than the interest rate on the central bank's liabilities. Simply signaling the commitment makes attacks less likely and lowers the "wobbly bubble risk premium" the EMDE country has to pay on its public and private debt.

Note that the effectiveness of accumulating official reserves might be partially undone via borrowing by private citizens and corporations in U.S. dollars. This is another reason to limit private borrowing in U.S. dollars. Absent any friction, a sort of Ricardian equivalence result might emerge, stating that an increase in official reserve holdings emboldens private agents to borrow more in U.S. dollars, rendering reserve holdings ultimately ineffective. This shows the importance of domestic capital (inflow) control measures to limit borrowing by private firms and citizens in U.S. dollars. That is, the government can implement ex-ante preventive measures to support the value of its safe asset through international capital flow cycles.

## Adding a Financial Sector to Study Domestic Macroprudential Policy

### Amplification mechanisms

Capital control measures limit the international borrowing of private citizens and firms. Macroprudential measures limit borrowing more generally among domestic agents denominated in domestic currency as well as in foreign currency. Macroprudential policy can be applied to borrowers, such as by restricting the leverage of firms or households. However, it is often easier to implement by limiting the financial sector's lending activity.

To study macroprudential policies, we incorporate a financial sector in the international framework of Brunnermeier and Sannikov (2019). We follow the framework developed in the I Theory of Money (Brunnermeier and Sannikov, 2016a). Let us consider here an environment in which citizens may diversify some of their idiosyncratic risk away by issuing long-term, defaultable nominal debt to domestic banks. Domestic banks fund themselves using short-term nominal deposits (inside money) in domestic currency. In addition, firms and banks suffer from the "original sin" by issuing U.S. dollar-denominated debt abroad. It is easiest to think of the U.S. dollar as the numeraire asset.

Figure 4 depicts the same balance sheet structure as in Figure 2, except now the EMDE's consolidated balance sheet is split between the balance sheet of the consolidated household/firm sector and a balance sheet for the banking sector.

When the domestic currency depreciates, all domestic firms' and banks' assets and liabilities decline in value except for their U.S. dollar-denominated liabilities — the consequence of the original sin. The firms' reduction in net worth increases their default probability, which hits banks' balance sheets on top of the initial shock they experience from their currency mismatch.

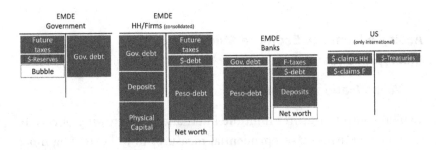

**Figure 4.** Balance sheets with financial sector in temptation phase

Amplification effects kick in due to the paradox of prudence on the side of the banks. Banks try to be micro-prudent, which makes the total system riskier, i.e., it is macro-imprudent. As banks scale back and shrink their balance sheets, they lend less. This lowers investment and growth, further increasing default risk. Banks then take additional losses on their balance sheets, which in turn makes them cut back further on lending and deposit-taking.

The reduction in deposits reduces money supply, a special form of domestic safe-asset supply. The fact that individuals and domestic firms can off-load less (default) risk to banks increases safe-asset demand. Without a foreign safe asset, the U.S. Treasury bond, or capital (outflow) controls, this would lead to disinflationary pressure, which is the primary outcome in advanced countries like the U.S. Hence, without policy intervention, banks' liabilities (their deposits) increase in value, amplifying the adverse effects even further.

For EMDEs, the picture can look very different absent capital controls. Domestic safe assets (government bonds and deposits) compete with U.S. Treasuries and might lose their safe-asset status (albeit not their money status as a medium-of-exchange instrument). This causes inflationary pressure, further devaluing the domestic currency and leading to capital flight to the U.S. Whether this is a mitigating or amplifying force depends on the environment. It is worthwhile to separate various channels through which banks are affected.

If the inflationary devaluation is unexpected and doesn't trigger a policy tightening, banks' nominal assets and domestic-denominated liabilities decline almost in lockstep in real value. However, since firms owe less in real terms, their default risk declines. Hence, ignoring losses due to the original sin, banks' assets decline by less and banks' net worth benefits from that effect. If the policy rate reacts, then banks' assets and liabilities are affected. The change in the real value of banks' assets depends on whether they are floating or fixed, i.e., whether interest payments on the assets adjust or not. In the latter case, banks make capital losses on the asset side. Whether they can make up for this by holding the deposit rate down depends on banks' market power vis-à-vis depositors.[10]

The additional inflation amplifies the exchange rate depreciation, which, in turn, is due to the larger knock-on effects caused by the original sin of dollar-denominated liabilities.

Overall, the loss of banks' net worth amplifies the crisis, possibly triggering a twin crisis (Kaminsky and Reinhart, 1999). When sovereign debt loses its safe-asset status (i.e., its bubble component) and banks own domestic government bonds, a doom/diabolic loop between banking risk and sovereign risk kicks in, which was prevalent during the Euro crisis. Since the doom loop reduces economic growth in the EMDE, the "bubble condition" for the safe asset, $r < g$, is even more difficult to satisfy.

### Monetary policy and macroprudential policy interaction in the presence of capital outflow controls

In a world in which capital is prohibited from flowing freely across international boundaries, it is easier for an EMDE to preserve the safe-asset status of its government debt. As long as the EMDE is not totally isolated and some banks have some dollar debt, a U.S. interest rate hike hits their balance sheets. As they shrink their balance sheets, they diversify less idiosyncratic risk away and push the risk on to the firms and households. With increased (idiosyncratic) risk exposure, firms and households tilt their portfolios more toward the domestic safe asset. Given capital outflow controls, fleeing into U.S. Treasuries is not feasible, and hence the only option domestic agents have is to flee into the domestic government bond. This makes it easy for the EMDE to preserve its safe-asset status. Indeed, (as explained in the I Theory) deflationary pressures instead of inflationary tendencies are the more likely outcome. Deflation (i.e., an appreciation in times of crisis) is one of the hallmarks of a safe asset — the good-friend analogy.

---

[10] The market power of banks plays an important role in understanding the reversal rate of interest analyzed in Brunnermeier and Koby (2019).

The objective of both monetary and macroprudential policy is to redistribute risk in such a way that endogenous risk is reduced. This lowers the overall amount of risk that agents have to bear and therefore reduces the price of risk. With lower total risk and a lower price of risk, the risk premium (which is the product of total risk and price of risk) is also reduced.

The obvious monetary policy in a world suffering from deflationary pressures is to stimulate and encourage higher inflation. The "inflation tax" makes holding domestic safe assets less attractive compared to physical capital. This also lowers the risk premium on physical capital and impacts the wealth distribution dynamics between banks and the rest of the economy. Quantitative easing (QE) measures involve the purchase of capital that can't be sold short. QE can be used to redistribute wealth toward the balance-sheet-impaired sectors as long as it involves assets for which financial markets are not perfect, e.g., when the asset is subject to short-sale constraints.

Note that **monetary policy** distorts the portfolio choice by changing the risk-free rate and the risk premium. Importantly, when using monetary policy to distort the portfolio choice, one has to reward the agents by granting them a risk premium. These agents earn this extra risk premium and hence become wealthier over time. That is, monetary policy has some impact on the wealth distribution. In contrast, quantity restrictions, like many **macroprudential measures**, directly limit portfolio choice and do not require a reward in the form of a risk premium. Hence, they can be implemented without inducing a particular dynamics of wealth. Of course, macroprudential policy also affects equilibrium prices and hence has redistributive effects.

### Dilemma and the interaction between monetary policy, macroprudential policy, and capital controls

In this section we assume that no capital controls are imposed. That is, (i) firms and banks can borrow in U.S. dollars in the boom phase and (ii) hold the U.S. safe asset, i.e., they can move into U.S. Treasuries as the global safe asset in times of crisis.

While macroprudential policy measures limit overall borrowing by firms or banks, capital controls limit foreign borrowing. The key difference is whether debt is denominated in the domestic currency or in U.S. dollars. As an aside, even if international borrowing is denominated in a domestic currency, it is less stable since foreigners are more likely to withdraw their funds in times of crisis (due to asymmetric information and monitoring frictions).

Granting citizens and firms access to the foreign safe asset, the U.S. Treasury bond, significantly complicates matters for policymakers, even though the exchange rate is fully floating. The first major difference is that now, in times of crisis, the economy experiences inflation pressures and a currency devaluation driven by the flight-to-safety into the foreign safe asset. Now, the government bond loses in real value during crisis times (when marginal utility is high), i.e., the covariance is reversed, destroying one of the hallmarks of a safe asset.

Our analysis that combines the I Theory of Money and the International Monetary Theory (Brunnermeier and Sannikov 2016a; 2019) provides a nice framework for understanding why the Mundell-Fleming trilemma is more realistically a **dilemma**, as Rey (2013) puts it. That is, even though the exchange rate is fully flexible, the competition with the U.S. Treasury severely limits the monetary policy space of the EMDE. Policymakers face a "Catch-22": price stability calls for tighter monetary policy, but this hurts banks' capitalization, triggering the adverse amplification loop described above. Or put differently, an accommodative monetary policy to help the banks is difficult to implement since it makes the domestic safe asset vulnerable to the loss of its safe-asset status. Accommodative monetary policy might trigger a sudden collapse (as the bubble component of the government debt bursts). The EMDE faces not a Mundell-Fleming trilemma but a dilemma since, despite a flexible exchange rate regime and an open capital account, redistributive monetary policy is severely restricted.

Are the other policy instruments also limited like monetary policy with open capital accounts? Ex-ante macroprudential policy measures that, for example, constrain leverage during booms still work well. Indeed, with a lower leverage ratio the economy is less prone to amplification and hence the EMDE is less likely to lose its safe-asset status. Having a tighter macroprudential regulatory framework during the boom phase makes it possible to fight capital outflows with a smaller amount of reserves.

Ex-post macroprudential policy in the form of **financial repression** that requires banks to hold domestic government debt steers the demand for safe assets toward the domestic safe asset. In the extreme, financial repression that forces domestic agents to hold so much in domestic government bonds that they have no resources left to buy foreign assets implicitly also imposes capital controls.

In conclusion, the macroprudential and capital control policy measures are substitutes, though imperfect ones. In contrast, monetary policy is a complement to macroprudential policy and capital controls. Stricter macroprudential policy and/or capital controls creates needed policy space for monetary policy.

## Improving the Global Financial Architectures with GloSBies

Issuing a safe asset has a lot of advantages. The sudden erosion of the safe-asset status accompanied with a sudden stop and outflow of credit is very costly for EMDEs. The recent and most dramatic capital outflows out of EMDEs are an example case in point of the current instability of the financial architecture. Figure 5, Panel B compares the recent outflows of funds from emerging markets in billion U.S. Dollars with amounts during previous crisis periods.

Active intervention can reduce the likelihood of sudden stops. However, a global financial architecture that is self-stabilizing and does not need active policy intervention would be superior. Note also that the core of the problem is typically not the shortage of safe assets per se but the fact that safe assets are not symmetrically supplied around the globe all the time.

So far, the focus of the international monetary system has been on leaning against these flight-to-safety capital flows. The IMF offers

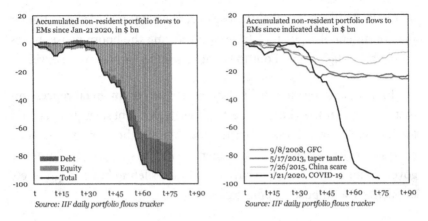

**Figure 5.** Capital outflows from emerging markets in $ bn after Jan 21st, 2020
*Source*: Institute of International Finance (IIF)

various lending facilities that allow governments to borrow in order to counterbalance these capital outflows. Similarly, international swap line arrangements among various central banks allow central banks to offset sudden capital outflows. Indeed, recent interventions by the U.S. Federal Reserve helped stabilize the situation significantly.

Absent these facilities, countries' primary precautionary strategy is to acquire large reserve holdings in good times, which they can deploy in crisis times in order to lean against sudden outflows. The Southeast Asian crisis in 1997 was a wake-up call for most emerging economies. IMF funding came attached with conditionality and hence was not very popular in Asia. Many EMDEs subsequently opted for a self-reliant precautionary **buffer approach** by building up large reserve holdings. Holding reserves also incurs carrying costs for the emerging economy, as the interest on safe foreign reserve assets is typically significantly lower than that on domestic assets. This drains resources, lowers a country's fiscal space, and hence, paradoxically, can make a crisis more likely.

An alternative, the more direct **rechanneling approach**, is to address the root of the problem — namely, that safe assets are asymmetrically supplied. The alternative institutional arrangement involves introducing Sovereign Bond Backed Securities (SBBS) in order to rechannel the destabilizing flight-to-safety capital flows as proposed in Brunnermeier and Huang (2019). Instead of facing cross-border flows from emerging economies to some advanced economies, one could redirect these capital flows to move across different asset classes. The "rechanneling approach" involves tranching the domestic sovereign bond into a junior and a senior bond. Since the latter does not lose its safe-asset status, this is a strictly superior solution.

### Tranching the national asset

Inflation that arises when investors flee the currency devalues the bond exactly when good-friend safety is needed most. This makes it challenging to maintain safe asset status. Outright default makes it equally challenging. Intuitively, the safe asset[11] can exist only if

$$r + \text{default risk premium} + \text{inflation risk premium} < g,$$

where $r$ is the real risk-free rate. To obtain the quoted nominal yield on the government bond, one has to add the expected loss rate, expected inflation, and possibly risk premia for other sources of risk.

Note that for the U.S., inflation is depressed during the global financial downturn and hence the inflation risk premium is negative, making it easier for U.S. dollar assets to satisfy the above inequality.

More importantly, for the EMDE this raises the question of whether it is possible to allow for default, avoid inflation, and nevertheless have the ability to issue a safe asset. The answer is yes, in theory, if one makes use of tranching. That is, EMDEs can issue junior bonds that are subject to default, which protects the other government bond, the senior bond. For the senior bond, a default on the junior bond is now good news, as it lowers the EMDE's overall debt level. In addition, investors can now flee into the EMDE's senior bond instead of the U.S. Treasury bond, reducing the pressure on the exchange rate and, with it, the inflation push. In other words, the default risk premium is now off-loaded to the junior bond. The

---

[11] Let us focus on consol bonds.

senior bond does not need to offer any default risk premium, making it easier to satisfy the above safe-asset condition.

If the EMDE were to offer an inflation-indexed senior bond, it becomes even easier to satisfy the above condition. The inflation indexing serves as a commitment to default on the junior bond instead of inflating the currency in order to repay both the junior and senior debt.

So what is the catch? The EMDE government has to commit to (i) always first defaulting on the junior bond and leaving the senior bond unattached, and (ii) more important, the government has to commit to not issuing a bond that is even more senior than the existing senior bond. This commitment problem is discussed in the corporate finance literature in Bizer and DeMarzo (1992) and in international sovereign debt literature. Furthermore, it should not undermine the seniority structure by issuing bonds with shorter maturity that is de facto senior to the more long-dated senior bond, i.e., the government should avoid a maturity rat race as discussed in Brunnermeier and Oehmke (2013). The answer to this commitment challenge is GloSBies, discussed in the next subsection.

### GloSBies

Instead of a single country offering both senior and junior bonds, an international special-purpose vehicle (SPV) could be established in order to buy a fraction of EMDEs' sovereign bonds, pool them, and tranche them into a senior and a junior bond. The senior bond is then the Global Safe Bond (GloSBies) for and from emerging economies, as proposed in Brunnermeier and Huang (2019). Figure 6 depicts the balance sheet of the SPV.

This structure resolves the commitment problems discussed above, as the consortium running the SPV is now able to exclude an EMDE if it were to issue a super-senior bond. In addition, tranching a pool of emerging-market government bonds, instead of those of a single country, exploits diversification benefits if the pool contains bonds from sufficiently heterogeneous EMDEs.

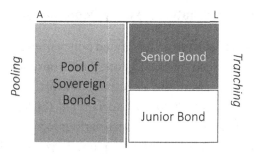

**Figure 6.** Global safe bond: GloSBies SPV balance sheet

The GloSBies structure is analogous to the Sovereign Bond Backed Securities (SBBS) or to the European Safe Bonds (ESBies), proposed for the Euro area by Brunnermeier *et al.* (2011). The Euro area suffered similar flight-to-safety capital flows from its peripheral countries to a few core countries. While within the Euro area there is no exchange rate risk, for the global SBBS the junior bond also has to absorb currency risk if the underlying national bonds are denominated in local currency.

SBBS have a second advantage besides rechanneling flight-to-safety capital flows: as shown in Brunnermeier *et al.* (2016), SBBS can eliminate the doom (diabolic) loop between sovereign and banking risk that arises when banks hold domestic sovereign bonds that are subject to default risk. As default risk rises and the sovereign bond price tanks, banks suffer losses, thus increasing the likelihood that the government will have to bail them out, which in turn lowers the sovereign bond price. Brunnermeier *et al.* (2017) studies diversification and contagion interactions, carries out numerical simulations, and analyzes various implementation details of SBBS for Europe.[12]

In Asia, the Executives' Meeting of East Asia-Pacific Central Banks (EMEAP)[13] is involved in the so-called Asian Bond Fund. This fund pools bonds from 11 countries, but does not tranche the pooled cash flows into a senior bond that could serve as a regional safe asset.[14]

---

[12] The European Union Commission refined the SBBS proposal and in May 2018 proposed the necessary regulatory changes.

[13] See http://www.emeap.org.

[14] In 2009 the introduction of a similarly structured Latin America Bond Fund was studied.

## Conclusion and International Policy Coordination

In this paper we considered an integrated policy framework that studies the interaction between monetary policy, macroprudential regulation, foreign exchange interventions, and capital controls. Unlike existing IMF works such as Basu *et al.* (2020) and Adrian *et al.* (2020), we depart from the New Keynesian framework in which various forms of price stickiness play an important role. We think understanding various forms of price stickiness is important but here we deliberately take a safe asset and risk perspective.[15] Monetary policy tries to influence not only the risk-free rate but also various risk premia. Citizens save for precautionary reasons in the safe asset, which provides insurance services. This increases the value of the safe asset, i.e., it lowers its interest rate. When a country's government bond competes with the U.S. Treasury bond as a safe store of value, deflationary pressures during crises reverse into inflationary pressures, undermining the EMDE debt's safe-asset status.

We outlined the subtle interactions between various policy instruments. Typically, ex-ante bank capital requirements and macroprudential measures are substitutes, which together are complements to monetary policy. Interestingly, our approach provides a framework for understanding why the Mundell-Fleming trilemma reduces to a dilemma. That is, a floating exchange rate does not necessarily grant an EMDE the possibility of independent monetary policy. GloSBies that pool and tranche the sovereign debt of several EMDEs might be a way forward for a global financial architecture in which the supply of safe assets is more symmetrically distributed.

---

[15] As an aside, let's highlight further similarities between the New Keynesian approach adopted in Basu *et al.* (2020) and Adrian *et al.* (2020) in which the form of the price stickiness plays the central role and a setting in which only financial frictions are at center stage. Issuing a long-term bond and committing to a periodic interest payment shares some aspects with wage stickiness. To see this, consider a firm that produces a certain output by either buying a machine financed with fixed monthly annuity payments over, say, three years or by hiring a worker whose wage is fixed for the next three years. Both arrangements are indeed similar except that quantity adjustment might be more or less costly depending on whether firing a worker or selling off a used machine is more costly.

Our framework also raises important questions about any spillovers of U.S. monetary policy and the desirability of international economic policy coordination. First, should debt bubbles be treated as desirable ways to expand financing to EMDEs, or should they be treated as signs of instability? Should the U.S. take into account that raising U.S. dollar rates might burst safe-asset bubbles in EMDEs? Is providing U.S. swap lines an attractive alternative? Or should the U.S. even try to prevent safe-asset bubbles from emerging in EMDEs? And second, how should EMDEs protect themselves against U.S. monetary policy cycles?

All these questions are critical to understanding how international capital flows can promote global growth rather than threaten price and financial instability.

## References

Abreu, D and Brunnermeier, MK (2003). Bubbles and crashes. *Econometrica*, 71(1), 173–204.

Adrian, T, Erceg, C, Lindé, J, and Zabczyk, P (2020). "A Quantitative Model for the Integrated Policy Framework." IMF Working Paper 20/122.

Basu, S, Boz, E, Gopinath, G, Roch, F, and Unsal, F (2020). "A Conceptual Model for the Integrated Policy Framework." IMF Working Paper 20/121.

Bizer, DS and DeMarzo, PM (1992). Sequential banking. *Journal of Political Economy*, 100(1), 41–61.

Brunnermeier, MK and Koby, Y (2019). The reversal rate of interest. Working Paper, Princeton University.

Brunnermeier, MK, James, H, and Landau, J-P (2019). The digitalization of money. Working Paper, Princeton University.

Brunnermeier, MK and Niepelt, D (2019). On the equivalence of public and private money. *Journal of Monetary Economics*, 106, 27–41.

Brunnermeier, MK and Morgan, J (2010). Clock games: Theory and experiments. *Games and Economic Behavior*, 68(2), 532550.

Brunnermeier, MK and Huang, LY (2019). A global safe asset from and for emerging economies. Monetary Policy and Financial Stability: Transmission Mechanisms and Policy Implications. Santiago de Chile: Central Bank of Chile, 111–167.

Brunnermeier, MK and Oehmke, M (2013). The maturity rat race. *The Journal of Finance*, 68(2), 483–521.

Brunnermeier, MK and Sannikov, Y (2016a). The I theory of money. Working Paper, Princeton University.

Brunnermeier, MK and Sannikov, Y (2016b). On the optimal inflation rate. *American Economic Review Papers and Proceedings*, 106(5), 484–489.

Brunnermeier, MK and Sannikov, Y (2019). International monetary theory: A risk perspective. Working Paper, Princeton University.

Brunnermeier, MK, Garicano, L, Lane, P, Pagano, M, Reis, R, Santos, T, Thesmar, D, Van Nieuwerburgh, S, and Vayanos, D (2011). European safe bonds (ES-Bies). Euro-nomics.com.

Brunnermeier, MK, Garicano, L, Lane, P, Pagano, M, Reis, R, Santos, T, Thesmar, D, Van Nieuwerburgh, S, and Vayanos, D (2016). The sovereign-bank diabolic loop and ESBies. *American Economic Review Papers and Proceedings*, 106(5), 508–512.

Brunnermeier, MK, Langfield, L, Pagano, M, Reis, R, Van Nieuwerburgh, S, and Vayanos, D (2017). ESBies: Safety in the tranches. *Economic Policy*, 32(90), 175–219.

Brunnermeier, MK, Merkel, S, and Sannikov, Y (2020). The fiscal theory of the price level with a bubble. Working Paper, Princeton University.

Calvo, GA (1988). Servicing the public debt: The role of expectations. *The American Economic Review*, 78(4), 647–661.

Kaminsky, GL and Reinhart, CM (1999). The twin crises: The causes of banking and balance-of-payments problems. *American Economic Review*, 89(3), 473–500.

Keynes, JM (1936). The General Theory of Employment, Interest and Money. London: Macmillan.

Obstfeld, M (1996). Models of currency crises with self-fulfilling features. Papers and Proceedings of the Tenth Annual Congress of the European Economic Association. *European Economic Review*, 40(3), 1037–1047.

Rey, H (2013). Dilemma not trilemma: The global financial cycle and monetary policy independence. In *Global Dimensions of Unconventional Monetary Policy*. Proceedings of the Economic Policy Symposium at Jackson Hole, Federal Reserve of Kansas City.

Printed in the United States
by Baker & Taylor Publisher Services